LEARNER-CENTERED TEACHING

Lineberger Memorial Library

Lenoir Rhyne University

Lutheran Theological
Southern Seminary

4201 North Main Street, Columbia, SC 29203

LEARNER-CENTERED TEACHING

Five Key Changes to Practice

Second Edition

Maryellen Weimer

JOSSEY-BASS
A Wiley Imprint
www.josseybass.com

7/13 Amazon $29.98

Published by Jossey-Bass
A Wiley Imprint
One Montgomery Street, Suite 1200, San Francisco, CA 94104-4594—www.josseybass.com

Limit of Liability/Disclaimer of Warranty: While the publisher and author have used their best efforts in preparing this book, they make no representations or warranties with respect to the accuracy or completeness of the contents of this book and specifically disclaim any implied warranties of merchantability or fitness for a particular purpose. No warranty may be created or extended by sales representatives or written sales materials. The advice and strategies contained herein may not be suitable for your situation. You should consult with a professional where appropriate. Neither the publisher nor author shall be liable for any loss of profit or any other commercial damages, including but not limited to special, incidental, consequential, or other damages. Readers should be aware that Internet Web sites offered as citations and/or sources for further information may have changed or disappeared between the time this was written and when it is read.

Jossey-Bass books and products are available through most bookstores. To contact Jossey-Bass directly call our Customer Care Department within the U.S. at 800-956-7739, outside the U.S. at 317-572-3986, or fax 317-572-4002.

Wiley publishes in a variety of print and electronic formats and by print-on-demand. Some material included with standard print versions of this book may not be included in e-books or in print-on-demand. If this book refers to media such as a CD or DVD that is not included in the version you purchased, you may download this material at http://booksupport.wiley.com. For more information about Wiley products, visit www.wiley.com.

Library of Congress Cataloging-in-Publication Data
Weimer, Maryellen, 1947–
  Learner-centered teaching : five key changes to practice / Maryellen Weimer.—Second edition.
      pages cm
  Includes bibliographical references and index.
  ISBN 978-1-118-11928-0 (hardback); ISBN 978-1-118-41903-8 (ebk.);
  ISBN 978-1-118-41616-7 (ebk.); ISBN 978-1-118-43369-0 (ebk.)
  1. College teaching.   2. Learning, Psychology of.   I. Title.
  LB2331.W39 2013
  378.1'2—dc23
                                    2012041888

Printed in the United States of America
SECOND EDITION
HB Printing   10 9 8 7 6 5 4 3 2 1

CONTENTS

Honoring the memory of
Barbara Robertson Friz
October 10, 1909–October 20, 2009

PREFACE TO THE SECOND EDITION

Welcome to the second edition of *Learner-Centered Teaching: Five Key Changes to Practice.* If you haven't read the first edition or haven't read it for a while, let me start by explaining why I've opted for the learner-centered name. A variety of terms are being used to describe these approaches to teaching: *learning-centered, student-centered learning, student-centered teaching,* or just plain *student-centered,* usually as contrasted with *teacher-centered.*

I think it's important to keep the focus on the learners, our students. However, when *student* gets incorporated in the description there's a tendency to end up in heated discussions about students as customers, and should educators be trying to satisfy them, and are student-customers always right, and is education a product, and if not, what do those tuition dollars buy? Those discussions have merit and should be occurring, but they are not what learner-centered teaching is about. The focus needs to stay on learners and the kind of instructional strategies that support their efforts to learn.

Why not use the *learning-centered* label, then? Learning is an abstraction. It's not a word that points us directly toward its meaning. Faculty belong to a culture that thrives on theoretical, abstract ideas. With the focus on learning, we are likely to find ourselves discussing more and better learning at some abstract level. We don't need learning connected to teaching via some intellectually captivating conceptual framework; we need instructional policies and practices that directly affect how much and how well students learn. What we call something will guide how we think about it—so what something is called matters. Calling this learner-centered teaching keeps us focused on what this way of teaching is about.

What Makes the Second Edition Better

What makes this edition better? A variety of things do, starting with arguments that are tighter and clearer. Some of these changes arise from the fact that extensive lecture-based teaching is becoming increasingly difficult to defend. There is more research documenting that this method encourages superficial learning, along with an inability to retain and apply what has been learned. And there is growing evidence that learner-centered approaches produce a different kind of learning, develop learning skills, and move students in the direction of autonomy and independence as learners.

This edition is stronger because it incorporates more of the experiential knowledge base. That addition is the result of my ongoing conversations with faculty about learner-centered approaches—how they are using them, what happens when they do, what unresolved issues have emerged, and what recommendations they would offer others. Their views and experiences have deepened my understanding of learner-centered teaching. Improvements in the experiential knowledge base are also the result of the prolific number of pedagogical articles that report on the design, use, and assessment of learner-centered approaches. These ways of teaching are being used across the disciplinary landscape by faculty at all kinds of institutions teaching all kinds of students.

I believe this edition is stronger because it tackles with more vigor what hasn't changed since the 2002 edition, and, regrettably, that includes almost everything targeted for change in the first edition. Evidence in Chapter Two, on research, and in the five chapters on key changes verifies that despite more widespread use of learner-centered approaches, instruction overall continues to be mostly teacher centered, faculty are still making most of the learning decisions for students, content still centers the instructional universe, teachers are still doing too many of the learning tasks that students should be doing for themselves, and students are still not regularly encouraged to assess their own work or that of their peers (which is different from grading it).

That's the stand-back, view-from-across-the-room picture of instruction in higher education. Up close, there are signs of change.

"Learner-centered" has become something institutions aspire to be—it's trendy now and along with that come the proverbial blessings and curses. As the conversation about being learner-centered continues, more people hear about it, and after consideration they try out some of its approaches. That's on the blessing side. One of the curses of this increased "popularity" involves a definitional looseness resulting from widespread use of the term. At this point, the learning-centered label is close to synonymous with active learning and is applied to almost any strategy that engages students and mentions learning. I think this edition is stronger because it seeks to reclaim and advance definitional clarity. Learner-centered teaching has characteristics that make it unique and that differentiate it from active learning and other forms of student engagement.

I have enjoyed revising, rewriting, and rethinking the content of this book more than I expected I would. It is exciting to see an orientation to teaching evolve in ways that make it more substantive and intellectually viable. It is also satisfying to see how much we have learned and challenging to realize how much we still don't know and need to learn.

CONTENT OVERVIEW

The details of what's new in this edition are best described in an overview of the chapters ahead. Content in Chapters One and Two was drawn from Chapter One in the first edition. Chapter One now contains the story of how I became a learner-centered teacher and a description of where these ideas originated and on what they are based.

Chapter Two is essentially a new chapter. It introduces a sample of the research on and research related to learner-centered approaches. A significant amount of research has been completed since 2002. The chapter samples what's been done; it does not comprehensively review the literature. As discussed in the chapter, comprehensive reviews of this literature base present sizable logistical challenges. Work on learner-centered approaches is being done across a wide range of disciplines. Tracking everything down is a daunting task even with search technologies. Equally challenging is integrating and comparing results. Researchers define learner-centered differently; some don't use any of the terms to describe treatments that most would call learner-centered. They test hypotheses using many methodological approaches. The work includes qualitative and quantitative analyses. Research on learner-centered teaching is not a systematic progression with one set of findings leading to the next set of research questions. Chapter Two looks more like a crazy quilt than a patterned design. Nonetheless, I think most will find the research sampled there constitutes an impressive array of evidence. It was the prevalence of new research and its intriguing array of findings that finally persuaded me to prepare a second edition.

If I could pick the chapter I would most like those interested in learner-centered teaching to read, it would be Chapter Two. Faculty have a long history of avoiding educational research, and they continue that research avoidance by not reading the wave of discipline-based pedagogical scholarship spawned by the scholarship of teaching movement. This is to their disadvantage and the detriment of instructional practice. What we do in the classroom can be verified (maybe even vindicated) by quantitative and qualitative analyses. Research adds validity to what have been asserted to be "best practices." Knowing what we know, in this case about learner-centered teaching, confirms what we propose and values what we do.

The heart of the book remains, as it was in the first edition, the Five Key Changes to Practice chapters in Part Two. These are the areas of my practice that changed when I moved from a teacher-oriented approach to a learner-centered one. This way of organizing learner-centered changes has been used by others, and I use it regularly when I speak about learner-centered teaching—the structure seems to work, so I have retained it.

Each of those chapters has been significantly revised. Early in each I explore what has and hasn't changed since 2002. Unfortunately, most of the attitudes that prevent learner-centered changes still prevail. What has changed is the number of new strategies, assignments, activities, and approaches that teachers are using to realize the changes explored in these chapters. Each chapter ends with an Implementation Issues section. These sections incorporate some of the content from Chapter Nine in the first edition along with new ideas and information.

The book ends with a chapter on resistance (both that displayed by students and that expressed by colleagues) and a more detailed chapter on the developmental issues involving the design and sequence of activities and assignments that advance learner development in a planned and systematic way. It suggests good places to begin the transformation of students from passive, dependent learners to autonomous, self-directed ones. The chapter also addresses developmental issues experienced by faculty.

This edition does not contain a chapter on Making Learner-Centered Teaching Work. Some of that content is now incorporated in the Implementation Issues section of each of the Five Key Changes to Practice chapters. Since 2002 I have written a book (Weimer, 2010) devoted to the ongoing growth and development of college teachers, and much of its content explores the process of implementing instructional changes. Treatment of these topics in the new book is much more thorough and well documented than it was in the previous edition.

Most of the appendixes remain in the new edition. Fifty percent of the references listed at the end of the book have been published since the first edition came out. I hope the highlights of them that I have incorporated in this book will motivate readers to consult these excellent sources.

One final note: I revised this edition after retirement. I'm still teaching—at least that's how I think of my ongoing work with faculty—but I'm not teaching undergraduates. When I wrote the first edition, I was teaching undergraduates, so descriptions of what I did in the classroom were in present tense. I've kept them that way in this edition.

AUDIENCE

Like the first edition, this book is for faculty. However, it's not a book exclusively for learner-centered teaching converts. It's also a book for faculty who think learner-centered ideas might be of interest, but they have questions and concerns. Are these ways of teaching that retain high standards and intellectual rigor? Are they ways of teaching that pander to students and encourage the sense of entitlement that so compromises the educational enterprise? Does this way of teaching diminish the role and importance of teachers? The book offers answers to these questions. It is a book for those interested in learning about these instructional approaches. It's even a book for those who may not think they're interested in learner-centered teaching but who are concerned about students—their passivity, lack of motivation, disinterest in learning. It's for teachers who wonder if there might be better ways to connect students with the power and joy of learning.

I suspect, though, that most readers will have an interest in the topic. A lot will have tried some of these approaches and are reading in order to move their practice forward. I've tried to respond to that audience by including many new assignments, activities, and approaches in this edition. If you've read the first edition and wonder if it's worth your time to read the second, the author is probably not the best person to ask. I will say, though, that my goal was to write a significantly revised second edition— one that merited a reread.

Readers interested in the topic will also include some beginners—something all of us once were. This is a book for beginners, as well. It presents lots of experiences of other beginners—you can learn from us, including from our mistakes—and it offers advice on getting started, including identification of specific strategies, assignments, and activities that are good places to launch learner-centered teaching.

ACKNOWLEDGMENTS

First off, a heartfelt thanks to the many faculty and administrators who purchased copies of the first edition. It gives this author great pleasure to meet readers and see copies of the book that have obviously been read. I hope this book continues and furthers interest in the topic.

This edition took much longer to prepare than I anticipated. I kept finding new material and wanting to significantly rewrite the old. Higher Education Editor David Brightman at Jossey-Bass was patient and constructively persistent. As the years of our collaboration lengthen, my respect for and appreciation of him only grow. Aneesa Davenport, also at Jossey-Bass, is an organizational and detail wizard whose commitment to book projects expedites their preparation. In addition to these and other impressive professional skills, she is a person of grace and charm.

Husband Michael and brother Mark are my fine family support. Mark provided careful help with the references. I dedicated the 2002 edition to my much-loved and greatly admired Aunt Barbara. She died ten days past her one-hundredth birthday, and this edition honors her memory. Her mind left before her body, which was a tragedy I had not anticipated. But my book was beside her bed when she died. Her caregivers told me she carried it with her even when she could no longer say why.

January 2013
Maryellen Weimer
Marsh Creek, Pennsylvania

THE AUTHOR

In 2007 **Maryellen Weimer** retired from Penn State as Professor Emeritus of Teaching and Learning. For the last thirteen years of her career at Penn State, she taught communication courses, first-year seminars, and other courses for business students at one of Penn State's regional campus colleges. In 2005 she won Penn State's Milton S. Eisenhower award for distinguished teaching.

Before returning to full-time teaching, Weimer was the associate director of the National Center on Postsecondary Teaching, Learning and Assessment, a five-year, $5.9 million, U.S. Department of Education research and development center. Prior to that, she spent ten years as director of Penn State's Instructional Development Program.

Weimer has numerous publications—including articles in refereed journals, book chapters, and books reviews—and service on the editorial boards of journals. She has consulted with over five hundred colleges and universities on instructional issues. She regularly keynotes national meetings and regional conferences.

Since 1987, she has edited *The Teaching Professor,* a monthly newsletter on college teaching with 15,000 subscribers. She has edited or authored ten books, including a 1990 book on faculty development, a 1993 book on teaching for new faculty, and a 1995 anthology edited with Robert Menges, *Teaching on Solid Ground.* She was primary author of a Kendall-Hunt publication, *Teaching Tools,* a collection of collaborative, active, and inquiry-based approaches to be used in conjunction with *Biological Perspectives,* an NSF-funded introductory biology text created by Biological Sciences Curriculum Studies (BSCS). Jossey-Bass published her book *Learner-Centered Teaching: Five Key Changes to Practice* in 2002, her next book, *Enhancing Scholarly Work on Teaching and Learning,* in 2006, and a 2010 book, *Inspired College Teaching: A Career-Long Resource for Professional Growth.* Her blog, Teaching Professor (found at www.facultyfocus.com), has more than 75,000 subscribers.

LEARNER-CENTERED TEACHING

PART ONE

FOUNDATIONS OF THE LEARNER-CENTERED APPROACH

CHAPTER ONE

LEARNER-CENTERED TEACHING: ROOTS AND ORIGINS

This chapter tells two stories. It recounts how I became a learner-centered teacher and it shares a bit of the origin and history of learner-centered ideas. The story of learner-centered teaching begins long before my efforts to focus on student learning. The approaches I started using rest on a collection of educational theories—some comparatively new; others established and venerable. These theories help explain why and how this way of teaching promotes learning. Knowing a bit about them makes it easier to decide whether this philosophy of teaching fits currently held beliefs or whether teaching using these approaches would represent a change in educational philosophy. The theoretical framework also offers criteria that can be used to assess the effectiveness of what has been implemented. Finally, knowing about the theories makes it easier to trace the origin of the various lines of research written about in Chapter Two.

The interplay between my story and these theories is interesting. I didn't start out aspiring to become a learner-centered teacher. I didn't even realize the changes I was implementing could be called that. Like many midcareer faculty, I was looking for new ideas—partly out of my need for growth and change, and partly because a lot of what I saw in classrooms seemed so ineffective. I opted for ideas I liked and ones that I thought I could make work. It took some time before I saw that the approaches I was using shared common elements, and it took even longer before I discovered that what I was doing rested on strong theoretical foundations. Once I discovered these things, I felt vindicated. What was happening in my classroom wasn't some sort of fluke. Students were responding as they did for good reasons—but that's not where my story begins.

The next section contains my story. It includes examples that illustrate learner-centered approaches, and they give an early sense of how learner-centered teaching might be defined. I also highlight each of the five areas in which I implemented changes. These areas are the subject of the five chapters in Part Two and are really the heart of my exploration of learner-centered teaching. Discussion of the theories follows my story, and examples are included in that discussion as well. They build some context around the theories and make it a bit easier to assemble a learner-centered framework out of the various theories.

A PERSONAL HISTORY

Like most important life lessons, what I have come to believe about learner-centered teaching grew out of a serendipitous confluence of events and experiences. The ones I consider most important are so overlapping and intertwined that a stream-of-consciousness recounting would more accurately describe how they occurred. However, in the interest of coherence, I will recount each of them separately.

EVENTS AND EXPERIENCES: WHAT MOTIVATED THE CHANGE

My transformation began in 1994, when, after a number of years working in faculty development, on educational research projects, and occasionally teaching upper-division and graduate courses, I returned to the classroom to teach entry-level, required courses. It was one of those midlife career moves motivated by the realization that the time for doing things no longer appeared limitless. As I took stock and tried to decide what I wanted to do with the rest of my career, it became clear that the most important and personally satisfying work I had done was in the classroom. I decided to return, finishing out my career as it had started, teaching undergraduates.

I went back wanting to teach differently, even though I wasn't terribly clear in my thinking about what was wrong with how I taught or how I wanted change. I thought more about students and the fact that their lack of confidence prevented them from doing well in the basic communication courses I taught. They needed to find their way past self-doubt, awkwardness, and the fear of failure to a place where they could ask a question in class, make a contribution in a group, and speak coherently in front of peers. It came to me that I might address the problem by giving the students a greater sense of control. What if I presented them with some choices and let them make some of the decisions about their learning?

My first semester back in the classroom I decided to try this approach in my 8 a.m. section. I designed a beginning public speaking course that had only one required assignment: the dreaded speech. They had to give at least one. The rest of the syllabus presented them with a cafeteria of assignment options: a learning log; group projects of various sorts; credit for participation and the analysis of it; critiques of peers; conducting an interview, being interviewed, or both; and conventional multiple-choice exams. A version of this syllabus appears in Appendix One. As can be seen there, each assignment had a designated point value, and it was not a case of do-it-and-get-full-credit. Students could opt to complete as many or as few assignments as they wished, depending on the course grade they desired. Each assignment had a due date, and once the date passed, that assignment could not be turned in.

The first couple of days, students were totally confused. I remember a conversation with one about whether the exams were required. "They must be required. If the tests are optional, no one will take them." "Sure they will. Students need points to pass the class." "But what if I don't take them?" "Fine—do other assignments and get your points that way." "But what do I do on exam days?" "You sleep in!" Several students said they couldn't decide which assignments they should do and asked me to make the choices for them. Even more wanted me to approve the collection of assignments they had selected.

Once the confusion passed, what happened the rest of the semester took me by surprise. I had no attendance policy, but I got better attendance than in any other class I could remember.

More students (not all, but most) started to work hard early in the course, and some students determinedly announced that they would do every assignment if that was what it took to get enough points for an A. I was stunned by this change of attitude—students willing to work and without complaints? The high energy level and sense of optimism I usually saw in students those first few class days continued well into the course, and even as the stress of the semester started showing, this class was different. These students were more engaged. They routinely asked questions, sustained discussion longer and in the end disagreed with me and other students far more than I remembered other beginning students doing. No, it wasn't instructional nirvana—there were still missed deadlines, shoddy work, and poor choices made about learning, but these things happened less often. I was definitely onto something and decided I would continue to experiment with the course.

About this time, I was asked to review a Brookfield (1995) manuscript under contract with Jossey-Bass and subsequently published as *Becoming a Critically Reflective Teacher*. I reference it in almost everything else I write. Few things I have read before or since have so dramatically influenced my pedagogical thinking. First off, I discovered how much about one's own teaching could be learned through critical reflective practice. Brookfield describes methods that allow teachers to dissect instructional practices so that the assumptions on which they rest can be clearly seen. Since then I've learned much more from other adult educators who study, describe, and promote both this kind of critical reflection and the transformative learning it often produces (Mezirow and Associates, 2000; Cranton, 2006). Transformative learning is one of the theories I'll be discussing subsequently in this book. But it was Brookfield who first enabled me to hold a mirror up to my teaching. The instructional image I saw was not what I expected. It was far less flattering.

I saw an authoritarian, controlling teacher who directed virtually everything that happened in the classroom. I made all the decisions and did so with little regard as to their impact on student learning and motivation. Almost totally focused on teaching, I had created a classroom environment that showcased my pedagogical prowess. Student learning just happened automatically, an outcome of my devotion to excellent teaching. It didn't matter where I turned the mirror, I never saw anyone other than the teacher.

Before Brookfield, I fussed around with some interesting new strategies; after Brookfield, I tried to transform the teacher. Shaping up the course turned out to be a whole lot easier than "fixing" my very teacher-centered methods. Flachmann (1994) captures exactly how I felt then:

> I'm a little embarrassed to tell you that I used to want credit for having all the intelligent insights in my classroom. I worked hard to learn these facts . . . I secretly wanted my students to look at me with reverence. I now believe that the opposite effect should occur—that the oracle, the locus and ownership of knowledge, should reside in each student and our principal goal as teachers must be to help our students discover the most important and enduring answers to life's problems within themselves. Only then can they truly possess the knowledge that we are paid to teach them [p. 2].

Another wise teacher makes the point this way: "I've come to realize that it is not so much what students know but what they can do. Likewise, teaching is not about what I know but what I enable others to do" (Phelps, 2008, p. 2).

Another event during this period also strongly influenced my thinking. For years my husband, Michael, had wanted to build a wooden boat. He collected books, bought plans, subscribed to *Wooden Boat* magazine and faithfully watched *Classic Boat* on TV when it was on Speedvision. Then we bought a piece of property on an island. We planned to build a house there and needed a boat big enough to haul supplies to the site. Armed with a set of blueprints (selected after having reviewed hundreds), Michael started building the hull of a wooden boat. New words crept into his vocabulary. Over supper, he chatted on about battens, chines, sheer clamps, the kellson, and garboard. Next, the hull was covered with marine plywood, not something easily obtained in landlocked central Pennsylvania. The whole neighborhood showed up to help turn the hull. Then it was time to construct the floor, design the cabin, and rebuild the motor. Every step was accompanied with a whole new set of tasks to learn.

During the evenings he watched videotapes demonstrating fiber-glassing techniques. Every day some new marine supply catalog showed up in the mailbox.

After hours of work that extended across months, *Noah's Lark* emerged, a twenty-four-foot, lobster-style wooden boat. She had a sleek white hull and dashing yellow stripe, a beautifully finished ash cabin, and she was powered by a fully rebuilt but not terribly fuel-efficient MerCruiser. She rode the water gracefully, rose to plane with style, and made her way through white caps and choppy water with steady certainty. She reliably towed barge loads of building supplies, always turning heads at the public launch. The bold asked, "Where did you get that boat?" "Built her," my husband replied, unable to hide the pride in his voice.

It takes far more time and money to build a wooden boat than I imagined. Beyond those surprises, I marveled at the confidence my husband brought to the task. Where did it come from? On what was it based? He had never built a boat—houses, yes; furniture, yes; but not a boat. As the project progressed and charges on the credit card mounted, I felt it financially prudent to ask, pretty much on a monthly basis, "Do you know what you're doing?" "Is this really going to be a boat we can use?" His answer was always the same, "No, I don't know what I'm doing, but I'm learning. Of course it will turn out. We need a boat, don't we?"

There was an irony I didn't miss—actually, it stuck in my craw. Michael is a college graduate. He acquired a degree in industrial engineering in his early thirties, and college was not the experience that had developed his confidence as a learner. In fact, quite the opposite had occurred. He graduated from college feeling that he just made it, keenly disappointed with what he had learned and stressed by the conditions under which he was expected to learn. He credits experiences with his father for developing his confidence. It irritated me that his college experience had undermined his beliefs about what he could do. College should be the time and the place for students to develop the learning skills on which that confidence rests.

While ruminating, I tried to imagine which of my students might tackle a complicated learning project about which they knew little. No one came to mind. I saw nothing in my students or myself, for that matter, that resembled the confidence and perseverance with which my husband confronted his need to learn how to build a wooden boat. That led me to think about what kind of classroom experiences would develop this self-confidence and these sophisticated learning skills. I couldn't answer that question right off, but I did become persuaded that one of my tasks as a teacher was developing learning skills and the confidence to use them.

Setting that goal changed my thinking about many aspects of instruction. I began to see course content in a different light. It moved from being the end to being the means. It went from being something I covered to something I used to develop learning skills and an awareness of learning processes. I stopped assuming students were learning how to generate examples, ask questions, think critically, and perform a host of other skills by seeing me do them. If they were going to develop those skills, they needed to be the ones practicing them, not me. I saw evaluation as something more than the mechanism that generated grades. It became a potent venue for promoting learning and developing self- and peer-assessment skills.

As my teaching transformation continued moving in the learner-centered direction, I realized how little I actually knew about learning. Brookfield's well-referenced book introduced me to all sorts of new sources. At the same time, interest in learning swept across higher education. For a while there, it almost felt as if learning had just been discovered—or maybe rediscovered. There were all sorts of things to read, and I read them in an unsystematic way, just allowing one source to lead to another. As I learned more about learning, I discovered that the new approaches I was adopting rested on a variety of educational theories, many supported by research.

ORGANIZING WHAT I LEARNED

I didn't try to organize the hodgepodge of learner-centered strategies and approaches I was implementing until I started working on the first edition of this book. It was then I saw that those changes could be grouped around five key aspects of instructional practice. Those five areas have continued to structure my thinking about learner-centered teaching. In both the first edition and this one, there is one chapter about each area. I consider those five chapters the heart of my work on learner-centered teaching.

Since they are so central, these aspects of instruction merit an introduction now. I start with how learner-centered teaching changes *the role of the teacher.* I didn't start with this chapter in the first edition, but I do in this edition for two reasons. It's a good place to start because it makes sense to faculty. Teaching that promotes learning is not teaching that endlessly tells students what they should do and what they should know. Rather, it promotes learning by facilitating the acquisition of knowledge. The hard and messy work of learning can be done only by students. And I start here because changing the role of the teacher is central and significant. I'm not sure that it's the first thing that needs to change. But the other changes cannot be executed if the role of the teacher stays the same. It's significant because although this change may be easy to accept intellectually, most of us have discovered practicing facilitation in the classroom is anything but simple. It presents teachers with an ongoing set of challenges.

Changing the *balance of power* in the classroom requires a bigger conceptual stretch. Teacher authority is assumed—taken for granted so often that most teachers have lost their awareness of it. Whether they realize it or not, teachers exert enormous control over the learning processes of students. They decide what students will learn and how they will learn it. They set the pace and establish the conditions under which the learning will take place. They regulate the flow of communication in the classroom, and finally they certify whether and how well students have learned. What does that leave for students to decide? Ironically, what's left is the most important decision of all: students decide whether or not they will learn. But even though teachers can't guarantee learning outcomes, they can positively influence students' motivation to learn when they give students some control over the learning process. The challenge for learner-centered teachers is finding those strategies that give students control and responsibility commensurate with their ability to handle it. The goal of learner-centered teaching is the development of students as autonomous, self-directed, and self-regulating learners.

The *function of content* stands as the strongest barrier to changes that make teaching more learner-centered. Teachers have lots of content to cover, and when students are working with new and unfamiliar content, they don't cover it as efficiently as faculty. Learner-centered courses still contain plenty of content, but teachers *use* the content instead of covering it. They use it as they always have—to develop a knowledge base—but they also use content to develop the learning skills students will need across a lifetime of learning. Equipping students with learning skills makes it possible for them to learn content themselves—sometimes within the course itself and regularly after it.

Learner-centered teachers institute changes that make students more *responsible for learning*. They work to create and maintain climates that are conducive to learning, whether students meet in classrooms or online. Teachers and students have become too dependent on extrinsic motivation to power learning. Students do things for points, grades, because they'll be quizzed, or there's some other kind of requirement. Without those sticks and carrots, learning activities grind to a halt. Students need to orient to learning differently. Learner-centered teachers let students start experiencing the consequences of decisions they make about learning, like not coming to class prepared, not studying for the exam, not contributing in groups. And learner-centered teachers work to do a better job of conveying the love and joy of learning. Teachers spend lifetimes learning and never even think about points.

Finally, learner-centered teachers revisit the *purposes and processes of evaluation*. Starting with the purpose, teachers evaluate what students know and can do for two reasons. They have a professional obligation to certify mastery of material, but teachers also use assessment activities like exams because preparing for them, taking them, and finding out the results can all promote learning. The goal of the learner-centered teacher is to maximize the learning potential inherently a part of any experience where students produce a product, perform a skill, or demonstrate their knowledge. As for the processes of evaluation, at issue here is the lack of opportunities students have to develop self- and peer-assessment skills while in college. Because grades retain such importance, teachers must grade student work. But mature learners have self-assessment skills and can constructively deliver feedback to others. Learner-centered teachers design learning experiences that give students opportunities to explore and develop these important skills, and they seek out strategies and approaches that do not compromise the integrity of the grading process.

Since publication of the first edition, this organizational scheme for considering learner-centered approaches has been used by others in presentations and publications. This typology continues to make sense, so it provides the structure for this second edition as well.

AND THE LEARNING CONTINUES

I taught another five years after publication of the first edition of *Learner-Centered Teaching.* I continued to refine the techniques I was using and implement new ones. I couldn't say exactly when, but at some point the collection of techniques I assembled stopped being interesting things to do and became a teaching philosophy. As such, it ended up influencing how I thought about every aspect of my instructional practice. So many things changed that I hardly recognized the teacher I had become.

Before retiring, I made several other realizations about this approach to teaching. First, it is not an easier way to teach. It requires sophisticated instructional design skills. When students are doing more learning on their own, what and how they learn is directly linked to the activities used to engage them. They will learn more and learn it better if those activities are well designed, whether they are done in class or at home. So many of the instructional activities I used were things students did in many other classes—multiple-choice exams, research papers, group presentations. I used them without thinking that their features could be manipulated and changed in ways that affected what and how students learned. When I reconsidered those assignments and activities, it wasn't always apparent what changes would result in better learning experiences. I discovered by trial and error and by soliciting lots of feedback on the changes from students. I stopped asking them whether they "liked" a particular activity and inquired about its impact on their efforts to learn.

In addition to requiring more upfront planning time, learner-centered teaching is more difficult because it is much less scripted.

You don't go to a classroom or online with a carefully prepared lecture—one with all the examples, transitions, questions (maybe even answers), links to previous material, sample problems ready to go on visually impressive PowerPoint slides. You go well prepared with a repertoire of material at your disposal—you have a carefully packed tool box, and, like any expert working on location, you know what you'll need most of the time. Even so, chances are that some days you won't have everything you need. In this case, you trust your experience with the content, with learning, and with students. Something else from the tool box may work or you'll be able to make do until you can get what you need.

I also came to realize that in learner-centered classrooms teachers don't work alone. Students become learning partners. They explore with teachers what will help them better understand an issue, a theory, or a problem. Never before did I feel this sense of partnership with students. Focused on more and better learning, we all made suggestions and offered feedback. And we all celebrated those breakthroughs to understanding and insight. It brought a kind of invigorating energy and spontaneity to the classroom, and it was exactly what I needed to sustain my interest, enthusiasm, and love of teaching during those last years I was in the classroom.

As my experience with learner-centered approaches grew, I found myself attracted to classroom activities that pushed and challenged me. I kept wanting to try new things. The positive experiences I had implementing them—even those that didn't work well—are the reason why I now routinely recommend the infusion of learner-centered approaches as the antidote to teaching that has become more ho-hum than imaginative. I felt better about myself as a teacher during those last few years than at any other time of my career.

Before I retired, I also came to understand that this way of teaching offers a deeper kind of personal satisfaction. This isn't teaching that features pedagogical showmanship. It's not about the teacher performing. It's about students learning and teachers making contributions that help learning happen. You can do things as a teacher that directly affect how much and how well students learn content. Sometimes students even fall in love with what has captured your intellectual imagination. You can also help students develop learning skills that change how they approach every learning task. You can help them learn to read critically, challenge assumptions, ask good questions, and evaluate answers. You can help students grow and develop as human beings—you can change their lives, and that's what makes teaching such a worthwhile endeavor. It is work that makes a difference.

Since retiring, I am continuing to work in this area, motivated in part by the interest it has sparked in others. I've written other books, but when I'm asked to speak, it is almost always about learner-centered teaching. These ongoing discussions with various faculty groups have continued to change my thinking about learner-centered teaching and were another motivation for doing a new edition of this book.

My thinking on the topic has also been enriched by much new literature published since the first edition. There are books and articles, some accounts of how learner-centered approaches succeeded, and some describing how they failed. There are descriptions of new techniques, some innovative and some modest alterations of common practices. There is much more research, some of it in education, but a lot based in the disciplines. Some studies report the effects of a particular technique on learning outcomes; others report on the impact of a variety of learner-centered changes implemented in a single course. Because this research exists in so many different disciplines, many of the questions and findings are not known by those in other fields, even though they share the same interests and could learn much from each other's work. The research employs so many different methodologies that it can't be integrated empirically, but its many findings can be reported and implications for practice explored. I saw this as another reason to revisit a now dated book and prepare a new one.

As I begin working on this new edition, our house on the island is almost finished. Michael built a huge fireplace in the front room. It rests on and circles around the giant boulder that is the back wall of our house. We think we have something of an Extreme Home. Perhaps you will see us on that television show some day. It was another of those projects that involved much learning, experimenting, heavy lifting, and spectacular results, once the smoke started reliably ascending the chimney. And downstairs in the workshop a second incarnation of *Noah's Lark* is taking shape. With the first boat, as Michael explains, "I didn't learn everything I needed to know the first time." When a wooden boat sits in the water and out in weather for the four summer months, rot becomes an issue. This *Noah* began with the same hull plan, but she looks different and has significant design changes. "I'm building this one to last fifteen years." We shall see. And after the new *Noah*, there's a 1961 Chris Craft awaiting restoration in the other garage bay. "How do you restore a very old wooden boat? I don't know. There's lots I have to learn."

THE THEORIES BEHIND LEARNER-CENTERED TEACHING

To make the transition from this personal history to a discussion of relevant theories, let me distill what I have come to believe are the key ingredients of learner-centered teaching. It is teaching focused on learning—what the students are doing is the central concern of the teacher. Being "focused on learning" is easily understood at a superficial level, but its delineation reveals more details and intricacies:

1. It is teaching that engages students in the hard, messy work of learning.
2. It is teaching that motivates and empowers students by giving them some control over learning processes.
3. It is teaching that encourages collaboration, acknowledging the classroom (be it virtual or real) as a community where everyone shares the learning agenda.
4. It is teaching that promotes students' reflection about what they are learning and how they are learning it.
5. It is teaching that includes explicit learning skills instruction.

There's much more about all of these intricacies in the chapters ahead.

At this point the consideration is how these key characteristics of learner-centered teaching grow out of and uniquely integrate a number of different educational theories. Although any number of us who use learner-centered approaches would claim that for us they function as the philosophy that drives our instructional decision making and grounds our practice, learner-centered teaching is not described in the literature as an educational theory or philosophy. Rather, it is regularly tied to existing theories like those briefly highlighted next.

ATTRIBUTION THEORY AND SELF-EFFICACY

When applied to education, Attribution Theory identifies what students attribute their success or failure to. Heider (1958) is credited with originating the theory. It was developed further by Wiener (1986) and researchers like Covington (1992). When students try to explain an academic outcome (like how well they did or didn't do on an exam), they generally attribute it to either ability or effort—how competent they are or how hard they tried. We've all seen how strongly attributions influence student behavior. Students regularly show up in our classes convinced they can't do something—write, solve problems, dance, or give a speech. A fine teacher of developmental writing once told me that the toughest challenge teaching deficient writers was persuading them that they could indeed write. How can you write if you don't have the ability? Some of these beliefs we see in ourselves. I am no good with computers. I can't make most technology tools work. When my husband is gone, I don't watch TV because I can't figure out how the silly remote control works. Are all thirty-five of those buttons really necessary?

Attribution Theory also explores how the cause (or source of the attribution) is tempered by what Weiner (1986) identified as control, stability, and locus. Is the cause under the student's control? Students tend to see ability as something they are born with, not something they can control. Is the cause stable or does it fluctuate? If a lack of ability is what causes you to do poorly in math, that cause is stable and unlikely to change, which makes it tricky to explain success unless you attribute it to blind luck. Is the locus associated with internal factors or external ones? For example, believing that the teacher put "tricky" questions on the exam or included problems not like those assigned as homework allows the student to blame external forces for poor performance. It also illustrates how locus mediates cause attribution.

Self-efficacy, not unrelated to Attribution Theory, has to do with students' beliefs about their capabilities—whether they can learn something. Bandura (1997), whose work in the area is most influential, has shown that what students believe about what they can and can't do influences all sorts of academic decisions from choice of major, to participation in activities, to their pursuit of job interviews. The power of these beliefs is illustrated by things like test anxiety, where a student may know the material very well but because the testing situation raises all sorts of doubts about capability she performs poorly.

Because beliefs about self-efficacy are formed from a variety of different sources of information, teachers and classmates can be instrumental. To build a sense of self-efficacy, students need to be in learning situations that "(1) construe ability as an acquirable skill, (2) deemphasize competitive social comparisons and high-light self-comparison of progress and personal accomplishment, and (3) reinforce the individual student's ability to exercise some control over the learning environment" (Stage, Muller, Kinzie, and Simmons, 1998, p. 26).

The bottom line is that many students do not have much faith in themselves as learners. Learner-centered approaches respond by challenging those beliefs with things like carefully sequenced assignment sets, which increase the likelihood of success, with clear demonstrations of how effort makes a difference, and with teaching that lets students own the responsibility for learning and for the decisions they make about learning.

RADICAL AND CRITICAL PEDAGOGY

This educational theory was first and now most famously articulated by the Brazilian educator Freire in a 1970 book, *Pedagogy of the Oppressed* (rereleased in 1993 by a U.S. publisher). The central tenet of radical or critical pedagogy (I will use the terms interchangeably, although those who work in this area make distinctions between the terms) rests on the idea that education is a vehicle for social change. Stage, Muller, Kinzie, and Simmons (1998, p. 57) elaborate: "Education's role is to challenge inequality and dominant myths rather than socialize students into the status quo. Learning is directed toward social change and transforming the world, and 'true' learning empowers students to challenge oppression in their lives."

Freire's equation of education with social change grew out of his experiences teaching illiterate peasants to read, a skill they then used to challenge corrupt political regimes that had long repressed them. Those who view the growth of knowledge as an objective, rational process oppose attaching this "political" agenda to education. The critical pedagogues counter that all "forms of education are contextual and political whether or not teachers and students are consciously aware of these processes" (Stage, Muller, Kinzie, and Simmons, 1998, p. 57). Tompkins (1991, p. 26) offers a clear description of how this political agenda manifests itself in every classroom. "I have come to think more and more that what really matters . . . is not so much what we talk about in class as what we do . . . The classroom is a microcosm of the world; it is the chance we have to practice whatever ideals we cherish. The kind of classroom situation one creates is the acid test of what it is one really stands for."

As you might suspect, this theory does not endorse teaching as the transmission of knowledge from authorities. Aronowitz (1993, p. 89) explains Freire's intentions for the classroom: "He means to offer a system in which the locus of the learning process is shifted from the teacher to the students. And this shift overtly signifies an altered *power* relationship, not only in the classroom but in the broader social canvas as well."

The idea of education as a vehicle for social change is not a dominant feature of current learner-centered practices. Those of us who use these approaches, especially in more egalitarian countries and cultures, are not trying to educate the masses so that they can redress social injustices. That may be an implicit goal of all education, but it's not the reason usually given for adopting these approaches. The interest is more in overcoming students' predilection to passivity. We are trying to teach in ways that encourage students to accept responsibility for learning. We want them to leave our classes believing that what and how they have learned enables them to figure out more things on their own and for themselves.

My experiences talking about learner-centered teaching have convinced me that the power issues raised by this theory are a central concern to faculty. Time and again in workshops, teachers tell me that students are not ready to handle learning decisions. They are unprepared and not motivated. They need and want teachers who tell them exactly what to do and how they must do it.

This transfer of power to students realized initially by giving them some control over learning decisions is further addressed in a masterfully edited conversation between Freire and Horton (Horton and Freire, 1990). Horton's theories of education emerged out of his work preparing disenfranchised African Americans to pass voting tests. Both Freire and Horton shared power with the poorest of poorly prepared students, those who could not read. And did they find that even these students could be trusted with decisions about their learning? They did indeed, and when students were so trusted, their motivation to learn increased dramatically.

Radical pedagogy challenges many common assumptions about who is responsible for what in the teaching learning process. It is a theory that questions the role of teacher authority in student learning experiences and one that challenges teachers to explore ethically responsible ways of sharing power with students. Making all the learning decisions for students may be what they want, but it is not an approach that develops confident, motivated learners. Radical pedagogy is about changing the power dynamic in classrooms for the benefit of students and learning.

Feminist Pedagogy

Feminist pedagogy is also about changing the power dynamic in the classroom, but for reasons that have more to do with teachers than with students. Like radical pedagogy, this theory finds that most teaching is too authoritarian. Power in the classroom is not equitably distributed, and the imbalance negatively affects learning outcomes, especially for women. Higher education has a history of male domination, and the forms patriarchy entrenched in society have found root in the academy and its classrooms. As a result, students (usually females, especially in male-dominated fields) are treated differentially. Their learning is inhibited by power structures that protect the powerful.

Feminist pedagogy sees patriarchy as of a perversion of power. Those in power love and protect their power to the disadvantage of those they control. They resist giving up power, not admitting their love of power, but instead offer up reasons why those in their classrooms are not capable of making decisions for themselves. Said more bluntly, the power issue is more about faculty and less about students.

Being in control in the classroom does come with a seductive set of advantages that include being able to set the agenda, direct the action, squelch most forms of dissent, and showcase one's intellectual and pedagogical prowess. The benefits of being in control may be the reason some teachers object to learner-centered approaches that require them to share power. This theory prompts individual teachers to explore the real reasons why learner-centered approaches seem untenable.

In feminist classrooms, teachers are facilitators of learning. More metaphorically, the teacher is like the maestro who directs others to make music or the gardener who prepares and plants, feeds, and waters, trims and prunes, making it possible for flowers to bloom with beauty and fragrance, or the midwife who brings experience and expertise to the birth of learning.

Feminist theory also critiques the competitive aspects of education. It posits that education does a much better job of teaching students to compete than to cooperate. Although not a feminist scholar, Kohn (1986) amasses a persuasive collection of evidence against the competitive aspects of educational practices such as grading on a curve. Learner-centered approaches encourage cooperation. They value the learning that occurs when students collaborate and work best in classrooms where learning can happen anywhere and should happen everywhere. Feminist hooks (1994, p. 12) describes these classrooms as "radical spaces of possibility."

Because the messages of both radical and feminist pedagogy are confrontational and the agenda political, discussion of them mostly occurs in venues far removed from the classroom. As a consequence, most faculty are unfamiliar with work done in these areas, even though many learner-centered ideas can be traced back to these theories. These more democratic and equalitarian views of education call into question traditional power structures and the role of teacher authority. They propose that students be empowered to accept responsibility for learning and that teachers are successful when they are no longer needed.

CONSTRUCTIVISM

At the core of this currently prominent educational theory is the relationship between learners and content. "Constructivist approaches emphasize learners' actively constructing their own knowledge rather than passively receiving information transmitted to them from teachers and textbooks. From a constructivist perspective, knowledge cannot simply be given to students: Students must construct their own meanings" (Stage, Muller, Kinzie, and Simmons 1998, p. 35). Fosnot (1996, p. 29) expands this description by explaining that learning "requires invention and self-organization on the part of the learner. Thus teachers need to allow learners to raise their own questions, generate their own hypotheses and models as possibilities and test them for validity." This theory of education and learning rests on the work of a variety of psychologists and philosophers, most notably Piaget, Bruner, von Glaserfeld, and Vygotsky.

Unlike critical pedagogy and feminist pedagogy, which are almost never mentioned in the work of practitioners, constructivism is regularly offered as a justification for using learner-centered approaches. The approaches associated with constructivism often involve group work, although those writing about the theory more regularly refer to the act of individual learners connecting new information to what they currently know in ways meaningful to them. The distinction is something of a moot point, because when students work together in groups, each group member still deals with content individually, relying on his or her own experiences and understandings.

Early on, the group work most often associated with constructivist theories was collaborative learning, as promoted by Bruffee (1993), who advocated that student groups explore complex, cross-disciplinary problems. With a teacher or teachers among them as master learners, these groups would search for new, integrated, and often innovative solutions to the problems. This early work spawned a variety of learning community models that use course structures to connect students, content, and teachers in exploratory learning situations. Learning community experiences are now part of college curricula at many institutions.

The idea that students might be involved in knowledge construction fits comfortably in the humanities and social science fields, where content supports more tentative and less definitive conclusions. It is more difficult to see how knowledge can be "socially" constructed in science, math, and engineering fields, where there are more "right" answers and much less disagreement about the status of knowledge. As a consequence, objections to constructivist theories came first from these fields, although at this point they have been raised by educators in many fields.

One of the objections raised first involves the inefficiency of letting students discover knowledge for themselves. It takes time and often includes time wasted pursuing answers in places where they won't be found. Courses are sequenced assuming that a specified amount of content has been "covered" and can be built on in the next course, although most teachers have discovered content covered does not always mean content learned or remembered. Constructivists respond that in the process of figuring things out for themselves, students develop valuable learning skills. They learn problem solving by solving problems, even when they don't always do it perfectly; they learn to ask questions by asking questions; they learn to evaluate answers by evaluating answers; they learn to think critically by thinking critically.

It has been practitioners who have pointed out the importance of balance between the student's need to discover and the teacher's need to tell. Chemistry faculty members Ditzier and Ricci (1994, p. 687) write: "It takes all of our pedagogical skills to discover, on a daily basis, the right mix of interaction and passive observation that balances the need to present the chemists' elegant way of thinking with the importance of fostering student creativity." In the classroom, it doesn't have to be either-or; it can be a balance of both. Sometimes the content itself makes clear when students should simply be told an answer and when they should be working to discover it on their own.

A second objection involves the role of the teacher in learning environments where students are doing the messy work of learning for themselves. Those who object say it isn't fair or ethical to give students a complicated problem and then let them sink or swim. Constructivists respond that this isn't what they are proposing; they want teachers to *support* learning, rather than *direct* it. Duffy and Raymer (2010), writing about inquiry-based learning, an example of a constructivist approach, explain that the guidance provided to learners is a critical part of the method: "However, the guidance is focused on promoting students' critical thinking rather than telling them what to do or what to pay attention to" (p. 4). Instructors using constructivist approaches do lecture, but generally this direct transfer of information occurs after students have grappled with the issue, after they have a sense of what it is they need to know. The benefit of waiting is that once students realize they need to know something, they listen attentively for the answers.

And finally, some object because they think constructivism means that teachers must give equal weight to whatever students propose, that every construction of personal meaning is acceptable, even those that aren't right or very good. This objection culminates with the assertion that constructivism dilutes the intellectual integrity of course content. It sacrifices academic rigor and standards.

The constructivists see this as another prevarication of what they are proposing. Constructing knowledge does not mean the learner makes up the knowledge—it's something much closer to positioning the new knowledge so that it connects with something already known and therefore makes sense to the learner. Teachers should pay attention to student understandings, not because they are viable alternatives to well-established facts, but because the way students think should shape the way they are taught. Moreover, once students have arrived at a conclusion or decided on a meaning, challenging their thinking is the next step in the process. Teachers should question students and design activities that require students to explain and defend what they propose. The goal is to get students to see quality variations among solutions.

Cooperative learning—a form of group work with a tightly prescribed task, interdependence among groups members, but individual accountability—has been used widely in the science disciplines in part because it responds to some of these objections. However, most cooperative learning structures are only marginally constructivist. Recent years have seen the rise of a wide range of group work models (Process-Oriented Guided Inquiry, or POGIL; Guided Inquiry; and Peer-Led Team Learning, or PLTL; among others), which blur the distinctions between collaborative and cooperative learning. Most of these new models do retain the core ingredients of constructivism—students in groups are working on open-ended problems, they are accessing and organizing information they discover, and they are crafting their own solutions. New research highlighted in the next chapter documents how amazingly effective some of these approaches can be.

Beyond use by individual faculty, constructivist principles have been used to realign whole curricula, course sequences, and multiple sections of individual courses. For an example, see Ege, Coppola, and Lawton (1996), who used constructivist theories to redesign the introductory organic chemistry course taken by all chemistry, biology, and premed majors at the University of Michigan.

Constructivism closely aligns with many learner-centered practices. Most fundamentally, it proposes that students must be interacting with the content—something far different from the passive receipt of information from an authority. In the constructivist interaction, students connect new material with what they already know. They may mold and shape the new information so that it fits with what they already believe and know, or they may use the new information to reshape, enlarge, and deepen their current understandings. A form of the verb "to construct," this is about students building knowledge with the guidance of teachers who have built knowledge structures out of this material previously.

TRANSFORMATIVE LEARNING

Transformative learning theory is based on constructivist assumptions, according to Cranton (2006, p. 23), an adult educator who has done much work in this area. It is about learners constructing personal meaning and doing so through processes of examination, questioning, validating, and revising—what adult educators call critical reflection. But it is the conclusion of the reflection process that differentiates transformative learning from constructivism. As the name indicates, this is learning that transforms, that changes learners in deep, profound, and lasting ways. Often what changes are taken-for-granted beliefs, unchallenged assumptions, and habits of the mind never before questioned. Sometimes this learning can be the result of a single event—what Mezirow and Associates (2000) call a "disorienting dilemma"—or the transformation can take place gradually, over time, as events and experiences trigger more critical reflection. Either way, this is the kind of learning that changes what people believe, how they act, indeed, who they are. It should be the ultimate objective of education, especially higher education.

This is another area of theory and research not generally known by those interested in learner-centered teaching, even though the practitioner literature is filled with accounts of changes in learners that those in adult education would call transformative. Unfortunately, teachers typically attribute changes that are transformative to chance—changes happen or they don't; they can't be planned or controlled. When teachers take this view, they don't think about specific things they might do to promote, advance, and otherwise increase the possibility of transformative learning experiences. So even though there is evidence (ably summarized by Pascarella and Terenzini, 1991, 2005) that college experiences change students, there's a possibility of more transformative learning experiences if teachers see a role for themselves in promoting it.

There's also a strong possibility that because learner-centered approaches focus the student so directly on learning, they lead students in the direction of transformative learning experiences. These are approaches that encourage reflection, critique, and the development of self-awareness. Learners can be transformed across a broad range of areas, according to adult education theory, and it may be that learner-centered approaches increase the likelihood of various kinds of transformative experiences.

Most of us using these approaches have seen them transform what many students believe about learning. Once they start taking responsibility for learning and making some of the decisions associated with it, they begin to see what they can accomplish when they are independent, self-directed learners. At some point there really is no turning back. I was abruptly confronted with this once in my graduate course on college teaching. We had invited a renowned scholar to class to discuss questions students had raised about some of his research and writings. He arrived and proceeded to lecture from a carefully prepared set of notes. Shortly after he began, a student interrupted, "Doctor, we asked you to class because we have questions we'd like to discuss with you. We'd prefer to deal with our questions and share ideas with you." The scholar was clearly taken aback, but a discussion did follow, and after class he remarked to me, "I've never had students do that to me before, but their questions clearly indicated they didn't need to listen to a lecture on the topic."

Although learner-centered approaches do transform beliefs about learning effectively, they don't transform all students. Perhaps they would if students experienced them more regularly in the curriculum, or if we knew more about which designs and what sequences had the greatest impact, perhaps we could better promote transformative learning. Even so, enough is known to justify the purposeful intervention of teachers to learning that changes students in these deep and profound ways.

Moreover, experience with learner-centered approaches doesn't just transform students. This way of teaching can also transform what teachers believe about learning and their role as teachers. I've already described how profoundly it changed my beliefs about teaching and practices in the classroom. These equally profound changes are also regularly described in the practitioner literature, but again, teachers do not identify what happened to them as a transformative learning experience. For examples, see Tompkins (1991), Mazur (2009), and Spence (2010).

This book begins with my first learner-centered teaching experiences and then subsequent discovery of the theories on which these approaches rest. As my experiences have unfolded and as learner-centered ideas have linked with various education theories, there is no neat, orderly progression of experiences, ideas, or connections. Things are more muddled and messy than clear and coherent. And the hodgepodge nature of this knowledge domain continues in the research realm, as the next chapter reveals. Learner-centered teaching was not discovered, explained by a theory, and then proven with a systematic line of research. But despite the inherent messiness of how one teacher stumbled onto these ideas and how the ideas themselves loop over and under, around and through a variety of educational theories, there is support—theoretical, empirical, and experiential—that these approaches to teaching promote more and better learning for students.

CHAPTER TWO

RESEARCH: EVIDENCE THAT LEARNER-CENTERED APPROACHES WORK

Considerable research justifying the effectiveness of learner-centered approaches exists. A significant amount has been published since the first edition of this book. In fact, the growing body of evidence supporting the effectiveness of these approaches was what finally convinced me of the merits of a second edition. This chapter will summarize a sampling of that work, updating what was highlighted in the first edition and introducing new findings.

I can imagine a number of faculty reading that opener and thinking that this might be a chapter to skip. Most faculty don't enjoy reading research unless it's in their area of scholarship or on a topic of intense interest. With research on teaching and learning, whether it's done in the field of education or by practitioners in the disciplines, there's another reason it isn't read. Many faculty don't think it's very good and don't think there's much to be learned that might benefit what they do in the classroom.

The neglect of research on teaching and learning is understandable to some degree. Educational research, like research in all our fields, is not uniformly good. The research methodologies, always presented in excruciating detail and with lots of jargon, are frequently unfamiliar. The implications of findings are not routinely spelled out. This research, again like much done in our disciplines, better informs subsequent research than practice. But I don't think that justifies the neglect of research on teaching and learning.

Here are just some of the benefits that come from knowing something about research relevant to learner-centered teaching. If you aren't using any learner-centered strategies, the research findings may offer evidence that convinces you to try some of these approaches. If you are using some of them, understanding more about the design features that make them work and the learning outcomes they most often affect can increase the effectiveness with which you use them. If you believe in learner-centered teaching and want to advocate for these approaches, even just informally recommend them to a colleague, your advocacy will be more effective if you know something about how they've been tested and the kind of evidence that supports how well they work.

Two final benefits are more broadly applicable but still relevant to learner-centered teaching. Because research on teaching and learning remains so little known, much instructional practice is not evidence-based. That seems very ironic in an academic culture where evidence is revered. Teaching is devalued and learning is compromised when practice is not guided by what is known about making both effective. Knowledge of the research can motivate the kind of changes that will make instruction more evidence-based. And finally, reading educational research relevant to learner-centered approaches just might convince you that there's other research on teaching and learning worth your time. Beyond these benefits, my goal for this chapter is to present an interesting, succinct, nontechnical summary of research—one that will keep you awake and intrigued.

The chapter does not contain a comprehensive review of the literature on learner-centered approaches. I don't have enough time left in my career to put together that kind of review. The research justifying these approaches has been done in all sorts of different fields, starting with education and its various subfields and ending with practitioner pedagogical research now being done in virtually every discipline. Finding everything—or just finding most things—is a daunting task. I'm pretty certain I read more on this topic than most folks, and I'm constantly finding things I haven't read and should have known about.

In addition to the research being located in many different places, there are all sorts of different techniques, strategies, and approaches that fall under the learner-centered umbrella. I will write more subsequently about how this definitional looseness makes it difficult to determine whether something is or is not learner-centered. At this juncture, it's a question of what to include in the review when we are confronted with such a wide array of options. I've opted for important, high-quality, interesting work—actually, I find much of what I'm going to write in this chapter fascinating, but then one must be careful of hyperbole in academic books.

Reviews of research often integrate findings using quantitative methods like meta-analyses, but the diversity of research relevant to learner-centered approaches rules out any sort of quantitative analyses. Too many different research methodologies have been used. The goal of most research reviews is to integrate what is known as a way of making clear what is not known and thereby helping to direct the research agenda. That's not what practitioners need to know about the research on learner-centered approaches. They need to understand the kind of questions that have been addressed by the research, what answers have been found—which, for educational research, with its lack of definitive conclusions, always means the answer supported by the weight of the evidence—and, most important, what they should be doing about the results. Those are the questions that should be answerable by the end of the chapter.

RESEARCH UPDATES

The 2002 edition highlights research done in three areas that merit updating: deep and surface learning, faculty orientations to teaching, and self-regulated learning. The research in each of these areas has been conducted in education and fields related to it. It is not research on learner-centered approaches per se, but focuses on the principles that learner-centered approaches exemplify.

DEEP AND SURFACE LEARNING

This work, reasonably well known among faculty (though for most the knowledge doesn't extend much past the difference between the two approaches to learning), was launched with a particularly seminal study by Marton and Saljo (1976; updated and analyzed in Marton, Hounsell, and Entwistle, 1997). They had students read material from an academic text and then asked them to describe what they had been reading. Ramsden (1988, p. 18), another important scholar working in this area, has succinctly summarized those first findings: "They found evidence of *qualitative* differences in the outcome of students' reading. The differences were not about how much the students could remember, but about the meaning the author had tried to convey. Some students fully understood the argument being advanced and could relate it to the evidence being used to support it; others partly understood the author's message; others could only mention some of the remembered details."

When students concentrated on memorizing the facts, focused on the discrete elements of the reading, failed to differentiate between evidence and information, were unreflective and saw the task as an external imposition, Marton and Saljo characterized their approach as "surface" learning. When students focused on what the author meant, related new information to what they already knew and had experienced, worked to organize and structure the content, and saw the reading as an important source of learning, Marton and Saljo characterized the approach as "deep." Ramsden (1988, p. 23) further outlines the differences between the two approaches. For students using surface approaches, "texts were a flat landscape of facts to be remembered, rather than an area dotted with salient features representing principles or arguments around which stretched plains of evidence."

Ramsden (1988, p. 271) also sees connections between deep learning and transformative learning: "Learning should be seen as a qualitative change in a person's way of seeing, experiencing, understanding, conceptualizing something in the real world—rather than as a quantitative change in the amount of knowledge someone possesses." Deep learning is what helps students achieve education's broadest and most important goals. "Higher education should . . . be concentrating on helping students develop skills, attitudes, knowledge, and understanding that will be of maximum value beyond academe; not just an induction into the world of work in a specific profession, but also an effective preparation for life in the 21st century" (Entwistle, 2010, p. 20).

"Since the original naturalistic experiment, the distinction between deep and surface approaches has been widely confirmed across most subject areas," according to Entwistle (2010, p. 24). That confirmation comes from instruments (Biggs, Kember, and Leung, 2001; or Tait, Entwistle, and McCune, 1998, reprinted in Entwistle, 2010, pp. 53–54) that reliably indicate whether students are using deep or surface approaches. Teachers can use these instruments to give students feedback and encourage them to explore the more productive approaches of deep learning.

The research on deep and surface learning has resonated with faculty. Most see all too many students focused on memorizing material without much, if any, understanding of what they are memorizing. Surface learning approaches result in material being retained briefly, and most faculty have seen that firsthand as well. The question, then, is whether learner-centered approaches promote deep learning. And the most convincing evidence that they do is found in research on faculty orientations to teaching.

FACULTY ORIENTATIONS TO TEACHING

As early as 1988 (Greeson), research was showing that there was a relationship between teacher-centered or student-centered approaches and the type of learning experiences that students reported. In that study, student-centered instructional approaches were preferable across a number of different variables. Those early results have been confirmed consistently, starting with Kember and Gow's (1994) study of teachers and students within departments. Their results "suggest that the methods of teaching adopted, the learning tasks set, the assessment demands made, and the workload specified are strongly influenced by orientation to teaching. In departments where the knowledge transmission orientation predominates, the curriculum design and teaching methods are more likely to have undesirable influences on the learning approaches of students. Departments with a greater propensity toward learning facilitation are more likely to design courses and establish a learning environment that encourages meaningful learning" (p. 69).

In the late 1990s, Trigwell and Prosser with various colleagues developed an Approaches to Teaching Inventory (revised in Prosser and Trigwell, 2006), which identifies the extent to which a teacher is oriented to information transmission and teacher-focused, or oriented to conceptual change and student-focused—in the parlance of this book, whether the instructor is teacher-centered or learner-centered. In 2010, Trigwell reported on five research studies that administered this instrument to faculty at the same time their students completed an approaches-to-learning instrument (such as Biggs, Kember, and Leung, 2001) and then compared the results. Several of these studies were impressively large: one involved 46 college science teachers in 48 classes with 3,956 students (Trigwell, Prosser, and Waterhouse, 1999); another involved 55 large first-year courses, taught by multiple teachers across a range of disciplines, generating data from 408 teachers and 8,829 students (Trigwell, Prosser, Ramsden, and Martin, 1999).

About the results from all these studies, Trigwell (2010) writes, "Together these studies indicate, with classes as the unit of analysis, that an information transmission/teacher-focused approach to teaching is strongly and positively associated with surface and non-deep approaches to learning, and that a conceptual change/student-focused approach to teaching is positively associated with deep and non-surface approaches to learning" (p. 121). Trigwell offers a description of the student-focused orientation that confirms it is what this book refers to as learner-centered teaching: "When teachers report that they have the student as the focus of their activities, where it matters more to them what the student is doing and learning than what the teacher is covering, when the teacher is the one who encourages self-directed learning, . . . where the teacher provokes debate, uses a lot of time to question students' ideas and to develop a 'conversation' with students in lecture, then his or her students are less likely to adopt a surface approach and more likely to adopt a deep approach" (p. 121).

This research offers a convincing commendation of learner-centered approaches. When they are used, the claim can be justifiably made that they promote a different, deeper, and better kind of learning. It is a kind of learning that lasts, and learning that enables higher education to achieve some of its broadest and highest goals.

INDEPENDENT, SELF-DIRECTED, AND SELF-REGULATED LEARNERS

Early in my faculty development career, I encountered the idea of autonomous learning in the work of Boud (1981), whose edited anthology describes how education typically makes students very dependent learners. They depend on the teacher to identify what needs to be learned, to prescribe the learning methods, and finally to assess what and how well they have learned. Many arrive in our classrooms needing teachers to tell them virtually everything—how many words their paper should contain, what font they should use, how many references it must include, and how wide they should make the margins. If these details are not specified, students will ask and be upset if they must make these decisions.

Because we so seldom see self-directed learners in our college classrooms, we forget how effectively some individuals do learn on their own. Whether it's a self-taught gardener, bird enthusiast, master knitter, or garage-based boat builder, some learners take their avocations to high levels of knowledge and skill. Many of the characteristics of independent learners have been identified through research that analyzes how these self-taught learners operate. This and other research is summarized in a 1991 book by Candy, *Self-Direction for Lifelong Learning*. An appendix contains Candy's Profile of the Autonomous Learner, which lists over one hundred "attributes, characteristics, qualities, and competencies" (p. 459) used by and in research to describe the autonomous learner. This appendix ends up being a unique summary of the research and an apt description of the "perfect" student, the one we'd all love to teach.

Zimmerman (2002), who has also done extensive research in this area, offers a clear definition of what he calls self-regulated learning. He says it is "not a mental ability or an academic per-formance skill; rather it is the self-directive process by which learners transform their mental abilities into academic skills" (p. 65). This characteristic of learners is variously named: self-directed learners, autonomous learners, independent learners. The differ-ences, more subtle nuances than substantive distinctions, coalesce in what Zimmerman (2008) describes as the overarching research question: trying to understand "how students become masters of their own learning processes" (p. 166).

Zimmerman's 2002 article offers a succinct and clear overview of research on self-regulated learning. It's definitely worth consulting if this area is of interest. He identifies three findings that have emerged out of this research. First, "self-regulated learning involves more than detailed knowledge of a skill; it involves the self-awareness, self-motivation, and behavioral skill to implement that knowledge appropriately" (p. 66). Research also confirms that self-regulation is not a trait that some people have and others don't. And finally, whether or not a student is motivated, self-regulated learning depends on self-efficacy beliefs and intrinsic interest.

As with deep and surface learning, researchers have developed a number of instruments that they have used to determine the extent to which students are self-regulating. These include the Learning and Study Strategies Inventory (better known as LASSI; Weinstein, Schulte, and Palmer, 1987), the Motivated Strategies for Learning Questionnaire (MSLQ; Pintrich, Smith, Garcia, and McKeachie, 1993) and the Self-Regulated Learning Interview Scale, which uses a structured interview to present students with six study problems to which they verbally respond (Zimmerman and Martinez Pons, 1986, 1988). Like the deep and surface learning instruments, these instruments are great resources for teachers. If students complete one of them, teachers benefit by discovering the extent to which their students are using self-regulating strategies, and students benefit just as much, if not more, by becoming aware of the strategies they use and more effective alternatives.

Zimmerman (2008) summarizes research on four questions currently being explored empirically. Until recently, researchers have relied on student self-reports of what they are doing when they study. Now there are software programs that enable students to use many of the strategies associated with self-regulation, and those programs allow researchers to track which of the strategies students use as they study. The question is whether congruence exists between those self-reports and the actual use of the strategies. So far, the results are mixed. The second question: If students use self-regulated learning strategies at home or in the library, for example, does that improve their overall academic achievement? Early research answers are yes. The third question is particularly relevant to learner-centered objectives: Can teachers modify what they do in the classroom in ways that increase self-regulated learning among students? Yes, they can. And finally, what role do students' motivational feelings and beliefs play in initiating and sustaining changes in their self-regulation of learning? Research now indicates a close relationship between self-regulated processes and sources of motivation.

As a result of research on self-directed learning, many now propose that a formal educational experience should enable learners to identify what they need to know and decide how they will learn it—whether they are confronted with learning tasks in the classroom, at home, on the job, or subsequently throughout life. However, Zimmerman (2002) points out that despite research findings showing conclusively that self-regulation leads to greater academic success, "few teachers currently prepare students to learn on their own" (p. 64). He elaborates: "Students are seldom given choices regarding academic tasks to pursue, methods for carrying out complex assignments, or study partners. Few teachers encourage students to establish specific goals for their academic work or teach explicit study strategies. Also, students are rarely asked to self-evaluate their work or estimate their competence on new tasks" (p. 69).

These approaches that prepare students to learn on their own are inherently a part of learner-centered teaching, which involves students in decision making about learning, encourages collaboration, offers explicit instruction on learning skills, and provides opportunities for self- and peer assessment. The value of having students able to learn for themselves is not something most faculty need research to verify. We know that our students will change jobs, many of them more than once, and that ongoing learning will be a part of every job, indeed of life. It is obvious that the success of our students depends on their ability to be lifelong learners.

Research findings on deep and surface learning, faculty orientations to teaching, and self-regulated learning support the use of learner-centered approaches. The work on faculty orientations establishes that if teachers' primary focus is on covering content, students respond by memorizing the material, often with little or no understanding. When teachers are learner-centered, focused on developing understanding of the material and committed to helping students gain mastery over their learning processes, students learn the material at a deeper level and begin managing their learning in ways that lead to their autonomy and independence as learners.

NOTEWORTHY REVIEWS OF RESEARCH

Reviews of research summarize and integrate findings, making clearer the status of knowledge within a particular domain. Most of the time reviews are written for those doing the research or with related research interests. Rarely do these reviews explore the implications of findings and even more rarely are reviews written expressly for practitioners. The three reviews in this section are notable exceptions, and all three report on research relevant to learner-centered teaching.

REVIEW OF RESEARCH ON MOTIVATION

Most faculty struggle against pervasive amounts of student passivity. How can these students be in college and yet be so unmotivated to learn? All of us who teach poorly motivated students need to know as much as possible about research in this area, and Pintrich (2003), an educational researcher known for his work on motivation, has published an outstanding research review. He considers research relevant to seven key questions about motivation:

1. What do students want?
2. What motivates students in classrooms?
3. How do students get what they want?
4. Do students know what they want or what motivates them?
5. How does motivation lead to cognition and cognition to motivation?
6. How does motivation change and develop?
7. What is the role of context and culture?

Unlike so many reviews, Pintrich spells out instructional implications of the research on motivation. For example, in response to what motivates students in classrooms, Pintrich identifies a set of generalizations supported by the research, beginning with "adaptive attributions and control beliefs motivate students" [in classrooms] (p. 673). In summarizing the research that supports this claim, he writes, "the general trend is that students who believe they have more personal control of their own learning and behavior are more likely to do well and achieve at higher levels than students who do not feel in control" (p. 673). And what "design" principles does he recommend based on this finding? "Provide [students] opportunities to exercise some choice and control." So what many of us have observed in the learner-centered classroom is supported by the research. When students can make some choices about how they learn, and when they have some control over their learning processes, their motivation to learn increases.

There is much, much more in the Pintrich article. However, I would be less than honest if I said it was easy reading. It's not, but if gaining a better understanding of the role of motivation in learning is of interest, there aren't many sources more definitive than this one. And effort expended reading this review is rewarded with clear suggestions on what should be done about the research findings.

REVIEWS OF RESEARCH ON ACTIVE LEARNING

Research on active learning covers a large domain and is as diverse and disorganized as any crazy quilt. The problems begin with the many different definitions for active learning and are exacerbated by all the different strategies to which the active learning label is attached. Then there are the multiple methods used to study the effects of active learning experiences. And finally, some sort of study of active learning has been undertaken in almost every discipline. Who would even attempt to review this domain?

The two reviews I'm about to highlight were authored not by educational researchers, who one might argue are the scholars best positioned to attempt such a review, but by a chemical engineer and a med school physiologist. Neither is a typical review of research articles, and each is constructed quite differently. Both were written for faculty audiences and, despite their different approaches, both come to the same conclusion. If there are ever any doubts as to what active learning accomplishes or if there's a colleague who's yet to be convinced that there's evidence supporting the claims regularly made about active learning, these articles settle the issue. Both merit discussing further, because active learning is to learner-centered teaching as bread is to butter.

Prince's review (2004) begins with definitions and follows with an excellent discussion of what makes the research on active learning so difficult to consider collectively. For example, there's the problem of defining what's being studied. He uses Problem-Based Learning as an example. It's an approach that has been widely used and studied, but there is no agreement as to the core elements of this strategy, which makes generalizing from the various studies difficult. Then there's the problem of measuring "what works." Assessing that "requires looking at a broad range of learning outcomes, interpreting data carefully, quantifying the magnitude of any reported improvement and having some idea of what constitutes a 'significant' improvement" (p. 225).

Using clear definitions and establishing qualifying criteria, Prince looks at two major categories of research on active learning: (1) active learning strategies that get students involved in lectures and (2) student engagement activities, including collaborative learning, cooperative learning, and problem-based learning. His reviews of research in each of these areas are clear and easy to understand. For an overall conclusion, he writes, "although the results vary in strength, this study has found support for all forms of active learning examined" (p. 229). A bit later he observes: "Teaching cannot be reduced to formulaic methods and active learning is not the cure-all for all educational problems. However, there is broad support for the elements of active learning most commonly discussed in the educational literature and analyzed here" (p. 229).

Michael's review (2006) also begins with definitions—for active learning and student-centered instruction. The definition for active learning, from the *Greenwood Dictionary of Education*, indicates that it is a "process of having students engage in some activity that forces them to reflect upon ideas and how they are using those ideas." It continues with a list offering examples: "Requiring students to regularly assess their own degree of understanding and skill at handling concepts or problems in a particular discipline. The attainment of knowledge by participating or contributing. The process of keeping students mentally, and often physically, active in their learning through activities that involve them in gathering information, thinking and problem solving" (p. 160).

That's a noteworthy definition for a couple of reasons. First of all, there is a tendency among faculty to think that active learning is about activity—getting the students to do something. What they are doing matters less than the fact that they are no longer passive. This definition makes clear that when the word "active" is combined with "learning," what students are doing matters. They should be engaged in activities that involve reflection, assessment, and learning tasks associated with mastery of the material. Said differently, not all things called active learning are focused on learning. Learner-centered teachers are interested in those that are learning-centered.

Michael (2006, pp. 160–165) includes in his review evidence from the learning sciences, cognitive science, and educational psychology. He distills the research from those fields into five principles, which he describes as "key findings" that support active learning:

- Learning involves the active construction of meaning by the learner. Learners construct meaning by combining what they currently know with the new information they are acquiring. This makes learning a personal process and rules out any idea of learning as the mere transmission of knowledge.
- Learning facts and learning to do something are two different processes. This explains how students can know the facts and still not be able to do anything with that information.
- Some things that are learned are specific to the domain or context (subject matter or course) in which they were learned, whereas other things are more readily transferred to other domains. In order to successfully transfer knowledge from one situation to another, students need to practice.
- Individuals are more likely to learn more when they learn with others than when they learn alone.

- Meaningful learning is facilitated by articulating explanations, whether to one's self, peers, or teachers. Constructing these explanations also gives students practice in using the language of the disciplines.

His review includes a section that highlights evidence that active learning works in the sciences. He explains how educational research is different from research done in the sciences and why teaching and learning phenomena are difficult to study. He concludes, "There *is* evidence that active learning, student-centered approaches to teaching physiology work [the evidence he summons supports this as a general conclusion], and they work better than more passive approaches" (p. 165).

DISCIPLINE-BASED RESEARCH IN SUPPORT OF LEARNER-CENTERED APPROACHES

Some of the best discipline-based research in support of learner-centered approaches involves three highly structured forms of group work, and most of the research on their effectiveness has been done in the sciences. A fine article describes and compares these pedagogies of engagement: Problem-Based Learning (PBL), Process-Oriented Guided Inquiry Learning (POGIL), and Peer-Led Team Learning (PLTL; Eberlein, Kampmeier, Minderhout, Moog, Platt, Varma-Nelson, and White, 2008). These are by no means the only group structures that incorporate learner-centered strategies. Prince and Felder (2006, 2007) offer two comprehensive reviews of what they call inductive teaching and learning methods which, in addition to the three group structures I'm summarizing here, include Project-Based Learning, Case-Based Teaching, Discovery Learning, and Just-in-Time Teaching. The Prince and Felder articles are full of references that describe programs using all these group structures as well as empirical studies of their effectiveness.

Problem-Based Learning (PBL) was first used in medical education. Groups of medical students tackled an open-ended problem, often a patient with a variety of confusing symptoms. In

PBL, the problem comes first, which means students learn content on a need-to-know basis. As it was developed, PBL was a lectureless pedagogy. In the years since its introduction, PBL has been used widely in many fields beyond medicine. With undergraduates, the problems are messy, real-world situations that require students to integrate knowledge across courses and sometimes even from several fields. Wider use has also prompted the development of different forms of PBL, making it difficult to compare research results.

Process-Oriented Guided Inquiry Learning, which usually goes by the acronym POGIL, originated in chemistry and involves students working together during class on specially designed materials. They work through a set of carefully crafted questions, the guided inquiry, which follow a three-phase "learning cycle." First students explore, then they invent, and finally they apply. Examples of POGIL materials as well as references and other resources can be found at this website: www.pogil.org. Instructors function as facilitators, supporting the groups in a variety of ways and occasionally presenting material in lecture format. Students are assigned roles such as manager, scribe, spokesperson, or librarian. This approach has been used with undergraduates in chemistry, physics, math, computer science, engineering, environmental science, education, anatomy and physiology, and marketing.

Peer-Led Team Learning (PLTL) also originated in chemistry. It involves the use of trained student facilitators—students who have completed the course with high grades. These student facilitators, or peer leaders, meet once a week for two hours with six to eight students currently enrolled in the course. They work on faculty-prepared problems related to text material, lectures, and homework problems. The peer leaders encourage students in the groups to use collaborative learning approaches such as brainstorming, round-robin problem solving, reciprocal questioning, and forms of think-pair-share. In some cases, the PLTL sessions occur entirely outside of class, sometimes they replace a regularly scheduled recitation session, and in other cases one hour of lecture per week is eliminated to make time for the PLTL session.

The Eberlein, Kampmeier, Minderhout, Moog, Platt, Varma-Nelson, and White article (2008) contains a detailed table that compares and contrasts these three approaches. They say that of the three, "PLTL involves the least and PBL the greatest departure from traditional instruction" (p. 270). Given the characteristics of learner-centered teaching, all three qualify as learner-centered approaches, although that label is not regularly attached to them in the literature. Students are actively engaged with the material, they have varying degrees of control over the learning processes, and they are not only learning material, but learning processes like how scientists approach and solve problems. Each of the methods has been studied empirically, and a summary of findings for each of the three follows.

PROBLEM-BASED LEARNING

PBL is the oldest, most widely used, and most well researched of these three group structures. Several review articles on PBL have been published: Vernon and Blake (1993) looked at thirty-five medical school studies of PBL published between 1970 and 1992. Albanese and Mitchell (1993) reviewed literature on implementation and outcomes, again in medical education. Dochy, Segers, den Bossche, and Gijbels (2003) did a meta-analysis of forty-three studies of PBL, including a number that were conducted in disciplines other than medicine.

In the literature, definitions of PBL are fairly consistent, but at the point of implementation, much variation occurs. Prince (2004) explains why this is a problem: "The large variation in PBL practices makes the analysis of its effectiveness more complex. Many studies comparing PBL are simply not talking about the same thing. For meta-studies of PBL to show any significant effect compared to traditional programs, the signal from the common elements of PBL would have to be greater than the noise produced by differences in the implementation of both PBL and the traditional curricula" (p. 228). This caveat should be kept in mind whether we are considering PBL studies collectively or individually, and it helps to explain the inconsistency in results across studies.

Even so, the research results should not be ignored, as they do document important outcomes that occur when students work collectively on solutions to PBL problems. Vernon and Blake (1993) report improved student attitudes about their programs and a statistically significant improvement of PBL students in clinical performance, although some have argued with that finding. The Dochy, Segers, den Bossche, and Gijbels (2003) review finds a "robust positive effect from PBL on the skills of students." They use the library more, read their textbooks more, have better class attendance, and study for meaning instead of memorizing. Prince and Felder (2006) describe the results of the Dochy, Segers, den Bossche, and Gijbels analysis as "unequivocal: 14 studies found a positive effect and none found a negative effect . . . The positive effect of PBL on skill development holds regardless of whether the assessment is concurrent with the instruction or delayed" (p. 129). It is not surprising that PBL develops skills so effectively. It is a learner-centered method that puts students much more in charge of their own learning.

But not all the findings on PBL are positive. Some studies (seven out of ten in the Albanese and Mitchell, 1993, review) report that students in PBL programs scored lower than students in traditional programs on tests of science knowledge (remember that the reference here is medical education). Dochy, Segers, den Bossche, and Gijbels (2003) report a similar finding, but describe the overall effect of PBL on knowledge acquisition as "non-robust" (p. 533). Prince and Felder (2006) elaborate: "When only true randomized tests are included, however, the negative effect of PBL on knowledge acquisitions almost disappears, and when the assessment of knowledge is carried out some time after the instruction was given, the effect of PBL is positive. The implication is that students may acquire more knowledge in the short term when instruction is conventional but students taught with PBL retain the knowledge they acquire for a longer time" (p. 129).

Prince (2004) offers this summary of PBL research overall: "While no evidence proves that PBL enhances academic achievement as measured by exams, there is evidence to suggest that PBL 'works' for achieving other important learning outcomes. Studies suggest that PBL develops more positive student attitudes, fosters a deeper approach to learning and helps student retain knowledge longer than traditional instruction" (p. 229).

PROCESS-ORIENTED GUIDED INQUIRY

Process-Oriented Guided Inquiry (POGIL) has been used by over one thousand teachers. It has also received $2 million in National Science Foundation funding, as well as other grant support. Research on this learner-centered group strategy contains an equally impressive list of results. For starters, it improves academic performance. Here are a couple of examples. In a first-year anatomy and physiology course (J.P.P. Brown, 2010) where 50 percent of the lectures were replaced with in-class POGIL activities, overall course scores increased from a mean score of 76 percent to 89 percent. And scores on the same multiple-choice final increased from a mean of 68 percent to 88 percent. The rate of students earning Ds or Fs dropped significantly as well. In a medicinal chemistry course (S. D. Brown, 2010) where students spent approximately 40 percent of their time working collectively on guided inquiry materials, mean exam scores for students in the two guided inquiry sections were almost 3 percentage points higher than students in the traditional section, and the final grade distribution in the POGIL sections were in the A to B range, compared with the other section, where grades were in the B to C range. And finally, in a professional selling course in marketing, faculty researchers (Hale and Mullen, 2009) document these results: "This innovative teaching method has reduced absenteeism, motivated students to become active learners and increased student performance in our classes" (p. 73).

Researchers consistently report that student attitudes toward the approach are positive, with students saying that working through materials with other students helps them understand the content better. In one study (Straumanis and Simons, 2008) involving over one thousand students at a number of different institutions, fewer than 8 percent of the students were negative about the approach. This compared with 30 percent who reported negative attitudes toward traditional lectures. In another analysis (Minderhout and Loertscher, 2007), 80 percent of the students said that aspects of POGIL experiences such as group problem solving and skill exercises helped their learning.

J.P.P. Brown offers this summary: "Although POGIL requires a great deal of effort and a careful introduction to students who might be skeptical of a novel and unfamiliar classroom experience, its benefits cannot easily be disputed" (2010, p. 155).

PEER-LED TEAM LEARNING

Since its development in the early 1990s, this strategy has been used widely across a range of institutions including community colleges and research universities. Gosser, Kampmeier, and Varma-Nelson (2010), the early developers of the approach, write that they ultimately "lost count of the number of PLTL (peer-led team learning) implementations, but a conservative estimate is that at least 200 faculty from more than 150 institutions are implementing PLTL, with 2,000 trained leaders conducting workshops for over 20,000 students per year" (p. 376). Early on, the developers assessed the effectiveness of this group structure by looking at student success in the general chemistry course for which it was developed. The percentage of students receiving As, Bs, or Cs in that course increased from 38 percent to 58 percent. Many of those implementing the approach have also tracked its impact on student success, and the overall average increase in the percent of students receiving As, Bs, and Cs is 14 percent.

More convincing than the reported increases in grades are the results of a variety of carefully controlled and empirically robust studies (Tien, Roth, and Kampmeier, 2002; Baez-Galib, Colon-Cruz, Resto, and Rubin, 2005; Lewis and Lewis, 2005; McCreary, Golde, and Koeske, 2006; Wamser, 2006; Hockings, DeAngelis, and Frey, 2008; Lyon and Lagowski, 2008). All of these studies report positive results for students who participated in the peer-led sessions.

Studies of this group method address one of the major objections faculty raise when considering learner-centered approaches: "I won't get the content covered, and that means students won't learn as much." In their Lessons Learned section, Gosser, Kampmeier, and Varma-Nelson (2010) conclude: "Lecture can be reduced without compromising content if the time is spent on activities that promote active engagement of the students with the subject matter and with each other" (p. 378). The studies referenced above support this claim in a variety of different ways. Here's one illustration: Lewis and Lewis (2005) used the PLTL model in a general chemistry course. In their experimental group, 100 students had two fifty-minute lectures per week and one fifty-minute peer-led session. In the control group, 190 students had three fifty-minute lectures. Students in both groups took the same four exams and final. Students in the experimental group had higher mean scores on every exam, including the final: "fears that students who had less exposure to lecture would learn less proved to be groundless in this study" (p. 139). Given the chance to continue the PLTL sessions in the second semester of the course, 85 percent of the students said they would and 76 percent of them believed that working in the group was beneficial. Only five (of the experimental group) reported that the group slowed them down.

Before concluding this section, I would like to highlight one more study of unstructured group collaboration. This study, done in chemistry (Cooper, Cox, Nammouz, and Case, 2008), looked at how work in groups affected problem-solving strategies and abilities. The study used a software system that allowed researchers to follow how students moved through a problem and model their progress as they worked on multiple problems. Based on earlier research, this team knew that students "stabilize," or settle on a strategy or approach, after working on about five versions of the problem. They wanted to know whether working in a group would change the "stable" strategies of individuals, particularly the less effective strategies.

The findings were quite remarkable. Using over 100,000 performances by 713 students, "we have shown that we can improve student problem solving by having students work in collaborative groups. These improvements are retained after grouping and provide further evidence of the positive effects of having students work in groups" (p. 871). Researchers found that most students improved by a factor of about 10 percent, including many of the students who had previously settled on ineffective strategies.

Why does working with others have such a positive influence on problem solving, an influence strong enough to remain even after the group member has returned to individual problem solving? The research team suggests some reasons. First, in groups students have to explain things to each other. That articulation helps those who hear it and those who make it. In a group, students must elaborate and critique each other. That further analysis aids understanding.

The evidence highlighted here and more like it offer convincing evidence that students can learn from and with each other in a variety of group structures. Many of the results document significant gains in content knowledge. Virtually all of them document important gains in the development of skills like questioning, critical thinking, problem solving, and knowledge integration and application. The evidence makes it difficult to explain why more faculty are not using learner-centered approaches like these.

STUDIES OF INDIVIDUAL LEARNER-CENTERED COURSES

Highlighted in this section are studies of individual courses in which a collection of different learner-centered strategies were implemented and empirically analyzed. In most cases, the learner-centered version of the course can be compared with previous or current sections of the course where the approaches were not used. The studies also illustrate different kinds of courses where learner-centered approaches have been incorporated, such as large courses.

SIX STUDIES OF BIOLOGY COURSES

An impressive amount of research has been done on mostly large and mostly introductory biology courses. These are well-designed studies with findings that deserve to be taken seriously. Faculty often dismiss pedagogical research not done in their discipline, and while it is true that we cannot be certain that the methods tested in one field will work with different content, a different teacher, and different students, most of the methods used in these studies are common ones—ones that are being used with many different kinds of content. The other very encouraging aspect of this work in biology is its response to the common faculty question of whether you can use learner-centered approaches in large classes. The brief highlights that follow include classes sizes, overview of the learner-centered strategies, and approaches incorporated and the results.

Armbruster, Patel, Johnson, and Weiss (2009) describe a series of changes implemented in 170- to 190-student introductory courses for biology and premed majors. Their course redesign consisted of three elements: they reordered the course content so that it could be taught as broad conceptual themes; they incorporated active learning (including clickers with participation points for answers) and group problem solving into every lecture; and they worked to create a more student-centered learning environment with course goals, helpful vocabulary handouts, and formative weekly quizzes. These changes significantly improved student satisfaction with the course including levels of interest in the course material, self-reported learning, ranking of classroom presentations as stimulating, and the overall evaluation of the instructor. As for academic performance, the same final exam questions had been used in a section of the course taught without these changes. Students in the redesigned course performed at statistically significant higher levels: "our positive results illustrate how changing the instructional design of a course, without wholesale changes to course content, can lead to improved student attitudes and performance" (Armbruster, Patel, Johnson, and Weiss, 2009, p. 204).

In another one-hundred-student general biology course, the professor (Burrowes, 2003) instituted a number of group learning strategies including regular problem-solving activities completed in the groups during class, a quizzing mechanism where one group member took the quiz for the group, a group test-retake with a small bonus point incentive, and a number of other changes involving how content was presented in class. This experimental section was compared with a similar-sized section taught using a traditional lecture approach. Students in the experimental section out-performed students in the control section at statistically significant levels on all three exams. They also out-performed students in the control section at statistically significant levels on questions testing conceptual understanding, which led the professor to conclude that "in-class practice of problem-solving techniques does help to develop skills for scientific thinking" (Burrowes, 2003, p. 498). They did better on the test-retake activity, and their attitude toward biology was significantly better than those in the control group.

Freeman, Haak, and Wenderoth (2011) tested whether highly structured course designs that included reading quizzes, extensive in-class active-learning activities, and weekly practice exams could lower the failure rate in an introductory biology course for majors. The course was offered every quarter and enrolled almost 2,100 students the year during which the study was completed. These experimental sections were compared with primarily lecture-based sections with fewer exams. "When we controlled for variation in student ability, failure rates were lower in a moderately structured course design and were dramatically lower in a highly structured course design" (p. 175). They also report that they "found no evidence that points for active-learning exercises inflate grades or reduce the impact of exams on final grades" (p. 175).

Knight and Wood (2005) modestly changed an upper-division lecture course on developmental biology. They still lectured 60 to 70 percent of the time, but the rest of the time students did problem solving, using a cooperative learning model. As for results, their findings suggest "that even a partial shift toward a more interactive and collaborative course format can lead to significant increases in student learning gains" (p. 304).

They use these results to "propose a general model for teaching large biology courses that incorporates interactive engagement and cooperative work in place of some lecturing, while retaining course content by demanding great student responsibility for learning outside the class" (p. 298).

Ueckert, Adams, and Lock (2011) report on a major redesign of an entry-level course for majors. This biology course enrolls nine hundred students in the fall and five hundred in the spring. It is taught in three to five sections by a variety of instructors. Redesign tasks included development of a common syllabus, a table of specifications (which identifies key concepts, desired skill levels, and amount of time devoted to each concept), and a course assessment tool. They incorporated a variety of learner-centered activities including think-pair-share, clickers, and small-group work, all described in detail in the article. They collected and analyzed data from three years before the change and for three years after it. The percentage of students who dropped the course decreased by statistically significant amounts, and the percentage of As and Bs increased, also by statistically significant amounts. They use the adjectives "long," "slow," and "challenging" to describe this revision process.

Derting and Ebert-May (2010) were interested in a different kind of research question: "Is the infusion of two new introductory courses early in a student's curriculum, both based on learner-centered inquiry-based principles, associated with long-term understanding of biological concepts and biology as a process of inquiry?" (p. 463). They note that most studies analyzing the impact of learner-centered course revisions focus on short-term changes. Did final exam scores improve, was there evidence of skill development, or did student attitudes about the course change? Derting and Ebert-May "studied a revised biology curriculum implemented at the beginning of the biology major" (p. 463). The revision involved development of two new courses, both using a number of different active-learning and inquiry-based approaches. In one of the courses, students posed their own research questions and hypotheses. They developed research proposals and critiqued those of their peers. They collected and analyzed data and presented their findings.

The researchers employed two assessment tools to ascertain the impact of the new courses across a five-year period. They assessed student understanding of biology as a process of inquiry (using a Views about Science Survey for Biology) and student knowledge of biological concepts at the end of the major (using a version of the Major Field Test in Biology). Simply put, their results "showed that an intense inquiry-based learner-centered learning experience early in the biology curriculum was associated with long-term improvements in learning" (p. 462). "Transformation of introductory biology curricula . . . through learner-centered inquiry-based teaching may have the potential to profoundly impact learning by all students and even become a tipping point for departmental change" (p. 471).

Study of an Algebra Course

At the University of Missouri-St. Louis college, algebra—required for several majors, a prerequisite for calculus, and a key course for students in math, science, business, and a variety of parapro-fessional programs—had a success rate of 55 percent (Thiel, Peterman, and Brown, 2008). Faculty redesigned the course. The three fifty-minute lecture periods were reduced to one and were replaced with two computer-lab sessions, where students learned math by doing math. In the labs students used software that included explanations, tutorials, practice problems, and guided solutions. They could also do their homework in the lab, collabo-rating with other students or soliciting help from the instructor, a graduate student, or peer tutor (one of whom was present during the scheduled lab sessions). Students also took weekly online quizzes, four exams, and a comprehensive final.

"The redesign has significantly changed the role of the instruc-tors and teaching assistants. They used to spend their time lecturing, writing assignments and exams, and grading. Now they focus on guiding students through the course via the weekly meeting in a lecture room and then working individually with students in the [math technology] learning center. The greater emphasis on individual instruction and one-on-one interactions with students is a change that most instructors find very reward-ing" (pp. 46–47).

As for the results, over a three-year period student success improved from 55 percent to 75 percent, "with no decrease in course rigor, as demonstrated by student scores on a final exam that included the same types of problems during the redesign period as before it" (p. 46).

STUDIES IN PHYSICS COURSES

Some years before there was much work at all on learner-centered approaches, specifically peer learning, Harvard physicist Eric Mazur (2009) had dramatically changed the way he taught and was collecting data on its effects. He describes his approach giving students "the opportunity to resolve misunderstanding about concepts and work together to learn new ideas and skills in a discipline" (p. 51). Of the findings from his work and those who have replicated his approach, he writes: "Data obtained in my class and in classes of colleagues worldwide, in a wide range of aca-demic settings and a wide range of disciplines, show that learning gains nearly triple with an approach that focuses on the student and on interactive learning" (p. 51). This short article, which recounts the transformation of his pedagogical approach, includes references to the studies that support his claims of significantly improved learning outcomes.

For a very specific example of another learner-centered approach used in physics, consider this study of two large sections ($N = 267$ and $N = 271$) of the second term of a first-year physics sequence. Sections were compared to see if "deliberative practice" improved student learning (Deslauriers, Schelew, and Wieman, 2011). Deliberative practice (a cognitive psychology concept) in this course took the form of "a series of challenging questions and tasks [that] require the student to practice physicist-like reasoning and problem solving during class time while provided with frequent feedback" (p. 862). Students in the experimental section used deliberative practice for one week, learning the same content that was being covered by lecture in the control section. "We found increased student attendance, higher engagement and more than twice the learning in the section taught using research-based instruction" (p. 862).

The studies described in this section illustrate what happens when a variety of learner-centered strategies are incorporated in a course. Positive results on learning outcomes were reported for large courses, for beginning courses, for courses with high failure rates, for major courses, and for required courses. The results were positive even when a small number of changes were implemented, and the results were enduring when the course design changes were substantial.

WHAT DO STUDENTS SAY ABOUT LEARNER-CENTERED APPROACHES?

Faculty using learner-centered approaches frequently experience student resistance, a topic dealt with at length in Chapter Eight. Initially, students want learner-centered teachers to do what teachers do in many other courses—tell them everything they need to know about the content and their assignments. Do students ever come around? At some point do they begin to see that what teachers are trying to do actually helps them learn the material? Of the studies reported in the previous two sections, many of the researchers did solicit responses from students as to the merits of these various learner-centered approaches, and uniformly the student response was positive. In many cases, students reported that they struggled with the new approaches initially, but as their experience with them accumulated, they did find them beneficial.

Supporting that response, but with a bit more detail, is a descriptive analysis (Terenzini, Cabrera, Colbeck, Parente, and Bjorklund, 2001) that compared the experiences of engineering students enrolled in courses that were part of a National Science Foundation project (Engineering Coalition of Schools for Excellence in Education and Leadership, or ECSEL) with the experiences of students in regular engineering courses. The project aimed to improve undergraduate engineering courses by incorporating active and collaborative learning experiences.

Survey data were collected from 339 students in seventeen ECSEL courses at six different institutions and from 141 students in six non-ECSEL courses. Among other questions, the survey asked whether students believed that they had made progress in a variety of learning and skill development areas as a result of taking that particular course.

Students in the ECSEL courses reported significant advantages: "ECSEL students reported learning advantages in three areas: design skills, communication skills, and groups skills. The advantages enjoyed by ECSEL students were both statistically significant and substantial" (p. 129). For example, ECSEL students reported learning gains in communication skills 11 percentile points higher than their peers in the non-ECSEL courses; in design skills ECSEL students reported learning gains 23 percentile points higher; and in group skills they reported gains 34 percentile points higher. "These learning advantages remained even when differences in a variety of student pre-course characteristics were controlled" (p. 123).

CONCLUSION

Sometimes it is best to let the evidence speak for itself, and this chapter may be one of these cases. We've covered a lot of territory here and explored what seems to me is a convincing body of evidence supportive of the learner-centered approaches advocated in this book. I am happy to let the evidence speak for itself, confident that faculty readers can review, critique, and evaluate it.

However, I am not going to close the chapter without raising the question asked by an impressive group of science educators and academic leaders (Handelsman, Ebert-May, Beichner, Bruns, Chang, DeHaan, Gentile, Lauffer, Stewart, Tilghman, and Wood, 2004) in the prestigious publication *Science*. Their audience is scientists, but the question can be asked of any academic scholar: "Why do outstanding scientists who demand rigorous proof for scientific assertions in their research continue to use, and indeed defend, on the basis of intuition alone, teaching methods that are not the most effective?" (p. 521). I suggested some answers in the chapter's introduction. Maybe they don't know there is research, or they don't read the research—maybe they've tried and found it difficult to understand—or perhaps they don't think the research is very good. This chapter is an attempt to challenge the legitimacy of those reasons so that the question realizes its powerful potential and motivates changes in practice.

PART TWO

THE FIVE KEY CHANGES TO PRACTICE

CHAPTER THREE

THE ROLE OF THE TEACHER

I didn't begin Part Two with this chapter in the previous edition. But I usually start here in my sessions with faculty because it's an easy place to begin understanding what learner-centered approaches involve. For most, it is a familiar place. The facilitative teaching role has been proposed for years, and the ideas it represents are not philosophically at odds with what most faculty believe about teaching and learning. So it's a good starting point.

That doesn't mean it's a role teachers find easy to execute. It is not the way most of us were taught and not the way we teach most of the time. Despite that, becoming a facilitator of learning is an essential part of being learner-centered. The success of the other four changes depends on how well the teacher can transition to this role. The goal for this chapter, then, is to describe what it means to be a facilitator of learning, document the continued reliance on roles that are more teacher-centered, offer a set of principles that illustrate how the learner-centered role looks when it's executed, and conclude with questions raised when the role is implemented.

WHAT NEEDS TO CHANGE?

What happens in the typical college classroom? Who's delivering the content? Who's leading the discussions? Who's previewing and reviewing the material? Who offers the examples? Who asks and answers most of the questions? Who calls on students? Who solves the problems, provides the graphs, and constructs the matrices? In most classrooms, it's the teacher. When it comes to who's working the hardest most days, teachers win hands down. Students are there, but too often education is being done unto to them. Rather than being active participants in the process, they passively observe what the teacher is doing.

Learner-centered teachers work hard too, but they realize that students need to be working on learning-related tasks as well. They see the teacher's primary task as facilitating or supporting the learning efforts of students. Even though this idea of the teacher as a facilitator is not new, there is a difference. When written about previously, it was proposed as an alternative, one among a number of roles a teacher might choose or rotate between. In the learner-centered classroom, being a facilitator of learning is more a requirement and less an option.

Previous descriptions of the facilitative role often use metaphors to reveal essential features of this approach to teaching. Fox (1983) compares a teacher who facilitates learning to a gardener. Gardeners deservedly get credit for what they enable flowers or fruits to accomplish, but they are not the ones who bloom and bear fruit. Teachers create conditions that foster growth and learning, but it is the students who master the material and develop learning skills.

Facilitative teachers have also been compared to guides, and many useful insights derive from this metaphor. Guides show those who follow the way, but those who follow walk on their own. Guides point out the sights; they've traveled this way before. Guides offer advice, they warn of danger, and they do their best to prevent accidents. Likewise, learner-centered teachers climb with students. Together they ascend what for many students are new and high peaks.

Hill (1980, p. 48) offers an especially eloquent description of the shared vulnerabilities inherent when teachers and students climb together: "The Teacher as Mountaineer learns to connect. The guide rope links mountain climbers together so that they may assist one another in the ascent. The teacher makes a 'rope' by using the oral and written contributions of the students, by forging interdisciplinary and intradisciplinary links where plausible, and by connecting the course material with the lives of students." Marini (2000) revisited this metaphor and draws still more comparisons.

Relatedly, those who facilitate learning have been compared with coaches. Barr and Tagg (1995, p. 24) write, "A coach not only instructs football players . . . but also designs football practices and the game plan; he participates in the game itself by sending in plays and making other decisions. The new faculty roles go a step further, however, in that faculty not only design the game plans but create new and better 'games,' ones that generate more and better learning."

Spence (2010, p. 3), in his excellent essay on the incomparable UCLA basketball coach John Wooden, says that Wooden thought coaching was teaching: "He dealt with players individually, working to deliver instruction when it would produce learning. His success depended on knowing the limits and capacities of each player . . . He believed that if you didn't pay attention to what students did and then correct and instruct them, there was no teaching. As he put it, if the students have not learned, then the teacher has not taught." Spence notes that "Our classrooms are a long way from Wooden's practices. But shouldn't they be more alike? Shouldn't they be learning spaces where students can try, fail, and be instructed? What I learned from the Coach was the necessity for a teacher to enter the learners' experience. I needed to observe and listen until I knew their strengths, weaknesses, and uniqueness. That requires intense work, but doesn't it reflect the duties of our profession?"

Eisner (1983) compares the teacher to a maestro before an orchestra. The teacher, like the conductor, stands behind a podium that holds a complicated score—the content to be taught that day. In front of the conductor there's an orchestra composed of individuals who play different instruments, have different levels of ability, and have practiced to varying degrees. The teacher-conductor has fifty minutes to prepare the orchestra to make music with the score. I love the grand possibilities of this metaphor.

But my favorite metaphorical description of learner-centered teaching is the teacher as midwife. I've seen the metaphor attributed to a number of different authors, but I first read it in an essay by Ayers (1986, p. 50). He writes, "Good teachers, like good midwives, empower. Good teachers find ways to activate students, for they know that learning requires active engagement between the subject and 'object matter.' Learning requires discovery and invention. Good teachers know when to hang back and be silent, when to watch and wonder at what is taking place all around them. They can push and they can pull when necessary—just like midwives—but they know that they are not always called upon to perform. Sometimes the performance is and must be elsewhere."

I think of the teacher-midwife as being there at the birth of learning. The midwife isn't giving birth. It is up to the learner to master and deliver this material, but the midwife is such a resource. She brings much previous experience, expertise, assurance, and calmness. She's been alongside many other students as they've struggled with this material. She knows when it gets really hard and has strategies she can suggest that help learners break through to understanding. And when that understanding is finally born, she is there to celebrate all that moment means to the learner. It's a beautiful metaphor.

These metaphors offer inspirational insights into the teaching role that facilitates learning. They are limited by their focus on what teachers *are,* as opposed to what they *do*; teachers are like gardeners, guides, coaches, conductors, and midwives. But how do teachers garden, guide, coach, conduct, or midwife in the classroom? In order to implement the role, teachers need to know what facilitators do, and a simple, straightforward summary is the best place to begin: they engage and support students in the hard, messy work of learning.

What makes this learner-centered role preferable to the more teacher-centered ones is that it more effectively promotes learning, and it does so for two reasons. First, teachers are focused on what *the students* are doing, instead of what they themselves are doing (Biggs, 1999a, 1999b). They see how students are learning or not learning the material, what learning skills they do and don't have, and this input allows them to adjust teaching so that it more effectively promotes learning. Spence's description of Wooden's approach to coaching illustrates this perfectly. The coach is not worrying about how he's coaching; he's observing the players, and that focused observation allows him to offer feed-back that helps the players execute more successfully.

Second, perhaps even more important, facilitative teaching promotes more learning because students are engaged in learning tasks. They aren't just copying down teacher-provided examples, but generating their own. They aren't just recording what the teacher does as she works through a problem, they are working problems on their own or with other students. They are asking questions, summarizing content, generating hypotheses, propos-ing theories, offering critical analyses, and so on.

I really understood this concept after reading the work of Biggs (1999a, 1999b), and I remember my first attempt to make the change. I thought it would be easy to implement. I introduced an important concept, explaining it carefully, asking and solicit-ing questions, before saying to students, "Now, what we need are examples. They will help you really understand this. So, what would be an example that illustrates this concept?" Nothing. Wait patiently. Encouragement. "It doesn't need to be a perfect example—share whatever's coming to mind." Nothing. More waiting. Time to reach for that back-pocket ace in the hole. "Well, you know often examples are used on the exams in this class. You really ought to have some examples in your notes." Finally, Al, who was a bit anal-retentive and always anxious when the action in the class slowed, tentatively raised his hand. "Thank you, Al!" As soon as I heard the example, I had that sinking feeling. It wasn't a good example. It took us another three or four minutes to get it to a place where I felt I could even write it on the board. After finishing, I remember looking down at my notes and seeing three really excellent examples there.

Should I have shared them? Yes and no. Perhaps I should have started by giving the students one of my examples—for the purposes of illustration and to get them thinking in the right direction. But the students should not just have teacher examples in their notes. They need some of their own—some that make sense to them—that connect what they already know with the new concept. And they don't learn how to do the hard intellectual work that generating good examples requires if all they do is copy down examples provided by the teacher. Moreover, the best time to practice generating examples is in class, when the teacher is there to suggest ways of finding them and with feedback that improves their quality.

Learner-centered teaching isn't an all-or-nothing proposition. Sometimes teachers need to do learning tasks for students. They need to provide solutions, answer questions, illustrate points, and demonstrate critical thinking. That's a legitimate part of teaching. But they shouldn't be doing these tasks all or even most of the time. Ultimately, the responsibility for learning rests with students. Learner-centered teaching promotes learning by directly engaging students in those tasks that expedite deep and lasting learning.

WHAT HASN'T CHANGED?

Given the considerable attention learner-centered teaching has received and the salience of the premises on which it rests, we might expect that teaching in higher education has become more learner-centered. Unfortunately, little evidence supports that conclusion. Most of the data indicate continued reliance on teacher-centered instructional approaches. The evidence is not found in one comprehensive survey, but is persistently present in many different analyses, as these examples illustrate.

EVIDENCE OF TEACHER-CENTERED INSTRUCTION PROVIDED BY FACULTY

In 1998, 76 percent of faculty (including new faculty) listed the lecture as their instructional method of choice (Finkelstein, Seal, and Schuster). Although it is possible for students to be actively involved in lectures, more regularly lectures are teacher-centered, with students passive recipients of knowledge. Has that percentage changed during the intervening years? We don't know. A survey like this has not been completed recently, so data are not available to compare with this historical benchmark.

Work has been done in some disciplines. A survey of faculty teaching undergraduate economics courses completed in 1995, 2000, 2005, and 2010 (Watts and Schaur, 2011) has investigated the teaching and assessment methods faculty report using in those courses. Amazingly, in each of these surveys faculty report devoting 83 percent of class time to lectures. Across the years there have been some increases in the reported use of other more learner-centered strategies, but the researchers conclude: "Although it is possible to make a reasonable case for the assertion that the gradual changes noted in teaching and assessment methods (particularly in the last two surveys) can be expected to continue, the larger and more powerful part of the picture . . . is that the preferences, incentives, and constraints that lead most economists to use 'chalk and talk' teaching methods should not be underestimated" (pp. 307–308).

Walczyk and Ramsey (2003) surveyed full-time science and math faculty at four-year institutions in Louisiana, asking about learner-centered techniques (which they defined and illustrated), and they found that use of these strategies was "infrequent" (p. 567). They concluded that "lecture-recitation-evaluation is alive and well in college science and math classrooms, even in schools whose primary emphasis is not on research" (p. 579).

In a qualitative interview study, researchers aimed to better understand the views of inquiry held by faculty who teach undergraduate science courses (Brown, Abell, Demir, and Schmidt, 2006). Specifically, they were interested in faculty perceptions of inquiry-based lab activities—those lab experiences where students actually use the scientific method to investigate phenomena and solve problems. This approach to lab work is often contrasted with "recipe"-type lab exercises that produce predetermined outcomes.

Faculty from a variety of different kinds of institutions were interviewed, and their general conclusion was that inquiry-based approaches are "more appropriate for upper level science majors than for introductory or nonscience majors" (p. 784). "Although faculty members valued inquiry, they perceived limitations of time, class size, student motivation, and student ability. These limitations, coupled with their view of inquiry, constrained them from implementing inquiry-based laboratories" (p. 784).

EVIDENCE OF TEACHER-CENTERED INSTRUCTION PROVIDED BY STUDENTS

A survey of 922 students asked for their assessment of undergraduate science classes (Kardash and Wallace, 2001). A factor analysis of the eighty-item survey instrument yielded six factors, including one called passive learning. "The mean of 2.81 [out of 6 on a Likert scale] on the Passive Learning scale clearly indicates that a majority of science classes remain primarily lecture driven and focused on the acquisition of facts" (p. 208).

The Terenzini, Cabrera, Colbeck, Parente, and Bjorklund (2001) study of engineering students referenced in Chapter Two asked students for feedback about courses that were using active and collaborative strategies, which they compared with feedback from students in regular courses. Listed next are a sample of items with the mean scores (out of 4.0) of students in the experimental courses and in regular courses and the effect size, which is calculated as percentile points. All the differences in these mean scores are statistically significant, and the percentile points favor students who were experiencing active and collaborative learning activities in their courses.

There are opportunities to work in groups	3.51	2.20	+39
We do things requiring students to be active participants in the teaching-learning process	2.92	1.91	+35
Instructor encourages students to listen, evaluate, and learn from the ideas of others	2.98	2.11	+31
Instructor guides students' learning activities, rather than lecturing or demonstrating course material	2.74	1.99	+28
I interact with instructor as part of this course	2.71	2.01	+26

These data not only indicate students' positive perceptions of learner-centered approaches, they also paint a contrasting picture of classrooms where professors are more active than students.

CLASSROOM OBSERVATION DATA

Research in the early 1980s documented that faculty devoted a small amount of time to classroom interaction. Fischer and Grant (1983) made 155 visits to 40 college classrooms at different institutions, across a range of disciplines, and at course levels from introductory to advanced. In those classrooms, professors talked almost 80 percent of the time, four times more frequently than students in classes with an average size of forty-seven. Students were not participating more in upper-division major courses than in lower-division courses. A 1996 observational study (Nunn) of twenty social science and humanities classrooms found that teachers devoted only 5.85 percent of total class time to student participation. That's approximately one minute per forty minutes of class time. Fritschner's observational study (2000) of 344 class sessions reports that when interaction was occurring, 47 percent of the time teachers were asking questions or commenting in response to student questions or responses. Even when students were interacting in these classrooms, during those exchanges faculty were still doing almost 50 percent of the talking.

Among data based on classroom observations is perhaps the most disturbing study of all (Ebert-May, Derting, Hodder, Momsen, Long, and Jardeleza, 2011). It's a large and complex study of biology faculty who attended workshops designed to move them from teacher-centered to more learner-centered ways of teaching. The workshops involved several days of instruction, and in response to survey data collected subsequently, a significant majority (89 percent of one cohort) said they had implemented reforms like those proposed during the workshops. A cohort of participants were asked to videotape their teaching (four times at designated intervals up to two years after their workshop experience). These tapes were analyzed using an instrument designed to measure the degree of active learning and student involvement observed in the classroom. "Observations . . . indicated that a majority of faculty (75 percent) implemented a lecture-based, teacher-centered pedagogy" (p. 555). These findings raise questions about the viability of workshop experiences and about the disconnect between faculty perceptions of their teaching and the reality of what was observed, but the study is cited here as observational evidence supporting the continued use of teaching methods that are not learner-centered.

ANALYSIS OF AN ARTIFACT OF TEACHING FOR EVIDENCE OF ACTIVE LEARNING

Archer and Miller (2011) assembled a collection of syllabi from "gateway" political science courses, the large introductory courses that are often the only courses taken in the discipline. They were interested in how much active learning occurred in those courses and decided to take a look at syllabi, pointing out that "while syllabi cannot fully convey what occurs in the classroom, they do provide a summary of instructor intentions, desired learning outcomes, and pedagogical approaches" (pp. 429–430).

Using Google and the Syllabus Finder tool, they acquired 491 syllabi from 238 different institutions, including a representative sample of institutional types. They analyzed these syllabi, looking specifically for indications that simulations, structured debates, and the case method would be used in the course. They explain why these particular techniques are well suited to the content of these courses and generally well known within the discipline. They found these activities were rarely proposed in their collection of syllabi; simulations were included 7.7 percent of the time, structured debates 4.7 percent, and case methods 3.7 percent. "Overall, 14.7 percent of all gateway courses in the sample employed one or more of these three active learning techniques" (p. 431).

What's referenced here is representative of a much larger collection of studies done in different fields and using a variety of methodologies. No single study establishes that college teaching remains teacher-centered, but the absence of data documenting widespread use of learner-centered approaches and evidence like that highlighted here support the contention that what's occurring in most college classrooms has not changed all that much since the first edition of this book was published.

WHY HASN'T TEACHING BECOME MORE LEARNER-CENTERED?

If learner-centered approaches more effectively promote learning (documented by research in Chapter Two) and the idea of facilitating learning makes good intuitive sense to faculty, then why aren't we seeing more change in the way students are being taught? Perhaps what makes sense intellectually has turned out to be tougher to implement than most of us expected. Here are some reasons why teaching has not become more learner-centered.

WHY FACULTY PREFER MORE TEACHER-CENTERED ROLES

The transition to learner-centered teaching has showed many of us just how much we like being the center of action in the classroom. With a captive audience, we simply cannot pass up the opportunity to show our stuff. With me, it's telling stories. I love to spin a tale (always true, of course), and as the years have accumulated, so have my stories. Some I've told enough to have perfected the punch lines. On a good day, even with a dead class I can tell one of those stories and suddenly the class comes to life. I feel such a sense of accomplishment when raucous laughter sweeps across the room. And students remember my stories. Years later when I meet them, they remind me of the "dishwasher" story. The problem, of course, is they rarely have retained the point of the story, so all my rationalization about stories being nails on which I hang all sorts of conceptual stuff (I love that metaphor—Amstutz, 1988) is really just an excuse for me to flaunt my storytelling prowess.

I don't believe learner-centered teachers are forever forbidden from telling stories or whatever else they enjoy and do well in the spotlight. That's like trying to diet and saying no chocolate ever, under any circumstances. Besides, some of my stories work—they make the points easier to understand and remember. Rather, it's about honestly analyzing my motives for telling a story and making sure I'm telling it to facilitate learning, not because I want to see if I can still make people laugh.

A second reason faculty stay with the more traditional roles finds voice in King's (1993) often quoted article title, "From Sage on the Stage to Guide on the Side." The facilitative role seems less glamorous, possibly even less important. Is that so because we tend to think the teaching role is more important than it actually is? Despite our involvement in and control over virtually all aspects of instruction, we cannot guarantee delivery of the product. A student cannot be forced to learn. A teacher cannot learn anything for a student. Students completely control the most important part of any educational experience. We might like to think that the instructional universe circles around us, but students are the stars in the larger learning galaxy.

With a more realistic understanding of our place in the educational universe, we can revisit our notion that facilitative teaching roles are somehow diminished or less essential in the learning process. Quite the opposite is true. Most women panic at the thought of giving birth without some sort of guide alongside. Only daring hikers ascend new and treacherous peaks alone. No orchestra makes music long without a conductor. Teams without coaches do not have winning seasons. True, facilitative roles are less about the thrill of performance, but they do offer the chance for teachers to be more intimately involved with students' learning. Teachers are credited with what made learning possible. Students learn because of us, not in spite of us.

There is another darker reason that prevents some faculty from moving to more facilitative teaching. Teacher–student relationships can become entangled with issues of codependency and the various psychological benefits that accrue to both parties when relationships are dependent. For the student, there is freedom from responsibility. Assignments are easier when the teacher has decided on all the details. For faculty, there are more unpredictable teaching variables nailed down, fewer loose cannons, and less vulnerability, plus the feeling of importance associated with making decisions for others. But for both parties, dependent relationships are basically unhealthy, ultimately limiting the potential for personal growth on both sides.

THE FACILITATIVE ROLE IS MORE DIFFICULT

Facilitating learning involves skills rarely practiced. It can feel awkward and uncomfortable. Because teachers think only or mostly about their performance, they aren't terribly objective or insightful as to why the new role causes discomfort. They just know it didn't feel right, didn't seem to go all that well, so they probably can't teach this way and had best go back to what they do know before they end up looking foolish in front of students, God forbid. Understanding how this role works and what makes facilitation a more difficult way to teach partly explains why more teachers haven't embraced the role and why many report less-than-positive first experiences.

First off, this is a much less scripted way of teaching. You don't go into the classroom with everything planned. You do go to class well prepared, but if part of the plan is to ask students for examples, you don't know what they'll come up with, and chances are good they'll propose an example that you've never considered or they'll offer one of marginal quality. Either way, you'll need to respond, and you'll be doing that without the benefit of advance preparation.

More challenging for me was the regular confrontation with the messiness of learning. Lecture content may be causing great confusion, but students are so good at faking attention and not asking questions that we discover there's a problem when we grade their exams. If students are engaged in group work and executing the assigned task poorly, that feedback is in your face. And recognizing the mess is only the first step. You've got to do something about it. Should you point it out? Do you clean it up? Make them clean it up? As we'll discuss in the upcoming Implementation Issues section, the answers to those questions aren't always easy or obvious.

These challenges are made worse by student resistance to teaching focused on facilitating learning. They don't want teachers who expect them to come up with the examples, do the problems, or explain concepts to each other. That's the teacher's job, and it's what "good" teachers are supposed to do, more than one student has pointed out to me. This way of teaching means more work for students. It's much easier to copy examples than to come up with them. It's also safer because there's less chance for error. You've got the teacher's examples—how could they possibly be wrong? All of Chapter Eight is devoted to student resistance, including how it manifests itself, how teachers can constructively respond to it, and how it usually dissipates when the teacher remains committed to the role. It deserves mention here only because student resistance is one of the things that makes the facilitative role more difficult to implement. You're trying something new, feeling a certain amount of trepidation, and at the very time you need support, you're having to deal with all sorts of objections.

Learner-centered teaching is not an easier way to teach. Some teachers sense this and avoid it; others experience it and back away. Interestingly, though, when asked, many faculty offer another reason for not trying learner-centered approaches. I hear it all the time in my workshops: "My students just can't handle the level of responsibility you're proposing. There's no way I could use this approach. They're just not ready for it." There are developmental issues involved, to be sure, and all of Chapter Nine is devoted to the discussion of them. But I also think that sometimes this objection is more an excuse and less a reason. The real reasons are discussed in this section, and they are more about the teacher than the students. After all, as I already pointed out in Chapter One, Freire and Horton successfully used these approaches with the poorest of poorly prepared students.

FACILITATIVE TEACHING: PRINCIPLES THAT GUIDE ITS IMPLEMENTATION

Implementing the role of teacher as facilitator can be guided by a set of principles that describe what learner-centered teachers do when they teach. As with any role, there is not one single, correct way to execute it. The principles are what make the role recognizable, but examples are what make it individually unique. There are all sorts of ways individual teachers can engage students and support their efforts to learn. The role is most effectively executed when teachers find ways that work for them, fit with the content they teach, and serve the learning needs of their students.

PRINCIPLE 1: TEACHERS LET STUDENTS DO MORE LEARNING TASKS

I've already previewed this principle. Teachers need to stop doing so many of the learning tasks for students. Teachers should not always be organizing the content, generating the examples, asking the questions, answering the questions, summarizing the discussion, solving the problems, and constructing the diagrams. The key word here is "always." On occasion (and in some classes there may be lots of occasions) teachers need to do all of these things for students. The principle is about gradually doing them less, until the point is reached when doing them is the exception, not the rule.

For example, at the end of a class discussion, it shouldn't always be the teacher who summarizes. I once observed a teacher letting students summarize via a unique but very effective strategy. It was an English lit class, and students were discussing part of a novel. They were seated in a U formation and contributed their ideas without being recognized. As they spoke, the teacher jotted their comments on the board. She did not speak, but focused on getting the essence of their contributions recorded. After about ten minutes, she said to the class. "Where are we? We need to think about this exchange and see if we can come to some sort of conclusion. Please review these notes I've made on the board." After a minute of silence, she said, "Anybody see any connections between these comments?" As students ventured connections, she drew lines, circles, added numbers, occasionally revised and some-times erased. Gradually some conclusions emerged. She asked students to get them in their notes in their own words and then she had three students put their summary statements on the board. The class proceeded to discuss the merits of each. They finally generated one that integrated several of their individual ideas.

The part of the demonstration that spoke to me was how effectively the recording role removed her as the focal point of the discussion. Students were directing their comments and responses to each other. On most days in my class, it does not matter where I stand in the classroom, students only talk to me, but then I realized that I was the only one responding to their comments. Sure enough, once I stopped doing that so regularly, they started talking to each other.

Black (1993) avoids doing all the problem solving work in his organic chemistry class with the following strategy. He arrives in the room early and writes problems on all the available board space. As students arrive, pairs of them are randomly assigned to work one of those problems. By the time class begins, eight to ten students are at the board working problems and they continue to do so for the first five or ten minutes of class. Black circulates around the classroom talking with other students and checking with those doing the problems. If they are stuck, he may offer a hint or ask a leading question.

"As work finishes, students other than those at the board are called upon . . . to analyze or comment on a given problem and its answer . . . I help by providing questions to direct their assess-ment of the answer. Is the solution correct? Could it be better? If they do not think it is right, then what is the problem and how can it be fixed? What is the central idea? What principle is involved? How would you have done it?" (Black, 1993, p. 143). Note how his questions focus on the problem-solving process, not just the right answers.

Once you start thinking about them, there are all sorts of learning tasks teachers can get students doing—summarizing at the end of the period, reviewing at the beginning of the next, predicting experimental results, proposing possible theories, gen-erating hypotheses, evaluating results. Will they do these tasks as well as the teacher? Almost guaranteed they won't, but with prac-tice they will improve. This way of teaching promotes learning by simultaneously developing learning skills and fostering content acquisition, as is fully explained in Chapter Five.

PRINCIPLE 2: TEACHERS DO LESS TELLING SO THAT STUDENTS CAN DO MORE DISCOVERING

Teachers have a terrible propensity to tell students too much. Say we have planned an in-class demonstration. We tell students what we're going to do, we do it, and then we tell them what hap-pened. We tell students when and how they should study and we tell them not to cram or procrastinate. We tell students to do the reading or the homework problems and not to come to class unprepared or late. We tell them how long their papers should be, what font they should use, and exactly how to submit their online submissions. What do students have to figure out for them-selves? Does this much telling promote learning? How does it affect the development of students as learners?

This much telling can become a vicious circle. Most of us spend a lot of time preparing detailed syllabi that describe every aspect of the course. But we still have to "go over" it in class because students won't read it. Sure, we editorialize, elaborate, and answer any questions, but mostly we're repeating the written text. After we're finished, it's not so much that students won't read as they don't have to. I sometimes wonder whether this lengthy discussion of what's written in the syllabus isn't part of the reason students continue to ask us questions that are answered in the syllabus. And, of course, most of us answer those queries.

There are alternatives that are more learner-centered. The syllabus for my entry-level speech communication course is long and complicated (see Appendix One). I pass it out as students walk in on the first day. They have ten minutes to give the syllabus a quick read, after which I encourage them to ask questions. Invariably, there are no questions, even though this class has many unusual features—students select the assignments they will complete, they may take a group exam and self-assess their participation. But students are cool; they act laid back. I sense they don't want to ask questions on the off chance they'll get out of class early.

The first year I tried this approach I had no backup plan, so in the absence of any questions I caved in and went over the syllabus. I was so disgusted with myself that almost immediately I settled on a different approach. Next semester, there were also no questions. "Fine," I said. "Understanding the syllabus is a very important part of being successful in this course, and because part of my job is to help you be successful, let's do a short quiz and see how well you do understand the syllabus." I routinely use this approach now, and the response is always less than enthusiastic. But I keep smiling. They don't know that I don't intend to grade the quiz. Once they're finished, I encourage them to compare answers with those around them and to change any of their answers if they wish. Next I put the quiz up and have the class vote on the answers. For items without a clear majority, I instruct students to check the syllabus and we'll begin with those questions next class period.

This approach to not "going over" the syllabus produces two results that make me think it's successful. It generates good discussion about the class and its structure. At some point students do start asking questions, which I challenge the others in the class to answer. If they aren't coming up with the answer, I direct them to the relevant passage, they to read it, and then I ask someone to answer in their own words. Second, students start the course having looked at the syllabus for course-related information. I reinforce this behavior when I introduce new assignments. Students take out their syllabi, read the description of the assignment, and then ask any questions they have about it. If a student asks me a question that is answered in the syllabus, I use humor, mentioning my advanced age and impending retirement, and saying that if they want the right answer they should take a look in the syllabus. But my favorite indication of success is what the students' syllabi look like at the end of the semester. They look used—not the clean, unmarked virgin text I used to see.

We should be hearing the "let them discover" mantra in many instructional situations. If a student asks a question that's ably answered in the text, refer them to the text. You might follow up with a question the next day to see if they looked up the answer. If previously covered course content emerges in a new context, have students find the previous information in their notes. Students also need to "discover" and accept responsibility for the decisions they make that affect their learning. Chapter Six discusses this topic in detail.

To help break the "telling" habit, I love an approach that Shrock (1992, p. 8) uses: "Students say that my office reminds them of granny's attic: books and papers share space with political posters, Depression-era advertisements, campaign buttons, and ERA pennants . . . But the most important sign is not politely historical, but fiercely oriented to the present and future. It refers to the constant challenge of student-centered teaching; it is deliberately placed at the side off my office door (above the light switch) so that it is the last thing I see before I head for class. In my own plain writing, the sign silently but simply insists: 'Why are you telling them this?'"

Principle 3: Teachers Do Instructional Design Work More Carefully

When students are busy working during class and the teacher is not, many of us feel guilty, as if we somehow aren't fulfilling our professional obligations. During those moments we tend to forget all the time and effort involved in the design and preparation of the activities that now engage students. The instructional design aspects of the teacher's role are an integral part of learner-centered approaches. They are the vehicles through which learning occurs.

Fink (2003) describes the process as "creating significant learning experiences," which is very different from having students do what they did last semester and what they do in most other classes.

Well-designed learning experiences have four characteristics. First off, these learning experiences (be they assignments or activities) motivate student involvement and participation. The objective is to draw students in, so that they are engaged and energized almost before they realize it. Second, as suggested previously, one of the best ways to accomplish the first objective is with assignments and activities that get students doing the authentic and legitimate work of the discipline. Wiggins and McTighe (2005) explain: "Instead of reciting, restating or replicating through demonstration what he was taught or already knows, the student has to carry out exploration and work in the discipline" (p. 154). Students are doing (at their level, of course) what biologists, engineers, philosophers, political scientists, and sociologists do. Third, well-designed assignments and activities take students from their current knowledge and skill level to a new place of competence, and they do so without being too easy or difficult. Also essential here is the need to sequence a set of learning experiences so that they build on each other. Some examples of how to do this are included in Chapter Nine. And finally, these are experiences that simultaneously develop content knowledge and learning skills. There is much more about this aspect in Chapter Five.

These characteristics set high standards, and it is unrealistic to achieve them all with every activity and assignment. Nonetheless, they should be benchmarks for the activities and assignments we currently use and the new ones we design. Learner-centered teachers do not underestimate the intellectual challenges involved in designing experiences that promote deep learning and skill development.

These kinds of learning experiences necessitate approaching design tasks with creativity and ingenuity, as well as with the recognition that good designs are evolutionary. After trying them out, original plans are changed, using feedback from students and the teacher's own sense of what did and didn't work. Let me illustrate with an activity I developed that went through at least six iterations before I got it to the place where I felt it achieved the learning goals I had set for it.

I use a case study that Silverman and Welty (1992) developed to stimulate faculty discussion. It involves a student who charges the teacher gave him a racially motivated grade at the same time a learning disabled student got preferential treatment. Students read the case before coming to class and they come prepared to take a side. I structure the discussion using Frederick's (1981) forced debate method. I create a center aisle in the room and then face the chairs toward this open space. As students arrive, they sit on the side that corresponds with the position they have decided to take. They then talk to each other about the reasons they are on one side or the other. If they change their minds at any time during the discussion, they move to the other side of the room.

I am the recorder, dividing the board in half and noting the arguments on their appropriate side. Once I stop hearing new arguments, I have each side convene to discuss which of the arguments on their side they think are strongest and how they would answer what they believe are the best arguments on the other side. Then a volunteer from each side role-plays a discussion between the teacher and the student who is challenging his grade.

Usually the discussion starts slowly, but because students care about the fairness of grades, they warm up and pretty soon the ideas are flying back and forth. They argue, refute arguments, summon evidence, make points, and state opinions, with many more students participating than is usually the case in class. Some change their minds and move to the other side. Others inch their seats closer to the other side, indicating that they aren't quite as convinced as they were when the discussion started. I hear great examples that I use subsequently when we are learning about arguments, fallacies, and evidence.

It's a great strategy and can be used with many kinds of content. If it's of interest, I'd recommend the work of Herreid (1994, 1999, 2007), who proposes a number of related strategies for using cases in science classes. The activity I developed combined a couple of existing resources into an experience designed to develop argumentation skills. I added the role-play component at the end because the activity seemed unfinished, and the role-play allows students to see how "preparing" for a conversation improves the quality of it. I fussed with how to set up the room and assumed several roles myself before opting to be the recorder. My written record helps students review the arguments. All of these design features make a difference. None of them is particularly unique, but experiences that promote learning are carefully constructed so that their various components work together to enhance the learning potential of the activity.

Principle 4: Faculty More Explicitly Model How Experts Learn

Teacher-facilitators demonstrate how skillful learners approach learning tasks. This is most successfully modeled by doing some legitimate learning in the class, but if it's an entry-level course that's been taught multiple times, a lot of new learning for the teacher may not be possible. We tend to know the content in these courses very well, but every now and then a student asks a new question or offers a different example and our response can demonstrate how an experienced learner handles new ideas and information.

Almost as effective as "learning" in a course are explicit discussions of the learning processes the teacher uses. When solving a problem, you can say out loud what is going through your mind. You can tell students how you confront a difficult and confusing problem, and explain what you do when you get stuck or come up with the wrong answer. It also helps to remember what it was like when you first confronted this material. Was it confusing? Was it frustrating? Did you understand it right away? What mistakes did you make? What helped you finally figure it out? Students are encouraged and helped when teachers model by recounting their first experiences with the material.

Students also need to see examples of learning as hard, messy work, even for experienced learners. An English colleague once shared how her students found the revising and rewriting process time-consuming and depressing. They had written the paper, thought it was finished, and now they had to make all these changes. They must be terrible writers. Their perspective changed considerably when she shared feedback from an editor on one of her papers. By golly, the teacher had to revise and rewrite virtually her whole paper, and that wasn't because she was a poor writer.

Teachers provide students with a powerful model when they, too, are engaged in learning, and I don't mean more learning of that discipline-based knowledge already known and loved. When teachers are learning new material in different fields and outside their comfort zones, students are helped in two ways. First, new learning reconnects teachers, who can easily forget what it feels like to be a student, with those feelings of confusion, frustration, despair, and accomplishment. I completed two undergraduate science courses after this book was first published. I remember the first time in astronomy when I raised my hand and asked what seemed to me a perfectly cogent question about something I didn't understand. The teacher replied that he didn't understand the question. I rephrased it. He answered, but what he said made no sense to me at all. To my amazement, I smiled, nodded, and said thank you. Since that day, I've tried to follow up with every student who smiles, nods, and says thank you for an answer.

A couple of my very favorite pedagogical articles report the experiences of faculty members taking courses with students in disciplines other than their own. English professor Starling (1987) takes a three-course business sequence as part of a learning community, and English professor Gregory (2006) enrolls in an acting class. Both articles are rich with insights gained through the experience, and I would have to agree. My experiences in undergraduate astronomy and chemistry were the most exhilarating and humiliating of my recent professional life. They took me and my teaching back to bedrock.

To sum up, then, students benefit when their teachers are learning (whether it's in a course they're teaching or taking, or on their own), because those teachers have fresh experiences being students. The students also benefit because they see that learning anything new takes work, isn't all that easy, and often involves errors. My lab partners "outed" my ignorance in the first-year seminar I taught that accompanied the chemistry course. At the end of each lab exercise there was an extra-credit "thinking" question, and as lab partners we could collaborate on the answer. I proposed a possible answer to my partners, and they agreed without question. After all, they had a teacher in their lab group. Of course, the answer I proposed was wrong, and as one of my partners announced in seminar, "We just found out that Mary-ellen doesn't know how to answer the thinking questions."

PRINCIPLE 5: FACULTY ENCOURAGE STUDENTS TO LEARN FROM AND WITH EACH OTHER

Faculty frequently underestimate the value of group work. When I recommend it, there are always a variety of reasons suggested why teachers should avoid it. Teachers are welcome to their opinions, but those opinions are at odds with a substantial amount of empirical evidence. Much research (just a bit of which is highlighted in Chapter Two) establishes that a range of different group structures enable students to learn from and with each other. It is absolutely true that good group-learning experiences require planning and effort from the teacher. Again, the design of the group task is one of the keys to making it successful, as is the willingness to help students learn how to function effectively in groups. None of us is born knowing how to work in groups. It is another skill that has to be learned.

Many students resist group work, and often the very best students are the most vocal in their objections. They have a litany of stories to tell about bad experiences in groups—most involving other members not doing their fair share of the work, missing deadlines, and otherwise letting the group down. A lot of these experiences are the result of poorly designed group work and teachers not empowering students to deal with group dynamics issues. Students end up believing they can do better work on their own and are only persuaded by a group experience that visibly demonstrates how groups can do more and better work than individuals.

I try to demonstrate the value of collaboration in a venue that students take seriously: exams. In my course, they can choose to be assigned to a study group that participates in a group exam experience. Each study group prepares some review materials for the rest of the class, and beyond that it's up to the group to decide if they will spend time studying together. Some do; others don't. Those who spend more time working together tend to do better, as research on cooperative learning documents (for an example, see Hsiung, 2012). Because group exams are a new experience for most students, I keep the grading stakes low. Good group performance gets rewarded; poor group performance is not punished. The grading bonus works like this. All students take and turn in the forty-question multiple-choice exam during the first half of the period. Then they convene as a group and do the same exam together. I grade the individual exams first and calculate an average score for the group. Then I grade the group exam. If the group score is higher than the individual average, that difference (usually between four and twelve points on this eighty-point exam) gets added to each individual score.

Group exams and various scoring mechanisms have been used by others. Benvenuto (2001) uses an approach like this in chemistry but with weekly quizzes. In his engineering course, Mourtos (1997) pegs the grading bonus to the amount of independence among group members. A bonus is awarded only if all students in the group score at a certain level on the exam.

I love watching students do the group exam. They hunker down together around it. Their discussion starts out with a quiet intensity, but almost immediately disagreements erupt and the debate starts. It's nearly impossible to get my beginning students to disagree with each other. They don't like conflict with their peers and try hard to avoid it in class. In this case, it happens without them even noticing. Best of all, they are discussing course content with passion, and that, too, is a nearly impossible accomplishment.

Students analyze this group exam experience after their exams have been returned. Those who have received bonus points have tangible evidence that being in a group helped them. Most can explain why the group did or didn't do better than they did individually. Participation in the group exam is an option (I'll be explaining assignment selection in Chapter Four), and routinely it's the very brightest students who select not to participate in the group exam experience. When I ask them why, they are quick to explain: "I just learn better on my own, Dr. Weimer." "I don't really have time to work with a group." I respect their choice but do my best to confront them with evidence that I hope causes some dissonance. For example, during the exam debrief I list the five highest exam scores and then I check off which are group scores and which are individual scores. Invariably three or four are group scores. And I'm not beyond sending those very bright independent operators an e-mail suggesting they might want to comment on those scores when they write their learning log entry on the exam.

Negative beliefs about group work merit revisiting by both students and faculty. The pedagogical literature is replete with descriptions of substantive group tasks that faculty have designed and implemented with success. A number of those are referenced in Chapter Two, and others will be described in subsequent chapters. Bottom line: students can and do learn from and with each other.

PRINCIPLE 6: FACULTY AND STUDENTS WORK TO CREATE CLIMATES FOR LEARNING

This principle is explored fully in Chapter Six, so it only needs an introduction here. Learner-centered teaching is much less about discipline (or *classroom management,* as it is euphemistically called) and much more about creating climates that promote learning. Teachers do take a leadership role in creating those climates, and they also bear some responsibility for maintaining them. But the climate in the classroom is something jointly created by the teacher and the students. The goal is to get students to the point where they start accepting some of the responsibility for what happens in class.

PRINCIPLE 7: FACULTY USE EVALUATION TO PROMOTE LEARNING

This principle is also the subject of a subsequent chapter (Chapter Seven). However, up front I need to be clear that the principle does not mean that faculty do less grading. That responsibility remains as it always has been. The difference is that teachers see that learning is potentially present whenever they evaluate student work. They can provide feedback and design follow-up activities that increase the likelihood that students will learn from the experience and be able to improve as a consequence of it. Part of this involves the recognition that students need to learn to assess their own work as well as that of their peers. No, they don't give themselves and others grades, but they can be engaged in activities where they look critically at their own work and that of their peers.

These seven principles provide an illustration of what learner-centered teaching looks like in action. They further delineate the various aspects of the facilitative teaching role: resource person, mentor, instructional designer, and expert learner. It is a different role, but it is no less important, less essential, or in any other way a diminished form of teaching. It is a role that directly and effectively links teaching to learning.

INTERESTING IMPLEMENTATION ISSUES

Several intriguing implementation issues emerged during my early attempts to teach in more facilitative ways. In one class I was using a fairly straightforward group activity, and what transpired seemed equally straightforward, but I struggled to answer the questions it raised. Later I realized that these questions are central to the successful implementation of teaching roles that focus on students and what they are doing. But let me start with what happened.

I was using an in-class, two-period, small-group activity. Students had completed the first half of the task and now needed to take their work to the next level. To guide that process, I had responded to each group's work with a several-paragraph memo. I handed each memo to someone in the group as I quickly reviewed the task. They had twenty minutes to read the memo, discuss the issues it raised, and then revise what they had submitted previously. All groups but one proceeded the same (sane) way: one member read the memo to the rest of the group.

Up front to my left sat a group populated (by accident) with a very shy crowd. The person to whom I had given the memo proceeded to read it to herself while the rest of the group waited patiently. When she finished, without comment, she passed the memo to the person sitting next to her, who also proceeded to read the memo silently.

At first I was amazed. What were they thinking? Well, clearly they weren't thinking. Why weren't they looking around at the other groups? Usually students so reliably take their lead from what everyone else is doing. Why didn't somebody in the group say something? Could they all be that reticent? I went from amazed to perplexed. What should I do? Should I intervene? That seemed like a step back—the teacher jumping in and fixing the problem every time students make a bad decision. But the quality of their work and their potential to learn from it were being compromised by this silly approach.

The dialogue in my head continued. What should I do if I intervened? What could I say without conveying how stupid I thought their approach was? Maybe they should know I thought they had made a poor decision and somebody in the group had to have figured that out. More important, what could I say that wasn't just telling them they had a problem. I was afraid if I asked, "How are you doing?" they would all nod and say "fine." Maybe I could ask, "Do you understand the task?" "Yes." "Well, how much time do you have left, and how much do you still have to do?" That still seemed pretty close to teaching as telling.

I ended up doing nothing, and they ended up doing poor work. I don't know if they ever made the connection between the way they approached the task and their resulting low grade. I'm not optimistic. I expect most of them had yet another experience that confirmed what they already suspected about the futility of trying to get anything done in a group. But my inept response to this group and their conclusion about the experience are not really the salient issues here. What happened in that group raises three fundamental questions about executing the facilitative teaching role.

DO YOU INTERVENE AND, IF SO, WHEN?

Those two questions are so interconnected they can be considered jointly. If this approach to teaching is about letting students discover and experience the consequences of their decisions, should teachers intervene? You could argue that they should not. Every intervention compromises the potential of students to learn from their mistakes, and we can all list powerful lessons learned from our own mistakes.

With beginning students (the student population I know best), I have to believe the answer isn't strictly yes or no. Most certainly I can and should intervene less than I did when teaching as telling was my modus operandi. But with beginning students (or maybe all students) there are occasions that warrant intervention. The trick is deciding which occasion and when in the course of the event the intervention should occur. In some cases the need is more obvious than in others. We intervene when a decision will hurt a student—they want to sign up to take eighteen credits and work thirty-five hours a week. We intervene when the decision of some students compromises the learning potential of others— the students in the back row who routinely chat and disrupt class. We intervene when students' efforts to figure something out produce such enormous frustration and anxiety that the learning potential of the experience is compromised—anger regularly gets in the way of learning. But in other situations the need for teacher action is less clear, and the consequences of intervening are more mixed. Would a set of guidelines help? Possibly. Even better might be more thinking about and discussion of examples like the one just shared. It illustrates how teachers must make difficult decisions about isolated, context-dependent, and frequently ambiguous situations that simply happen.

HOW BEST TO INTERVENE?

If the ethical responsibilities and compromised learning potential of an experience necessitate intervention, what form should that teacher intervention take? I have pretty much described just telling them. Perhaps that's appropriate occasionally, but when we do it all the time students come to rely on the teacher to tell them what they should and shouldn't be doing. Mature learners need to be able to figure that out for themselves. It's better to ask students questions that lead to the needed insight and understanding.

There's an additional timing question linked to the question of how. Should you intervene while students are making the error or wait until after they've made the mistake? That's another "it depends" answer, but you can make the case for waiting until after if they are trying to figure out what went wrong and there's the potential of learning from their mistakes. I must admit that I don't have a lot of good answers to this question, even for this second edition. As with the previous two questions, this one also deserves thoughtful analysis before and after it happens in class.

As the many topics addressed in this chapter illustrate, the role of learner-centered teachers is not all that easy to execute. It demands that teachers move from teaching that focuses on what they are doing to teaching that responds to what the students are doing. The goal is to engage and support students in learning. A set of principles have been proposed as a way of showing more concretely what teachers who facilitate learning do. Examples also illustrate the role in action, and those offered are but a few of many possible applications.

Some teachers avoid the role because it seems to diminish the importance of the teacher, but as I've endeavored to show in this chapter, it is an equally important and essential role. Students can learn on their own, but for the vast majority of today's college students, teachers are a must. We haven't yet figured everything out yet, but we've figured out enough to know that learner-centered teaching offers intriguing challenges and unique rewards. We also know it's a role that promotes learning.

CHAPTER FOUR

THE BALANCE OF POWER

Although most faculty are at least somewhat comfortable with the idea of a role change that might more effectively facilitate learning, the notion that the balance of power in the classroom needs to change is new and unsettling. From my experience writing and talking about the topic, I've learned that the best way to prevent outright rejection is to ease into the idea with a couple of questions.

How would you characterize your students? Are they empowered, self-motivated learners who tackle learning tasks with confidence and ingenuity? A few perhaps, but many of today's college students are anxious and tentative. They begin courses hoping that they'll be easy and worrying about what they'll do if they're difficult. Most can list a number of things they aren't good at or can't do. They look for majors that require few math and science courses, and they do their best to avoid courses that require a lot of writing. Most would rather not speak in class, and their idea of a good class is one where the teacher tells them exactly what to do. These are generalizations, but for many students education is something that happens to them, and most of the time it's a rather boring, unpleasant experience.

When my colleagues and I bemoan students' lack of confidence and their very passive "whatever you say, Prof" attitudes, we wonder what we can do to overcome this complacency that so compromises students' efforts to learn. That's a good question, but I don't think it's the right one. We need to be asking something more difficult: Why are students like this? Why are so many anxious, indecisive, and unsure of themselves as learners? Even more pointedly: Is there something about the way we teach that makes students dependent learners, that inhibits their development, making it so they can't learn unless teachers tell them what and how? Queries like these lead directly to issues that involve the balance of power in classrooms.

WHAT NEEDS TO CHANGE AND HASN'T: TEACHER CONTROL

Our authority as teachers is so taken for granted that most of us are no longer aware of the extent to which we direct student learning. But answers to a simple set of questions make it very clear. Who decides what students will learn in the course? That is, who makes the decision about what content will be included in the course? Who controls the pace at which that content is covered? That is, who sets up the calendar for the course? Who decides how the students will learn the content? That is, who determines what activities and assignments students will complete? Who sets up the conditions for learning? That is, who establishes course policies on things like attendance, participation, due dates, and rules for conduct in class? In the classroom itself, who controls and regulates the flow of communication? That is, who decides when students will participate, recognizes volunteers, or calls on those who don't volunteer? And finally, who decides how well students have or have not learned the material? That is, who determines the grades?

Respected chemistry educator Bunce (2009) makes the same point this way: "Students 'know' that the course belongs to the teacher: the teacher determines policy, due dates, the difficulty of the tests and the value of each assignment/test. The teacher also decides what material is important and how it will be presented. No one asks students what they need to learn. Typically they have no voice in how things are done, nor are they likely to volunteer any suggestions for fear that it would be viewed as impudent" (p. 676).

For tangible evidence of the propensity to control students and their learning, we need look no further than the course syllabus. Even mild-mannered, normally gentle faculty resort to edits, demands, and directives that set down the law for students. "No late papers accepted, ever, under any circumstances." "Don't ask for extra credit. Time and energy should be spent on regular class assignments." "Failure to participate will lower your grade." "Do not talk in class. You are here to listen and learn." "You must do the reading before you come to class. Telling us what you think without having informed your opinion wastes valuable class time."

In two powerful articles Singham (2005, 2007) decries what syllabi have become: "They list assigned readings but not reasons *why* the subject is worth studying or important or interesting or deep, or the learning strategies that will be used in the course. The typical syllabus gives little indication that the students and teacher are embarking on an exciting learning adventure together and its tone is more akin to something that might be handed to a prisoner on the first day of incarceration" (2007, p. 52). He continues: "a detailed, legalistic syllabus is diametrically opposed to what makes students want to learn. There is vast research literature on the topic of motivation to learn, and one finding screams out loud and clear: controlling environments have been shown consistently to *reduce* people's interest in whatever they are doing, even when they are doing things that would be highly motivating in other contexts" (2007, pp. 54–55).

Faculty firmly establish who's in charge with policies that address all manner of individual behaviors and classroom issues. There are faculty who will not teach if students wear baseball caps or chew gum in class. I recently saw a syllabus that admonished students to bathe before coming to class. The instructor explained that several years ago a student routinely arrived in class with offensive body odor. She added the policy, and so far it's worked— no smelly students in class since then. If discussion ever flags in one of my workshops, an energized exchange can always be generated if I inquire about cell phone policies, despite the fact it has been months since I've given a session where a faculty phone has not interrupted the proceedings. Singham (2007) describes something he calls "syllabus creep," whereby "faculty keep adding new rules to combat each student excuse for not meeting existing rules" (p. 55). I can't document with a study that the number of policies per syllabus has increased since the 2002 edition of this book, but I'd be willing to bet a chunk of my retirement that the number hasn't decreased.

Most faculty willingly acknowledge that they exercise considerable power over student learning, but they strongly resist any suggestion that the amount is excessive and possibly detrimental. In an August 24, 2011, Teaching Professor blog post (www.facultyfocus.com) I encouraged readers to revisit syllabi with a set of questions that inquired about tone, whether the document conveyed excitement about learning, whether all the course decisions should be made by the teacher, and whether students had ever been asked for feedback on the syllabus. The post generated considerable response, some positive, but a lot strongly defending the syllabus as a contract. "If the purpose of your syllabus isn't to state your requirements in such a way that it is a defense again shenanigans, I would suggest you are a very new prof." "My syllabus is not a place to give them warm fuzzies. It's a place to list contract-style exactly what they need to accomplish to get the grade . . . It's not a sales pitch for Happy Teddies Kindergarten." "This is the kind of touchy-feely nonsense that engenders the entitled attitude we face in the classroom."

Comments like these make clear why faculty think they must assert control: students need it. They can't be trusted to make decisions about learning or to respond maturely in less than fully controlled learning environments. They don't respect authority; they don't have good study skills; they aren't well prepared; they have no interest in the content area; they take courses to get grades and don't care about learning. All they want out of education is a good-paying job.

These characteristics are typical of college students—we could debate exactly how many—and they are issues that must be dealt with if students are to be entrusted with decisions about their learning. But the fact that students need to be prepared to handle learner-centered approaches does not justify making all the decisions for them. Mallinger (1998, p. 473) points out that "the argument for instructor-directed leadership assumes that students are not *capable* [emphasis added] of expanding their maturity level."

The second reason faculty control so much of what occurs in the classroom is because they always have. It's what teachers are supposed to do. Braye (1995, p. 1) explains: "a 'good' teacher dominates the classroom and its elements. She prepares lesson plans for efficient use of class time, prescribes course objectives, and disseminates information clearly and effectively so that students may learn it quickly, remember it well, and reproduce it upon demand." For years I followed this script, thinking I was doing what students needed teachers to do. It never occurred to me that the way I controlled students and their learning processes might be a detriment, or that the way I was teaching might benefit me more than them.

Here's an example of the kind of unsettling discoveries an examination of my practices revealed. I regularly waved off student questions until I had thoroughly made my point. I didn't want to be interrupted. When I was finished, then I asked for questions. I quickly glanced around the room and, seeing no hands, I asked a question, called on a student (no time to wait for volunteers), barely acknowledged his response, and moved on. I couldn't spend more time on this topic if I was going to get through all the content. Thinking about this made me angry and a bit embarrassed. Being this much in control without knowing it wasn't something I expected to find out. And using this much power just because teachers always have didn't seem like a very good reason.

Finally, faculty exert control over learning and students because of vulnerabilities that are an inherent part of teaching. We teach who we are, which means we can be hurt and so we are cautious. But this vulnerability and its associated fear are things more often felt than understood by teachers. One of my colleagues discovered this in a recurring bad dream about teaching. It's the first day of his large entry-level business logistics course. He's going through his usual intro, pointing out that he's a full professor and no longer has to teach beginning classes, but he chooses to do so because the content is so important. Somewhere in the middle of these promotional messages, a student whose face he can never quite make out stands up and loudly declares that the instructor is bogus, a great big fake, and ought to be removed. Students have paid for and deserve better. As this student agitator energizes the class, they surge toward the front of the room. My colleague wakes up kicking and screaming, as he is bodily removed from the class.

I laughed when I first heard the story in this dream, probably because it seems so antithetical to his teaching persona. But it's a dream rooted in reality. If students wanted to bodily remove the teacher from the classroom, even in reasonably small classes there are enough of them to accomplish that feat. Teachers may exert lots of power, but they are still never completely in control of a class. Most of us have felt this vulnerability when, for instance, we add an assignment not listed in the syllabus or publicly chide a student for the infraction of some rule. If students challenge a teacher's authority, most teachers feel obligated to respond by exercising more power, and that starts an upward spiral that almost never ends positively.

Worried about these challenges, teachers are motivated to do what they can to prevent them. Ironically, the more controls they put in place, the more likely students are to resist. The ironclad syllabus that handcuffs students to the course defines the teacher–student relationship adversarially. It all but dares students to challenge the teacher's authority. Some of the theories highlighted in Chapter One and some of the research reviewed in Chapter Two document that students' motivation, confidence, and enthusiasm for learning are all adversely affected when teachers exert control, and students end up feeling powerless.

But this isn't the ultimate irony. Despite making most of the learning decisions for students and controlling most aspects of the learning environment, students still get to make the decision that matters most. They, and they alone, decide whether or not they will learn. Teachers cannot learn for students or force learning on them. There are strong negative consequences if students decide not to learn—they don't get credit and have wasted money on the course. They get failing grades, which jeopardize their college and professional careers. Or they leave the course with little knowledge and few skills, and therefore struggle in subsequent courses. But some students choose these consequences anyway. In reality, the balance of power in the classroom favors students. They can render teaching pointless by not learning.

In sum, faculty continue to exert much control over the learning processes of students. Even though they do so thinking this benefits students, more often it is a detriment to deep learning and the development of learning skills. Making the learning decisions for students creates dependent learners, and tight control of the learning environment negatively affects the motivation to learn. To justify this use of power because students cannot be trusted to make learning decisions or to act responsibly assumes students cannot learn either of these important skills. Not only is this a poor reason, it is probably not the real reason faculty feel the need to control learning processes and what happens in class. Teaching exposes vulnerabilities: students can successfully challenge a teacher's authority. And they can refuse to learn, thereby showing that despite having great power, teachers are still powerless to ensure the ultimate goal of education.

CHANGING THE BALANCE OF POWER

When teaching is learner-centered, power is shared with students, not transferred to them wholesale. Faculty still make decisions about learning, just not all of them, and not always without student input. Even so, the change raises ethical issues about teacher responsibilities—what it is teachers are obligated to provide learners. Those who object to learner-centered approaches worry that students end up running the class and teaching themselves. And it is true that the ultimate goal is to equip students with the learning skills they need to teach themselves. Autonomous, self-directed learners don't need teachers, or need them much less. But the process of becoming an independent learner is a gradual one, and most college students start out being very dependent learners.

In learner-centered classrooms, power is redistributed in amounts proportional to students' abilities to handle it. Parents of a teenager with a new driver's license don't hand over the keys to the family car Friday night and say, "Have a nice weekend. We'll need the car back Monday morning." The strategies shared in this book give students some say, but not the power to decide everything. Students are not running the class, and teachers are not abrogating legitimate instructional responsibilities.

Here's an example that illustrates how this change in the balance of power works. Beginning students who have never taken a sociology course have neither the knowledge nor the experience to select a textbook for the course. Asking them to do so would be ethically irresponsible. But let's say the sociology teacher surveys a variety of texts and selects five books that would accomplish course goals and meet student learning needs. Students in the course could then be formed into textbook review committees, provided with rubrics identifying the characteristics of a good text, and as a class tasked with making and justifying a textbook recommendation. I have a colleague who routinely uses this method to select course texts. To his repeated surprise, students seldom recommend the text he expects they will pick. He also says that students in subsequent sections look at the text differently when they know students helped to select it.

In this example, students are given a limited amount of power, and the design of the activity guides their decision making. In my course, I let students decide which assignments they will complete (save one that is required), but their decision making is constrained by several design features. Students choose their assignments, but the assignments selected must be completed as they are designed. With some assignments, though, they can decide how much they will do. For example, in the learning log assignment, students determine which and how many of the entries they write. In addition, every course assignment has a due date (including the log entries), and after that date the assignment cannot be completed. I know that my beginning students have trouble with time management, and I don't want them trying to do a course worth of work during the last two weeks. I also don't want them doing lots of the assignments without devoting significant time and energy to each. So, for any assignment to generate points, students must earn at least 50 percent of the points. If the work is not passing, no points are awarded.

Determining how course content will be learned is a decision appropriately made by mature, responsible learners. It is not a decision that the vast majority of beginning students should be making. But if beginning students are to develop into mature learners, if they are to begin managing their own learning, then they must be given some control over it. And if teachers want to learn how to facilitate learning, they must be willing to transfer some decision making to students. Like students, the best way for teachers to learn is by releasing control gradually.

Students don't always see the benefits of this change. Initially they are confused. Some resist by pointing out the teacher is not doing her job, which is really about giving power back to the teacher. The fear that students will use the power they've been given to overthrow or otherwise compromise the teacher's authority is unfounded, at least in the experience of many of us who have shared power with students.

I let students set the participation policy in my course. There's more about how this works in the next section. As they work through the details—questions such as should the teacher call on students or only recognize volunteers, should students lose points if they give a wrong answer, and is attendance part of the participation grade—students frequently defer to me or question the process. "Why are you asking us? These are things teachers decide." Dependent learners prefer teacher-centered classrooms because that's what they're used to and they don't have to take responsibility for decisions made by the teacher.

When it becomes clear to students that the teacher will not make the decisions she has asked them to make, they use this new power tentatively and with some anxiety. They want feedback and need reinforcement. If that's provided, they move forward with a bit more confidence. Then one day, seemingly all of a sudden, students get it, or at least a number of them do, and that critical mass generates an energy and enthusiasm that often ignites the rest of the class. No, instructional nirvana does not descend. Not everybody gets it. Some activities and assignments still bomb. But the class is different in very positive and convincing ways. I will mention four of them.

When I started letting my students select their assignments, quite frankly I didn't expect to see much of a difference. In reality I was giving them a very modest amount of control. But right away there was a noticeable change in their level of motivation; they were willing to do more work. Before I began letting students select assignments, I required completion of between ten to twelve, depending on the semester. After they began selecting assignments, on average students completed more than thirteen assignments, and nobody complained about how much work the course involved. My experience and that of others is confirmed by Pintrich's (2003) work on motivation, reviewed in Chapter

Two, as well as the research on independent learners that is also highlighted in that chapter.

Next I observed that having some control also affects how students learn the material. It makes it easier to connect with the content, to see its relevance, and to want to apply what's being learned. More than once I remember reflecting that knowledge is power, and my students were exercising their knowledge and power with purpose, and sometimes even with poise. And, of course, the experience of making some decisions informs subsequent experiences making other decisions.

Power sharing creates a more positive and constructive classroom environment. There is a stronger sense of community—a greater sense that the class belongs to everybody. Students see more clearly that they, too, are responsible for what happens in class. Routinely the class participation policy that students set in my course has a plank that the teacher will call on students only when they volunteer. Much to my surprise, more than once when I asked a question and was getting no response, someone spoke up, reminding the class that I had agreed not to call on students and somebody better volunteer.

When students share power in the classroom, when they are entrusted with some decision making and feel a sense of control, there is less disruptive behavior. When they don't feel powerless, they have fewer reasons to challenge authority. Power sharing redefines the teacher–student relationship, making it less adversarial. Classroom management changes from needing policies that prevent misconduct to a quest for procedures that promote the climate for learning. Chapter Six explores these classroom climate issues more fully.

Given these positive responses—more motivation, better content connection, a stronger sense of the class as a community, and fewer classroom management issues—it is not surprising that teachers also benefit when they share power with students. It's a pleasure to work with students who are less passive, more interested, and willing to work! Their responses motivated me. I prepared more, searched harder for new activities, and was willing to take greater risks. I never felt that I had lost power in those classrooms where I shared it with students. Ironically, I usually felt more in control. When I did ask students to do something, they willingly complied.

In a nutshell, when power is shared, what happens in the classroom changes. Teachers and students behave differently. I tolerate more noise in my classroom. To outsiders, I suspect it looks chaotic. Students work in groups, and they talk to people in other groups. Before class they wander around, talking to each other. Sometimes they sit on the table in the front of the room and rearrange the chairs so that they are no longer in neat rows. They write announcements on the board. They act like they own the place. I will never forget the day a peer reviewer arrived in class only to be accosted by a student. What was he doing in class? After explaining, I heard the student tell my colleague that it was "definitely an unconventional class with a lot of weird assignments," but I shouldn't get in trouble because it was really a very good class. I didn't know if I should be horrified or thrilled.

REDISTRIBUTING POWER: EXAMPLES

What kind of assignments and individual classroom activities responsibly give students more control over learning processes? That's the question this section aspires to answer. The examples it contains are organized around the four areas identified in the chapter introduction as places where teachers typically make decisions for students: (1) the activities and assignments of the course, (2) course policies, (3) course content, and (4) the evaluation of student learning. The section includes examples that offer students different amounts of decision making, thereby giving teachers choices that align with students' and teachers' readiness for power-sharing options.

ACTIVITIES AND ASSIGNMENTS

I've already mentioned that I let students in my beginning courses select the assignments they will complete. These assignments are described in the syllabus that appears in Appendix One. I make the process administratively easy by not using formal contracts. Students are welcome to add assignments, exchange assignments, or do fewer assignments as the course progresses. I grade student work using an absolute grading standard, which I include in the syllabus. From day one, students know how many points they need to earn for each letter grade.

Even though I don't want to be bothered with having to keep track of who's doing what assignment, my beginning students still need to be encouraged to do some course planning. So in their first log entry students make some initial assignment choices and share their reactions to being able to make these decisions. Some of their reactions are not very encouraging. They say they plan to do the easy assignments (although there is some disagreement as to which ones are easy). They also plan to select those assignments they "like," with little insight that these choices relate to their learning preferences. They believe a teacher might use this approach because "you like students and want to give us a chance," or "you don't want any student blaming you for a bad grade."

What is encouraging is their response to the final log prompt: "How do you think this strategy will affect your performance in the class?" "I think this structure will really help me. It puts me in charge." "With this class, it's up to me, and although that scares me, I really think that's the way it should be." "I'll have to see, but I think I'm really going to work hard in this class. I feel like I have a chance." "I will do every assignment if that's what it takes to get an A in this course. I am motivated."

I didn't admit in the first edition of the book that when I first started using this approach, I didn't fully understand the design implications. I just thought it was a neat idea that might motivate some students to work a bit harder. What I came to realize was that this approach presents the teacher with some fairly complex design challenges. You have to ensure that completion of any possible combination of assignments achieves the course goals. This makes having a clear set of course goals essential, and it necessitates a thoughtful analysis of each assignment as well. If I were doing this over, I would implement the assignment selection approach more gradually, giving students options between several assignments before letting them select all the assignments. It is also possible to give students options within an assignment. The same design principle applies. Each option must achieve the assignment's overall goals, and each option must be equally time-consuming and intellectually challenging.

Some faculty let students determine when assignments are due. This works well for papers. With assignments that run parallel with the content, they give students a window (say a week) during which the paper is due. For faculty who believe teaching students to meet deadlines is important, students are asked to designate their due date within this window and to identify the penalty if they miss that deadline.

With more experienced students and larger projects, students can be given time management responsibilities for the entire project. I have a colleague who does this in a 300-level business course. In this group task, students must prepare a major report that attempts to persuade a business to locate a manufacturing facility in the county. The first graded part of the assignment is a memo from the group in which they identify the major steps necessary to complete the project, the order in which they need to be completed, a tentative timeline, a proposed division of labor, when and over what they would like instructor formative feedback, and a final delivery date for the report.

It is also possible to let students make some decisions about the weight of their assignments. If regular quizzes or homework assignments are part of the course and they normally count for 5 percent of the grade, students might be allowed to use them for 10 percent of the grade or more, with a corresponding percentage taken off the final or unit tests. In my graduate course on college teaching, students complete five different assignments. Each one of those assignments is worth 10 percent of their grade. I give them the other 50 percent of their grade and let them distribute it among the five assignments. I recommend they make that distribution using a needs assessment. In five years, what do they anticipate they will most need to know about college teaching? Knowing that, they can more easily determine which of the assignments will best provide that knowledge. Dobrow, Smith, and Posner (2011) report that interest in the course and interest in taking other courses in the area was significantly higher for students who were able to determine, within designated ranges, the weight of three major assignments in an MBA management course, compared with students not given this choice.

COURSE POLICY DECISIONS

I have also written a bit about how students set the participation policy in my communication courses. Let me add more details about how this works and some of the lessons I've learned. I use a round-robin cooperative learning technique to start the class working on the policy. Students work in groups of four, with each student being given a different question about participation. I have them answer questions like: What behaviors should count positively toward participation credit? Should some participation behaviors count more? If so, which ones? What behaviors should cause students to lose participation credit, and how much credit should they lose? How can the teacher and other students encourage participation? Each student asks every other person in the group their question, they take notes on the answers, and they answer everyone else's questions.

Next, all students with the same question form a new group in which they share the responses they've collected. Their task is to construct a group answer that integrates the most common responses, as well as other good ideas that the group supports. They submit their answer, and I respond the next period with a memo to each group that raises questions and asks for elaboration. In their groups students provide this clarification and then post their answers, which we discuss further. Using the student responses, I prepare a draft policy, which I distribute. The class may discuss it further before they vote to accept or reject the policy.

My first surprise was how regularly students came up with policies that closely parallel the ones I've been using for years, although there has been an occasional surprise. One class proposed that right and wrong answers would count equally. My first thought: I'm glad I don't teach math. Then I spent a good deal of time wondering whether I could endorse such questionable policy. I shared my misgivings with the class and asked for their rationale. Two responses persuaded me that I could live with the policy, at least for that semester. One student explained that if you give a wrong answer and the teacher goes to great lengths to correct you in front of everyone else, it takes a good deal of courage to raise your hand next time. Another student, one of those very bright students who can be simultaneously loved and hated, pointed out that teachers repeatedly tell students that they shouldn't be afraid to make mistakes because so much can be learned from them. "Now, if I'm going to make a mistake in class, and the whole class is going to learn from it, then I should get credit for it." I decided the point was his.

Constructing this policy routinely demonstrates how readily students want to return the power to the teacher. Initially, they propose parts for the policy that are decidedly vague. "Students should get credit for trying." When I object, asking how I'm supposed to know if a student is trying, they promptly respond, "You decide. You're the teacher." I try to make them understand with an absurd example. "You want me to decide? Okay, I can do that, but let me tell you something. Every semester I have engineers in this class and I never had one who tried to participate. Right now, I'm telling you no engineer is getting credit for trying." They naively protest. "You can't do that. You're the teacher. You have to be fair." At that point, some of them start seeing how making the policy specific can actually protect them.

Students almost always decide that the teacher will only call on volunteers. That has also surprised me and prompted serious thinking about what's referred to in the literature as "cold calling." Why do faculty call on students when they don't volunteer? Sometimes it's the only way to get students to participate. Or it's a way to handle the overparticipation problem—those few students who are willing to answer any and every question. Howard, Short, and Clark (1996) found that 28 percent of the students made 89 percent of the comments in the 231 class sessions they observed. In another study, Howard and Henney (1998) report an average of 31 student contributions observed per class. Twenty-nine of these (that's 92 percent) were made by five students.

When asked, most faculty say they call on students because they are trying to encourage participation. If students are "encouraged" by being made to speak when they haven't volunteered, they will come to realize they can contribute, and that will motivate them to volunteer. For years now I've been looking at the research on participation and trying to find a study documenting this assumption. So far I haven't found one. Instead, what I think students learn from this practice is how to speak up when somebody calls on them. Unfortunately, in their professional lives there won't be a teacher to call on them, even though they may need to speak up.

Further thinking has led me to wonder if cold calling might actually benefit teachers more than students. It's awkward and uncomfortable to ask a question and have no one answer. It feels like time is being wasted, although most faculty wait so briefly, the time wasted is minimal. It can also feel like a thinly veiled threat to the teacher's authority. Let's not answer and see how she handles it. But just as soon as the teacher calls on a student, the teacher no longer has a problem. Now the pressure is on the student to come up with an answer.

I have also noted (with pleasure) that most of the policies students generate in my classes address the overparticipation problem. They propose that "lots" of people will participate, but that nobody will participate "too much." I point out that people who overparticipate in class (and elsewhere) frequently don't know they have a problem and so we need to make clear when it is a problem. How many contributions per seventy-five-minute period is too much? They come up with some arbitrary number, which we incorporate into the policy. Its effect is quite dramatic. I see those overparticipators keeping track of the number of times they have contributed. That's precisely the kind of self-monitoring that needs to occur. I wish the same policy could be instituted in faculty committee meetings.

One final surprise: generating the participation policy makes students more aware of the participation dynamic in the classroom. They start thinking about participation in terms of behaviors: asking questions, answering questions, asking follow-up questions, responding to each other, offering examples. It's almost as if they are seeing participation in action for the first time. Again, I don't want to imply that participation perfection has come to pass in my classes. It hasn't. There are still students who never say a word (and it's a communication class), still questions I can't get anyone to answer, and still comments that take the discussion off topic. Even so, this redistribution of power has made for better interaction in my classrooms. Woods (1996) reports similar outcomes in a senior-level engineering class where he let students design the instrument used to assess their involvement in class discussions.

Participation is not the only policy students can be given a role in creating. Benjamin (2005) has developed an exercise that gets students articulating goals for the course, which he then integrates with his. DiClementi and Handelsman (2005) report on their experiences letting students set classroom management policies in a number of areas. Initially they had students propose policies, which the teacher would then decide to accept, reject, or revise, as a guard against students' proposing something inappropriate. Surprisingly, though, they report that student policies were so consistent with their own that at some point they dropped the teacher approval mechanism.

Even cold calling need not be a do-it-or-don't-do strategy. Welty (1989, p. 47) created something he calls "cool" calling. Before class begins, he posts a question and then he tells three students that he'd like them to begin the discussion with some answers to that question. Dealing with class announcements and other logistical details first gives students a little time to think of what they might say in response to the question. It's another example of giving students just a bit of control and a chance to improve their answers.

COURSE CONTENT DECISIONS

When I talk with faculty about involving students in decision making related to their learning, the idea of letting them make decisions about content meets with strong resistance. Faculty know so much about the content, and students know so little that I now wonder if this isn't why it seems completely irresponsible to give students any say over content. And those feelings are only strengthened by the amount of material contained in our courses. None of it can be deleted, and there is absolutely no time to add extra topics, even when students indicate interest in them.

But we already do let students make some content-related decisions. We let them choose topics for their speeches, select subjects for their artwork and write papers, even major research papers, on content they wish to explore. Some teachers let students choose among a collection of readings. And there are other time-efficient, small content decision possibilities. I had a teacher who let students identify the topics to be covered during an exam review session. E-mail makes it easy for students to identify potential topics. When I first started using this strategy, I did so with the goal of being more learner-centered. I discovered that it is also an excellent feedback mechanism. You learn what students think are important topics and what content areas they aren't sure they fully understand.

Chapter Seven discusses several strategies faculty use that involve students writing test questions. This review mechanism encourages students to focus on questions instead of answers. My students memorize all sorts of material, but often can't put the answer together with the question. If the writing test questions activity includes a feedback component, it also helps students answer for themselves the frequently asked question, "What do I need to know for the exam?" If some (even just a few) student-generated questions (or versions of them) end up on the exam, that gives students a bit of content control, and it becomes an activity they take very seriously.

Black (1993) gives students more content control in a restructured organic chemistry course. Content is "covered" in the text—meaning he doesn't give lectures on topics that are explained in the book. He describes what happens in class: "Currently, the class is run much like a discussion section . . . I generally query the students at the beginning of each class to determine what they are having trouble with, and what they want to talk about. From their suggestions, we make a list of topics, and during the class I try to address the problems they are having with these topics, perhaps by clarifying and explaining, providing examples, or whatever else I can do to help" (p. 142). If this sounds like a recipe for disaster, Black says that's not what happens. "Interestingly, the course does not collapse when I come in and ask what students want to talk about, because it is always in the context of the current chapter, and the schedule for working on those chapters is in the syllabus. Going to class each day is a pleasure, and always somewhat different. I am relaxed, enjoy the time, and it shows to the students. I feel no pressure to enter a mad race to cover the material; rather, we work together on what is currently their work" (p. 144).

Tichenor (1997) describes how students were involved in the design of labs in a physiology course. Chapter Two highlights a study (Thiel, Peterman, and Brown, 2008) conducted in a math course where faculty meet in class once a week. The other class sessions are held in a lab where students are working on problems. These students do not decide what problems they will work, but they do determine what content gets covered in the class session by identifying the problems they can't solve, the solutions they aren't sure of, and the questions they need to have answered.

In some situations students can make major content decisions about a course. My graduate course on college teaching counts as graduate credit, but is not required by any graduate program. This means I am not beholden to any department to cover certain topics. I have generated a long list of potential topics and readings for the course. For their first assignment, students write a short paper that explains why they are in the course, what they hope to learn, and what content they think might help them accomplish their learning goals. These papers are shared with classmates, and a list of potential topics is generated. Groups and individuals prioritize the topics and, using their lists, I identify the topics that will be covered in the course, create a calendar, and assemble a collection of relevant readings. If majority interests have ruled out a topic of interest to an individual, I encourage that student to use one of the assignments to explore the topic.

EVALUATION ACTIVITIES

Assessment offers yet another challenging arena for involving students in decision making. The assessment of learning has long been the exclusive domain of faculty. And the pressure on students to get grades compromises their ability to be objective about their work. Nonetheless, there are ways to get students involved in assessing their own work and that of their peers. Chapter Seven is devoted to this topic. It contains a variety of examples and discusses the issues involved.

Several syllabus-related activities simultaneously involve students in decision making about the assignments and activities of the course, its policies, the content, and assessment strategies. They are offered here in a summary of some ways power can be redistributed. Johnson (2000, p. 1) lets students help him design the syllabus for the course. He prepares a syllabus before class and distributes it the first day, but across the top of the first page he writes "DRAFT." He begins class by having students interview each other, talking about what they want to learn in the course. They share what others have said, and Johnson writes what he hears on newsprint. Then students assemble in small groups and with the draft syllabus in hand they respond to this prompt: "Building on your own needs, the results of our interviews, and my commitment to include your input, how would you revise the course?" Students are welcome to offer revisions to any part of the syllabus. Johnson reports that they make a variety of suggestions, many of them excellent. "I cannot recall a case where the students tried to find the easy way out, or to water down the course" (p. 1). He carefully considers their input and revises the syllabus, including as many of their recommendations as he feels he justifiably can. It's a great example of involving students in course decision making while still retaining enough instructor control to guarantee course integrity.

Since the 2002 edition, other examples of related syllabus activities have appeared in the pedagogical literature. Hudd (2003) gives students in an introductory sociology course a "skeleton" syllabus that contains the topic for each week, along with text and supplemental readings. There are no assignments listed on the syllabus. Working in groups, students are tasked with creating them. "While students infrequently generate an innovative idea (e.g., an in-class group exam), the vast majority of assignments are fairly traditional and discussion focuses on preferences for exams, papers, or oral presentations, as well as the timing and weighting of these various assignments" (p. 198). The article contains a wealth of detail associated with the design and implementation of the activity. Student response has been "overwhelmingly positive," and Hudd notes that the activity teaches other lessons, as illustrated by this student comment: "It was like giving us the power, which was a different thing. Instead of just walking to a class and receiving an agenda, we made our own" (p. 200).

Gibson (2011) challenged sophomore-level students in a sociology of aging class to design the course so that it would be personally meaningful to them. She acknowledges that some might argue that giving students the power to establish course objectives compromises the integrity of the course. However, because of her experience, she believes that "it is possible to meet academic and accreditation requirements, empower students, and achieve learning at the same time" (p. 96). Logistically, she presented students with fifty possible course objects and twenty-two different assignments (all listed in the article). Students set deadlines for the assignments and prioritized their importance. She then weighted these assignments according to their priorities. Again, student response was very positive.

Finally, Mihans, Long, and Felton (2008) report on the involvement of students in the redesign of a largely unpopular elementary education course. Students and faculty jointly participated in a committee that undertook the course redesign project. They write: "We questioned whether undergraduate students had sufficient pedagogical expertise and disciplinary knowledge to fully participate in the design of a university course. We also questioned whether we were willing to relinquish control over the process of restructuring a class . . . We knew that we had to be *truly* willing to share power with the students and not simply give lip service to collaboration. Were we really willing to defer to the students when we disagreed—and should we?" (p. 2). Their experience answered all these questions positively. The article describes the process they used to create a syllabus for the new course. It also explores the issues involved in this kind of power-sharing activity.

INTERESTING IMPLEMENTATION ISSUES

The most fundamental implementation question is the one this whole chapter aspires to answer: Can a set of learning activities and experiences be designed to responsibly give students more control over the decisions that affect their learning? I encourage further discussion and exploration of the examples included in the chapter as you seek to answer that question.

Three other questions emerge out of experiences using the examples highlighted in the chapter:

1. How much power is enough to motivate students?
2. How much decision making are students ready to handle?
3. How do teachers know when they've abrogated legitimate instructional responsibility?

I didn't have very concrete answers when I wrote the first edition. I was hoping that during the years since then better answers might become available, but the literature on learner-centered teaching has yet to deal with these questions substantively, despite their importance.

HOW MUCH POWER IS ENOUGH TO MOTIVATE STUDENTS?

If having power (in decision making, for example, as the chapter proposes) motivates learners, how much power does it take? For instructors using these approaches, the question can be answered pragmatically. They can give students some decision-making discretion and see when and how their motivation is affected. Some of the research highlighted in Chapter Two hints at the answer—several studies report better grades (which suggest more learning) and more positive attitudes as a result of even very modest decision-making discretion (Armbruster, Patel, Johnson, and Weiss, 2009; J.P.P. Brown, 2010; S. D. Brown, 2010; Gosser, Kampmeier, and Varma-Nelson, 2010, for example). That certainly has been my experience as well. But we need more than individual answers. We need principles and guidelines that can be used to establish professional norms and standards.

Related is the question of the amount of decision making it takes to motivate an individual student versus how much it takes to positively affect the class. I felt as though I redistributed enough power to motivate most students, but that amount did not positively affect all students. Students still fail my courses. They choose not to work or do such a miniscule amount that they do not learn enough to pass the class. I find myself wondering whether they needed more control, whether they'd been given too much, or whether they failed for factors totally unrelated to the power and control issues.

This quandary leads to the question of whether decision making could be given to students differentially. Could some students be given more control and others less, or would this violate the principles of fair and equitable treatment for all students? More fundamentally, is this even pragmatically possible, given the size of most classes?

HOW MUCH DECISION MAKING ARE STUDENTS READY TO HANDLE?

The amount of decision making needed to motivate students must be balanced against their intellectual maturity and ability to operate in conditions where they have more freedom but also more responsibility. The question is how teachers objectively determine which decisions students are ready to make on their own and which decisions they need instructor guidance and feedback on.

This question is important because, as those who object to learner-centered approaches are quick to point out, students are not well prepared to make decisions about learning. Even in those areas that they do control, like deciding how they will prepare for an exam, most teachers have seen evidence of poor decision making. In my communication and first-year seminar courses, I have students prepare a study game plan for an upcoming exam. It involves a timeline and a list of activities they will use to prepare for the test. I am always amazed by the number who tell me this is the first time they have developed such a plan. And I am always dismayed by the number who report after the exam that they didn't follow any part of the game plan. They did what they normally do: wait until the night before and then try to learn (more like memorize) everything they think they need to know.

Beyond their lack of good study skills, students also have very little or no experience making decisions related to their learning. They are used to educational experiences where teachers decide everything, from the page length of each paper to whether a student has the intellectual wherewithal to major in a particular field.

Without strong study skills and previous decision-making experiences, the chances that students (especially beginning ones) will make bad decisions is high. Should teachers let students make some of those bad decisions in the hopes they will learn from them? If so, what kind of decisions? Almost every semester I have some students who participate regularly in my communication courses, but they didn't select this assignment option. When I point out that their contributions are precisely the ones called for by policy, meaning they could be getting points for what they are doing, most readily admit they have made a mistake. I don't let them add the option after the fact, but maybe I should.

A few of the mistakes students have made in my courses have had serious consequences. I had one student who failed because he had twenty-five points less than he needed to pass. When he showed up at my office surprised and dismayed, I asked him, "How many points did you have?" "I don't know. I never added them up. But if I had known I was short, I would have done more work." This experience caused me to wonder if I should be distributing point totals to students throughout the semester. I hadn't thought that was necessary because I give them a grid on which to record their points, and every time I return an assignment I remind them that if they keep track of their points, they will know exactly where they stand in the class. Most students have no trouble with the system. In fact, they regularly tell me how well it works for them. How they are doing in the course is not a mystery, and that makes it easier for them to focus on the work of the course.

Nonetheless, the reaction of this student with twenty-five points less than he needed to pass has caused me considerable consternation. Was keeping track of his points beyond his ability level, or was he just lazy and irresponsible? I don't know how teachers figure out something like this before or after the fact. And this example also illustrates the individual-versus-class dilemma. What about those situations where most of the class can handle the decision, control, or power they've been given, but some students cannot? These are both pragmatic and theoretical questions for which we need answers.

HOW DO TEACHERS KNOW WHEN THEY'VE ABROGATED LEGITIMATE INSTRUCTIONAL RESPONSIBILITY?

As already noted, those who write about self-directed, autonomous learners see teachers ultimately being phased out of the learning process. However, teachers don't need to retire just yet. Most of our students are years away from having the skills and intellectual maturity necessary to assume full responsibility for their own learning. But the point is this: ultimately, there are no responsibilities currently assigned by the teacher that cannot at some point be relinquished to learners. So we compromise our instructional responsibilities not by what we hand over, but by the timing of that transfer.

Given our discussion of where we start with most students, there are areas where teachers need to retain some control—and possibly a significant degree of control. For example, so long as grades are used as gatekeepers to subsequent educational experiences like graduate and professional schools, teachers must retain control of the major components of the assessment process. Given the way the curriculum is organized in some majors and programs, when courses are taken in sequence and where faculty have agreed that certain topics belong in certain courses, teachers are irresponsible if they let students change course content. And with very beginning, very developmental college students, teachers need to retain significant control over the design and structure of course activities and assignments. From the teacher's perspective, then, in addition to assessing the ability of a group of students to handle making certain decisions, the teacher also needs to consider these larger contextual issues.

In some situations it's easy to see that a teacher has inappropriately relinquished power and control. I once had to find a replacement for an ill faculty member. Students strongly objected to the newcomer, who was not honoring the absent teacher's course policies. "We get to grade our own group work," they told me. I didn't understand. "You mean you assess what the other groups do and then the teacher considers your feedback when group grades are assigned?" "No, we grade the other groups and those are the grades." "What do you use for criteria?" "We just give them the grade they deserve." "Do you ever give groups less than Cs?" "No, we only give As and Bs." No wonder they wanted that policy continued.

In less extreme cases, the decisions are more difficult, which justifies regularly revisiting these ethical responsibilities. I do have to be honest, though, and admit that I'm not worried about teachers abrogating legitimate instructional responsibilities. Most faculty control decision making about learning so completely that the possibility they will relinquish too much power too fast seems very unlikely. It's a bit like those faculty members forever fearful that if they tell a joke, they will "entertain" students, thereby totally compromising their credibility as educators. Of course, it depends on the situation, but I do not believe that the examples included in this chapter compromise a teacher's instructional responsibilities.

I'd like to have been able to offer more definitive answers to the questions raised in this section. Perhaps asking the questions is more important than suggesting "right" answers. They are questions that can be profitably asked by individual faculty members as they explore the changes they might implement in this area. But they are also questions we should be exploring collectively, as those of us committed to learner-centered teaching seek to develop the knowledge base on which our practice should rest.

In conclusion, learner-centered teaching changes the balance of power in the classroom. It requires that faculty give students some control over learning processes. In most college classrooms, power, authority, and control remain firmly and almost exclusively in the hands of teachers, and retaining this much control is what continues to make instruction very teacher-centered and what makes students very disconnected from learning. Power can be responsibly shared with students, and doing so often produces some astounding results. Teachers give away control, but it comes back to them as great respect from students who are motivated, engaged, and sometimes even loving learning.

CHAPTER FIVE

THE FUNCTION OF CONTENT

If the influence of power on learner-centered teaching decisions is subtle and unassumed, the impact of course content is direct and unequivocal. Learner-centered approaches are less efficient than didactic instruction. They take more time, which decreases the amount of content that can be covered in a course, and for many faculty that makes this way of teaching untenable. The amount of content in a course is a matter of instructor credibility, program reputation, and professional responsibility. If the prescribed amount isn't covered, students struggle in subsequent courses or, even worse, they will fail the exams that certify they are prepared for their professions. Concerns about content are not trivial—for those committed to getting it covered and for those of us who want to change how it functions in courses.

This chapter begins by challenging entrenched thinking about content—not by recommending courses without plenty of it, but by offering reasons why the current thinking about coverage no longer makes good sense. The chapter also explores how the function of content broadens when teaching is learner-centered. It offers a variety of examples to illustrate, and it concludes with questions raised when content assumes an expanded role in the course.

Several months back someone sent me a copy of an online exchange that had taken place between a group of faculty who were reading the first edition of this book. "I had all sorts of problems with the chapter on content," one of the participants wrote. "Teaching less content will decrease the integrity of our courses, lower academic standards, and poorly prepare students for their careers." Is that what this change in the function of content will do? Do learner-centered approaches compromise what and how students learn content? Those are the questions to take with us as we explore a different role for content in the learning experiences of students.

WHAT NEEDS TO CHANGE?

What needs to change is our thinking about content—specifically the notion that it is something we "cover" and the assumption that more content is always better. "Covering" content is an ingrained and unquestioned part of our thinking. How many times do we make or hear comments like these? "Today we're going to cover . . ." "I covered that material just before the last test." "With these curricular changes, we've got to decide what we're going to cover in each course." "I can't believe how much content she's covered since the last test!"

"Covering" the content is a metaphor—we don't literally cover it. We are speaking figuratively. Wiggins and McTighe (2005) unpack what's implied by the metaphor. "The word *cover* refers to something on the surface, like a bedspread. Applied to teaching, it suggests something superficial. When we 'cover' material . . . we end up unwittingly focusing on the surface details, without going into depth on any of them" (p. 229). Cover also means to "travel over," as in we "covered" this many miles today. "When talking about covering a lot of ground, whether as travelers or teachers, we may have gone far, but that doesn't mean we derived any meaning or memorable insights from our 'travels'" (p. 229).

Coverage does not necessarily equal learning, something most teachers recognize. "Teaching, on its own, never causes learning. Only successful attempts by the learner to learn cause learning. Achievement is the result of the learner successfully making sense of the teaching" (Wiggins and McTighe, 2005, p. 228). We know that, but covering the content has become a teacher responsibility. Students may fail to learn or understand what we have covered, but that is their problem—not ours. We can face ourselves, our colleagues, and our professions knowing that we have done what teachers are supposed to do. Less often do we confront ourselves with the fact that when little or no learning results from teaching, teaching serves little or no purpose.

Rather than being a topic of substantive exchange, content coverage is usually cocktail conversation. It's a discussion of how we've fallen behind, mostly because students aren't as dedicated to the content as they need to be, and how in the world will we get through it all before the semester ends. Most faculty readily admit that there's too much content in their courses, and some (depending on the number of cocktails) confess that they really would like to cut down on what they cover. But these conversations haven't had much impact on how we think about content or what we do with it in our courses.

And it's not a topic written about with any regularity in the pedagogical literature, although there are a few exceptions. In the years since the first edition, some interesting articles have appeared in *The Journal of American History* (which is not a pedagogical periodical, but regularly includes a section of teaching articles) that address coverage in the introductory survey courses of the discipline. One article (Sipress and Voelker, 2011) notes that "criticisms of coverage-oriented history teaching have abounded for over a century" and then proceeds to offer a "genealogy of the coverage model" (p. 1051), starting with concerns voiced in the late 1800s. In a 2006 article Calder writes: "When I claim that the typical, coverage-oriented survey is a wrongheaded way to introduce students to the goodness and power of history, I am not saying anything outrageous or new. But pedagogical inertia happens. While everything else touching the survey has changed— think back to the days . . . when classroom technology meant pull-down maps and chalkboards . . . —the old routines of coverage remain firmly in place" (p. 1359).

This change is not about courses without plenty of robust, intellectually challenging content—I feel the need to keep repeating that. It's about challenging the coverage metaphor—the idea that the kind of learning we espouse happens when faculty "cover" content by telling students about it. Finkel (2000) says that "to carefully and clearly tell students something they did not previously know" is for most faculty a "fundamental act of teaching"

(p. 2). And that's the thinking that needs to change. Thinking that content is there to be "covered" does not cause us to use the content in ways that promote learning or develop important learning skills.

The opposing metaphor proposes that teachers "uncover" content. As the cartoon caption below a professor standing squarely in front of a blackboard with problem parts showing on either side proclaims, "Aim not to cover the content, but to uncover part of it." Although this contrasting version captures the essence of learner-centered thinking about content, the necessary change is clearer if we abandon all forms of the metaphor. It's not about covering content but about using it to accomplish two goals. We use content to develop a knowledge base, just as we always have. Students shouldn't have courses in biology, sociology, physics, or anything else on their transcripts knowing nothing about those fields. But we also use content to develop the learning skills students need for the lifetime of learning that awaits them after college.

Related and equally antithetical to learner-centered teaching is the assumption that more content is always better. "Good" courses are packed, indeed overflowing, with content. Even at research universities, where pedagogical sins abound, the one instructional offense to avoid is teaching courses without lots of complicated content. The text for that introductory chemistry course I took was 838 pages long. The book measured 8–1/2 by 11 inches, and the font size was about 8 point. It was enormous. We got through almost three-quarters of it, although doing so was an exhausting marathon.

The question about content that we should be asking but never do is, How much is enough? It's a particularly salient question when asked about those survey courses that are typically the only encounter that students have with a discipline. To overview any discipline in fifteen weeks is to fly over the content at great heights and high speeds. And those disciplinary landscapes continue to expand, dividing into subfields and specialties, and sometimes separating into new disciplines.

What if our introductions of students to our fields were characterized by the features of a good introduction of one person to another? A good introduction offers a few details about the new person that makes her sound interesting—someone you'd like to meet and possibly get to know. Intriguing details are inherently a part of every discipline—that's why we love ours so much. A good introduction also identifies some common ground shared by the two people. "You are both from the West Coast." "You two share an interest in Northwest wines." "Tam knows several of your friends." These connections make starting the conversation easier. We could connect students with our content in the same way. "You'll be interested in chemistry because you ingest a multitude of chemicals every day. How many of you had cereal for breakfast? Have you ever read the list of ingredients on the box? Those words you can't pronounce—chemicals, right? What are they, and should you be having them for breakfast?" I'm paraphrasing a great introduction to chemistry I once heard in a course. What doesn't characterize good introductions is a rapid recounting of the person's entire life history including a hundred and one details, many of which don't seem particularly interesting or all that relevant.

I loved the chemistry content I learned—it enabled me to understand the essentials of global warming and ozone depletion. I did my term paper on acid rain in the Adirondacks. I know why I should be driving an economy car and paddling our boats. But I often felt I was the only student in the class who saw the relevance of chemistry. The rest of the students were there to survive a required course. By the time it was over and they had met chemistry, they knew they didn't like her, sold her book back, and happily looked forward to forgetting whatever they might have learned about her. We can't afford to have students leaving chemistry, biology, psychology, economics, or any other discipline with minimal knowledge and those kinds of attitudes.

How much content is enough? It's not just a question to be asked about courses for nonmajors. The question is relevant to every course we teach. We also need to ask it of our degree programs and professional accreditation requirements. Despite the question's relevance, few, if any, criteria offer guidance that help faculty determine appropriate amounts of content. Take away the more-is-better assumption and we have no idea how much content is enough in any kind of course. It simply is not a discussion we've ever had, and for the reasons explored in the next section, it's a conversation long overdue.

What needs to change? The answer is simple: our thinking about content. Why isn't it changing? That answer is not simple: we can't change something we never think or talk about substantively. We have comingled content coverage with instructor identity and course reputation. If we change the function of content, we risk compromising the credibility of both. And the content is what we know and love. Why in the world would we want to teach less of it? There are reasons; let's see if they're persuasive.

WHY IT NEEDS TO CHANGE

Thinking about the function of content needs to change for several reasons, beginning with the fact (and it is a fact) that content coverage simply does not promote deep and lasting learning. Carvalho (2009) correctly observes: "We as teachers are preoccupied in making sure that we expose the students to as much of the information as is available, often neglecting how much our students are able to apply the information. Teachers budget their time in class in favor of comprehensive coverage of the material and at the expense of ensuring learning and application" (pp. 132–133).

Research continues to document that when faced with a blizzard of information, students memorize, give back the details on exams, and then mostly forget them. "Educational research over the past twenty-five years has established beyond a doubt a simple fact: What is transmitted to students through lecturing is simply not retained for any significant length of time. Consult your own experience. How much do you remember from all that you were told in high school and college?" (Finkel, 2000, p. 3).

Let's look at one specific research example. Bacon and Stewart (2006) studied marketing majors taking a course in consumer behavior—a course in their chosen field, ostensibly an area of interest, and with content relevant to professional practice. Using an interesting longitudinal design, the researchers found that most of the content covered in the course was lost after two years. Among a series of recommendations, they propose that faculty sacrifice breadth for depth in courses. "It is important to remember that although we hate to 'give up' some of our favorite topics, the topics that are only covered in passing are not meaningfully retained. Thus, we have already been giving them up; it just has not been obvious. To avoid giving up everything, a few important topics must be covered in more depth" (p. 189).

Most of us don't need a long list of references documenting how much course content students forget. We see the evidence firsthand. Two weeks after an exam when we ask students to recall something they "learned" for it, they look confused, think maybe they've heard the term, but the silence is long as they try to recall what it means and to see how it relates to what we are talking about now. Ditto for the next course in the sequence. There sit students who got As and Bs in the prerequisite course, and yet when you ask a prior knowledge question, you're lucky if anybody even ventures a guess. Covering content does not develop the knowledge base or learning skills that students need to take with them from a higher education experience. And that is the most fundamental reason why we need to think about doing something with content other than covering it. But it isn't the only reason.

There is simply too much content now to teach students everything they need to know about anything, and knowledge continues to grow exponentially in all our fields. After college, students face a lifetime of learning. When I first interviewed Knapper (Weimer, 1988) about his and Cropley's book, *Lifelong Learning in Higher Education* (1985, now in a third edition, 2000), he characterized our thinking about teaching students what they need to know as "education by inoculation," explaining that giving students a "dose" of content and hoping that will be all they need is flawed thinking. College graduates need to leave us knowing as much about *learning* content as they know about the content itself.

Faculty have also long assumed that students pick up the learning skills they need in the process of learning—that as they solve problems, they develop problem-solving skills, or as they observe a faculty member thinking critically, they figure out that's how they ought to be thinking. That's the route most of us took to becoming sophisticated learners. And it continues to be true for some students. They tend to be the brightest students, and most of us know only too well that those aren't the majority of students in college today. All students (yes, even very bright ones) develop learning skills better when they are taught explicitly— when they don't develop by chance but are an intentional part of the instructional process. Learner-centered teachers use content to develop a knowledge base and the skills that sophisticated learners need.

In addition to the ineffectiveness of covering content, how much there is to teach, and the need for explicit instruction on learning skill development, there is one final reason why orienting to content as something to cover needs to change. Technology now makes vast amounts of content immediately available. I no longer need to go to the library! I can track down virtually every article I want to read online, and many of those articles contain links that lead me directly to the references. If I read an author whose work I think is good, a quick search identifies what else she's written. The differences technology has made are stunning, and they, too, raise a whole series of questions about the function of content in courses and a college education.

The amount of knowledge available, along with its easy access, means learners need to develop information management skills. Powerful search engines lead us to almost anything we might want to know, but they don't always lead to the best information. How do you find that? What separates credible sources from those that are not? How do we know when we have enough information? How can the vast amounts of information available on almost any topic be organized, integrated, and otherwise made useful?

Some of the questions raised by technology are more philosophical. Does the easy access to information mean students can know less? Do they need to know the date of the Louisiana Purchase or what it entailed when the answer to both questions can be found within seconds? Sanger (2010), best known as the cofounder of Wikipedia, says no to knowing less. Writing about the Internet, he argues that accessible information does not change what understanding requires. "Being able to read (or view) *anything* quickly on a topic can provide one with information, but actually having a knowledge of or understanding about the topic will always require critical study. The Internet will never change that" (p. 16).

As for whether these reasons are persuasive, I find it hard to imagine a more compelling mandate for change, and yet these reasons (which most faculty know) have not changed what the majority do when they design and deliver courses. Most don't opt for smaller textbooks or choose to cover less in class sessions. I've hinted at what keeps faculty very content-focused, but we need to explore that orientation more fully.

WHY IT ISN'T CHANGING

The allegiance to content begins in graduate school, where long years of course work develop content expertise almost exclusively. The typical academic begins and ends a career knowing a great deal of content, and most begin and end very much in love with their material. The typical academic also begins and ends a career with considerably less teaching and learning knowledge (and yes, there are exceptions). Some of that knowledge is accrued along the way, but for most (again, granting the exceptions) what is known about teaching and learning pales in comparison to content knowledge.

Being comfortable with content, we gravitate toward it. We understand concepts—we can explain how they work, why they're important, and what makes them really cool. But try explaining critical thinking—what it is, why it's important, and how you do it. When knowledge is tacit and actions are automatic (as critical thinking is for most academics), teaching someone else how to do it is not particularly easy, and that's why many faculty stick with what they know best and love most.

But the allegiance to content rests on more than a wish to avoid teaching outside the comfort zone. As noted earlier, content has become a measure of course and instructor credibility. Having lots of complex content in a course establishes its reputation for rigor. Any decrease in the amount of content is equated with a lowering of standards and diminished instructor credibility. That's a risk that few faculty (including those with tenure) are willing to take. In those cocktail party exchanges, faculty can accept in principle that the function of content needs to change, but as long as the current orientation to content prevails, they don't want to be the ones messing around with how it functions in their courses. And there are some legitimate concerns here.

If the course is part of a sequence and it's in a discipline where new content builds on previous content (like math), covering only ten chapters when the next course in the sequence starts with

Chapter Thirteen does a disservice to students. If the certifying exam that students need to pass in order to become registered nurses includes knowledge questions about various renal functions, and the faculty have decided to cover the kidneys less comprehensively, students may miss those and enough other questions to start regularly failing the exam, and that puts the program in jeopardy.

I'm really warning against conversion experiences where faculty find the reasons to change thinking about coverage so compelling that they throw caution to the winds and opt not to cover half the text. Maybe there is twice as much content in the course as there should be, but until we individually and collectively have answers to the how-much-content-is-enough question and until more faculty, disciplines, and programs are challenging the thinking about content, it pays to be sensible about how much content stays and goes in a course.

Nonetheless, I don't want to give anyone an excuse to continue to cover content without having thought about what's being done and why. Even if the courses taught are part of a sequence or courses in a program where the amount of content is dictated by certifying exams, the remainder of the chapter suggests ways to use learner-centered approaches even in very limited time frames, ways to more efficiently manage class time, and ways to make students more responsible for learning material on their own. Teachers can move a little or a lot in the direction of using content instead of covering it, so long as they start moving. To continue as oriented to content as we are compromises the integrity of the educational enterprise far more than decreasing the amount of content in a course ever will.

How Does Content Function in a Learner-Centered Course?

In learner-centered courses, content functions to accomplish two purposes: it is used to build a knowledge base and to develop learning skills. In building the knowledge base, learner-centered teachers opt for those instructional strategies that promote deep and lasting learning. They want students to understand the content so that it is more likely retained and more easily applied. Given research like that highlighted in Chapter Two, they know the best way to promote deep learning is by letting students use the content to do the work like that done in the discipline. From these experiences, students learn how to think like those in the discipline.

Most of us know firsthand that novices do not think about or use content the same way experts do. This means teachers must be realistic about how well students will do the work of the discipline. Calder (2006) writes of students in his introductory history course: "Can beginning students learn to do history the way professionals do it? Of course not. But my studies have found they can learn to execute a basic set of moves crucial to the development of historical mindedness" (p. 1364).

When students are learning by using the material, teachers are faced with the messiness of learning. In their first attempts to do literary criticism, use the scientific method, or analyze a case study, students make all sorts of mistakes, most of them egregious. That kind of incompetence can be difficult for experts to handle. This week I have been trying to teach my developmentally disabled brother how to more efficiently and safely use a paring knife to peel apples. I explain, I demonstrate, and then I hand him the knife. "No! Not like that! You're going to cut your finger." I try not to yell. How do I make him understand? What is so hard about what I've just showed him? It would be so much easier to just peel the apples. Dealing with the mistakes of novices requires teaching skills rarely used in teacher-centered classrooms. Teachers must work directly with students. They must be able to give constructive feedback, be patient, deal with frustration (theirs and the students'), suggest other approaches, encourage repeated attempts, and celebrate accomplishments, even small ones.

Fortunately, learning how to deal with students as they work with the content is addressed in the now vast literature on active learning, even though initially interest in active learning wasn't about providing opportunities for students to practice with the content. Most active learning strategies are learner-centered, but teachers didn't start using them because they wanted to focus more on learning. They saw the strategies as an antidote to passive learners. It was in the process of using them that many teachers came to understand how effectively they motivated students and encouraged a different kind of learning. As a consequence, interest in active learning has remained high for several decades, so that the pedagogical literature is full of active learning strategies, including many that give students carefully designed opportunities to use content in ways that develop their understanding of it. This literature also offers helpful advice to teachers looking for ways to intervene constructively when novices are working with content that is new to them.

As important as promoting deep understanding of the content is in learner-centered environments, the content is also used to develop learning skills. And, as already noted, achieving this goal is challenging—perhaps even more challenging than teaching for understanding. Most teachers find students' lack of basic learning skills frustrating. By the time they reach college, students should have been taught how to read, calculate, and communicate in writing. Berating and bemoaning the demise of basic education is a favorite faculty discussion, but any points made lose their significance in light of another reality. When students graduate from college and they are still missing those basic skills, it's very clear that legislatures, employers, and parents hold higher education accountable.

Our thinking about basic skill development needs to change. Gardiner (1998) reports that in a sample of 745 undergraduates, only 14 percent said that they had been taught how to study. Kiewra (2001, p. 4), who has spent his career researching learning skills, asks this follow-up question: "How can strategy instruction be remedial if strategy instruction never occurred in the first place? The truth is strategy instruction is not remedial; it is enriching." You can't be expected to know how to take notes if you've never been taught. It's that simple for all sorts of skills that college students should have but don't.

In addition to remediating absent basic skills, learner-centered teachers also take seriously the development of more sophisticated skills that are unique to a discipline and the more generic skills that characterize all autonomous, self-directed learners. I still regularly refer to Candy's (1991, pp. 459–466) impressive profile of autonomous learners, which lists over one hundred research-identified competencies possessed by independent learners. They include skills like the ability to be methodical and systematic, to have well-developed information-seeking and -retrieval skills, and the ability to be flexible and creative.

Learner-centered teachers use content to help students develop a knowledge base, to remediate basic skill deficiencies, and to develop more sophisticated learning skills—how can they possibly do all these things in one ten- or fifteen-week course? I hear in the question a rising sense of panic. Advice and specific suggestions follow in the next section of this book, but first it should be understood that although the goals of using content to promote understanding and develop learning skills are separate, they can often be accomplished simultaneously, via the same activity. Having to teach content and develop various kinds of learning skills is more daunting when we think of the two dichotomously— either we're dealing with the content or we're developing learning skills. In a learner-centered environment, they can function in mutually reinforcing ways.

Here's a simple example that illustrates how that works. It involves the instructionally challenging last five minutes of a class session, when students are packing up mentally and physically. Most teachers devote that time to summary (although a few are still covering content), and in most classrooms it is the teacher who does the summarizing. Do students learn to summarize when they are only listening to their teachers doing it? By now you probably know the answer—they learn to do it better when they get to practice doing summaries. Maybe they are reviewing their notes and underlining the most salient points. Maybe they are talking with a partner about an unsolved problem that is similar but different from those just presented in class. Maybe they are generating potential test questions. Whatever the activity, it is engaging students with the content—they are reviewing material from this class session and they are reviewing it by using activities that develop their ability to summarize.

Using a single activity to accomplish both goals is a time-saving maneuver and more. It's also a bit like a successful marriage, where a synergy makes the two together better than each was separately. Being responsible for summary and review heightens students' awareness of themselves as learners. As they review their notes, they discover that some of the things written there don't make sense. Perhaps they haven't written enough, or what they have written doesn't mean anything to them. They might discover that talking with a colleague is a useful way to clarify understanding, or that framing a potential test question makes more sense than memorizing answers. Many of the examples that follow show how with just a bit of massage teachers can amplify and reinforce what students may be discovering about learning and about themselves as learners when they start doing learning tasks rather than having them done by the teacher.

In the chapter's opening section I asserted that this change in the function of content did not reduce its role but actually made it larger. This section makes clear how that happens. Content is not just covered in the learner-centered classroom; it is purposefully used to promote the kind of deep learning we associate with understanding and used to develop a range of learning skills. That's a larger, not a smaller, role for content.

DEVELOPING LEARNING SKILLS: GUIDELINES

How teachers and students use the content to develop understanding tends to be discipline specific. Teachers who know the content (and most faculty have great content expertise) can select the best examples, theories, concepts, readings, and problems that students can use to help them master the material. The advice a book like this can offer addresses more fundamental issues like the need for teachers to move away from so much telling and begin to let students use the content to explore how a discipline does its work. And a book like this can show faculty how the content can be used to develop learning skills, as the next two sections are devoted to doing. However, very few of the learning experiences proposed in the next two sections divorce learning-skill development from content acquisition. They are examples of using a single activity to build content knowledge and develop learning skills.

The first section offers a set of guidelines on learning-skill development that are helpful for two reasons, I think. I am well aware—despite my protestations regarding the amount of content in courses—that most faculty cannot lop off large amounts of course content, but will more likely be trimming bits and pieces off around the edges. This set of guidelines assumes there's still lots of content to teach in courses, but those teaching it are now interested in, if not committed to, seeing how it can be used to develop learning skills. Moreover, I do believe, even more now than I did when I first wrote the book, that worthwhile learning-skill development can be done in small increments and with minimal time allotments. Of course, more is better, but sometimes less can be better than none at all, and in this case it is.

Second, guidelines can be helpful to those new to explicitly teaching learning skills. Some of what can be done to develop learning skills and students' awareness of themselves as learners is simple and straightforward. Not all learning skills are complicated. There are some easy places for teachers and students to start. I'm hopeful that this makes these guidelines helpful and motivational.

Think Developmentally. Thinking developmentally begins with a clear understanding of those learning skills that students do and do not have. You want to begin a developmental trajectory from where students are—not wasting time pontificating about how they should be someplace else and not imagining that they can be moved on to sophisticated skills before they've mastered basic skills—but having verified with feedback where they are and where they next need to move.

Thinking developmentally also means thinking about the sequence of activities, assignments, and events that will move students along a skill development trajectory. Most students don't learn how to ask probing questions, construct analytical arguments, or integrate course knowledge all at once. It's a gradual process, but a process that is expedited when there's an order, as in a planned sequence of events that they move through. There is much more about sequencing learning experiences in Chapter Nine, which is devoted to developmental issues.

Target Skill Development. We start, then, by identifying those skills in need of development. Given the many skills most students lack, it's easy to come up with a lengthy list. Making the list is fine, but then it needs to be prioritized. What skills do your students most need to do well, given the content in this course? Those two or three skills are what they should be working on. Spreading our skill-development efforts too thin diminishes the powerful impact that can be achieved by a set of integrated activities designed to target a few critical learning areas. The skill-development deficiencies of most college students are numerous, but not everything that needs to be done can be accomplished in one course, even one taught by a great teacher dedicated to skill development.

Routinely Engage Students in Short Skill-Development Activities. Most teachers don't have whole periods they can devote to skill development. Part of what makes short activities still worth doing is that regularly addressing learning-skill issues creates expectations. Students begin to understand that they are learning content and learning how to learn the content. They start developing a sense of themselves as learners. Regular reminders and short activities build on each other to create a cumulative impact greater than that of isolated individual activities

Take Advantage of Those Ready-to-Learn Moments. There are times in a course when students are ready to learn—right before and after exams are probably the most obvious times. In addition to helping them correct knowledge errors, these can also be opportunities to explore approaches to study. Is using flash cards a good option for this content? What is gained by recopying notes taken in class? When a class is missed and notes are acquired from another student, does it matter whose notes you get? Do you understand those notes as well as the ones you take? You are noting by now that the teacher is not telling students to abandon flash cards, put the notes in their own words, or be in class, but the teacher is asking questions that encourage students to confront and respond to what they are doing.

Partner Positively with Learning Center Professionals. At virtually every college and university, teachers can partner with professionals in the learning center. It's great to have colleagues there who support what faculty are working on with students in the classroom. Unfortunately, some faculty believe the presence of a learning center absolves them of the responsibility to work with students on skill deficiencies. Learning center professionals will tell you that they are most effective at developing learning skills when they and faculty join forces, and much research confirms the viability of this conclusion. There are examples illustrating how this partnership can work in the next section.

Some faculty undermine the efforts of those in the learning center by making it a place where nobody wants to go. They announce in class: "Anybody with a score less than sixty on the exam needs to go to the learning center and get help." "If you're making all sorts of grammatical errors, you need to take this paper to the learning center and get your writing problems fixed." Announcements like these make the decision to get help a negative, demoralizing one, and as a consequence a lot of students don't seek help.

Yes, students need to grow up and face reality, but most of us know from experience that the students who need help aren't usually the ones asking for it. If we want to help those students learn to face reality, then we must better understand the issues related to help seeking. I have long recommended the excellent work of Karabenick (1998; also summarized in my November 11, 2011, blog post at www.facultyfocus.com). He differentiates between two different goals of help seekers: the "executive" help seeker who wants answers to the math homework so he won't have to do it, and the "instrumental" help seeker who wants to learn how to do the work himself.

Karabenick and colleagues study help seeking as a process, and they explore the factors that influence decisions at each step. The process begins with the student acknowledging that a problem exists and recognizing that getting help might alleviate the problem. Next is the rather complicated decision of deciding to actually get help. We live in a culture that prizes the ability to figure things out for yourself, and if you can't do that, asking for help undermines the sense of personal adequacy and becomes cause for embarrassment. You can be embarrassed that you need help and then afraid that when you ask for it, you still won't understand or be able to perform. If you can get through those feelings and commit to asking for help, the next question is whom you should ask. Karabenick has studied both the "formal" sources of help, like that provided by learning center staff and the professor during office hours, and "informal" sources, like other students or family. Those informal sources are less qualified to provide the help, but asking them is a lot easier.

The decision not to seek help when you need it is both immature and irresponsible. Nonetheless, it's a decision lots of students make. Teachers can influence that decision, though. What they say about getting help can motivate or deter students. If they present the learning center as a resource, a place with folks dedicated to helping students learn and a place that lots of students have found beneficial, that makes the decision to seek help there easier to make.

Some of you may think this is pandering to students. Perhaps it is, but how do we get faculty who need help with their teaching to seek it? Do we tell them they need it? Because most faculty are more mature than students, they may seek the help, but they don't come with very positive attitudes about improving. And don't we all know some who've been told this for years and still have yet to get help? I'm willing to pander a bit if that's what it takes to get students working on learning skills that are essential to their success in college.

Use Supplementary Materials to Support Learning Skill Development. All sorts of excellent supplementary materials are available for students' use in further developing their learning skills. They can be assigned for use outside of class, which means they aren't taking class time, and there's the added benefit that using them encourages students to take responsibility for developing their skills. Some of these supplementary materials teachers can develop. The advantage is that teacher-developed materials can target the skills needed in the course, and they can be developed to support particular assignments and activities. Appendix Two contains a variety of samples developed by teachers, all of which deliver good advice (some specific and some more generic) with style and respect.

The disadvantage of teacher-developed supplementary materials is the time required to create them. That problem does not exist with professionally developed resources, and many of these are available. Some are commercially available and must be purchased. The advantage is that these resources have an empirical track record and can benchmark the skills of individual students as well as the class as a whole. I regularly recommend inventories like the Learning and Study Skills Inventory (LASSI; Weinstein, Schulte, and Palmer, 1987), which gives students a comprehensive and constructive overview of their study skills. I also recommend the Perceptions, Expectations, Emotions, and Knowledge about

College Inventory (PEEK; Weinstein, Palmer, and Hanson, 1995), which helps students assess their thoughts, beliefs, and expectations about personal, social, and academic changes likely to occur in college. It's a great tool for helping students develop accurate expectations about what it takes to succeed in college. Learning center staff usually have a repertoire of surveys and inventories like these that they can recommend, and sometimes they will administer, score, and discuss results with students.

My *Inspired College Teaching* book (Weimer, 2010) references another source of supplementary materials, in Chapter Four, on Feedback for Teachers That Improves Learning for Students. The chapter offers descriptions and references to a variety of instruments developed for use in research projects. In the book I recommend faculty use them as formative feedback mechanisms. They provide valuable insights about students, learning, and the impact of teaching on both, but the results also effectively develop student awareness of themselves as learners. For example, there's a survey used in research that identifies the characteristics of assignments that encourage procrastination (Ackerman and Gross, 2005). Discovering those characteristics provides both faculty and students with useful information.

STRATEGIES THAT DEVELOP LEARNING SKILLS

The purpose of this collection of examples is to show the guidelines in action. Most of the collection focuses on the development of basic learning skills—the ones students frequently lack. Most are easily implemented, even by teachers new to explicit learning-skills instruction. And you can vary the amount of time you devote to them depending on the circumstances. Some work well in short time frames.

Developing Reading Skills. It's the first day of class in an entry-level course where many students lack college-level reading skills. You make a reading assignment and tell students to come to class with their books and having done the reading. The next day you start by opening your book to page 3, showing students that you have the second sentence in the first paragraph underlined. If your students are like most, there won't be many books in class, but they will perk up. "What page was that? What paragraph?" Most are noting what you have underlined, and you can imagine that sentence being marked in any number of books after class.

The payoff comes next class, where now you see a sizable number of books and markers. Students are thinking this could be the class of their dreams—the one where the teacher tells them exactly what to underline in the book. But it's not. Today you have students turn to pages 36 through 39, and you ask them what they have underlined. "You have everything on page 36 underlined? Is it all equally important? Let's talk for just a couple of minutes about how you decide what to underline."

The third day in class, there's a short lecture. It's followed by a question set like this: "How does the material I've just presented relate to what you read last night? Let's see if we can articulate that relationship. Does what I've said contradict or agree with what's in the book? Have I provided examples to illustrate concepts presented in the book? Did I repeat what's in the book? Why might it be important to understand the relationship between material presented in class and material contained in the book?"

You don't develop sophisticated reading skills with three short sequences like this, but you begin the process, and if students are regularly confronted with *how* they are doing the reading as well as what they are getting out of it, awareness begins to develop. If you are willing to devote more time and energy to building good, and even sophisticated, reading skills, there are a number of excellent assignment descriptions that can be recommended (Howard, 2004; Yamane, 2006; Roberts and Roberts, 2008; Tomasek, 2009; Parrott and Cherry, 2011). These articles contain detailed descriptions of the assignments and activities associated with them. Don't worry that the articles are written by faculty in other disciplines. I can assure you that these assignment designs will work well with a variety of texts and other kinds of assigned readings. Best of all, they have students engaged in work that develops reading skills and gets them coming to class having done the reading and prepared to discuss it.

Developing reading skills these ways illustrates a couple aspects of learner-centered teaching previously mentioned, and worth repeating. Most students don't do the reading just because the teacher tells them to. They've been told that in lots of other courses, but have discovered nothing happens to them if they come to class unprepared. In some of those classes they've even managed to get Bs on exams without reading. However, if they arrive in this class and the teacher is using the reading by referring them to specific pages and asking for discussion of the points made there, that action conveys messages that underscore the importance of the book. It also demonstrates that less telling and more actions-that-show can create a climate where students start acting more responsibly. They show up in class with their books. They underline and star the passages discussed in class. Some actually do the reading before class. Reading assignments like these are another example of the successful fusion of knowledge and skill development. Students are reading content they need to learn and learning how to read in ways that make it easier to learn.

Partnering with the Learning Center. I have a colleague in history who invites a learner center staff member to join a class session. He presents material, and the students and learning center person take notes. Students give a copy of their notes to the learning center staff member, who returns to class next session with some feedback on the notes, including examples (exemplary and less than exemplary) from their notes and hers. Material on various note-taking strategies is distributed and briefly discussed. The presentation takes about twenty minutes. The instructor uses this event to develop note-taking skills and to make students aware of all the ways the learning center can support their efforts to learn.

An activity like this could be formatted around other class events, like exams. Just before taking an exam, perhaps online, students can briefly describe how they went about preparing for the exam. Their descriptions, along with aggregate exam results, might be reviewed and discussed by someone from the learning center. The goal of the discussion is to answer this question: Judging by what you now know about exams in this class, what's the best way to prepare for the next ones? Or the exam review session could end with five minutes' worth of tips (more fully explained in supplementary materials posted on the course website) on dealing with exam anxiety.

Learning About Learning from Each Other. Sometimes the messages about how to learn are more effective when they come from someone other than the professor. A physics professor I once observed had the students who had done well on exams in class the previous semester write a set of study suggestions for students in the next class. He distributed these the week before the exam, with the former students identified along with their course grades (he had obtained their permission, of course). I happened to be in his class on the day when he passed out this material. The student response was pretty remarkable. Everyone was reading the handout. It was carefully put away in notebooks and book bags. And guess what sort of advice the former students offered? It was the party line regularly voiced by teachers! "Be sure you do the homework problems every night. Don't wait and try to do all the problems the night before the exam." "The best way to prepare for the exam is by doing practice problems." "Don't skip this class! You need to see him doing the problems." "Ask questions in class." "Make him do more problems if you don't understand."

Some faculty have students from one class write letters to students taking the class the next semester. The letters offer teachers great feedback, and they are equally valuable for students just starting the course. A compilation of excerpts can make an excellent handout, be posted on the course website, or be attached to the syllabus. Another faculty member I know invites three or four students from the previous class to an early session of the new class. He introduces the panel, explains that each of these students did well in the course, and then encourages current students to ask the panelists questions about the course. To ensure that the questions students most want answered get asked, he leaves the class, devoting the final fifteen minutes of a class session to this discussion. As I discovered when I tried this strategy, it takes a bit of courage to let this discussion happen without being present. It also necessitates the careful selection of panelists. But this approach adds a certain authenticity to the exchange. I worried that students might see it as a chance to get out of class early, but both times I used this strategy, discussion continued right up to the end of class.

The Learning Question. This is another strategy that can take very little time. It's most effective when it's done regularly. I call it the "learning question," which I tell students is a prompt not about what they are learning but a query as to what they are learning about themselves as learners. I ask the learning question after most class events. "So, what did you learn by working with other students on a group exam?" "So, what did you learn about discussion from that forced debate we did yesterday?" "Did you learn anything about how you make inferences from your results on the critical inference test?" Sometimes I put the learning question on the board, point to it as class begins, and ask for thirty seconds of silence during which students think about the prompt and how they'd respond. Sometimes I have them write down their answers, which I then collect. Depending on how much time I have, I will read all or some of those answers, perhaps sharing a few pithy insights from them next class. It's a simple strategy that can be used in many different ways. The more ways and times it's used, the more effectively it reinforces the underlying message: you are a learner with a set of learning skills that you can discover and develop.

Learning from Exam Results. Teachers give students tests because they must certify whether students have mastered the material, but exam experiences are opportunities for learning— the course content and more sophisticated study skills. For students, they are events that motivate learning. Chapter Seven discusses ways to maximize the learning potential of exams including review activities, the exam itself, and the debrief when the graded exam is returned.

Here, I'd like to highlight some strategies that can be used to help students confront what they should be learning from exam results, particularly when the results aren't all that spectacular. When students don't do well on exams, there's a tendency to blame the test—the questions were tricky, not like the homework, too hard, or not what they expected. Sometimes these things may be true, but more often the reasons for poor performance are related to how students prepared (or didn't prepare) for the exam. They could be included in Chapter Seven, but they're here because they illustrate yet another set of short, straightforward activities that confront students with the consequences of actions taken or not taken.

As explained in Chapter Seven, I don't "go over" the most often missed items. Students do that because they missed those items, not me. I also have students do some analysis of those items they missed. They begin by listing the number of each test question missed. I identify four or five frequently missed questions and indicate what day that content was presented in class. I have students look at their notes from each of those days. Were they in class? Did they get notes from someone else? Do they have what they need in their notes (or the notes of someone else) to answer the question? I use this activity to gently challenge the widely held student belief that you can miss class, get notes from somebody else, and be covered, and to confront the effectiveness (more often ineffectiveness) of student note-taking practices.

Next, students go back to the list of questions missed, and I read the list of test question numbers that came directly from the text. "Are you missing more questions covering material presented in class or material covered in the text?" Most of the time, they are missing more from the book. I ask students who didn't miss many of the book questions to share how they study the book. I ask how many in that group did not do the reading. I ask how many waited until the night before the exam to do the reading. Sometimes a student will attribute his good performance to luck. I ask, "How many of you who are satisfied with your grade would attribute your success on this exam to luck?" "Is luck something you want to depend on for the next exams?"

Finally, I have students look for those questions where they changed answers and how many times they missed or got the answer correct when they changed it. (If exams are given online, then students might not be able to track these changes.) I talk with them a bit about the mixed research results on this point and encourage students to make an individual assessment on this exam, subsequent ones in this class, and on exams in other classes. Savvy learners know whether or not it pays to change answers when they don't know the answer and can't figure it out.

At the end of the debrief period (which includes other activities described in Chapter Seven), I have students write a memo.

To: me

From: me

Re: Things I learned taking this exam that I'd like to remember when preparing for the next one.

Most students write with purpose during the allotted five minutes. I collect their memos. I may read a few of them, but I don't grade them. I return them at the beginning of the review session for the next exam. The majority of the class revisit what they wrote with considerable interest.

Writing to Learn; Learning to Write. I am a big fan of learning logs. They can be used to accomplish a variety of course objectives. As we have learned from the Writing-Across-the-Curriculum movement, when students write about the content, they are engaged in an activity that helps them learn the content and improves their writing. Learning logs are especially effective at developing learner self-awareness. Students can write about an activity that happened in class. After a group exercise, for example, they can summarize what the group decided or produced, they can write about how well the group functioned, but most important, they can be queried about what they did in the group. What did they contribute? How did they help the group? Was there something they wish they'd done differently after the fact? The success of logs at promoting these kind of insights depends on the prompts. As I learned, it takes time and repeated revisions to get a set of prompts that promotes self-awareness, but when the prompts are good, they do regularly result in insights.

Many teachers avoid logs because they are time-consuming to read and challenging to grade, especially when students are writing about their feelings, opinions, or experiences. Others can't imagine how logs work in courses where the primary activity is solving problems. Maharaj and Banta (2000) provide an excellent example of a log assignment developed and used in an engineering mechanics course.

Other teachers have developed efficient ways to handle log assignments. They can be collected at several designated times, not every day. The frequency and length of the writing can both be controlled. They need not be read and graded with the same intensity as research papers. I read log entries here and there, and I limit the number of comments I make. I've had good luck with a strategy shared by a colleague: don't write comments, write questions, and then have students write a log entry that answers one or all of the questions. Logs can be graded with rubrics that assess a whole collection of entries, as opposed to each one individually.

Two recent articles propose that students review a collection of log entries (in both of these cases students had been writing about assigned readings), and then in a paper reflect on how their thinking about course content had changed, how their understanding of certain issues had enlarged, and any evidence they could see of their growth and development as thinkers (Hudd, Smart, and Delohery, 2011; Parrott and Cherry, 2011). That final paper is what's graded. Thoughtful design of log writing can produce an assignment that promotes learning on several levels and that is also manageable for teachers.

IMPLEMENTATION ISSUES

The most important and challenging question that emerges when content starts being *used* instead of being *covered* is "How much content is enough?" Though I wrote about this at length earlier in the chapter, I could still write another section on its importance, how desperately it needs to be asked, and how bereft we are of answers. The lack of answers is particularly troublesome when changes are implemented and less content ends up being covered. We worry about what's being left out and wonder if we should feel guilty, especially when we'd really like to cut more given how well these new approaches engage students. Rather than revisiting a question already asked, let's consider another question closely related to it.

HOW DO WE CHANGE ATTITUDES ABOUT THE FUNCTION OF CONTENT?

For most of us who have implemented learner-centered approaches and seen the kind of results they produce, the switch from covering to using content makes perfect sense. But it's not a change that makes sense to many of our colleagues. Even though the discussion of learning continues across higher education, I don't think I've ever heard anyone suggest that developing learning skills might be important enough to warrant covering less content. How could students possibly learn more if you cover less? The question is how do we change these long-held attitudes about content, because until they do change, covering less content will be a decision that entails risk, which realistically means even those of us committed to these approaches will cut some content, but probably not much as we could or should.

I can't think of any easy way to change the prevailing content-oriented attitudes, but that doesn't excuse us from trying, and there are things we can try. First, those of us using content to develop knowledge and skills need to be able to describe and document what happens when we do. How do students respond? How does their performance change on tests, on papers, in groups, and in class? Is there support in the research literature and the practice of others for what we're seeing happen in our classrooms? What I'm proposing here goes beyond telling colleagues what a great idea this is and how there hasn't been anything quite as wonderful since they started slicing bread. Even though our experiences in the classroom have significantly changed the way many of us think about content, skills, and learning, that doesn't mean our experiences are all that persuasive to others. We are members of a culture that prizes evidence over assertions. We'll revisit this idea in Chapter Eight, which deals with resistance—evidence overcomes resistance better than anything else.

On the other hand, we should not let colleagues dismiss learner-centered ideas with proclamations about content-free courses. No learner-centered teacher that I know, and no literature on the topic that I've read, proposes courses without plenty of content. The arguments made in the opening of the chapter bear repeating. Content in every field continues to grow; we can't possibly teach students everything they need to know. And technology has changed the role of content, whether current practice acknowledges that change or not. But even with good reasons and evidence, I'm not sure that arguments will carry the day.

More often now, I hear myself challenging colleagues to try some of these approaches and see for themselves if and how well they work. The key here is being able to propose some fairly simple, easy-to-implement techniques and ones where the chance of success is high. You'll find some of these in Chapter Nine. Knowing what to recommend depends on knowing the colleague and his teaching situation. Most important, recommendations to others are more successful if the proposer has some experience making them work.

MAKING THE STRATEGIES WORK FOR ME

This particular implementation issue is relevant to any learner-centered approach. It's appropriate to discuss it here because the necessary adaptation is more crucial when content is involved. Many faculty are not as systematic as they should be when implementing a new idea. They get a good idea from a colleague, hear about one in a workshop, or read about one in a book. They like the good idea. It sounds like something they can use, and they adopt what I call the Nike approach to change—they just do it.

The success of any instructional alteration increases when its implementation is systematic, thoughtful, and planned. Most important, rather than just being done, the change needs to be adapted to fit the new situation, and that involves consideration of at least three variables. First off, the new strategy must fit the teacher—it must be something that person can do with confidence, something that fits comfortably with who they are and how they teach. Mostly we decide this with gut feelings. "Yes, that's a good idea. I could do that." It's interesting to reflect on a collection of those choices and what they tell us about who we are and how we teach.

The new strategy also needs to fit the configuration of the content we teach. How the content we teach is organized, how knowledge in a field advances, what counts as evidence—all these aspects of content are unique to our disciplines and have implications for how a strategy is used. And finally, the new strategy must fit the learning needs of students. It must be something they are ready to handle developmentally. It must be something that offers challenge, but not impossible difficulty. I have written at length about the change process and this need to adapt new ideas in my *Inspired College Teaching* book (Weimer, 2010). If the topic is of interest, you will find this discussion in Chapter Six, on Implementing Change Successfully.

Those who object to learner-centered approaches do so most often because these approaches change the function of content. They end up making teachers less content-oriented, less willing to make instructional decisions only on the basis of what students need to learn. Learner-centered teachers also care about how students learn. They see a larger function for content. They use it not only to develop a solid knowledge base but also to develop a range of learning skills so that students leave their courses with knowledge based on understanding and learning skills that lead to more learning. It's hard to imagine how that compromises course integrity, lowers academic standards, or poorly prepares students.

Nash (2009) writes a fitting conclusion to this chapter: "Often when I teach less, I find that I actually teach more. I call this a 'pedagogy of ironic minimalism.' Whenever I take the time to call forth what it is my students actually know, and whenever I intentionally minimize the 'endless breadth and depth' of my 'vast wisdom and knowledge' then my students learn the most."

CHAPTER SIX

THE RESPONSIBILITY FOR LEARNING

Although dissatisfaction with students is as old as the teaching profession itself, today's college students are challenging to teach for a unique set of reasons, most well known and already mentioned in previous chapters. Many are not well prepared for college-level work. They don't have good study skills and often lack essential background knowledge. Many attempt to combine higher education with full-time jobs and families. A lot see education as the pathway to jobs that pay well—they aren't especially interested in being well educated. Most college students are not confident learners. They tend to be passive, hoping that the educational decision making will be done by their teachers. Students are motivated by grades; most have yet to fall in love with learning. When they don't get good grades, students today are quick to blame everyone and everything other than themselves.

Listing all that ails college students is not difficult. More challenging and beneficial, but less readily apparent, are solutions and answers to the teaching problems presented by our students. How should teachers respond to their learning needs? What helps them learn? How can their missing skills be remediated? Can they be moved past the motivation to work only for points and grades? How do we get them to start assuming an active role in their educational experiences? Is there any way we can infect them with the love of learning that so inspires us? The questions lead to the central issue addressed in this chapter: students aren't accepting the responsibility for learning. They aren't seeing that learning is something only they can do for themselves. Instead they want teachers to make learning happen, and please let it happen via processes that are pleasant and painless.

Getting students to accept the responsibility for learning begins by getting teachers to recognize those instructional practices that make students dependent learners and contrasting these with practices that create classroom climates conducive to learning. The chapter proposes a series of principles teachers can use to build relationships that promote learning and then offers a range of activities illustrating the principles in action. Some of those activities involve teacher actions, and some join teacher and students in activities that make classroom climates places where students accept their learning responsibilities. As with other aspects of learner-centered teaching, there are implementation issues, and these are explored at the end of the chapter.

WHAT NEEDS TO CHANGE AND STILL HASN'T

If you've read the chapters before this one, it probably won't come as a huge surprise that I believe our response to student learning issues ends up being part of the problem. We do deserve lots of credit for being well intentioned. Most of us understand that if problems like those listed in this chapter's opening paragraph persist, significant learning in our courses, success in college, and success in the careers that follow will be seriously compromised. Our concerns have motivated a gradual, usually unconscious realignment of instructional policies and practices.

First, we try to rectify their inadequacies as learners by making clearer and clearer, more and still more explicit the terms and conditions for learning. If they don't know or won't make the decisions necessary to succeed in our courses, we'll make those decisions for them. And so, as already discussed in Chapter Four, we have instituted policies that mandate all manner of details related to learning: mandatory attendance, penalties for missed deadlines, required participation, and no makeup quizzes or exams. We partition assignments and set the due dates in installments to prevent procrastination and to ameliorate the effects of poor time management. We prohibit talking, texting, eating, drinking, coming late, leaving early, and anything else we can think of that diverts attention from course content. We stipulate assignment details: page length, font and margin size, number of and format for references. We employ elaborate strategies to prevent cheating. Most us are bending over backwards to get students doing what learning requires.

What can't be accomplished with policies and requirements, we go after with an array of extrinsic motivators. We use quizzes to keep students up with the reading, offer extra-credit points if they look up a reference, award bonus points if all the homework problems are correct, and record a check-plus for every contribution in class. Our classrooms have become token economies where students get points for every desirable action, and have points docked for undesirable actions. Our grading systems distribute points across assignments, activities, and classroom behaviors with precise and exquisite detail. In the chemistry course I took, lab reports were only worth 10 points out of 600 points possible in the course. However, each point was divided into tenths, essentially making the lab report worth 100 points, and students were not above passionately arguing for an additional .2 or .3 of a point.

Pike (2011) believes that point systems like these "end up training students to focus on the wrong things" (p. 4). Students think about their course work in terms of the points they will get for it, not because they see assignments as opportunities to learn important material. These systems "distract students from what should be motivating their learning" (p. 4). She calls the belief that grades motivate learning a "dead idea" in teaching. Grades motivate getting grades.

Are these ways of responding to passive, dependent learners working well? Do students end up learning in these rule-bound environments and as a result of the motivational sticks we wave about menacingly? They do—sort of. If students expect a quiz, they do the reading. If attendance is mandatory and points are at stake, they show up more often for class. But do these short-term victories lead to the ultimate goal? What kind of students are we seeing in our senior seminars and capstone courses? Are they intellectually mature, responsible learners who will do what needs to be done in the absence of requirements and policies? Can they organize and execute learning tasks on their own? Are they curious, imaginative learners—ones who eagerly anticipate a lifetime of learning?

I wonder why we don't view the ongoing issues with classroom management—including student incivility, disruptive behavior, and the many derogatory characteristics now regularly attributed to millennial students—as signs that these approaches aren't all that effective. The faculty I encounter are eager to talk about classroom management—how many policies they should have, which ones work, does anybody know how to get students to stop texting, and why in the world don't college students go to the bathroom before class? It's not a conversation about less policies and not a conversation that questions the assumptions inherent in the policies. It's usually about adding more policies or finding the ones that work. Shouldn't our continuing preoccupation with classroom management issues tip us off that there might be problems with our approach?

Whether we're trying to prevent disruptive behavior, motivate preparation, or inculcate integrity, exerting more control is not the answer. It locks teachers and students into a vicious circle. The more structured we make the environment, the more structure they need. The more decisions we make, the less able they are to make decisions. The more extrinsic their motivation, the less intrinsic their commitment to learning. The more often we do learning tasks for them, the less likely they are to assume the responsibility for learning. The more control we exert, the more controlled they become. We end up with students who have little commitment to learning and who cannot function in less than totally structured learning environments.

The solution is not to immediately abandon policies, rules, or extrinsic motivation. Again, it is about a different way of thinking, a recognition that rules and requirements may produce results, but they cost us and our learners dearly. We should be relying on them less and using them more judiciously. We should be identifying alternatives—ones that create climates conducive to deep, lasting learning. "Interesting and relevant assignments, timely feedback, connection between student and teacher, connection among students, meaningful use of time—these things motivate learning" (Pike, 2011, p. 6). Learner-centered teaching is about creating classrooms in which students begin to mature and act more responsibly about their own learning and toward the learning of others.

CLASSROOM CLIMATES THAT PROMOTE STUDENT RESPONSIBILITY FOR LEARNING

The nature of this change begins with an exploration of what is meant by a "climate" for learning. With that understanding, the next question is how teachers create, maintain, and advance climates that motivate students to accept the responsibility for learning and to develop as self-directed learners. Classroom climate is an intriguing metaphor. It simultaneously hinders and helps our understanding of those classroom conditions that promote autonomy in learning.

CLASSROOM CLIMATE: DEFINITIONS AND DESCRIPTIONS

When I work with faculty on defining classroom climate, I start by trying to illustrate how the metaphor obfuscates meaning. Even though we regularly talk about classroom climate—or the "environment" for learning or the "atmosphere" within departments or at the institution—we aren't referring to meteorological phenomena. When I point that out and ask what the metaphor refers to, the question is usually followed by a period of silence, after which folks start venturing short answers; "feeling comfortable," "a safe place," "respect," "good rapport." The answers identify characteristics of the climate. They don't say what it is.

Fortunately, classroom climates have been studied empirically, first at the primary and secondary level, but also at the postsecondary level as well. In the absence of more recent work, I still rely on the excellent research of Fraser. He starts with the premise that classroom climate consists of a series of complex psychosocial relationships that exist between the teacher and the students, collectively and individually, as well as the relationships between and among students. Fraser, Treagust, and Dennis (1986) developed and empirically validated a College and University Classroom Environment Inventory (CUCEI) that measures and compares preferred and actual classroom environments. The forty-nine-item instrument consists of seven subscales that can be thought of as answers to the "What is it?" question:

1. Personalization, defined as opportunities for interaction between professor and students and the amount of instructor concern for students
2. Involvement, defined as the extent to which students actively participate in all classroom activities
3. Student cohesiveness, meaning how well students know and are friendly to each other
4. Satisfaction, defined as how much students enjoy the class
5. Task orientation, being how clear and well-organized class activities are
6. Innovation, defined as the extent to which the instructor plans new and unusual class activities and uses new teaching techniques and assignments
7. Individualization, or the degree to which students are allowed to make decisions and are treated differentially, according to their individual learning needs

Winston and others (1994) developed a similar instrument.

When completing the Fraser inventory, students identify the features of their "ideal" classroom and then they provide feedback on the environment in a particular class. Students do not rate as ideal the now common rule-oriented, requirement-driven, and teacher-controlled classroom. Fraser has also used the instrument to measure faculty perceptions of their classrooms and then compared those with student perceptions. The results are a bit troubling: "Teachers tend to perceive the classroom environment more positively than did their students" (Fraser, Treagust, and Dennis, 1986, p. 45).

Research on classroom climate indicates that these psychosocial relationships strongly influence learning outcomes. Fraser writes: "Use of student perceptions of actual classroom environment . . . has established consistent relationships between the nature of the classroom environment and various student cognitive and affective outcomes" (1986, p. 45). When students are in a classroom environment they prefer, they achieve more.

And the "weather" metaphor helps us understand why. Weather influences behavior in direct ways. When it's cold outside, we put on sweaters, jackets, and socks. Our response is automatic. Come October in Pennsylvania, we store our flip-flops. Certain classroom "climates" can have the same direct impact on learning. Students don't procrastinate. They aren't just looking for an answer and satisfied with the first one they find. They aren't copying somebody else's work. There is something they need to know. It's obvious, it's important, and they are ready to learn. Sounds a bit like instructional nirvana? Yes, well, on most days and in most classes, the temperature for learning probably isn't this hot.

The metaphor also makes clear that the "climate" in a classroom doesn't "cause" learning any more than cold weather bundles us up. Rather, it motivates us to take action. We put on coats, gloves, and hats. The objective is to create conditions in the classroom that motivate students to take action. We need to create those conditions that make them want to engage in the hard work of learning.

Despite the fact that the metaphor has complicated the task of defining classroom climate, it offers still more rich insights. Whether it's a physical classroom or a virtual one, the climates for learning are not created by announcement but by action. If you want a good climate for learning in your classroom, you do not get it by including two lines in the syllabus saying that there will be one. It results from actions (and sometimes from inaction). You do things that help create it and, once it has been created, you continue with actions that help sustain it. And finally, as we are learning about the climate in our physical world, the responsibility for it is shared. Teachers can provide leadership, but the climate in the classroom is cocreated with students. Early in my career, I heard a wise teacher tell a class, "This is not my class; it is not your class; this is our class, and together we are responsible for what does and doesn't happen here."

CLASSROOM CLIMATES THAT MOTIVATE STUDENTS TO ACCEPT THE RESPONSIBILITY FOR LEARNING

The goal is clear. We want students to function as responsible learners. We want them to be independent, autonomous, self-directed, and self-regulating learners. These are the attributes that Zimmerman (1990, p. 4) says characterize self-regulated learners: "They approach educational tasks with confidence, diligence, and resourcefulness…Self-regulated learners are aware when they know a fact or possess a skill and when they do not…Self-regulated students proactively seek out information when needed and take steps to master it. When they encounter obstacles such as poor study conditions, confusing teachers or abstruse text books, they find a way to succeed." More recently Macaskill and Taylor (2010) have proposed this operational definition: "Autonomous learners take responsibility for their own learning, are motivated to learn, gain enjoyment from learning, are open-minded, manage their time well, plan effectively, meet deadlines, are happy to work on their own, display perseverance when encountering difficulties and are low in procrastination when it comes to their work" (p. 357). The only problem I see with these descriptions is that they describe so few of our students. Macaskill and Taylor's article includes a brief survey (psychometrically sound) that measures learner autonomy and can be used to give students a sense of what autonomous learners do and teachers some feedback as to whether their students are autonomous.

If classroom climate is built on relationships (between teachers and students and between students themselves), then what kind of relationships promote the development of learners who fit these descriptions? Let me suggest five features of relationships that promote the development of responsible learners and create classroom climates with good weather for learning.

Logical Consequences. We need to let students start experiencing the consequences of the decisions they make about learning. Do you have students who come to class unprepared? They haven't done the reading or completed the homework problems? Do you have a strongly worded statement in the syllabus that tells students to come class prepared? And have you reinforced that message with an equally strong verbal statement? And yet students still come to class unprepared, some making that admission without embarrassment. Why is that?

Yes, they are busy. Yes, some of them are lazy. Yes, lots of them are working and have families. But I don't think those are the real reasons. They come to class unprepared because lots of other teachers have told them the same thing, but when they show up to class unprepared there are no consequences. They sit quietly and keep a low profile when the teacher asks questions. Most of the time they don't get called on, and if they do, they appear scared or confused and the teacher moves on. It's a straightforward manifestation of the old adage, "actions speak louder than words." Students act in response to what we do, not what we say. We do nothing, so they get away with doing nothing.

Examples of how teachers absolve students of consequences are multiple. Say it's a class where students have a habit of arriving late. They saunter in nonchalantly during the first five or ten minutes. Teachers stop doing anything important at the beginning of the period. Students figure that out, so there's no problem being late. Without realizing it, teachers reinforce behaviors that make students less responsible for what they need to do as learners. Coffman (2003) offers another example: "Even something as insignificant as bringing pencils for your students to borrow on exam days teaches students that they don't need to be responsible for bringing them" (p. 3).

Contrast these examples with a math class I once observed. I was surprised when I arrived five minutes before the class was scheduled to start to find that most of the students were already there. So was the instructor. He had the homework assignment up on an overhead. It included some problems not in the book. He left it up for several minutes after the class started, but then took it down and never put it back up. Arrive late to that class and you missed the assignment. It was then your responsibility to get it from somebody else or see him after class.

Every decision students make about learning has consequences, but we no longer let them experience most of them. We hesitate, and not without good reasons. Who wants to hurt students, make them defensive, or otherwise diminish their commitment to college. How students experience the consequences of their decisions matters and needs to be thought through carefully. Is public humiliation justified when a student arrives late to class? How does that exchange affect the rest of the class? Rest assured: dress down a student for any infraction, and the rest of the class is all ears. Does it make a difference if the student is beginning or ending a college career, if the class is large or small, if the student is one you know well or hardly know at all, if this is the first or fifth time late? Decisions about consequences are never easy. Nonetheless, the decision should always be in favor of consequences.

An unprepared student should not be able to sit comfortably throughout a class session. When I ask a question about the reading, if there is no response, I persist with eye contact directed at those students on whom I can usually depend on for an answer. If there is still silence, I write the question on the board and suggest that students might want to have it in their notes. I ask why the question might be important. I hint around that I've used a question like this on the exam. If none of this generates a response, I let the question stand unanswered. "We'll begin with that next period. And you know that I'll be depending on you for an answer." I am positive and patient in these exchanges, but absolutely relentless. I answer the questions I've asked students only on rare occasions. Think about it from the student perspective: What are the consequences of not answering questions the teacher asks? Usually there are none, and sometimes if you wait long enough, there's a reward. The teacher answers and always with the "right" answer.

Consistency. Teacher–student relationships where actions (and inaction) have consequences develop responsible learners. So do relationships characterized by consistency. It is terribly important that what the teacher says is reinforced by what the teacher does. For example, it says in the syllabus "no late homework accepted." In class you point this out, adding emphasis. "This means never, under no circumstances." A few days later, a student approaches you as class is about to begin. He has a litany of excuses, which he summarizes with this plea, "I do hope you'll accept this homework. I so need your feedback." You acquiesce, just this once. But your behavior has said loudly and irrevocably to this student and anyone else who saw it that you accept late homework. One single action can render a whole collection of announcements mute. The actions-speak-louder-than-words adage is well confirmed by research in the communication field (Knapp and Hall, 1992). When the sender contradicts a verbal message with a nonverbal action, the receiver believes the nonverbal message.

Consistency between what we say and do is relevant in many classroom contexts. If we say we want participation, welcome questions, and don't mind interruptions, but then proceed to cover content at horse-race speed, breathlessly ending with a call for questions and a quick glance around the room, we have conveyed a message, but not the one we initially stated. We've just made it abundantly clear that student questions, interruptions, and comments are only important enough for a minimal amount of time. And we cap off that message by saying "good" after our call for questions doesn't elicit any.

Consistency also means that students can depend on how the teacher relates to them. She's predictable, and all students are held to the same standards. They know what some answers will be, regardless of who asks the question. Expectations for students (and for the teacher) are clear and not compromised. That doesn't mean the teacher is anything but gracious and kind, but the teacher's actions are motivated by goals that transcend what individual students may think they need or why they believe established principles don't apply to them. The teacher relates to individual students and the class reliably and predictably. Her consistency models what she expects of students as mature, responsible learners.

High Standards. Those who argue against learner-centered teaching frequently raise concerns about standards. They equate being learner-centered with mollycoddling students, pandering to their need for grades, or seeing them as customers who've paid for a product. Quite the opposite is true of climates that motivate students to accept their responsibilities as learners. In learner-centered classrooms teachers have high standards, they believe their students can reach those standards, and they are committed to helping them do so.

Students may seem to like it when teachers make it easy. They clap when classes are cancelled. They smile when the paper doesn't have to include references, when the exam is postponed, or a chapter is taken off the syllabus. They discuss who teaches the "easy" sections of courses. Are faculty really all that different? We sigh with relief when a committee meeting gets cancelled, a deadline is extended, or we don't get assigned to yet another search committee. Isn't this just some version of the venerable pain-versus-pleasure principle? Sometimes students deserve more credit than we give them. They do understand that easy courses and teachers with low standards compromise the value of educational experiences. That may seem to be what they prefer, but the research says that they do know the difference.

From the empirical work on student ratings we have learned that high ratings don't go to teachers of the easy courses, even though many faculty still think they do. In general, easy courses are not rated as highly as courses with rigor and standards (for large comprehensive studies, see Marsh and Roche, 2000, and Centra, 2003; for examples of individual studies, see Jansen and Bruinsma, 2005; Dee, 2007; and Martin, Hands, Lancaster, Trytten, and Murphy, 2008). These findings are corroborated by the literature describing the implementation of learner-centered practices, and whether that's determining a classroom policy, setting assignment deadlines, or generating quiz questions, students will step up to the plate. Students don't take advantage of the situation and opt for easy alternatives. Teacher standards and expectations call them to better work, especially when, as discussed in Chapter Three, the teacher facilitates their learning endeavors.

So many faculty seem to have lost their way with standards. They focus on upholding standards, rather than setting standards and then upholding students' efforts to reach them. It isn't always clear what standards they are upholding, but they are high standards, they never change, and most of today's college students cannot achieve them. But they are standards the teacher fondly remembers reaching, and there have been a few students, most from bygone years, who have also reached these marks, but today these standards only show the woefully compromised intellectual caliber of college students.

Standards can be high, but they should not be unattainable. Goals at impossibly high levels do not motivate student effort.

Reachable high goals do. In climates that promote learning, standards are not immutable laws. They evolve as content changes and as the knowledge and skills needed to succeed after college change. Most important, after having set realistic and challenging goals, the teacher builds a relationship not with the standards, but with the students. Learner-centered teachers uphold high standards but they also hold high beliefs in what students can accomplish. When students see that the teacher is on their side and committed to their success, it motivates and inspires effort. When teachers believe in students, students start believing in themselves and start acting like the learners we want them to become.

Caring. Professors need to care about students, and various studies indicate why. An excellent article by Meyers (2009) summarizes and integrates this research. One of the examples cited there (Wilson, 2006) found that students' perceptions of professors' positive attitudes toward them (meaning the profs were concerned about their students and wanted them to succeed) accounted for 58 percent of the variance in student motivation. Benson, Cohen, and Buskist (2005) found that when teacher–student rapport increased, students enjoyed the class more, their attendance improved, as did their attention during class, they studied more, and were more likely to take additional courses in the discipline. Meyers summarizes these and other studies in this way: "Despite the fact that students are acutely aware of whether their professors care about them, professors do not necessarily prioritize this aspect of teaching to the same extent" (2009, p. 205). A surprising number of teachers convey messages that students take as indications of not caring. Hawk and Lyons (2008) asked over three hundred MBA students if they ever had the feeling that a teacher had "given up" on them and their learning in a course. Forty-four percent of the students said yes.

Some faculty find the need to care about students troubling. Their job is to teach, not to care. Students should be able to learn, whether or not the teacher is caring. Others maintain that they do care. They show it by always coming to class prepared, by regularly updating course materials, and by providing students with timely feedback, but their students don't appreciate these efforts or see them as expressions of concern. Still others worry that caring crosses professional boundaries, involving them in the personal lives of students, or it compromises academic standards and course rigor. The Meyers (2009) and the Hawk and Lyons (2008) articles highlight research that identifies a variety of behaviors frequently associated with caring. They include things like using personal examples, incorporating humor, calling students by name, conversing informally with students before or after class, smiling, and moving around the classroom. It is difficult to imagine how actions like these compromise the intellectual integrity of the course, cross professional boundaries, or are beyond the capabilities of faculty.

Like many aspects of teaching, care for students can be expressed in different ways. There are even options for those with teaching styles not particularly nurturing or supportive. These can be things as simple as an occasional kind comment, a bowl of candy set beside the student chair in the office, or conscientious responses to e-mail queries. Expressions of caring do need to be genuine, but they can be varied and should fit comfortably with your teaching personae.

Meyers (2009, p. 209) makes one final point worth mentioning: "A cycle often emerges in which students reciprocate the care that they receive from their professors in ways that renew purpose and give faculty a sense that they are making a difference in students' lives in important ways." Said more simply, students aren't the only ones who benefit when care is expressed.

Commitment to Learning. When teachers are committed to learning and visibly demonstrate those commitments, it motivates students and changes how they orient to learning. Commitments to learning can be made visible in many ways, starting with the suggestion made in Chapter Five—regularly and repeatedly asking the learning question "What are you learning?" in this class, in your other courses, from your friends, at work, at home, as you read, and online.

For most teachers, it's easy to use course content to demonstrate commitments to learning. We sometimes forget that our love of the material can strongly affect students. How many of us found our way to this field because we had a teacher who madly loved the content? We may be a bit reluctant to show this emotional attachment. We've spent years (for some of us, that's *many* years) studying what look to others like pretty esoteric knowledge domains. When we try to explain these areas of expertise to others, it quickly becomes clear that they don't understand, don't want to understand, and don't know how this could be of interest to somebody else. Students react with the same bewilderment, except that sometimes their response feels more like disdain. I've written elsewhere of my colleague at Penn State who devoted his career to the study of water beetles. I interviewed a student taking his class who commented, "You want to tell the guy he should get a life, but you just can't because it's obvious those beetles are his life."

Despite the eccentricities of what we study, passion for the material can motivate students, and it, too, can be expressed in a multitude of ways. It doesn't have to be an opulent display of enthusiasm, dramatic evocations, or wild gesticulation. I observed a math class once where the professor was doing what's usually done in those courses—working through a problem, explaining the steps, and filling two sections of the board before finally arriving at the answer. He wiped his chalky hands on his pants and made a half-hearted attempt to tuck in more of his shirt as he walked to the side of the room. He stared at the problem for several seconds and then said to the class, "Do you see that symmetry? It's really beautiful and that's why I love math." I didn't see the symmetry, but I think some of the students did. And all of us got the message. With simple but genuine authenticity, this more disheveled than dynamic professor had shared something about his content that captivated him.

Students also benefit by seeing a professor's more general commitment to learning. If the professor can talk about what he is currently trying to master, or if she provides explicit learning skills instruction—whether that's critical thinking, problem solving, analysis of evidence, or knowledge transfer—students start to see that learning matters. They become more aware of themselves as learners. They begin to understand that how they study does make a difference, in their grades, yes, but in a larger sense as well. The learning skills they can acquire in college are of use and value subsequently. Of course, this doesn't happen all at once, and it doesn't happen for every student. But when part of the teacher's relationship to and with students involves a highly visible commitment to learning, it will have an impact on most students.

Some of you will have noticed that each of these relationship characteristics is descriptive of teachers. Content in this chapter's opening section makes clear that classroom climate is not something the teacher creates alone, and these teacher characteristics don't contradict that point. Rather, they illustrate the leadership role learner-centered teachers take in both creating and maintaining classroom climates that promote learning, as Hilsen's (2002, pp. 150–155) extensive list of Suggestions for Establishing a Positive Classroom Climate also show. Students look to faculty for leadership throughout the course. They are influenced by the ways faculty propose to define relationships with them. The point of this section is that those relationships can be designed in ways that encourage students to take the responsibility for learning. They are relationships that promote the development of autonomous, self-directed learners, and in those classrooms the "warm weather" makes everyone more productive.

Student Involvement in Classroom Climate

Beyond the teacher–student relationships that promote learning are activities that involve students in creating, maintaining, and enhancing climates conducive to learning. Like faculty, students understand classroom climate more intuitively than explicitly. Activities early in the course can raise their awareness and motivate positive contributions. Regular input from students can help maintain and even further enhance those conditions that increase commitments to learning. The activities that follow describe how students can be involved in accomplishing each of these goals. Some of the activities accomplish more than one of the goals, and all of them build on each other. The more time the teacher devotes to involving students in classroom climate issues, the more ownership they feel for the class and the more responsibility they assume for making the class a good place for learning.

Involving Students in Creating the Classroom Climate

My favorite activity for introducing students to the idea of classroom climate is simple and generally takes less than fifteen minutes. I write in large letters on a section of the board, "The best class I've ever taken" and on a section next to it, "The worst class I've ever taken" (actually, since I work at a public institution, I frequently write "The class from hell"). Beneath each heading I write "what the teacher did" and "what the students did." I tell students that I will face the board and write what I hear them saying. I do not want to hear the name of any course or any teacher. They usually start with examples of things teachers did in their classes. When there's a pause, I jot a few things under "what the students did" in the best and worst classes I've had. In just a few minutes we have two very different portraits on the board. I conclude by moving to the "best class" section and indicate that this is why I became a teacher. "I want this class to be one of these best courses. But you know, I can't make that happen without you. Can we work together to make this a class where we learn a lot and enjoy doing so?"

I like the way this activity makes students aware of relationship issues that affect classroom climates. With their worst classes, students talk about teachers who didn't care—ones who made the classroom a place where students didn't want to participate or be involved. In their best classes, they describe how the teacher helped them learn, how they were motivated to work hard, and enjoyed attending class. The activity also makes clear that student actions influence what happens in class. It introduces students to the idea that teachers and students share responsibility for the atmosphere in a class. When time permits, we also discuss this idea.

Goza (1993) proposes a similar activity that she calls Graffiti Needs Assessment. She writes ten sentence beginnings on the top of a newsprint sheet (one sentence per newsprint page) and posts them around the classroom. The first few minutes of class students wander around the room meeting each other and writing endings to those sentence beginnings. She uses the exercise to generate information about student goals, to discover levels of background knowledge, and to begin to cultivate interest in course goals. You can use the activity for that purpose, adapt it to generate discussion about classroom climate and conditions for learning, or use it to do a bit of both. Here are some possible sentence stems related to climate issues: "In the best class I ever had, students . . ." "In the best class I ever had, the teacher . . ."

"I learn best when . . ." "I feel most confident as a learner when . . ." "I don't learn well in classes where . . ." "Classmates encourage me to learn when they . . ."

Research by Appleby (1990) can be used to structure a very different kind of climate-setting activity. Appleby's results are a bit dated now, but the underlying idea isn't. He surveyed a cohort of students asking them to identify the faculty behaviors that most "irritated" them. He also surveyed a faculty cohort asking them to list student behaviors that were irritating. Some of these behaviors are still annoying—students who talk in class, fall asleep, are late, leave early, are regularly absent, and those in class who look completely bored; and faculty who keep classes late, treat students like children, and are always right.

You can put students in groups, use some of these behaviors as examples, and ask each group to identify the five faculty behaviors students find irritating or faculty behaviors that get in the way of learning. Results from each group can be combined to create a top five behaviors list. Those can be shared with students along with the faculty members' list of the top five student behaviors that irritate or make teaching difficult. The objective is to get students to avoid those behaviors, and the bargaining chip is the faculty members' commitment to avoiding behaviors that annoy students and compromise their efforts to learn. This activity gets around the need to fill the syllabus with admonitions and prohibitions. There are still behaviors that are against the rules, but they've been identified via a process that makes both teachers and students accountable and responsible.

We learned from Fraser's (1986) research that classroom climate is also influenced by the relationships between and among students, and those relationships need to be cultivated, especially in classes where students don't know each other. Many faculty use icebreakers to start the process. A fine collection can be found in Barkley's *Student Engagement Techniques* (2010, pp. 115–120). I like icebreakers that are connected to the content. Eifler's (2008) speed-dating activity places students seated in two rows facing each other. Students have in their hand a copy of the course syllabus. Eifler asks two questions: one about something in the syllabus; the other is personal. Students must quickly answer both questions before those in one of the rows move one seat down and the new partners respond to a different set of questions. An activity like this not only gets students interacting with each other, it's another way for teachers not to have to "go over" the syllabus.

There are more activities highlighted in other chapters here that can also be used to help establish classroom climates conducive to learning. Letting students set one or several policies in the classroom, as described in Chapter Four, or giving students a role in creating the syllabus effectively establishes the shared responsibility for what happens in the classroom.

INVOLVING STUDENTS IN MAINTAINING THE CLASSROOM CLIMATE

Activities like those just described do help to create good classroom climates, but just like the weather, classroom climates can change, sometimes very quickly. Have an altercation with a student in front of the rest of the class, and you can feel the weather change. Sometimes the classroom climate changes more gradually—as when one season transitions to the next. Moreover, students and teachers experience aspects of the climate differently. Some are more sensitive to the "cold"; others more attuned to changes. To maintain the climate, teachers need a repertoire of activities that enable them to keep track of the environment in a class. It's risky to assume that faculty and student perceptions of what's happening are the same.

I still recommend that faculty use the College and University Classroom Environment Inventory (CUCEI) instrument (Fraser, Treagust, and Dennis, 1986) discussed earlier in this chapter. The instrument and instructions for scoring it are included in the research article. In addition to providing feedback on the actual climate in the classroom, it develops student awareness of what makes a classroom climate. As indicated earlier, researchers had students answer each item twice; once rating their ideal classroom climate and once rating the climate in this particular class. Those are useful comparisons. The value of this feedback is also enhanced when faculty complete the instrument. You can complete it the same way students do by indicating the ideal classroom climate and then your experience of the climate in this class. Comparing your results with the aggregated class results can make for an interesting and informative discussion (and you can do this online if you prefer not to devote class time to this activity). If you're interested in knowing how accurately you are sensing students' assessment of the climate in the class, you can complete the instrument predicting the class response before it is calculated. And if students complete the instrument more than once, changes in the climate can be tracked across time.

I've collected feedback on classroom climate using an adapted version of an assessment technique proposed by Garner and Emery (1993). They have students divide an 8–1/2-by-11-inch sheet of paper into three columns. They label the columns "Start," "Stop," and "Continue." Under "Start," I have students list things not present in the classroom environment that, if present, would enhance their learning. Under "Stop," they list aspects of the classroom climate that are detracting from their learning experiences. And under "Continue," they list things we are doing that contribute positively and should be retained.

Whether you use some sort of classroom climate inventory or some other formative feedback mechanism, it is essential that the results be shared with students. This isn't just useful feedback for the teacher. Whether the climate in a class is good, bad, or somewhere in between, students have contributed to whatever it has become. Sharing the information provides a perfect opportunity to challenge students to consider their contributions—how some actions inhibit the learning efforts of everyone and others can make the classroom an even better environment for learning.

INVOLVING STUDENTS IN ENHANCING THE CLASSROOM CLIMATE

Beyond creating a climate for learning in the classroom and taking actions to ensure that it is maintained, it is also possible to continue building the climate for learning so that it is even more conducive to learning. Returning once more to the weather metaphor, the "hotter" the climate for learning in a classroom, the more motivated students are and the more learning that usually produces.

Group work provides a specific example. As the course progresses and students gain experience working in groups, they can be encouraged to take more responsibility for what happens in the group. I challenge my students to think about the future when they work with others in professional contexts and there won't be a teacher nearby to fix group problems. Is marching into the boss's office to complain about group members who don't participate, don't come to meetings prepared, or don't deliver quality work what the boss will expect of college-educated professionals?

How can groups be empowered to handle these kinds of group dynamics issues? It starts with understanding that as group members they have individual responsibilities, and the group as a whole has collective responsibilities. What individuals have the right to expect from the group and what the group has the right to expect from individual members is articulated in a Group Members' Bill of Rights and Responsibilities, which appears in Appendix Two. This document can be distributed to groups when they first meet. They may be charged with discussing it, revising it, and signing off on it. Or groups can be challenged to create their own rights and responsibilities document. The presence of a document like this doesn't guarantee that the group members individually or collectively will act on their rights and responsibilities, but it improves the chances, and when they don't, it makes dealing with the problem easier.

In an upper-division course where the group project is long and complex, a colleague of mine has each group appoint a group process liaison. These liaison members meet collectively with the teacher once every couple of weeks. The group discusses various process issues like members who aren't delivering, difficulties the group may be having resolving differences, members who want to do all the work, groups that are procrastinating, and the liaisons, with the teacher's help, brainstorm solutions—what options the group might have for dealing with these problems. Liaisons report back to their group, discussing problems and solutions. Their challenge is to get the group to deal with the issues. With group work, the climate for learning is enhanced when groups become able to function effectively on their own.

The climate for learning in the classroom is also enhanced when individual students own their responsibilities. The best example here: students stop automatically blaming the teacher or the test for their poor performance. Getting students to understand that they made decisions that contributed to poor exam performance isn't always easy, but here are some ideas. If class size permits, invite students who've done poorly to meet with you during office hours. Extend this invitation via e-mail or in a personal note on the exam, not by telling them in class to come and see you. If you want to opt for a more strong-armed approach, withhold the grade until the student comes. You might need to withhold some excellent and average grades, too—not just the failing ones—or students will figure out what the routine is and become leery about coming to your office. Should students be required to come? I'd stop short of that. Coming to the office starts the process of assuming responsibility for the grade. Not all students will come. Teachers need to be realistic: we cannot help students who do not want help.

The conversation you do not want to have is one where the teacher tells the student what to do. The teacher needs to raise relevant questions: How did you study? What did you study? Why do you think your approaches didn't work? Did some of the things you did work better than others? The conversation also needs to be about the future: So, what should you be doing now to better prepare for the next exam? Does that include going to the learning center and seeing what help might be available there? The desired outcome is a specific game plan that includes concrete actions the student can take. The teacher can propose options and offer advice, but the student should develop the game plan.

Using a model like this, McBrayer (2001) conducted 547 conferences with students and reported that on average their next exam score in his introductory psychology course increased by ten points. Students who needed to schedule such a conference but didn't showed no consistent improvement on the following exams. More students might be motivated to have a postexam conversation if the teacher collected data like this and could report an average increase in the scores of students who availed themselves of this opportunity.

As this chapter section illustrates, activity options for creating, maintaining, and enhancing constructive classroom climates are many. So far, research is not forthcoming about how many activities or what combination of them is needed to produce those climates where students accept the responsibility for learning. Teachers will need to explore the effects of these activities for themselves. There are plenty of us who can report that they do change the climate in our classrooms in noticeably constructive ways. They are activities that encourage students to act more responsibly about their learning and the learning of others.

IMPLEMENTATION ISSUES

I'd like to consider several questions that emerge when classrooms become places that make students more responsible for their learning. The questions have philosophical and practical ramifications. Regretfully, I'm not sure that we're closer to answers now than we were when this book was first published.

In my experience, the first questions to emerge involved the process of weaning students and myself from the strong reliance on rules, policies, and extrinsic motivators that had long been part of students' learning experiences and my approach to teaching. You can't abandon the rules all at once. I struggled to discover the instructional activities and assignments, policies, and approaches that prepare the immature, often irresponsible student to accept the responsibility for learning. I also struggled with what I felt comfortable doing. In some cases that meant abandoning a policy, only to reinstate it the following semester. Specifically, the questions are these: Is it a matter of doing away with some rules, retaining others, but ending up with fewer rules overall? How do you decide which rules stay and which ones go? Or should you revise the rules so that they allow more freedom but at the same time hold students more accountable? Or is it some combination of deleting, retaining, and revising? Most of us are answering those questions for ourselves and doing so through a process of trial and error.

The second group of questions pertains to letting students experience the logical consequences of the decisions they make about learning. How many consequences should students (especially beginning ones) be allowed to experience, and what kind of consequences are appropriate? For example, if you know (on the strength of evidence, not just a general impression) that attendance strongly affects performance in your class, is letting students decide whether or not they attend ethically responsible? Most of us have seen too many students make the wrong decision and decide that attendance doesn't matter. Should we let beginning students make decisions that can mean they end up needing a fifth year to finish college or decisions that put their academic future in jeopardy? It's tempting to say no and institute one of those tough attendance polices that do get more students in class. But do students learn the larger lessons from tough attendance policies? Do they learn why being in class makes a difference? Do they start regularly attending classes regardless of whether or not there's an attendance policy? Here's the goal: let students experience enough consequences so that they learn the lesson before their poor decision making results in irreparable damage.

Finally, there's a philosophical question with lots of practical implications. If the ultimate goal of learner-centered instruction is for individual learners to manage their own learning, how does a collection of individuals functioning as a class limit, transcend, or otherwise affect the learning proclivities of individual learners? For example, if one student works well against a set of deadlines (they might even be self-imposed deadlines) and another functions best without the pressure imposed by deadlines, does the teacher set deadlines for some and not for others? What does that do to notions of fair and equitable treatment for all students? The question is philosophical, as we seek to understand how individual rights are positioned within a collective learning environment, and pragmatic, as we struggle with the viability of different rules for students enrolled in the same course.

This chapter began by challenging the typical faculty response to immature, unmotivated, unfocused, or ill-prepared college students. It proposes that rules, requirements, policies, prohibitions, and lots of extrinsic motivators make students more dependent on teachers. These strictures are part of the problem and not a viable solution. If the goal is to make students more responsible for their learning, then teachers must work to create conditions that influence student attitudes and action. Classrooms need to be climates with conditions favorable to learning. Learning in these classrooms is not forced. It happens as students respond to conditions that promote growth and learning.

Classroom climates grow out of the relationships between teachers and students and among students. Those relationships are defined by teacher and student actions. This chapter has discussed both, yet much of its content describes actions that *teachers* can take to make classrooms places where learning is the likely outcome of being there. In an excellent article, Ramsey and Fitzgibbons (2005, p. 335) point out that "in most of the writing on learner-centered education, the focus remains on the teacher." I remember reading that and thinking it was a critique that applied to this book and to this chapter. "In our view, such a focus objectifies students, distances teachers, and underemphasizes the most critical element in the classroom: learning" (p. 335).

After thinking about it more, especially as I revised this chapter for the new edition, I don't believe there is any other way. It is a joint endeavor, but the question is who takes the lead, makes make the first move, and proposes relationships that change the way teachers and students interact. Students are not in a position to create learner-centered classrooms. Students look to teachers for leadership, and when the goal is creating climates for learning, I believe the onus is on the teacher. We have a responsibility to do what we can to make classrooms places where learning and the efforts of learners are honored. Climates for learning become possibilities when teachers take actions like the ones highlighted in this chapter.

CHAPTER SEVEN

THE PURPOSE AND PROCESSES OF EVALUATION

To make evaluation more learner-centered, the purpose and processes involved need to change. In the realm of purpose, we need to better balance the two reasons why we grade student work. Teachers have the professional responsibility to certify the level at which students have mastered the material. And that purpose has come to dominate both faculty and student thinking about graded learning experiences. But students do work that teachers evaluate for a second reason: completing it promotes learning. The design of assignments influences what students learn, how well they learn it, and what skills are developed in the process, and these lead to the main point of this chapter. Activities and assignments can be designed to realize more of their potential to promote learning. Unfortunately, all too often it's the grades, not the learning experience, that matter most to students and teachers. Learner-centered teaching attempts to redress that imbalance with activities, assignments, and assessment strategies that include a stronger and more deliberate focus on learning.

As for the processes of evaluation, they need to involve students. That doesn't mean that teachers hand over grading responsibilities to students. In learner-centered classrooms, teachers are still in charge of grades. But students are involved in activities that develop their self- and peer-assessment skills. Leaving students out of the process lessens the chance that these important skills develop during college. Self- and peer-assessment skills develop best when they are taught explicitly and students have the opportunity to practice them.

The changes in the purpose and processes of evaluation are addressed in this chapter with a structure that by now is familiar. I begin with the problem—what needs to change and why it hasn't. Then the changes are described in detail and illustrated with examples. Finally, we look at the implementation issues that merit consideration.

WHAT NEEDS TO CHANGE AND HASN'T

Grades are important, undeniably so. They function as gatekeepers in, through, and out of postsecondary institutions. The more selective the college or university, the higher the entrance GPA required. Many institutions now control enrollment in majors, and acceptance depends largely on GPA. At the end, college GPA plays a significant role in determining postsecondary educational opportunities, including whether students can attend graduate school, med school, law school, and other professional programs. Many employers use GPA to decide who does and doesn't get a job interview. Grades matter, and only naive faculty make proclamations to the contrary. But learning matters more, especially in the long run. How long has it been since someone asked about your GPA?

Without question, grades are important, but it's still difficult to justify the level of importance ascribed to them, and for several different reasons. They don't measure all kinds of learning equally well. They do accurately document whether a student knows a set of facts at a certain time, not whether the student can remember or apply those facts outside the classroom. They can measure critical thinking, problem solving, logical reasoning, and the ability to synthesize and evaluate. Unfortunately, the questions included on most tests don't measure these higher-order thinking skills (Momsen, Long, Wyse, and Ebert-May, 2010). Rarely do grades give an indication of how well students can work together, or how committed they are to high ethical standards, or whether they see the value of civic engagement.

Grades very effectively indicate how good students are at getting grades. What Pollio and Humphreys wrote in 1988 is still true: "Grading outstrips both intercollegiate athletics and intramural sports as the most frequently played game on the college campus. It takes place in all seasons and everyone gets to play one position or another" (p. 85). Getting undeserved grades compromises the integrity of grades. And their objectivity can be eroded further when overworked professors get tired and are then influenced by how they feel about a student, what they like to read in a paper, or how they anticipate students will respond to low grades.

These are some of the reasons why grades shouldn't be as important as they are. Even so, the high value placed on them is not decreasing. Even if learner-centered teachers tried to change the importance attached to grades, there's not much chance they'd succeed. But they can work hard to resist and overcome three negative effects grades have on learning.

First, as faculty well know, the emphasis on grades causes students to work for grades and not for learning, or at least not for the deep, lasting learning equated with understanding. Faculty are less aware that some of their actions reinforce this misaligned student motivation. Research by Church, Elliot, and Gable (2001) documents that students are more likely to adopt performance goals (as in do things for the grade), than to adopt mastery goals (as in do things associated with deep learning) when the professor emphasizes the importance of grades and when the grading is perceived to be excessively difficult.

Faculty emphasize the importance of grades in more subtle ways as well. In several classrooms I've heard teachers asking students about content from an earlier part of the course. "Remember when we talked about X?" Students look confused and are slow to respond. The teacher prompts them by saying, "We talked about it just before the first exam." Student memories are not being triggered by locating this content alongside other content or by connecting it with larger course concepts, but by when that content was presented in relation to the exam. No, this isn't a major offense, but it does illustrate how the importance of evaluation events like exams permeates our thinking. We "position" the content around them.

As discussed in Chapter Six, we create elaborate point systems that put a grade value on everything students do (or don't do) in the class. We have designed these systems to clarify expectations, and they do, but not without creating an undesirable by-product: monstrous amounts of grade grubbing. You can get students to do almost anything for a point. I've been known to go into a class and offer an extra-credit assignment worth three points. "Anybody interested in doing it?" Hands everywhere wave enthusiastically. Next day I offer two points, and still there are many volunteers. I continue on and finally when I'm down to offering 0.5 of a point, some student will ask whether I'm trying to make a point about what students will do for a point or part of a point. I used to jokingly suggest to students grubbing for one or two more points that they might try "buying" them. But then one day an envelope containing $20 and a request for three additional points showed up in my mail.

There is no question that students are entirely too grade oriented. Many see their inherent worth as human beings reflected in a grade and are seemingly incapable of separating the performance from the person. We must work to help them gain a healthier perspective on grades, but some research indicates that students think faculty are just as grade oriented as they are. Of that finding Pollio and Beck (2000, p. 98) write, "the present situation seems to be that both students and professors want the same changes—stronger emphasis on learning, weaker emphasis on grades—and both seem to hold the other responsible for the present, less than ideal situation." Unfortunately, as the importance of grades increases, their role in promoting learning decreases. As a consequence, some students take little other than grades from their courses.

Excessive concern over grades causes a second student response that compromises learning. Grades confirm what many students suspect: it's ability (and sometimes luck) that determines grades—not effort, not good study habits, not hard work. Either they have the ability to learn math or they don't. Either they can write or they're entirely bereft of any writing ability. Attribution theory (discussed in Chapter One) explains this thinking, and research documents the extent to which students equate grades and ability. Covington and Omelich (1984) asked students to rate their ability to deal with content in a course taken the previous semester, estimate how hard they had worked, and report the grade they received. Assessments of ability accounted for 50 percent of the variance, with course grade and effort expended a distant second or third. Perry and Magnusson (1987) found that even the presence of an outstanding teacher could not dislodge the powerful results that occur when students believe academic outcomes are predetermined by factors beyond their control, like their innate abilities.

Classrooms where students are graded on a curve have especially pernicious effects on student beliefs about abilities and their motivation to learn. With a limited number of As possible, students who see themselves as intellectually inferior quickly give up and receive grades confirming just how woefully inadequate they are. Furthermore, the competitive environment in those classrooms creates a strong disincentive to collaboration, making it less likely that students will learn from and with each other. Learning ends up being an isolated, individual activity, much to the detriment of those students who learn well with others. Classroom policies, practices, activities, and assignments should be designed to showcase how effort makes a difference, how learning almost always requires hard work, and that what students learn is far more enduring than the grade they get for doing so.

Finally, the pressure to get grades motivates students to cheat. And cheat they do, despite gallant faculty efforts to prevent this assault on academic integrity. That students cheat has been documented by far too many studies to list. In most studies, the percentage of students who say they have cheated ranges from 40 to 60 percent. They report that their peers cheat more than they do. Allen, Fuller, and Luckett (1998) believe that self-reports of cheating tend to underestimate the actual number and percentage of students who cheat.

Since the first edition of the book, the easy access to information on the Internet has increased the amount of plagiarism. "Studies have shown that students do not perceive the same principles of ownership applying to web-based sources as conventional published materials" (McGowan and Lightbody, 2008, p. 273). Using a qualitative research design that gathered data via student focus groups and individual interviews, Power (2009) reports that students know plagiarism is something their professors don't want them to do, but they aren't always clear about what constitutes plagiarism and they report that they don't know how to avoid doing it. Using the cut-and-paste feature is so much easier than struggling to put the ideas of others in your own words.

Genereux and McLeod (1995) studied the circumstances most influential in spontaneous and planned decisions to cheat. The dependence on grades for financial aid and the impact of course grade on long-term goals were among the top five reasons for both decisions. Given our current financial realities, one can only imagine how powerfully those reasons influence decisions today. Results from a 2004 study of cheating behavior among business students "clearly demonstrates that students know what cheating is and that they believe it is morally wrong. But they continue to cheat because they feel that the benefits outweigh the potential costs, and they believe cheating to be the 'norm'" (Chapman, Davis, Toy, and Wright, p. 246). As one of the students they interviewed noted, "Cheating is not really considered a bad thing by students. Since everyone does it once in a while, it is kind of like going over the speed limit. Everyone knows that it is against the rules, but everyone still does it" (p. 236).

Students do not understand that in addition to compromising the integrity of the educational enterprise, cheating also hurts them. They aren't learning content they need to know. They aren't developing skills that they need to have. They aren't being honest with themselves and others about what they know and can do. And they aren't developing the confidence that comes from mastering material and successfully demonstrating skills. The belief that cheating doesn't matter, especially if it gets you a better grade, needs to change, and classrooms where learning is prized as much as grades challenge those damaging norms and mistaken assumptions.

In addition to better balancing the importance of grades and learning, we also need to give students a role in the evaluation process. Up to this point, students have had little or no involvement in the assessment process. In most courses they are not asked to look critically at their own work or the work of their peers, and for good reasons, some would argue. Given the intense motivation to get grades and their propensity to cheat, how can we expect them to handle a role in this important process with any sort of integrity or objectivity? Moreover, isn't certifying mastery of material a teacher responsibility? Yes, it is, but the question is whether it's possible for teachers to uphold the integrity of the grading process and still involve students in activities that build their self- and peer-assessment skills.

Research on self-assessment offers some answers. It is noteworthy that even though students are given few opportunities to evaluate their work, research interest in self-assessment is long-standing. Early work is summarized in a still regularly referenced meta-analysis done by Falchikov and Boud (1989). This review of forty-eight studies includes some expected results: correlations between the grades students give themselves and the grades teachers give them are low if the course is entry level and required. However, if it's an upper-division, major course, if the grading is done against specified criteria, and if students have a chance to compare their assessment with that of the teacher, correlations are much more promising.

Work done more recently also confirms that under certain conditions students can self-assess with some reliability. Kardash (2000) looked at fourteen research skills purportedly developed by undergraduate research experiences. Students rated themselves on these skills before and after an undergraduate research experience. Their faculty mentors also rated them on these skills. Kardash (2000, p. 196) reports "striking similarities" between the ratings, with both faculty and students giving highest ratings to the same five skills. Krohn, Foster, McCleary, Aspiranti, Nalls, Quillivan, Taylor, and Williams (2011) investigated a system whereby students reported their in-class, verbal contributions on a specially designed card that they then submitted for credit. The students did not know that observers in the classroom were also keeping track of their comments. "Agreement between participant and observer records of individual participation proved high overall, and students did not over report their comments under credit conditions" (p. 43). Edwards (2007) has developed a system in which students grade their homework and exams. He checks their grading, and reports "an overwhelming majority of students grade homework problems exactly or very closely to how I would have graded them" (p. 73). The same is true for their exams: "the majority of scores do not change with my rechecking" (p. 73). Students respond very favorably to Edwards's self-grading system, with many commenting how much they learn by correcting their own mistakes. When Edwards asked students about how much cheating they thought was occurring in the class, 88 percent said "none" or "not enough to worry about." Reports like these and others document that in some situations and under certain circumstances students assess their work honestly. They don't always give themselves the assessment they'd like to have whether or not they deserve it.

Given the possibility of involving students in assessment activities, we need to remind ourselves why they should be involved. The ability to accurately assess the quality of one's own work as well as that of others is a skill useful during college and in most professions subsequently. I now believe much more strongly than when I first wrote this book that those of us committed to learner-centered objectives must devote more energy to the development of these skills. Nicol and Macfarlane-Dick (2006) rightly observe that although many of us have changed our conceptions of teaching and learning, "a parallel shift in relation to formative assessment and feedback has been slower to emerge. In higher education, formative assessment and feedback are still largely controlled by and seen as the responsibility of teachers; and feedback is still generally conceptualised as a transmission process . . . If formative assessment is exclusively in the hands of teachers, then it is difficult to see how students can become empowered and develop the self-regulation skills needed to prepare them for learning, outside university and throughout life" (p. 200).

HOW THE PURPOSE AND PROCESSES OF EVALUATION CHANGE

Two problems with current practice have been identified. Mostly in response to external pressures, instructional policies and practices now place a disproportionate emphasis on grades, and these are compromising various learning outcomes. Second, excluding students from evaluation activities prevents the development of important self- and peer-assessment skills. In this section I will offer examples illustrating some of the ways learner-centered teachers address both these problems.

A BETTER BALANCE BETWEEN GRADES AND LEARNING

Let's start with grades. They are still important and still generated by teachers. Doing the work required in a course gets students grades, but it's also an opportunity for them to learn. The challenge is to acknowledge the importance of grades but retain a focus on what's being learned through these experiences. To meet this challenge, I've devised a set of principles that define a more balanced relationship between grades and learning. The principles can also function as criteria that help us identify and develop activities and assignments that achieve this better balance.

Harness the Power of Grades to Motivate Students. We know that grades motivate students. They are better at motivating effort in the direction of grades than learning, but grades do energize students. Teachers can use this motivation—yes, that means getting students to do things for points—but as they do, teachers should attempt to redirect that motivation by harnessing it to more productive outcomes. What I think faculty need to do with the motivation to get grades is a bit like going to the jailhouse to preach forgiveness. You're not there to release the prisoners; students still need to get grades. But you bring the liberating message that learning matters more than grades, especially from vantage points later in life. Examples illustrating how this principle can be realized follow here. But it is important to see positive possibilities in the motivation to get grades. It's energy that can be redirected toward learning.

Make Evaluation Experiences Less Stressful. Some of the learning potential inherent in evaluation experiences is compromised by the stress associated with them. Sarros and Densten (1989) asked students to rate thirty-four potential stressors. Nine of the top ten related to evaluation activities, including the number of assignments, taking exams, and receiving low grades on them. Afraid, anxious, and stressed-out students do not focus well on learning objectives. The goal here is not to entirely eliminate stress, because appropriate amounts of it pique performance. The problems begin when our students experience too much stress and they don't cope with it constructively. Many of the examples that follow illustrate how stress associated with evaluation events can be reduced without compromising what makes them challenging and rigorous.

Use Evaluation Only to Assess Learning. Some faculty have been known to use evaluation activities to advance hidden agendas. Very early in my teaching career, I had a class that I didn't think was taking the content all that seriously. It was a speech class, for goodness sake, and as one student told me, "I don't really need this class—I've been talking since I was three." These students needed to recognize that the content had substance and rigor, and so I gave a really "hard" test, not to measure how well they understood, but to show them that the content in this course wasn't easy. Unfortunately, that's not the kind of exam that promotes learning.

Excessively difficult exams should not be used to establish a course's reputation for rigor. When 75 percent of a class fails or gets really low scores on an exam after the teacher has made a good-faith effort to explicate the material, it means the teacher hasn't explained things very well, isn't very good at making tests, or is using exams to accomplish some purpose other than the promotion of learning. Yes, it is possible that 75 percent of the students did not study, but ulterior teacher motives are a more likely explanation. In its most egregious form, faculty or departments use courses to "weed out" students who, by some set of subjective standards, "can't do" physics, engineering, math, nursing, or some other course of study. Students may learn through courses and exams that their interests and talents lie elsewhere, but courses and exams should not be expressly designed to accomplish this end.

Another version of this hidden agenda problem occurs when faculty use evaluation experiences to "test" how far students can take the content. They include new kinds of problems—ones students should be able to solve if they apply what's been covered in class, but not the kind of problems students have seen before. If one of the course objectives is developing students' abilities to apply what they've learned to different kinds of problems, it's legitimate to test their ability to do so, but only when students have had a chance to practice those application skills. Problems solved in class and assigned as homework should involve application, and students should get formative feedback on their attempts. For evaluation experiences to promote learning, they must be designed for that purpose. Using them to accomplish other goals compromises the integrity of the process, increases student stress, and makes grades matter more and learning even less.

Focus More on Formative Feedback. We've all seen it happen. Hand back a set of papers with comments that it's taken many hours to provide and watch students quickly look at the grade and then stash the paper in their book bags. Maybe they read the comments later, but do they act on the suggestions and improve their next paper? Not as often as we'd like, and we've already explored some reasons why, but the point here is a different one.

Focusing more on formative feedback doesn't mean writing more comments or otherwise increasing the amount of feedback provided. It means thinking creatively about structures and activities that more effectively focus students on the feedback and not the grade. This approach can be as simple as separating the two—provide the commentary before the grade while students still have the chance to act on feedback and improve their grade, or provide the feedback without the grade, asking for a response to the feedback and then delivering the grade. It might be changing the format of feedback—writing students a letter or offering the feedback face-to-face.

Focusing on formative feedback also means thinking about the issue more broadly—beyond commentary that responds to a product. It is true that since the first edition of this book, class sizes have not gotten smaller and teaching loads have not decreased. Many of us do not have time to provide face-to-face feedback, and if we can't there is no reason to feel guilty about circumstances we do not control. However, we must not underestimate the power of a personal comment to affect a student, sometimes more profoundly than the grade. A quick compliment, a word of encouragement, noting accomplishments elsewhere on campus in an e-mail—these, too, are forms of feedback. They're disconnected from grades and effectively convey that some of the things students get from courses may be worth more than points and grades.

These principles can be simply summed up: students complete work that we grade because doing so causes them to encounter and learn the content. Learner-centered teachers work to maximize the learning potential that is inherently part of any graded assignment or activity without diminishing the importance of grades.

USING EVALUATION TO PROMOTE SELF- AND PEER-ASSESSMENT SKILLS

Since the 2002 edition of this book, there has been increased recognition that the feedback teachers provide students often has little effect on subsequent performance. In one study (Crisp, 2007), a cohort of undergraduate social work students got detailed feedback on a written assignment. Six weeks later, they completed a similar assignment and despite the feedback, grades for 66.7 percent of the students were within four percentage points on both assignments. "This study found only limited support for the idea that students respond to feedback by making changes which are consistent with the intent of the feedback received" (p. 571). We spend time and energy providing feedback, identifying what's right and wrong in the paper, project, presentation, exam, or essay assuming students will use this information to do better work next time. What's wrong with that assumption? Why don't more of our grade-motivated students make the changes that would improve their work?

In a thoughtful and well-referenced article, Sadler (2010) argues that "despite the teachers' best efforts to make the disclosure full, objective and precise, many students do not understand it appropriately because . . . they are not equipped to decode the statements properly" (p. 539). He says that teachers are spending too much time focusing on the composition of the feedback and not enough time helping students understand it. So what's the solution here? Should teachers spend more time telling students what the feedback means?

Telling is not the learner-centered way. Sadler says it bluntly: "Put simply, to depend on telling . . . as the main vehicle for promoting student improvement is to rely on the information transmission model for the development of significant assessment concepts" (p. 548). Its lack of success is documented by research and also by those subsequent assignments in which the same errors are repeated. Rather than teachers telling, students need opportunities to assess their own work and the work of others. They must learn how to recognize what's good, what needs to be fixed, and how to make it better. And how are those skills best developed? By practice.

As a result of the Writing-Across-the-Curriculum movement, more teachers have let students practice offering assessment feedback to their peers. Students read each other's papers before they're submitted and suggest ways the work might be improved. Teachers using this approach quickly learned that students don't offer good feedback automatically. Just as quickly, students concluded they didn't "like" critiquing the work of others if the task involved having to say something negative about it. They copped out: "Good paper. I don't see any problems," or they commented on minor issues like the placement of a comma. A lot of teachers found the quality of this feedback so discouraging and the student attitudes so negative that they pulled back from having students look at each other's work.

Actually, what happened here illustrates the point Sadler (2010) makes in his article. Students lack what he calls "appraisal expertise." Teachers have lots of it—we have graded more student papers, performances, projects, and presentations than we can count. And out of all that experience develops expertise. We know an A paper when we read one, and we can explain what makes it exemplary. Given their lack of involvement in evaluation activities, we shouldn't be surprised that students aren't very good at doing it—for their peers or for their own work. If we want them to make good judgments and offer quality feedback, then we need to use activities designed to develop these skills. We need to share assessment criteria with them, show how we apply them, and then give them the opportunity to practice. They need to be taught the principles of constructive feedback so that they make helpful comments that motivate improvement. Developing these skills is not an impossible task, and we aren't starting from square one.

Nicol and Macfarlane-Dick (2006), who see the ability to self-assess as a characteristic of self-regulated learners, point out that students already engage in some of this self-evaluation on their own. When they prepare a paper, for example, students decide if the paper is long enough, if they've used enough references, if their writing makes sense, and if they've included content they think the professor wants to read. These are self-assessments, not always detailed ones, and not always ones based on relevant criteria, but they are looking at their work with a critical eye. We can use this as a starting point, showing students how further development of these skills can help them learn more and get better grades. With better skills, they and their colleagues can exchange the kind of feedback needed to improve their work still further. Once students start giving and getting useful feedback, their motivation to work with each other increases significantly.

In sum, given the grading issues explored earlier, we can't give students free reign to grade themselves; given our professional responsibilities to certify mastery of material, we shouldn't. But does that prevent or excuse us from offering experiences that develop self- and peer-assessment skills? The next section contains a variety of strategies, approaches, ideas, and assignments that do develop these skills. I will leave you to decide if they are ways of involving students that still maintain the integrity of the grading process.

Using Exams, Assignments, and Activities to Promote Learning

This section contains a wide range of ideas on maximizing the learning potential inherently a part of evaluated student work. The examples illustrate how principles proposed in the previous section can be realized via activities and how the format and structure of traditional assignments can be changed to put more emphasis on learning. A good place to begin is with perhaps the most common and widely used of all evaluation activities: the exam.

Maximizing the Learning Potential of Exams

We have long assumed that the learning promoted by exams happens automatically. A completed exam shows what and how well the student has learned. We act as though the learning is entirely up to the student, forgetting that as instructional designers we have the power to shape these experiences. We can arrange and rearrange their various parts, and in so doing define the nature of that learning experience. The following activities illustrate ways to shape exam experiences that are more focused on learning.

Review Sessions. Some faculty don't have in-class review sessions because that means one less period for presenting content. The question is whether students benefit more from being exposed to additional material or from having a chance to organize, summarize, distill, and integrate the content they must learn for the exam. Should students do this summarizing and integrating on their own as they study? Perhaps. Will they learn to do it better if their efforts are guided by an expert who understands how the content domain is organized? Probably. Favero (2011) explains how his thinking about review sessions changed: "Like many teachers, I fought against trading 'content' or course time for an entire class period devoted to a review session. Over time, I came to the conclusion that if I wanted my students to become problem solvers, I had to provide them with low-stakes opportunities and time to solve them" (p. 248).

The typical structure of reviews also deters faculty from using them. The teacher goes over important and challenging content. Students are supposed to ask questions, ostensibly about what they don't understand. More often, though, they use the opportunity to try to ferret out what's going to be on the exam. "Will we need to know about cost-benefit analysis for the exam?" or a bit more cleverly, "How much detail will we need to know about cost-benefit analysis?"

There are other ways to structure review sessions. The teacher already knows the content and doesn't need to review it; students are the ones who need to review. The period should be designed so that students are doing the work, with the teacher providing guidance. They can be working individually or in groups, but they should be solving problems, answering old exam questions, writing possible test questions, or extrapolating key concepts from assigned readings. One of Favero's (2011) strategies begins with students' writing down the five most important facts, theories, or concepts from the material slated for this exam. Students discuss their lists with each other and then Favero does a quick tally of the items on their lists. If need be, he adds concepts students have missed, and then with the students he prioritizes the list. He uses the activity to focus student study efforts on the most important topics and concepts.

In the same vein, the preparation of study guides and review materials benefits students. Teachers already know how to prepare these materials. I hold my students responsible for text material we don't cover in class. The thought of having to decide what they might need to know from this undiscussed reading causes considerable consternation. To help them prepare and alleviate the anxiety, I put students in study groups, assign each group a different chunk of this text material, and task them with preparing review materials for the rest of the class. These materials are distributed before the exam, and if students use them to study, they grade and offer feedback on each group's material. The amount of points involved is small.

Students individually or collectively can be asked to write potential exam questions and bring them to the review session. Before using this approach, I didn't realize how answer oriented students are. They memorize lists and details, sometimes without really understanding what question the content answers. Writing potential test questions benefits students in two other ways. The exercise forces them to make decisions about what's going to be on the test, and it can clarify their thinking about what kinds of questions they will find on the exam. My beginning students write questions that test recall of detail and questions with one definitively right answer. Seeing samples of my questions alongside theirs shows them differences and usually motivates more serious exam preparation. "Your questions are a lot harder than ours." Some faculty (Green, 1997) take student development of exam questions even further, having students create questions for each content unit, assembling these in a database open to the whole class and then using a significant number of these questions on the exam. One caveat: don't expect students who haven't written tests questions previously to write good ones initially. It's another one of those skills that develops best when students are given some instruction and opportunities to practice.

Exams. Exams don't promote deep learning unless the questions challenge students to think, and there is evidence that test questions don't do that as regularly as they should. In one study (Momsen, Long, Wyse, and Ebert-May, 2010), researchers collected exams from 50 biology faculty teaching 77 different introductory biology courses. Their analysis of the questions on these exams revealed a stunning conclusion. "Of the 9,713 assessment items submitted to this study . . . , 93% were rated Bloom's level 1 or 2—knowledge and comprehension. Of the remaining items, 6.7% rated level 3 with less than 1% rated level 4 or above" (p. 437). Questions that test knowledge recall and comprehension encourage students to memorize details and develop a superficial understanding of the content, which they rarely retain.

Part of the problem here is straightforward: questions that challenge students to think are much harder to write, and that explains why there aren't a lot of them in the question banks provided by textbook publishers. It's not that multiple-choice questions are inherently less thought provoking. SAT and ACT questions are multiple choice, and many of those are challenging as the dickens. If exams are returned to students, then new questions must be generated for each new class. Good questions can be preserved if students have access to their exams (when they're returned and subsequently in the prof's office), but are not in possession of them. That way, questions can be recycled and across the years a collection can be developed, revised, and reused.

Exam circumstances are pretty much fixed. Students work alone within time constraints, without access to resources or expertise and under surveillance so that they don't cheat or cheat less. When you stop and think about it, you may conclude that there is something a bit artificial about how we test what students have learned. When in your professional life do you find yourself needing to demonstrate what you know within fifty minutes and with no access to information or others? To diminish student anxiety and to make testing situations a bit more realistic, some faculty let students prepare a crib sheet that they can use during the exam. Within certain size specifications, students may include any information—facts, formulae, graphs, quotations, and definitions—they think they might need to answer test questions. Assembling this information forces students to make choices about what they need to know, and it helps them assess the status of their understanding. Janick (1990, p. 2) notes the irony: "The development of a good crib sheet resembles its antithesis, studying." Some faculty have students submit their crib sheets with the exam and will use them to show individual students or the class as a whole that they had the information they needed on the crib sheet, but were not able to apply it. That can be useful feedback if students prepare crib sheets for subsequent exams.

In Chapter Three I described some group testing models. They illustrate effective ways to harness the energy that exam experiences produce and redirect it toward learning outcomes. Discussing content with other students promotes understanding. It clarifies details, raises questions, and offers an intense encounter with the content. Students regularly report that group testing models reduce exam anxiety as well (see Pandey and Kapitanoff, 2011, for an example).

Sundar described for me a make-a-final option she gives students in math courses (Weimer, 1989). These student-created finals are graded on things like problem development (assessed against course objectives), their solutions (including partial credit recommendations), and the point value assigned the problem (given its importance relative to other course content). The most persuasive aspect of this approach was the number of students who reported that they spent considerably more time preparing the final than they would have spent studying for it.

For another interesting alternative, see Ellery's (2008) article, which offers an exam scheme that incorporates a self-assessment component. Her approach responded to the poor quality of the essay exams her second-year students were writing. After one such exam, which 50 percent of the students failed, she delivered feedback (but not grades) on exam answers to the whole class (not on individual exams) and noted that the answers were not well structured, contained irrelevant content, and missed relevant content and that writing problems were compromising answer quality. In addition, she provided students with essay answer exemplars. Then she gave students the opportunity to write a second essay exam with different but equally difficult analysis and application questions. Students submitted both the first and second exam, but they selected which one they wanted graded.

Seventy-six percent of the students chose to write a second exam, and although many of them found the selection process difficult and anxiety provoking, 81 percent did choose the better of the two exams. As this and the other examples show, there are alternatives to our traditional testing methods. They merit consideration if the goal is to maximize the learning potential inherently a part of exam experiences.

Debrief Sessions. Typically teachers go over the most missed questions, offering explanation and elaboration. That approach does not take advantage of the learning potential that is still present after the exam. Teachers don't need to correct the answers—students do. Whether in groups or individually, students can be given the chance to find the correct answers and to fix their mistakes. Maybe that happens during the debrief session or maybe students do the work at home, completing it before the next class session. Maybe their grade isn't recorded until they've corrected their errors, and maybe it's a few points higher if they take care of all their mistakes.

This leads to the question of extra-credit opportunities associated with exam experiences. There isn't a lot of research on extra credit, but what there is documents that most faculty are pretty strongly opposed to giving students extra-credit options (Norcross, Horrocks, and Stevenson, 1989; Norcross, Dooley, and Stevenson, 1993). When I proposed in my blog that extra-credit options could be designed to offer students a second opportunity to learn the material, there was some support but more opposition (www.facultyfocus.com, July 20, 2011). The fear is that when extra credit is an option, students, who tend to believe all extra credit is easy, will rely on it and study less. I'm still on the side of well-designed, substantive extra-credit options being good second learning opportunities. Consider these examples and their ability to harness the grade motivation to productive learning outcomes.

Deeter (2003) attaches a blank sheet of paper to her exams. Students use the paper to list test items they weren't able to answer or answers they were unsure of. They take this sheet with them and have until the next class session to find the answers to those questions. They turn in their completed sheets, and Deeter reattaches them to their exams. She grades all the answers, giving partial credit for items answered correctly on the blank sheet. In the blog exchange, a faculty member outlined another option. Students first complete a quiz individually. They then meet with their learning team members and have a designated amount of time to discuss quiz questions. They are allowed to change answers or add material to answers during this time, but they make these changes using a red pen provided by the teacher. In these examples and similar ones, students regularly report that they learn much more when they have to correct their own errors than when they listen to the teacher explain the right answer.

Debrief sessions can also be designed to address some of the decisions students have made about preparing for the exam. Class attendance makes a difference. You can say this to students, but the message really hits home when you show them evidence. Take the five highest exam scores and list the number of times that group of students missed class. Take the five lowest scores and list the number of class sessions that group missed. Let the facts speak for themselves. Many students aren't taking enough notes in class. You can say that or you can demonstrate it. Pick a question that lots of people missed. Identify the date that material was covered and have everybody look at their notes. Do they have what they need there to answer the question? Were they absent and did they get notes from somebody else? Do they understand those notes? Quick discussions of topics like these can be concluded with students writing themselves a memo addressing "things I learned taking this exam that I want to remember for the next one," as explained in a previous chapter.

DEVELOPING SELF- AND PEER-ASSESSMENT SKILLS

Any given assignment or activity in the course can accomplish more than one learning objective. Exams promote content acquisition. They can also be used to develop learning skills, and they can incorporate self- and peer-assessment components, as the previous examples illustrate. The same is true when the goal is developing self- and peer-assessment abilities. Activities can be designed that promote skill development in these areas at the same time those activities accomplish other learning objectives. Many of the assignments and activities that follow illustrate how this works.

I continue to encourage review of these options. Remember the key question of this chapter: Do these ways of involving students in self- and peer-assessment activities retain the integrity of the grading process? Are they ways for students to develop important skill sets that don't compromise the ethical responsibility teachers have to certify mastery of material and give grades?

SELF-ASSESSMENT: DISCOVERING WHAT I DO AND HOW WELL I DO IT

Being able to look critically at your own work is easier once you've looked at the work of others, especially unknown others. If students aren't doing well writing essay answers, let them "grade" several (hypothetical or anonymous) essay answers. Maybe they first do this individually and then compare their assessments with others. I have found that given three answers at different quality levels, students do see the differences and do correctly identify the answer that is good and the one that isn't. They can use those sample answers to start identifying the specific things that make one essay excellent and another poor, and from there, with the teacher's help, they can begin to generate criteria for good essay exam answers. For most students, this is an illuminating experience on several fronts. They understand more clearly what the teacher "wants" in an essay answer. They realize they can begin to make accurate quality judgments about answers. And they can start applying what they're learning about answers in general to their own specifically.

The development of self-assessment skills also easily links with efforts to make students more aware of themselves as learners and more responsible for the decisions they make about learning. If students complete some sort of journaling assignment or prepare sheets that summarize and react to assigned readings (as Parrott and Cherry, 2011, describe and as discussed in Chapter Five), that collection of writings can culminate with students' reviewing what they've written and preparing a reflection paper that describes how their ideas have changed and their skills have developed.

When asking students to write about their skills, it is always good to ask them to identify those aspects of the skills that need further development. With assignments like these, it must be made clear to students that "points" are not awarded because they claim to have learned "so much" in this course, but on their level of insight and ability to summon evidence that illustrates and supports their claims.

A similar kind of reflection writing is possible after a performance, presentation, or other kind of activity. For example, if students have been involved in a group project that has extended across several weeks and involved production of a graded product, students can be asked to reflect on how well the group functioned and how their contributions helped and what they could have contributed to help the group even more. I use an interview assignment in my course. Students apply for "jobs" advertised by student groups. The groups interview various candidates and select one for the job. The interviewees write a paper in which they describe and assess the answers they gave to various interview questions. Most important, they say how they would improve their answer if they were ever asked the same question.

Here's an example that illustrates the myriad design details necessary if students are to actually be involved in the grading process. In Chapter Four I indicated that students in my introductory communication course create the participation policy that is then used to assess their participation. With that policy in place, students complete a self-assessment that clarifies how they typically participate in courses. They use that assessment to set concrete (as in measurable and observable) participation goals for this course. They must propose goals that are consistent with and advance the class-generated policy.

Shortly after developing these goals, I assign students who are doing this assignment a participation partner (remember that my students select the assignments they complete). The partners exchange (in writing) their individual participation goals. For the next two weeks the partners observe each other, recording any participation behaviors they observe. I am regularly amazed at how effectively peers motivate behavior change. Students who haven't yet spoken in class speak up the first day their partner is observing them. Students' responses more deliberately address the behaviors identified in their participation goals. There's always more interaction during those two weeks than at any other time in the course.

At the end of the observation period, each partner prepares a letter giving feedback on what they've observed. They must offer specific examples—no general commendations or condemnations. The letters they prepare are uniformly positive and constructive, often including encouragement if the partner is not achieving the goals. Students then use this feedback and their own assessment to prepare a progress report. I respond with my assessment of their progress in achieving their goals. If students are well on their way to accomplishing them, I encourage consideration of more challenging goals. I give them the option of making the assignment worth more points if they do opt for more challenging goals.

At the end of the course, students prepare a final self-assessment memo. Once again, the evidence included must be specific, including dates and descriptions of what they did. They end their memo by saying how many of the possible points they believe they've earned. Before reading these memos, I decide how many of the points I think they've earned. I keep track of who's doing what in the course via a log that I work on for five to ten minutes after each class. I share my points total, but so long as the student and I are within three points of each other, I record the amount that is higher. In the beginning I worried whether this approach would work, but consistently (usually 85 percent of time), across many semesters, students and I were within three points of each other. And when we aren't, under-evaluation is more of a problem than overevaluation and yes, it is more often female students who underestimate the worth of their contributions.

I would be less than honest if I didn't admit that this assignment went through many different iterations before becoming what I've described here. It's difficult to get assignments like this right the first time. But it ended up being an assignment that I felt accomplished a number of different goals. It offered students a substantive self-assessment experience. It made them aware of how they participate, and in most cases it developed a new level of participation skills that students recognized and reported on with pride. And perhaps best of all, it made for more and better interaction in the classroom.

Peer Assessment: Discovering That I Can Give and Get Useful Feedback

Even though many teachers have been disappointed with the quality of feedback students provide when they peer-review each other's writing, the problems can be remedied with better design of activities and a recognition that giving useful feedback is not a skill most students bring with them to college courses. Ever since I've heard it, I've endorsed Shelley's Twenty-Minute Rule (devised by E. Shelley Reid, who teaches English at George Mason University): "Anything you *really* want students to do on their own at a critically engaged college-student level, and that you suspect they might not have done before, you need to do together—in class—at least once—for twenty minutes." To prepare students to do peer reviews of writing, Reid recommends you start by generating and discussing criteria for evaluation, share and discuss "model" texts and include time for students to practice with those texts, and share and discuss appropriate comments. A great way to start discussion of appropriate comments is to ask students to share comments that faculty have written on their papers that were (or were not) helpful.

For students learning to critique each other's writing, Nilson (2003) suggests prompts that do not ask directly for judgments; that any student, no matter whether she knows the rules of the discipline or not, can answer; and that demand careful attention to the details of the work. Here are some examples from a much longer list contained in her article: What one or two adjectives (aside from "short," "long," "good," or "bad") would you choose to describe the title of this paper? Put stars around the sentence that you believe is the thesis statement in this paper. Highlight (in color) any passages that you had to read more than once to understand what the reader was saying. Bracket any sentences you find particularly strong and effective.

Writing-Across-the Curriculum is a well established movement at this point, and peer review has been one of the activities recommended from the beginning. Consequently, there are many fine resources that contain a range of examples and useful advice, and one of the best is Bean's now classic work *Engaging Ideas* (2011 for the 2nd edition).

The extended example I'm including here uses peer assessment in group work. It is regularly proposed as the antidote to the problem of group members free riding, although not everyone recommends using it or group grades, for that matter. Cooperative learning advocates believe that group work should be designed so that "individual accountability" is retained. In other words, grades are for individual work, not to be shared equally by group members who probably did not work equally. For a succinct and well-reasoned summary of this position, see Kagan (1995).

The arguments on both sides are interesting and worth reviewing before you decide whether to use group grades and peer assessment. There are places in the middle, and that's where I've ended up. The grade is divided into parts; one part is based on the product produced by the group, and everybody in the group gets that grade, and one part is an individual grade based primarily on peer-assessment feedback.

In the beginning students aren't all that excited about assessing each other's contributions in the group. There is a lot of back-scratching commentary: "Everybody contributed equally in this group. We all worked hard." One simple solution here is to have group members rate and rank the contributions of others. They rate on a scale from excellent to poor, and they can give as many "excellents" as they want, but they also rank the contributions of others from 1 to 5, and they can only give one 1, one 2, one 3, and so on.

This simple solution addresses the issue of who worked and who didn't, but it doesn't do much to develop peer-assessment skills or give students experience with exchanging feedback. It's best to start developing those skills by having students use a set of criteria to assess the contributions of their peers. From a comprehensive review of the literature, Baker (2008) identifies the eight most common behaviors that have been used to assess individual contributions to and in groups:

1. Attended meetings
2. Was dependable and met deadlines

3. Did quality work
4. Exerted effort, doing his or her fair share of the work and sometimes more
5. Cooperated and communicated well with members
6. Managed group conflict well
7. Made cognitive contributions
8. Helped establish group goals and identify and assign tasks

Baker includes long and short peer-assessment forms that use these criteria, and her article is an excellent resource.

Specifying how group members effectively contribute to group functioning enlightens individuals at the same time that it enables them to provide each other feedback. That feedback is most useful when there is still time for individuals to modify their behavior. Getting it after the project is completed is better than not getting it at all, but a formative feedback exchange after the group has started working together can keep problems from becoming serious and improve overall group functioning. If students are new to peer-assessment activities, they benefit from having a teacher facilitate their initial exchange of feedback. I have students assess the contributions of every member except themselves. They also answer a couple of open-ended questions that pertain to overall group functioning. I tabulate the scores and deliver the results to students electronically. Then I meet with each group. I open with some commentary about their responses to the open-ended questions. I ask if anyone has a question about the feedback they've received that they'd like to have the group address. And I usually wrap up the discussion with a bit about the value of groups regularly discussing the processes they're using, including how well they are or aren't working together.

It is possible to engage more experienced students in the process of developing the criteria they will use to assess each other's contributions. After they've been given the group project and have had a chance to develop a clear understanding of what it entails, they can be asked to identify what individual group members will need to contribute in order for the group to successfully complete the project. Here, as well, those of us who have tried this approach have not found that students take advantage of the opportunity. For the most part, they generate viable criteria. They can submit their proposed criteria for teacher review and approval, if you're worried. If they then use these criteria in their peer assessment, the assignment can culminate with them reflecting on the appropriateness of those particular criteria.

IMPLEMENTATION ISSUES

Two implementation issues merit a brief revisit, even though both have been raised elsewhere in the chapter. The first has to do with the importance of grades and student motivation to get good ones, whether or not significant learning accompanies the grade. Both are powerful forces, and efforts to focus students on learning often feel futile. Teachers' regular references to the importance of learning aren't always appreciated by students, and they don't seem to make any difference. It takes a lot of tapping on the stone before the piece finally breaks off. Getting the message through takes patience and persistence, and learner-centered teachers believe in the message. They don't give up, and in some classes with some students, the patience and persistence pays off. Students begin to see grades and learning in a better perspective.

The second implementation issue involves the careful and creative design needed if students are to play a part that counts in the assessment process. It's necessary because the emphasis on grades compromises students' objectivity. But it's worth pursuing because when their self- and peer-assessment activities count, students take those activities much more seriously. Letting their assessments count is a great illustration of harnessing the motivation to get grades and moving it in a more productive direction. As several examples in the chapter have shown, there are ways to get students involved, but the activity must be carefully and thoughtfully designed. If students are able to manipulate the assignment or activity to their advantage, then the integrity of the grading process has been compromised, and that's a problem.

In sum, this chapter has explored the final change needed to make teaching more learner-centered. The purpose and processes of evaluation need to change. Teachers grade students for two reasons: to certify the level at which students have mastered the material and because completing work that is graded promotes learning. Grades have become more important than learning to students (and to some teachers). Learner-centered teachers work to better balance grades and learning, the two purposes for evaluation. The processes of evaluation must also change. They should be used to help students develop self- and peer-assessment skills. The chapter offered many examples showing how teachers can focus students on learning and how students can be involved in assessment activities that build their skills. Do these activities compromise the integrity of grading processes? That's the question every teacher must ask when considering a role for students in this very important part of teaching and learning.

Despite what needs to change here—and for many teachers what this chapter proposes may seem like a lot—something very fundamental remains the same. Teachers are still responsible for ensuring that the grades students get are the grades they have earned. This chapter has shown how some teachers meet that responsibility at the same time that they focus on learning and give students opportunities to develop self- and peer-assessment skills.

PART THREE

IMPLEMENTING THE LEARNER-CENTERED APPROACH

CHAPTER EIGHT

RESPONDING TO RESISTANCE

Some faculty find the arguments for learner-centered teaching very convincing. With considerable enthusiasm, they start creating new assignments, developing classroom activities, and realigning course policies. By the time they've completed the planning process, they are just plain excited about launching what feels like a whole new course. They introduce these new course features on the first day, sharing with students their conviction that these changes will make the class so much better. And what happens? Students do not respond with corresponding enthusiasm. In fact, they make it very clear that they prefer having things done as they are in most classes. Teachers leave class disheartened. The student response feels like a personal affront.

And sometimes it isn't just students who object to learner-centered approaches. Colleagues, including some very senior and very experienced teachers, raise their eyebrows, shake their heads, and proceed to tick off a range of concerns. Maybe this way of teaching would work with very bright, very senior students, but who'd risk trying it with beginning students in a required, general education course? Or it's questions about getting the content covered—these active learning activities take a lot of time. Or it's about standards and reiteration of concerns about grade inflation. Or it's the hypothetical scenario of students getting out of control and taking over the class. To those new to learner-centered teaching, colleague concerns coupled with the apparent lack of student enthusiasm can raise serious doubts and challenge the once deeply felt and enthusiastic commitment to this way of teaching.

The resistance of students and colleagues is harder to deal with when it's unexpected. The purpose of this chapter is to prepare you to expect it. Any teacher trying learner-centered approaches should know up front that student and faculty resistance to learner-centered teaching happens regularly. It is a common, typical response, not some dreadful anomaly expressed exclusively by your students, your colleagues, or resulting from your instructional inadequacy.

The second purpose of this chapter is to help you deal with student and colleague resistance. The resistance of each is handled in different sections of the chapter, but the analysis used explores the same three areas for both. First, resistance is more easily answered once it is understood. Why are students and colleagues resisting? What fuels and feeds their objections? Second, how does the resistance manifest itself? What does it look like? What do students and colleagues say and do that indicates they are resisting? And finally, how should teachers respond to the resistance? What should they do? What should they say?

With students, there is good news. There are ways to address their lack of enthusiasm and preference for conventional teaching methods, and they work. Once students have experienced learner-centered approaches, once they understand the educational rationale behind what the teacher is asking them to do, they stop resisting and more than a few start endorsing these ways of teaching and learning. With colleagues, the results are more mixed. Since the first edition of this book, more teachers have tried these approaches, which makes it easier to find supportive colleagues, but as evidence included elsewhere in this edition indicates, most teaching is still not especially learner-centered, and teachers who haven't tried any of these approaches remain doubtful. I think most of us would agree that it's easier to convince students, but when either students or faculty resist, it's good to recognize and understand the response and even better to have some ideas about dealing with it.

Why Do Students Resist?

Student resistance has been studied by researchers and written about by faculty who've experienced it. Despite more literature, my favorite article on the topic remains the same. It's by Felder and Brent (1996) and aptly titled "Navigating the Bumpy Road to Student-Centered Instruction." Besides the copy in my files, I have a second dog-eared and almost completely underlined copy in my first-day folder, which I read once more as I prepare for class. Here's one of many important points made in the article: "It's not that student-centered instruction doesn't work when done correctly—it does, as both the literature and our personal experience . . . richly attest. The problem is that although the promised benefits are real, they are neither immediate nor automatic. The students, whose teachers have been telling them everything they need to know from the first grade on, don't necessarily appreciate having this support suddenly withdrawn" (p. 43).

Student resistance to learner-centered approaches is widely reported in the literature published before and since the first edition. Several accounts detail serious and ongoing student objections that are interesting to read, albeit a bit frightening. Resistance to the extent reported by these authors is not typical. In Noel's case (2004), in his assessment, too many learner-centered approaches were implemented too quickly. Albers (2009) redesigned an honors course that expected students to be more self-directed. They rebelled, much to her surprise. She assumed honors students would be open to learning experiences they could direct. In both of these articles the authors analyze why the learner-centered approaches they tried fostered so much student discontent. It takes courage to publish articles describing teacher attempts that aren't a smashing success. Moreover, they eloquently remind us how much can be learned from mistakes. I wish more of us would write about instructional changes that don't go as planned. There's more about these two fine articles in Chapter Nine, on developmental issues.

The more typical student response to learner-centered approaches involves resistance based on four reasons. The reasons are related and can be cumulative in their effect. It is also important to note that learner-centered approaches aren't the only aspect of instruction known to provoke student resistance. Some resistance to other aspects of instruction also derives from these reasons.

LEARNER-CENTERED APPROACHES REQUIRE MORE WORK

Learner-centered approaches involve more work for the teacher, especially in the design phase, but students resist because learner-centered approaches mean more work for them, and when they first encounter them, students feel they are being asked to do the teacher's work. Say you want your students to have five examples that illustrate a theory in operation. The easiest and most efficient way for students to acquire those examples is to have the teacher list them on a downloadable handout. It is much more difficult for the students to gather with a group of peers and generate examples. Who knows if they're the "right" examples or the ones that will be on the test? This is resistance to the hard work of learning.

And it's resistance for the right reason, from the teacher's perspective (and, we hope, some day from the students' as well). It's proof that learner-centered approaches engage students and get them working on learning tasks. As noted in Chapter Three, when students are generating examples, it's a process that helps them learn the content and it's a process that teaches them how to generate examples. With teacher feedback and guidance, they can learn to generate great ones.

LEARNER-CENTERED APPROACHES ARE THREATENING

Students also resist learner-centered approaches because they are afraid. What happens in most courses—indeed, what has happened throughout most of their education—is the same: teachers tell the students what to do. It's the standard routine and it's what students expect when they begin a new class. They arrive in this course and discover that what they know and find comfortable is being replaced with something new. This teacher has opened Pandora's box and out have popped all sorts of new policies, practices, assignments, and expectations. What are students supposed to do? Who's responsible for what now? What in the world does this teacher want?

These changes frighten different kinds of students. The really good students have been highly successful in the other learning paradigm. They know how that works and what they need to do to get good grades. In this course, the rules are different. Most feel frustrated and angry—they don't want to have to figure out how to play a new game. The students in class who aren't self-confident learners are also frightened. Keeley, Shemberg, Cowell, and Zinnbauer (1995)—who describe resistance to being taught critical-thinking skills and note that similar resistance is likely to occur with other learner-centered approaches—draw their explanation from psychotherapy literature: "Teachers of critical thinking and psychotherapists both *require* individual responsibility and self-direction from their students/clients, who often lack self-confidence. So students/clients must try things they are not yet good at. Relying on oneself rather than the expert is frightening. Becoming a successful critical thinker or client means taking risks and fighting fears of failure and of the unknown" (p. 141).

When fear is what's causing students to resist, the resistance grows out of the students' beliefs about themselves as learners. It's not a case of students objecting to an assignment, policy, or new expectation per se; it's the fear that they won't be able to deliver what they're being asked to do.

LEARNER-CENTERED APPROACHES INVOLVE LOSSES

Kloss (1994), who charts students' resistance to intellectual development, observes that whenever you move from one level of understanding to another, something is lost, something is left behind. "We as teachers need to remember that growth creates a sense of loss in students, the loss of certainty that has sustained them and been a refuge in an increasingly complex and confusing world" (p. 155).

Most of us can recall times on the road to maturity when we finally realized it was up to us—we had to make decisions for ourselves. I remember once speaking to my father about what seemed an especially important and unclear decision. I asked him what I should do. He said he would offer advice and share his opinion, but I would have to choose. I remember crying when I hung up the phone. It was so much easier when Dad just told me what to do.

Learner-centered approaches take students to new levels of responsibility. The ownership for what does and doesn't happen is much more obviously theirs. One of my students wrote in his journal: "In this class your destiny is very much in your own hands. I keep thinking I should like that, but I don't. I miss having things decided for me." Classrooms where teachers make all the decisions are safer, simpler places. Students may understand intellectually that the new approaches foster their personal development, but the feeling of loss is an emotional one that sometimes manifests itself as resistance.

SOME STUDENTS ARE NOT READY FOR SOME LEARNER-CENTERED APPROACHES

Chapter Nine considers the complex issues of development, including how we prepare students for and then push them toward increased responsibility and autonomy. With many students, we are starting close to ground zero. They are very dependent learners. Any number of the activities, assignments, and policies described here and elsewhere in the literature require a level of intellectual maturity that students simply may not possess. We don't start feeding babies solid food before they're ready—if we do, we usually regret it, and so it is with students new to learner-centered teaching. They resist, often telling us they can't do what we're asking. It takes wisdom to discern whether the resistance is to more work, based on fear, about loss, or is a legitimate objection to something the student is not yet prepared to handle. Chapter Nine explores the developmental issues related to learner-centered approaches and suggests activities that are good places to start when students are not intellectually mature learners.

RECOGNIZING RESISTANCE

Sometimes student objections are so obvious they can't be missed, but other times the resistance is expressed in ways that don't necessarily look like objections to learner-centered approaches. For example, my students don't say that they object to a particular assignment. Instead they fixate on the details. They ask question after question, simple questions, ones that strike me as absurd. Usually there are accompanying comments that they've never been asked to do anything like this before.

Kearney and Plax have identified a number of different types of resistance and shown that student resistance to many aspects of instruction is widespread (see the 1992 source, which summarizes several of their studies). They did not study resistance to learner-centered approaches exclusively, but three of the kinds of resistance they identify illustrate what resistance to learner-centered approaches often looks like.

Passive, Nonverbal Resistance

This type of resistance usually presents itself as the overwhelming lack of enthusiasm described earlier in the chapter. I will introduce a short in-class group activity and after I think everybody understands what they need to do, I'll say, "Okay, go ahead and get yourselves into groups. Get together with three or four other people and form a group." I have done this in classes where there has been absolutely no visible response. People just sit there, look at me, look at the clock, look out the window. "I need you to get into groups . . . please circle up your chairs and make sure everybody in the group knows each other." This request might be met with a kind of "minimalist" response. Some students sort of start looking at each other, making tentative nonverbal queries, "Wanna group?" Still, nobody moves any furniture. I now venture out into the class, smiling cheerfully, seemingly unaware and certainly undaunted by this less than enthusiastic response. "Bunch," I say, "Bunch. You folks a group? Well, get your chairs together . . . want me to arrange some for you over here?"

Their message is perfectly clear: "We don't want to get into groups." But no one has spoken this resistance. There is less risk involved when the message is communicated nonverbally. If the teacher directly asks a student, "What's the problem, Fred?" the response can be a verbal denial. "No problem, I'm going with these guys." Passive resistance is a way to object without having to own the responsibility for doing so. It presents teachers with a special challenge because students can maintain that it isn't happening.

Beyond this lack of enthusiasm, passive resistance presents itself in other ways—as excuses, for example. Students don't do what the teacher asks, but rather than saying how they feel, they offer excuses. "I had two tests to study for." "I had to work overtime." Or students may not comply, but pretend that they are complying. They'll get together in the group and chat amicably about everything but the task. Or students may passively resist by refusing to participate. They may be in class fully prepared, but refuse to ask or answer questions. They won't establish eye contact with the teacher. With passive resistance, the objections are made clear behaviorally, as opposed to verbally—the kind of actions that can be denied or explained alternatively if students are directly questioned about them.

PARTIAL COMPLIANCE

If teachers ignore students' passive resistance and appear as if they aren't getting the message, often students will up the ante and resist by doing the task poorly, doing it halfheartedly, or doing it very, very quickly—especially if they think they might get out of class early. Although I'm not sure how insightful students are about why they're doing what they do, the thinking goes something like this: "If we do a really crummy job with this, just barely, barely do what she wants, maybe she'll figure out that this isn't working and won't try it again." It isn't always easy to figure out whether this kind of response is about students who don't have much experience working in groups, don't have good group skills and therefore don't know how to do the task well, or whether it's a form of resistance. Sometimes I think it's a combination of both.

Partial compliance also manifests itself in many ways. Students may come to class prepared, but won't divulge what they do know. They'll mumble three words in response to an intriguing open-ended question. They'll do some of the homework but not all of it. The student may be very bright and capable, but resists by making only minimal effort. Sometimes partial compliance is indicated by the preoccupation with procedural details—endless questions about what "you" want us to do, discussion of alternative approaches, or questions of interpretation. The students comply by focusing on the task; they resist by discussing it to death. However, it's important to consider whether endless discussion of an assignment is a form of resistance or whether the assignment is confusing and unclear. Wise teachers don't make assumptions; they seek more feedback from students.

Open Resistance

The good news about open resistance is that you don't have to wonder whether it's resistance. The message is clear and usually delivered with emotion, sometimes lots of emotion. In the best-case scenario, the disgruntled student stops by during office hours to raise objections. Best-case scenarios aren't what usually happens, and that's the bad news about open resistance. It's voiced in class, delivered when you don't expect it, and conveyed without much finesse. "No other teachers expect us to work like this." "Why do we have to figure out the answer? You know the answer. Why don't you just tell us?" Adult students, paying their own tuition, can be particularly adamant when asked to work with a group of eighteen-year-olds. As one told me in front of the rest of the class, "I don't know a lot about this, but I do know that I don't have time to sit around with a bunch of kids who know less about it than I do." Or the comment one of my colleagues got: "We know why you have us do group work. Those are the days you didn't have time to prepare for class." Or the e-mail received by another colleague: "You need to understand that most students learn best when the teachers lecture. Our class is no exception."

There are very good answers to all these objections, but they don't always come to us the moment after an irate student has articulated an objection that suggests we may not be doing what the student believes teachers ought to do. Being defensive comes pretty naturally in situations like these, but even though the attacks seem personal, they're not. Resistance is based on reasons that have little to do with the teacher, as established in the previous section. Understanding both the reasons for resistance and the manifestations of it prepares us to consider responses. We are looking for answers that help students deal with their resistance.

OVERCOMING RESISTANCE

The best way to respond to resistance is with communication—a free and open exchange between and among everybody involved. I would characterize the needed communication in four ways and propose that resistance is best answered when teachers use all of these communication strategies. It is important to remember that overcoming resistance is not something teachers do for the students, but something they work to help students accomplish for themselves.

COMMUNICATE FREQUENTLY AND EXPLICITLY ABOUT THE RATIONALE FOR LEARNER-CENTERED APPROACHES

Learner-centered teachers explain the educational rationale behind what they are asking students to do. They do not assume that the reasons for or merits of an assignment or activity are obvious to students. Most of us have learned the hard way that they aren't. Typically students don't spend much (if any) time thinking about the rationale behind activities, assignments, or policies. They are more likely focused on grades and other anxieties, like trying to figure out what this teacher wants, not why she wants it.

Moreover, teachers don't regularly explain the rationale behind what they ask students to do and can be taken aback by the lengths to which they must go in learner-centered classrooms. New assignments, unfamiliar activities, and different policies must not only be explained in the rational, objective way teachers usually do, they must also be presented persuasively. Teachers need to make an attempt to "sell" students on the idea—or at least present the good and compelling reasons for an assignment, activity, or policy like this.

Along with efforts to persuade are nondefensive attempts to justify learner-centered approaches. "We both want the same thing: a course that is worth all that you've paid for it. My goal is to offer a course that promotes learning—lots of learning, deep learning, the kind we equate with understanding. And I want you to become sophisticated learners." "Yes, you are right. What I'm asking is more work for students. It would be easier if I just gave you examples, but how does that prepare you for the future, when I won't be there and you need examples?"

Closely related are messages that defend the approach, coolly and calmly delivered. "You know, I'm not terribly interested in whether you like this course, this assignment, or this activity. I care about how this course and what I'm asking you to do affects your efforts to learn. Are you learning this material?" "No, I'm not letting you form your own groups. In most professional contexts, we don't get to pick the people we work with. We are assigned to teams, groups, and committees and expected to work productively with people we don't know and sometimes we don't even like." Whether it's persuading, justifying, or defending, the messages are all about making the reasons why clear.

But alas, perhaps you've noted that I've just offered another example of teaching as telling. I know I did tell them when I first tried to get students to understand the rationale. Later on I started asking, rather than telling, and student responses were less insightful than I expected: "Why do you think a teacher would ask students to grade their own participation?" "Because you don't want us to blame you for bad grades." "Because you have to grade too many things and need help." "Because you like us and want to give us some control." "Because it's an interesting thing to do with participation." I was perplexed—should I revert to telling them the reasons? Most of the time I didn't. I went to the dark side instead and offered a few bonus points to anyone who could come up with the reasons. The rationale behind what we have students do remains a mystery unless we challenge them to explore and sort through the reasons.

COMMUNICATE MESSAGES THAT ENCOURAGE AND POSITIVELY REINFORCE

In my experience, resistance that arises from the fact that learner-centered approaches require more work is the easiest for students to overcome. If they stop and think about it, students can see the logic—in being able to figure out what's important in the reading, what's likely to be on the test, which examples illustrate the theory, or why they need to solve the problems. They are more quickly convinced if their repeated complaints don't prompt the teacher to tell them what they need to know. The more tenacious resistance rests on anxiety and fear, the discomfort of being asked to do new things and old things differently.

As facilitators of learning, teachers are on the side of students and can offer welcome encouragement and support. "I know this is pushing you, but I wouldn't be asking if I didn't think you could handle the assignment. You can figure it out." "Feeling frustrated and making mistakes are important parts of the learning process. See what you can learn from them."

Along with these encouraging messages, you need to give positive reinforcement when it's deserved. It's not deserved when it dishonestly praises behavior, actions, or contributions that don't merit commendation. It is deserved even when what worked, went right, or meets high standards is a small part of the total project. In fact, it is needed more in those circumstances where much of the feedback has to be negative.

To convince students and help them overcome the resistance they feel, teacher encouragement needs to rest on a firm and absolute belief in students' abilities to learn, to figure things out, and to develop into mature, autonomous learners. True, not all students will meet the challenge. In learner-centered classrooms, students still screw up, fail, and otherwise let us down. But that reality should not shake our faith in the ability of most students to learn well when we use these approaches. It is much easier to offer the kind of encouragement and support students need when you really and truly believe that these approaches help them become better learners.

SOLICIT STUDENT FEEDBACK ON THEIR LEARNING EXPERIENCES REGULARLY

Resistance is overcome when students are given opportunities to talk about it. Let them raise questions and voice concerns when a new assignment is given. Answer their questions calmly and thoroughly. As work on a project gets underway, ask students to talk about how it's going, whether through an online exchange or in class. If they need to vent, let them do so. Then refocus the discussion on what can be done about these frustrations. Are there changes that can be made at this time that might make the project a more profitable learning experience? Some of their suggestions may not be implementable, but their ideas merit our consideration.

Finally, after the project, activity, or assignment is completed, schedule debrief discussions. These benefit students and teachers. I recommend having these discussions right at the conclusion of the work, rather than waiting until the end of the course. The experiences are fresh in everyone's mind, and students are more motivated to talk at this point than later. The feedback may be written—if it is, open-ended questions reveal more than questions that ask students to rate experiences. What worked well? What needs to be changed?

I prefer having these kinds of debrief discussions in class. They're an opportunity for students to practice delivering assessment feedback (advocated at length in Chapter Seven), and they're part of building ownership for what happens in class. Everybody in class shared the experience, so let's talk about how it affected efforts to learn the content and what we learned about learning processes by working this way. To add substance to the discussion, you might task a group of students with evaluating the project. They might create and conduct a survey or interview classmates. Their presentation of the results is what starts the whole class discussion. Talking about their experiences with a project does much to diminish resistance to subsequent assignments and activities.

These conversations not only benefit students, they are of value to teachers as well. They are difficult only if you go into them assuming that you've designed a near-perfect learning experience. It's better to think of any learner-centered approach as a work in progress, one that you expect will evolve and change over time and in response to student feedback. You also need to be prepared to deal with feedback not always delivered constructively. As discussed in several different places now, learning to provide useful feedback is a skill that develops with practice. It's also good to have thought about how you will respond to suggestions that you can't implement—ones that compromise the learning objectives of the activity, for example. If you decide not to make a change that students propose, they appreciate knowing why. Conversely, you want to have these conversations expecting to hear some really good ideas, and chances are you will.

When teachers respond positively to student feedback, when they make changes, it motivates students in several ways. First, it encourages them to offer more feedback. Second, it increases their sense of responsibility for what happens in class. Soliciting and using their input provides concrete evidence that the teacher is letting students have a say in the way important things in class will happen. Now they, too, have a vested interest in the success of what's being tried. And finally, the opportunity to think about the design and redesign of learning experiences begins to prepare students for the time when they will design their own learning experiences.

RESIST THEIR RESISTANCE

Unhappy, whining, complaining students can easily get on a teacher's nerves. Consciously or unconsciously, that's part of the students' plan—wear the teacher down and watch her back down. And if she does, they have discovered that resistance works, so you can expect it to increase. Resistance diminishes when you resist it and soften your firm response with the communication strategies proposed in this section.

If a new assignment, activity, or policy isn't going as planned and is generating lots of complaints, it's tempting to give in to students. However, if you want to help them get over their resistance, you need to stick with the plan. That doesn't mean you can't make modifications or other modest changes. Backing down happens when the learner-centered features of what you're having students do are compromised—when they don't have to figure out the answers, work together in groups, provide each other feedback, make decisions about what they're supposed to do, and the like.

You may want to back down, having already decided this is one activity you won't be using ever again, but once it's been launched in a class, there is merit in staying the course and proceeding with confidence. You don't need to pretend that everything's working well when it isn't, but your confidence rests on the theory and research that support the effectiveness of learner-centered approaches and in your ability to help students "fix" or at least make better those aspects of the assignment, activity, or policy that they are finding frustrating or difficult.

Given the reality of student resistance, I don't think you can try learner-centered approaches halfheartedly. You can't be tentative about what you're doing. That only adds fuel to the resistance fire. You may feel like retreating, returning to a safer, saner way of teaching, but when you're working with students all they should see is your unwavering commitment to learner-centered goals. They get a sense of that determination and they back down.

As you experience and deal with student resistance, know that you are not alone. It has been the response in many classrooms, and most of us have also seen the resistance diminish— sometimes it completely disappears. And you will be pleased by what replaces it. Just as those of us committed to learner-centered approaches cannot return to how we taught before, students also find that they no longer want to learn as they once did. They chafe in classes where there are no choices, no focus on learning, no responsibility or autonomy. I remember one day when I was giving (what seemed to me) a short lecture. I could see students looking at each other. Then a hand went up tentatively. "Dr. Weimer, we have a lot of work to do in our groups, and isn't what you're telling us covered in the reading?" I was a bit offended—I thought I was adding new insights. What I should have been feeling was thrilled.

Faculty Resistance

Unfortunately, the chapter can't end on this high note. Some colleagues and administrators question these approaches, and their resistance is not as easily dissipated by open communication. As with students, the place to begin is by analyzing the bases of their resistance. On what grounds do they object? With these understood, ways of dealing with their resistance can be explored.

Sources of Faculty Resistance

Some colleagues resist because they find these approaches very threatening. Learner-centered teaching tests a teacher's mettle on several different levels. It deals with issues of power and authority. It takes away exclusive reliance on content expertise. It moves teachers into the unfamiliar domain of learning skills instruction. It raises questions about widely used instructional practices. As with students, developmental issues explain some faculty resistance. Not all teachers are ready for these approaches—some likely never will be.

However, you can be sure that when colleagues state the reasons for their objections to learner-centered approaches, they won't be telling you it's because they find them threatening or otherwise personally disconcerting. Virtually no self-respecting academic would admit to such an emotional, potentially irrational reason. You'll have to figure that out for yourself. Is this colleague resisting learner-centered ideas, or is she resisting because learner-centered approaches involve risks she's not yet willing to take.

Other colleagues resist for more objective reasons. They are concerned about what these approaches might do: potentially diminish the amount of content in courses, let students set course policies, devote class time to learning skills development, decrease the number of rules and requirements, and give students a role in self- and peer-assessment activities. For lots of faculty, these are pretty radical ideas, and they do raise lots of legitimate questions. As with students, this is resistance for the right reasons. These colleagues are asking questions that have answers, and their asking provides the opportunity to inform and possibly persuade others of the merits of learner-centered teaching.

DEALING WITH FACULTY RESISTANCE

Responding to the resistance of colleagues begins with being prepared—knowing something about the theoretical, empirical, and experiential knowledge bases on which these ideas about teaching and learning rest. The questions asked by those who resist can be answered, and there is much elsewhere in the book relevant to the objections regularly raised. If the resistance is based on fear, then arguments, good reasons, and evidence still may not carry the day. In those situations, you make the best case you can, leave it there, and keep backup strategies like these in mind.

Be Mindful of the Politics. Faculty can be very idealistic. Once convinced that they have truth on their side, they have been known to sally forth with the commitment of a crusader. If you're old, tenured, and energized by conflict, go forth and do battle with those who resist. But if you're not, don't ignore the political realities of your situation. If you don't get tenure, you won't be a learner-centered teacher at this institution. If you end up on the outs with your department chair, your merit raise (assuming such things still exist) might be even more disappointing than expected. Academic freedom is a wonderful thing, but we still live, work, and must survive in very political organizations.

Don't Try to Convert the Masses. This is kind of a second verse to being mindful of the politics. Those of us strongly committed to learner-centered approaches will be the first to tell you that we need many more faculty teaching like this. The pace of change is frustratingly slow. But pursuing others' teaching approaches with missionary zeal is not recommended. It regularly makes nonbelievers even more resistant and puts the missionary in harm's way. The principle we recognize with students finds application here: you cannot learn anything for students. Likewise, you cannot improve anybody else's teaching. They must be ready to do it themselves.

It is nice to have some company when we embark on a new way of doing things. The presence of others helps vindicate the decision to make these changes. However, sometimes the need to have others do as we do derives from lingering questions and self-doubt. Examine your motives for wanting to get others adopting these approaches. Learner-centered approaches are not "right" because lots of people are using them; they are "right" because they are grounded on empirical, theoretical, and experiential evidence. So don't seek the company of others for the wrong reason. Trying to convert them takes time away from the efforts needed to use learner-centered approaches effectively.

Use the Autonomy of Your Classroom. The autonomy of our classrooms isn't always beneficial, but it is in this case. What you do in your classroom is pretty much your own business. Even if the climate at your institution is not pro-learner-centered teaching, no one is likely to stop you from trying some of these approaches. You don't need to post a sign on your door announcing what you're doing. Just do it. I'm not suggesting being dishonest, but there's also no need for global announcements, especially if those in your world question changing your teaching in these ways.

Document the Impact of Your Approaches. Evidence persuades colleagues and administrators better than preaching. Don't tell them about what these approaches are accomplishing; collect evidence that demonstrates it. And here I am not referring to end-of-course rating data. Most institutions are still using forms that assume didactic, teacher-centered instruction. They contain irrelevant items, and they don't contain others about which feedback should be collected. Many institutions mandate the use of a particular form, so instructors can't opt to replace it with something else. If this is the case, then it is even more essential that teachers collect data that document the impact of these approaches.

That documentation might include samples of student work, including completed exams, papers, and projects. A collection of work from an individual student can be used to show progress. Documentation might also include surveys asking students to report on how the learner-centered aspects of the course affected their efforts to learn. It might be a study that compares student performance in learner-centered sections with the performance of others in sections that are more teacher-centered.

It's important to remember that documenting the impact of new approaches matters for two reasons. The discussion here focuses on collecting evidence that can be used to answer the resistance of colleagues—to satisfy others (including administrators) that this is a legitimate and effective way of teaching. That may or may not be the kind of data teachers need in order to understand the impact of a particular activity, assignment, or approach. When the agenda is further evolution of an assignment, activity, or other kind of learning experience, teachers benefit most from detailed, specific, and descriptive feedback from students. Decisions about what kind of data to collect should be governed by why the data are being collected.

Find Like-Minded Colleagues. Maybe no one else in your department is trying these approaches, but chances are very good that you're not the only one at your institution using them. And beyond your institution, there are many faculty experimenting with the kind of instructional strategies described here. They may not always call what they're doing learner-centered, but they are using strategies more focused on learning, and most are only too happy to discuss what they are doing and how it's working.

There is so much that can be learned from and with colleagues, and they don't have to be colleagues in your discipline. There are discipline-specific content issues, indeed, but there are also many aspects of learner-centered teaching that transcend disciplines. Resistance is one of them. Colleagues in other departments might have the perspective needed to help with resistance from departmental colleagues. They might have ideas about collecting data to document the impact. There are all sorts of reasons to look for like-minded colleagues wherever they may be found.

In conclusion, it's helpful to think about resistance positively. What can be learned when students or colleagues resist? The objections raised by others challenge us to keep looking at what we are doing and asking why. Resistance can be the force that motivates us to continue exploring the theory and research, learning more about what it means to be learner-centered and why teaching that way changes student learning experiences. We can learn how to respond effectively to student resistance. Most of us see it fade as students get used to learner-centered approaches— often it's gone well before that of our colleagues. Once students are on board, they won't let you go back. They will keep you moving forward, leaving the objections and resistance of colleagues whirling behind in a cloud of dust.

CHAPTER NINE

TAKING A DEVELOPMENTAL APPROACH

Developmental issues are not front and center in faculty thinking about students, learning, or instruction. Teachers know that eighteen- to twenty-two-year-old students "grow up" and otherwise mature in college. They also know that educational experiences help students in all age cohorts develop intellectually, but how the development occurs, what processes are involved, and how teachers can constructively intervene are not thought about very much or very specifically. As a result, most faculty have students do pretty much the same kind of activities and assignments, be they beginning students or seniors. They expect seniors to do more work and do it better, but much of what seniors do isn't all that different from what they did in their first college classes. In the early 1990s Erickson and Strommer (1991; revised and expanded edition, Erickson, Peters, and Strommer, 2006) authored an excellent book titled *Teaching College Freshmen,* which addressed the developmental issues that pertain to eighteen-year-old college students. I thought the book ought to be the first in a series that included volumes on teaching sophomores, then juniors, finally seniors, and maybe even graduate students. Faculty should be aware of developmental changes students are experiencing and how events in the classroom contribute to those processes.

Along with these more general maturation and intellectual development processes are issues unique to the transformation of dependent, passive, often not very confident students to motivated, autonomous, and self-regulating learners. Some is known about how students develop as learners, but the impact of particular instructional approaches, activities, and assignments on that development has not been studied as extensively as it needs to be. Much of what is suggested in this chapter derives from the observations and experiences of those of us who've tried to intervene in ways that promote the development of self-directed learners.

The chapter begins with what is known about how students develop as learners. Building on that knowledge, it explores how learning experiences can be designed to promote the development of learning skills and the overall growth of students as autonomous, self-directed learners. Curricula can also be designed to be learner-centered. Not very many have been, but if the learner-centered agenda is to advance beyond individual classroom experiences, then we must consider how learning experiences might be linked in courses that are sequenced. Developmental issues are relevant not only to students, but also to teachers. The chapter concludes with a discussion of those issues and teachers' responses to them.

THE DEVELOPMENTAL PROCESS: WHAT WE KNOW

We can start with some fundamentals. Those of us who have tried to move students in the direction of autonomy and self-regulation can tell you four things about the process. It's not automatic, it doesn't happen at a predictable pace, it's not linear, and it doesn't happen quickly. It's very difficult (maybe close to impossible) for students to become independent learners when someone else is making all the learning decisions for them. This makes giving students the opportunity to exercise some control a necessary but insufficient part of the process. Providing the opportunity does not guarantee movement in the desired direction. Despite being in conditions that cultivate autonomy and self-direction, some students remain very dependent learners.

Students do not become independent learners at a predictable pace. Sometimes progress is slow and steady, sometimes there's a growth spurt, and sometimes there's no sign of movement. These variable rates of growth can be seen in individual students as well as in the class as a collective entity. These growth rates are no doubt influenced by other maturation and intellectual development processes—in other words, everything else that is going on in the student's life. Teachers don't have much control over that, but growth rates are also influenced by something teachers do control, and that's the sequence of activities and assignments in the course.

The fact that students sometimes lurch forward and then fall back means they do not make linear progress in their development as learners. They can be experiencing a variety of learner-centered activities without any apparent impact, and then suddenly one day the light goes on—they get it and are way ahead of where they were the day before. However, the opposite is also true. If they make a bad learning decision and experience the consequences, or if an assignment pushes them beyond their comfort zone, they can quickly regress. They go back to asking the teacher to make their learning decisions. They want to be told what to do, and they want assignments they know how to do. Fortunately, for most students, these steps back are temporary.

Finally, most students grow to independence slowly. They become autonomous, self-regulating learners over time. Can they be transformed in one course? Generally not. In fact, sometimes the progress seems so minimal that it's discouraging. At those times it's important to remember that the influence of a teacher and experiences in a course don't stop affecting students when the course ends. Since the 2002 edition of this book, empirical evidence has arisen to support the long-term impact of learner-centered experiences. The Derting and Ebert-May (2010) study highlighted in Chapter Two used a robust empirical design to ascertain the effects of two learner-centered, inquiry-based courses taken by students early in their biology curriculum. As seniors, those students had high-level profiles on the Views about Science Survey for Biology (which indicates student understanding of biology as a process of inquiry) and higher scores on the standardized Biology Field Test than seniors who hadn't taken these two courses.

Learner-centered environments do change the majority of students, but they don't do so quickly, at the same pace, or consistently in the desired direction. Still, there is enough consistency in the ways students change to lead to the generation of a model.

Grow (1991) proposes a set of stages from dependence to self-direction. He describes this process "not as a definitive thing, but as another statement in the ongoing conversation of those who encourage self-directed, lifelong learning" (p. 147). Unfortunately, this "conversation" hasn't resulted in publication of other models or in research verifying this particular progression. Even so, Grow's model is widely referenced, attesting to its sensibility as a description of the stages through which learners progress. He observes: "A theory doesn't have to be right to be useful. Nearly every action we take results from a workable convergence of misconceptions" (p. 127).

Grow describes four points on the continuum between dependent and independent learning. In the first stage, students are *dependent* and not self-directed. He explains that they "need an authority figure to give them explicit directions on what to do, how to do it, and when" (1991, p. 129). To help them begin moving forward, Grow recommends that teachers "coach" these students. They should be kept "busy learning specific, identifiable skills. Set standards beyond what students think they can do, then do whatever is necessary to get them to succeed" (1991, p. 130).

At the next stage, students are *interested* and moderately self-directed. They are ready to begin setting goals for themselves. Their confidence and learning skills can be built by teachers who are enthusiastic about learning. Often students internalize their teacher's enthusiasm and find their own motivation by the time they have moved through this stage.

In the third stage, students are *involved* and at intermediate levels of self-direction. They begin to see themselves as participants in their own education. They want to know how they learn, and they begin applying and adapting generic learning strategies to their efforts to learn. At this stage students are more open to learning from and with others. Teachers should now function as co- or joint participants in the decision-making processes about learning. Students should regularly provide progress reports on their work so that teachers can offer advice and guide students in their decision making about learning.

Finally, students reach a level where they are *self-directed*. They can set their own goals and establish the standards their work must meet. Grow (1991, p. 135) explains that teachers at this level do "not teach subject matter but . . . cultivate the student's ability to learn." Teachers consult with students over the criteria, timelines, lists of potential resources, and possible collaborators. "A Stage 4 teacher might set a challenge, then leave the learner largely alone to carry it out, intervening only when asked to help—and then not help meet the challenge, but instead empower the learner to meet the challenge" (p. 136).

The stages proposed by Grow provide a useful framework, a place to begin exploring the developmental issues associated with encouraging independent, self-directed learners. But more work in this area is needed. Without it, we can suggest how teachers might intervene in the process, but we can't say with certainty when it's best to intervene, what assignments or activities should be used given the learner's stage of development, or what interventions effectively move stuck learners forward. Some of us have figured out ways to intervene that seem to work for our students and with the content we teach. Our examples are offered in the next section. Others may use them as starting places in their own exploration.

DEVELOPMENTAL DESIGN FOR ASSIGNMENTS AND ACTIVITIES

It makes sense that students' experiences with learning activities affect both their development as independent learners and their acquisition of learning skills. The question is how assignments and activities can be designed in ways that support the development of these goals. Two different design processes—one I'm calling progressive design and the other targeted learning skill development—offer a couple of possible answers.

PROGRESSIVE DESIGN

In progressive design, the students do the same activity or assignment more than once, often repeatedly, as in the case of reading quizzes. Those learning experiences can be exactly the same with only the content changing, or they can be designed so that each iteration emphasizes different learning skills along with new and potentially more challenging content. Let me use a straightforward example to illustrate.

In many disciplines (biology is a good example) where the content is categorized and characterized, matrices effectively summarize differences and similarities. Imagine a matrix that shows defining characteristics across one axis and categories on the other. Specific examples fit the cells where the characteristics and categories intersect. Sophisticated learners will see the value of a device like this for organizing content and will learn how to construct such tools on their own.

Dependent learners with less sophisticated learning skills can be taught how to construct a matrix incrementally, across a series of different activities, all of which involve matrices. You can start by giving students a matrix with the categories and characteristics included, but the cells empty. You might use it as a device to summarize content at the end of a period, filling in the cells with students' help, making the completed version available to them, and pointing out how efficiently it reviews and distills content. Next, give students a matrix with empty cells, only this time they complete it on their own during that summary time. Collect and share several matrices at the beginning of the next period to review the content and use the process, working with students, to construct a "correct one." This activity might be followed with one where half the class has a matrix with categories but no characteristics, and the other half one with characteristics but no categories. Have students work with partners to complete their half of the matrix and then have them join a pair with the other half and finish the matrix together.

At some point, students start working to complete matrices using text material instead of content being presented in class. They might be ready now for a matrix with the cells filled in but without any categories or characterizations. By this time students should be ready to start creating matrices on their own. Let that work begin in groups, and have the groups share their work with other groups. About this time as well, creating matrices might be part of a graded homework assignment or a quiz. If work involving creating or otherwise using matrices ends up on an exam, it further reinforces their value and importance.

An example like this illustrates the fundamental features of this progressive design process and models how activities and assignments can be sequenced so that each subsequent experience further develops the learning skill or focuses on a different part of it. All sorts of activities and assignments can be progressively sequenced in this way. Creation and use of concept maps is another good example—even a sequence of group activities can be designed with tasks that become more challenging and group processes requiring more group decision-making and responsibility. When you stop and think about it, the only benefit of replicating the same assignment is the opportunity it provides for practice.

Many of us do something similar when we partition assignments, say a large paper or semester-long group project. We break the larger task into its various components and sequence them along a timeline. A lot of us opted for this approach with papers because we couldn't stand to read another set written the night before they were due. Doing so improves the quality of the papers, and it models a progressive process for students. By the end of a college career, when learning skills are more advanced, one would hope students would be able to do this partitioning and sequencing for themselves. In capstone courses with final projects, preparation of documents that describe the planning process ought to be part of the assignment.

I do need to caution that the design task involved in creating a sequence of assignments that builds content knowledge, develops learning skills, and promotes autonomy is not always as easy as the matrix example makes it look. I learned this the hard way with my learning log assignment. As I initially conceived it, I imagined a very open-ended writing task that would allow students to respond to course content in whatever way was interesting and relevant to them. They could write a log entry about what happened in class, about text content relevant to the topic, or about examples from home, at work, or with their friends where they observed what we were talking about—I couldn't believe what a wonderfully open and freeing assignment I was giving them. The students didn't see it that way at all. Almost immediately, during class, after class, and in my office I started getting the question, "I don't know what you want in these log entries. What should I be writing about?" I went through my spiel again about this being an opportunity to take the content to a place of interest and personal relevance. I must have explained the goals of the assignment ten different ways. I wanted what they wanted, but the confusion, questions, and a general, classwide angst about the assignment continued.

I persevered, but the following semester I decided to take care of the problem, and my solution appears in Appendix One. If students didn't know what they should write about, well then, by golly, I'll tell them. Each log entry has a series of prompts, and students will write a paragraph that responds to each. Problem solved—no more complaints—but also no development of application skills, thinking about course content and personally applying it, and no student control over or decision making about the content of their entries (beyond deciding whether or not they'd write a given entry). Essentially my solution sacrificed almost everything that made the assignment learner-centered.

Over the next several semesters I worked to redesign the assignment so that in the process of writing entries students learned how to apply course content. I started out with prompts that told students exactly what to do. Then I wrote entries with multiple prompts and had students select the three they would write about. Then I wrote a series of prompts and gave students the option of revising them before responding. Then I identified general topic areas and had students write their own prompts. And finally the entries were blank pages. Students generated their prompts and responded to them. And when they arrived at that point, any number of students were happily reporting how much they liked being able to write and respond to their own prompts.

Successful progressive design depends on being able to look at an assignment that happens multiple times and figure out a viable sequence of experiences that develop specific skills and an overall progression that leads students in the direction of autonomy and self-regulation. It helps to think of this as an evolutionary task with the features of the assignment or activity being refined as their impact on student learning is observed and feedback from them is solicited.

Targeted Learning Skill Development

Beyond designing and sequencing individual assignments and activities so that they more systematically develop learning skills, learner-centered teachers also think about how all the activities and assignments in a course relate to each other. Too often students experience assignments and activities as isolated, unrelated events because basically that's what they are. We have students do different things as a way of keeping their interest (and ours), not because we have planned for those different learning experiences to work together to accomplish learning goals. By now this refrain is familiar (maybe too familiar): we are not the careful instructional designers we need to be.

Again, a simple, straightforward example illustrates how a collection of assignments and activities can in a more planned and systematic way develop learning skills. Let's use a fairly typical assignment set: three objective exams, two papers, and regular online quizzes that cover the assigned reading and participation in class. These assignments do develop content knowledge, but that isn't addressed here because content expertise is necessary for that discussion. This collection of assignments can also be used to develop learning skills. Potential skills to develop might include self-reflection (developing self-assessment skills), furthering critical-thinking skills, improving reading skills, cultivating more responsibility for what happens in class—it could be any number of skills. What it should not be is a large amorphous collection of skills that students will develop in some undifferentiated way, provided all goes well in the course. One course and one teacher cannot develop every learning skill that independent learners need. It's better to target skills, and the best ones to target are those essential to mastering the material in the course.

Let's say we decide to target the skill of self-reflection—specifically, we want students to be able to critically evaluate their preparation processes and to accurately assess the quality of their work. Both of these are big goals, and they describe skills most students do not have. Exhibit 9.1 contains a collection of activities that use this assignment collection to start the development of self-assessment skills, meaning with this assignment set we work toward achieving those goals, but usually stop short of accomplishing them.

Yes, these activities target skill development, not content acquisition. You are using content to develop skills, and time devoted to these activities is not time being used to cover content. Chapter Five contains the justification for doing so. Yes, these

Exhibit 9.1. Activities Within an Assignment Set That Develops Self-Reflection Skills

Exam Preparation

- Students prepare a study game plan that includes a timeline and the description of the study methods they plan to use. They attach it to their completed exam.
- Game plans are discussed by the teacher and students during the exam debrief. Were they followed? Which study methods worked? Which ones didn't work? Students write a quick analysis of their study game plan, which they must submit when they turn their exam back in if they want their exam score recorded.
- Game plan analyses are returned shortly before the next exam, and students use them to prepare a study game plan for the next exam.

Paper Critiques

- Students identify their paper's thesis statement (underlining works fine).
- Students put a star beside what they think is the best paragraph in the paper.
- Students identify the paragraph that they had the most trouble writing.
- At the end of the paper, students ask the teacher for feedback on some specific aspect of the paper.
- To have their grade recorded or in order to learn their grade, students respond to the teacher's feedback with a memo that identifies two or three areas targeted for improvement in the next paper. These targeted areas are listed at the top of the next paper.
- The teacher prepares a one-page handout using some of Nilson's (2003) peer-review prompts (see Chapter Seven for more details). Students partner, exchange drafts, and respond first in writing and then verbally to the prompts on the handout.

(Continued)

Exhibit 9.1. (*Continued*)

Quizzes

- Students complete a quick survey that asks about reading strategies: When are you reading? How much time are you spending? How do you interact with the text (underline, write notes in the margin, use class notes while doing the reading, or talk about the reading with a classmate)? The teacher tallies and discusses results with students, focusing on two or three concrete strategies that might improve quiz scores.
- Students who do well on the quizzes are asked to recommend reading strategies to other students.
- Students are given an opportunity to submit possible quiz questions (see Chapter Seven for more ideas on students writing exam questions).

Participation

- To prepare for a class discussion that explores participation as it is occurring in the class, students send the teacher an e-mail answering questions like these:

   List two or three things you've contributed to class over the past several weeks.

   Identify a comment made by another student in class that you remember, that helped you understand, or a question asked by another student that you wanted to have answered.

   Offer the teacher some suggestions that would increase the effectiveness of participation in this class.

   What could you do differently that would improve participation in this class?

- Discuss participation while it is occurring in the class. Use the feedback provided earlier. Conclude with two or three specific things that the class and the teacher will try to do to increase the effectiveness of in-class exchanges.
- The teacher regularly refers to comments and questions contributed by students in this class and previous classes, using them to illustrate the kind of student comments and questions that make participation valuable.

activities mean more work for the teacher. But as any number of the chapters explain, learning skills do not develop well without explicit instruction, and the workload can be designed so that it is manageable. Many of these activities produce work that need not be graded or work that can be responded to with quick and easy assessments.

Progressive design and targeted skill development as I've described them here are infrequent topics in the pedagogical literature. Their absence illustrates the chapter's opening assertion. The development of students as learners and the design of curricular experiences that contribute to that process are not often thought about by faculty. However, I'd like to mention a couple of exceptions. Even though their content is discipline-specific, they model the value and usefulness of this kind of pedagogical scholarship. As Buchler (2009) writes about developing the quantitative skills of math-averse political science students, "the primary obstacle to teaching quantitative methodology to math-phobic students is that they have never been taught how to learn math" (p. 527). His article identifies five misconceptions that political science students have about learning math (and these misconceptions aren't held exclusively by political science students). He then offers advice and strategies that teachers can use to disabuse students of these misunderstandings. It's an incredibly useful article that targets development of a particular skill with a progression of different activities.

Fitzgerald and Baird (2011), also political scientists, propose that teaching critical thinking is the most important job of teachers in this field. Many teachers in other fields would agree. Their article describes a set of assignments that involve four kinds of critical-thinking activities. What they propose is a bit discipline specific and not useful across fields, but one of the points made in their article is: "We propose that when faculty instructors develop effective activities for students, they make these plans widely available to their colleagues" (p. 619). Technology makes this a viable option, and any number of disciplines support websites that contain miscellaneous teaching resources. That's a start, but these instructors are calling for assignment collections that target the development of particular skills. Is there a discipline that wouldn't benefit from assignment collections that focus on the development of skills important to the discipline? This particular article also illustrates that these carefully designed, implemented, and assessed assignment collections are scholarly, intellectually challenging work. This should be scholarship that counts.

In sum, activities and assignments can be designed to advance the development of students as self-directed and self-regulating learners. Doing so means that their development results less from accident and more from purposeful planning. The challenge for learner-centered teachers is discovering how to successfully intervene in the process with carefully designed and sequenced learning experiences. In this section, we have explored the possibility of doing so with progressively designed activities and assignments, and targeted skill development.

DEVELOPMENTAL CURRICULAR DESIGN

Something else that hasn't changed much since the first edition of this book: most students are still experiencing learner-centered teaching one course at a time. When change occurs at the individual course level, students have learner-centered experiences by chance. They may have one learner-centered course, several, or none at all in their college experience. Evidence has been cited previously that one course can make a difference (Derting and Ebert-May, 2010), but there is little question that the impact would be considerably greater if students had more than one such course, and greater still if those courses were designed as a developmental sequence.

One area of change is worth noting: learning communities that link courses. A variety of learning community models are in use, and most of them involve courses that are connected by content and learning experiences. Students take a political science and composition course, and paper topics used in the composition course involve the political science content. However, there is not much in the literature suggesting that the learning experiences in these courses are purposefully designed to develop autonomous, self-regulated learning skills. If you're interested in determining how learner-centered a collection of courses, curriculum, or program is—or even how learner-centered your institution might be—Blumberg and Pontiggia (2011) have developed rubrics on twenty-nine components drawn from the five key changes identified in this book. They apply these rubrics to a curriculum to illustrate their use.

Two books published since the first edition begin to explore what it means to institutionalize learner-centered experiences. The first, *Leading the Learner-Centered Campus: An Administrator's Framework for Improving Student Learning Outcomes* (Harris and Cullen, 2010), discusses the kind of academic leadership necessary for the development of curricula focused on students as learners and the kind of institutional climate that motivates and rewards faculty innovation in this area. The second focuses on curricular development (Cullen, Harris, and Reinhold, 2012). It outlines the characteristics of learner-centered curricula, talks about developmental sequencing across courses, and, best of all, includes sample curricula. For faculty and academic leaders interested in learner-centered approaches being used in more than a few courses scattered across the curriculum, these resources contain much useful content.

GOOD PLACES TO BEGIN

I am frequently asked in workshops about good places to begin—which strategies work best when students have little or no learner-centered experiences and when teachers don't regularly use these approaches. Before the specific suggestions, let me make several recommendations about first attempts to implement learner-centered approaches.

Begin with an activity or assignment where the chance of success is high. Partly this is for the teacher's sake. If you try a learner-centered approach and it doesn't go very well, the motivation to try another one decreases. If you try something and it works well, that increases the motivation of the teacher and the students. So this decision is partly for the students' sake as well. When students participate in an activity or complete an assignment that represents a new kind of learning experience and they don't experience a sense of success and well-being, that's the match that lights the dry tinder called resistance.

For teachers, this also means beginning with an activity that feels comfortable—something you can see yourself doing successfully and something that fits your content and how you teach. For more experienced teachers, it's good to use some approaches that you've never tried before and that carry uncertain results. We need growth opportunities that stretch and pull us, just not at the beginning. It's best to start with something you can execute with poise and confidence.

If you need to find out whether learner-centered approaches work with your content and your students, start modestly. Despite the research evidence and the experiences of others who've found these approaches convincing, there's always that nagging question of whether they will work when I use them. The best advice in this case is to try out a couple—maybe even just one— and see how it or they work. Limiting the number makes it easier to give these new approaches your full, undivided attention, which also increases the chance they'll be successful. If you don't want to risk using a group exam, try group testing on a quiz. If you are worried about the kind of policy your students will propose, let them work on one, give them three possible versions and have them select one, or let them propose a policy subject to your approval. If letting students select assignments seems a bit much, have them make choices between several assignment options or between different versions of the same assignment. In other words, if you have doubts, hedge your bets. I have no qualms about this recommendation. The literature is replete with examples of small learner-centered changes that made enough of a difference to convert the doubters.

Balance student needs against your own. Many of the learner-centered assignments and activities described elsewhere in the book have students participating in new and different learning experiences—things they haven't done before, things that involve decision making, things that they are used to letting teachers do. It is important to consider how many of these new options students can handle in the beginning.

This recommendation continues my ongoing concern about teachers having conversion experiences, be it in a workshop or from reading a book. They see the light and are ready to light up their entire instructional world. They feel like changing everything and decide to start by changing many things. I wish I could require everyone who feels this way to read two articles that describe very unsuccessful experiences in which faculty implemented more learner-centered approaches than their students were ready to handle.

Noel (2004) writes of his experiences as a new Ph.D. teaching an MBA course not highly regarded by students and that he had not taught previously. "At the beginning of the module, I was excited and confident. At the end, I was exhausted and confused" (p. 188). The article describes what happened in-between, and it isn't pretty. He lists three erroneous assumptions made at the outset: he assumed that once he explained his new ideas for the course, students would embrace them; he assumed that bright, capable students would be up for the open-ended task he'd designed; and he assumed he was capable of pulling it off. "I had never been afraid to try new things in the classroom, although I had never done anything quite this radical before. I had certainly had problems in classes before, but I had never had one completely explode on me. I should be able to handle anything that arose." (p. 191). Thank you, Noel, for your remarkable level of honesty.

Albers (2009) volunteered to teach an upper-division honors social science seminar. She did so "with considerable excitement, viewing it as an opportunity to implement some new pedagogical approaches. The unexpected initial reactions of students constituted one of the most disappointing professional experiences of my long career" (p. 270). Her analysis of student response is insightful. "My attempt to change the normative 'professor' behaviors were [sic] based on the assumption that students would welcome the changes this wrought for them. Implementing such change quickly brought me into contact with the degree of comfort some students have with the predictability of existing roles" (p. 274). Thank you, Albers, for this insightful analysis of developmental readiness miscalculated.

In my experience I have found that a combination of new and familiar assignments and activities works best with beginning students. Students participate in a new kind of learning experience, and that's followed by something familiar. We do an unusual group activity in class, and the next day we're back to a familiar lecture-discussion sequence. Not everything in the course is new, but enough has been changed so that no student escapes the fact that this is not a business-as-usual course.

Exhibit 9.2 lists a number of potential activities for "beginners." These are good places for both faculty and students to begin. The chance that any new learning experience will succeed

Exhibit 9.2. Good Places for Teachers and Students to Begin

The Learning Question. Start regularly and frequently asking students about what they are learning and, even more important, how they are learning it. Ask them in social conversations during class and after every activity in class. Mention what you are learning and how. Ask students to write informally about how they anticipate learning a particular kind of concept, how they learn from the text, and how they learn from each other. Make the discussion of learning a theme of the course. (For a more detailed description, see Chapter Five.)

The Exam Review Session. Plan a review session in which students are doing the review: they are preparing study guides, writing possible test questions, identifying topics that need further explanation, and discussing with each other what they will need to know for the exam. (For a more detailed description, see Chapter Seven.)

Practice Grading. To help students understand what makes a good essay answer or an A paper, give them several anonymous answers or papers at different quality levels and let the students "grade" them, individually first and then in discussion with others. (For a more detailed description, see Chapter Seven.)

Course Goal Setting. Benjamin (2005) involves students in course goal setting. He shares with students a handout listing seventeen possible goals for the course. On the syllabus he lists his goals for the course and explains why they're important. Then he asks students to select the three goals on the handout that are most important to them. The ones getting the most votes are added to the syllabus. If needed, he adjusts course content, activities, and assignments to accomplish these added goals.

Before- or After-Class Session Reviews. During the last or first five minutes of class, plan an activity in which students review content presented during class or the day before. Maybe they underline and expand their notes. Maybe they compare notes with someone else. Maybe they generate potential test questions. Maybe they summarize the most important idea in 140 characters. It's also valuable for students to review material presented several days past, especially if understanding new content depends on knowing the old.

Assignment Choice. Take one assignment and redesign it so that it includes several options of possible topic choices and possible format choices. Any time students are given choices, they should be asked to explain and justify what they've decided to do. (For a more detailed description, see Chapters One and Four.)

Assessment Criteria. Involve students in setting the criteria that will be used to assess an assignment or activity. If the students will be discussing a reading, ask them what makes a student discussion worth listening to and participating in. Use their feedback to create a set of criteria you will use to assess their next discussion of an assigned reading. Hollander (2002) reports on doing this and then grading the discussion as a whole, rather than individual contributions to it.

Quiz Collaboration. Administer an in-class quiz. At the end, give students five minutes to talk with others about their answers. Then let them change any answers they wish, first adding a star beside any answer they changed, then noting their original answer and the changed answer. Changed answers count. In the debrief, there's a discussion about whether consulting with others helped or hurt and why.

Classroom Climate: Best and Worst Experiences. To help establish a climate for learning, facilitate a discussion of best and worst class experiences. Record them on the board so the differences are there for everyone to see. Or in groups, this can be a getting-to-know-each-other discussion during which students share best and worst group experiences. Or it can be an online exchange highlighting best and worst online group experiences. Or it can be identification of best and worst participation policies. The goal is to get students thinking about which experiences helped and which ones hindered their efforts to learn. (For a more detailed description, see Chapter Six.)

is enhanced when teachers make adaptations so that the activity or assignments fits the unique features of their teaching and learning situation. In other words, make these strategies your own.

The Developmental Issues for Faculty

One of the most interesting features of the Grow model introduced early in the chapter is Grow's (1991) contention that there is a parallel developmental trajectory for faculty. Faculty move through stages as they change from being teacher-centered to learner-centered. Blumberg (2009) has developed a collection of rubrics based on the five change areas discussed in Chapters Three through Seven. These rubrics do an excellent job of identifying developmental steps in the transition to learner-centered teaching. They make it easier for teachers to see where they are on that continuum. The rubrics are also helpful because they make clear that learner-centered teaching is not an all-or-nothing proposition. Teachers can be a little or a lot learner-centered in their practice. They can be at different levels, depending on the area—they might be well along in their efforts as a facilitator of learning and less far along in their use of self- and peer-assessment approaches. The basic message of the previous sections in this chapter is that teachers are well advised to move themselves incrementally along the continuum, rather than trying to jump from one end to the other in a single course. For most teachers, learner-centered teaching represents a paradigmatic change in thinking that is implemented via a range of new activities and assignments. Or, more simply, most teachers do not find making this change easy.

Grow (1991) identifies another mismatch problem also hinted at in previous sections. Student resistance is increased when teachers are further along the learner-centered continuum than students, and the further the two are apart, the greater the resistance. This is another reason why teachers must curb their desire to change too much too fast. Students do need to be pushed forward, but from where they begin, not where teachers think they should be or where teachers are themselves. The mismatches described by Grow can occur in both directions. Students experience frustration and disappointment when they are more learner-centered than their teachers.

Over the years I have had several interesting discussions about whether learner-centered approaches should be recommended to new faculty. Does implementing them successfully depend on a certain amount of experience and level of instructional maturity? This specific question hasn't been studied, at least in any research I could locate, but there is a related finding with relevance. Ebert-May, Derting, Hodder, Momsen, Long, and Jardeleza's (2011) study of workshops designed to help science faculty become more learner-centered found that novice teachers implemented more of these changes than experienced teachers. The research team wonders whether those who have taught longer have more difficulty implementing change and are less inclined to do so.

Whether experienced or inexperienced, teachers implementing learner-centered approaches beyond a few simple techniques must be reasonably confident teachers willing to take some risks. The reasons have already been explored. This is a less scripted way of teaching. Because what happens in class depends more on what students are doing, what happens in class is less under the teacher's control. The approach incorporates explicit skill instruction. There is student resistance to deal with. It takes a certain level of instructional maturity to handle change this significant.

I don't think successful implementation of learner-centered approaches depends so much on career stage as it does on the readiness of the individual faculty member. If you've read the book, are motivated to try some of these approaches, are willing to do more than you have been doing, have considered what you're getting into, and still want to grow and change instructionally, then you should proceed and do so with confidence. Not everything will go perfectly, but you and the students will learn and do better next time.

I used to think that someday I would finally be a learner-centered teacher. I would arrive. Flachmann (1994) disavowed me of this notion. His advice captures the essence of this chapter and one of the underlying themes of this book: development for teachers and students is about moving forward. "Good teaching is a *journey* rather than a destination. It's not a subway stop where, once you are there, you can cease moving forward . . . Inertia is an insidiously powerful negative force in teaching—the urge to keep doing things the way we've done them for years. It's a bit like belonging to the pedagogical equivalent of Alcoholics Anonymous: there's always a poor teacher in us just waiting to emerge. We have to resist the temptation to stay as we are, to rest at the bus stop" (p. 1).

I used that quote to end the first edition of the book. One reader called it a sharp-stick ending, and it is. Sometimes we need more than gentle reminders. But now I'm feeling the book should end on a more positive note. I have been inspired and motivated by Brookfield's (2006) powerful description of what learner-centered teachers do. The quote begins with a long list of Hollywood portrayals of strong teachers including *Goodbye Mr. Chips, To Sir with Love, Stand and Deliver,* and *Mr. Holland's Opus,* among others. Despite admiration, he says that for him they are bad role models. "Teaching is not about charismatically charged individuals using the sheer force of their characters and personalities to wreak lifelong transformations in students' lives. It's about finding ways to promote the day-to-day, incremental gains that students make as they try to understand ideas, grasp concepts, assimilate knowledge and develop new skills. All the small things you do to make this happen for students represent the real story of teaching. Helping learning is what makes you truly heroic" (p. 278).

Syllabus and Learning Log Entries for Speech Communications 100A

Welcome to Speech Communications 100A, a course that aims to develop your communications skills. Because everyone communicates all the time, the content of this course will be relevant to you after you graduate, as well as today. In this course you will become more aware of how you communicate and better able to communicate effectively. The course combines theory and practice, giving you the opportunity to apply what you have learned.

TEXT

The course text is *Communicate* by Rudolph F. Verderber (Wadsworth, 1995). Reading assignments should be done before coming to class. Please bring your text with you to class, as regular discussions of text content will occur during class.

COURSE ASSIGNMENTS

In this course, assignments are handled differently: you select the work you will complete, with one exception: all students must give an informative or persuasive speech. Bear these two rules in mind as you review the options that follow next:

1. At least 50 percent of the total points possible for each individual assignment must be earned; otherwise *no points* will be recorded for the assignment.

2. Once the due date for an assignment has passed, that assignment cannot be completed.

EXAMS

1. Test 1: a multiple-choice and essay exam including material from class and the text (80 points possible)
2. Test 2: a multiple-choice exam including material from class and the text the day they are assigned (80 points possible)

PRESENTATIONS

1. An informative or persuasive speech (five to seven minutes long) and a speech preparation sheet. **This is the only required assignment in the course.** (50 points possible for the speech; 10 points possible for the prep sheet)
2. Interviews (ten to twelve minutes long) conducted by classmates representing hypothetical corporations and organizations with open positions. You select the positions of interest and are interviewed by the group. See Small-Group Experience 2, in the next section, for more details on the groups. (Two interviews, 15 points per interview, each summarized in a short paper, plus 5 bonus points if you get the job.)

SMALL-GROUP EXPERIENCES

1. Test 2 Study Group. Be a member of a five- to seven-person study group who will jointly prepare for Test 2. After taking the exam individually, the group will convene and complete a group exam. Group exam scoring options will be described on a handout. (_____ points possible)
2. This assignment also includes a three-page typed paper that analyzes what happened in the study group in terms of (a) what the group did or didn't do that contributed to its success (or lack of success) and (b) what the individual group members did that contributed to the group's success or lack of it. *Note:* **this paper must be completed if exam bonus points are to be awarded.** (30 points possible for the paper)

3. Interview Group. With five to seven other classmates, be employees of a hypothetical corporation that will write a job description, prepare interview questions, and interview up to eight candidates for the job. A group grade will be based on a final report that includes (a) the job description, (b) interview questions, (c) a summary of interviews conducted, (d) justification for the person hired (30 points possible), and (e) an assessment of how well the group conducted the interview based on feedback from those interviewed (10 points possible). In addition, individual members' contributions to the group will be assessed by other members. (20 points possible; this makes the interviewing part of the assignment worth up to 60 points total)

LEARNING LOG

This assignment encourages students to explore how the course content relates to their individual communication skills. Each entry is written in response to a series of questions provided by the instructor. Entries may be handwritten or typed and should be about two pages long if handwritten or one double-spaced page if typed. Collections of entries are due on the dates specified in the course calendar. You may prepare all, one, or some of the entries. However, once a due date is past, those entries may not be submitted.

Entries are graded using the following criteria: (1) their completeness (meaning all the questions for a particular entry are addressed); (2) the level of insight and reflection (evidence of thoughtful responses); (3) the support provided for the observations and conclusions; and (4) the extent to which relevant course content (from class and the text) is integrated in the entries. (10 points possible per individual entry)

SPEECH CRITIQUES

You will provide constructive feedback to eight classmates on their informative speeches. You will use a form provided by the instructor, and after your critiques have been graded, they will be given to the presenter. *Note:* **you must do all eight critiques.** (80 points possible)

PARTICIPATION

Using the class-authored participation policy and a set of individually generated goals, your contributions to class will be assessed. *Note:* **participation cannot be added as an assignment option after February 3.** (50 points possible)

This assignment also includes a five-page typed participation analysis paper submitted in the following three installments on the due dates indicated on the course calendar:

Installment 1: one page that reacts to and assesses the class-generated policy and in which you generate your participation goals for the course

Installment 2: three pages, one of which is a letter to your designated partner providing feedback on his or her participation as you have observed it and two pages consisting of a midcourse progress report

Installment 3: one page that contains a final assessment of your participation in the course (a more detailed handout describing this assignment will be distributed later)

Note: **all three installments of this assignment must be completed if points for participation are to be earned.** (50 points possible for the paper)

BONUS POINTS

1. On several unannounced days, attendance will be taken. Those present will receive 5 bonus points. (up to a maximum of 25 points)
2. Additional bonus point options will be offered at the discretion of the instructor.

Following are some tips on developing a game plan for the course.

For the purposes of planning, circle the assignments you are considering doing and then total the points possible. Be realistic. It is highly unlikely that you will get all the points possible for the assignments. Check your total with the point totals needed for each grade (as listed in the next section). Be sure that you're planning to do enough assignments to get the grade you desire in the course. Keep track of your points as the course progresses (a point grid sheet will be provided later), so that you will know if you need to add more assignments.

Test 1	80 points
Test 2	80 points
Informational or persuasive speech and prep sheet	60 points
Interviews	30 points
Study group test bonus	15 points
Study group analysis paper	30 points
Interview group experience	60 points
Learning Log: 22 entries at 10 points per entry	220 points
Speech critiques	80 points
Participation	50 points
Participation analysis paper	50 points
Attendance bonus	25 points
TOTAL	**765 points**

GRADES

Grades for this course are assigned according to the following scale:

525 and above = A   378–412 = C
499–524 = A–   343–377 = C–
482–498 = B+   309–342 = D
465–481 = B   292–308 = D–
448–464 = B–   291 and below = F
413–447 = C+

Note: A day-by-day calendar of all course meetings follows. It lists content topics, activities scheduled for the class session, reading assignments, and assignment due dates.

LEARNING LOG ENTRIES
ENTRY 1

Develop a game plan for the course indicating which assignments you plan to complete. Why have you selected these options? What do you think your choices indicate about your learning preferences? Why do you think a teacher would give students a choice about assignments? How do you think this strategy will affect your performance in the class?

ENTRY 2

Why does the university require a course in speech communication? If this course wasn't required, would you take it? Why? (Or why not?) Overall, how would you assess your communication skills? Reread pages 22 and 23 in the text and set at least one goal for yourself in this class.

ENTRY 3

Write about your participation in college courses (or high school if you have no or limited experience with college courses). How much do you participate? Is that as much as you'd like to contribute? If it's not as much, what keeps you from saying more in class? What role should student participation play in the college classroom?

ENTRY 4

Think about your experiences working in groups: What made those group experiences effective or ineffective? What responsibilities do individuals have when they participate in groups? Can individual members do anything to encourage other members to fulfill these responsibilities?

ENTRY 5

Take a look at the definition of *leadership* that appears in the chapter on leadership in groups (pp. 241–259). Summarize the definition in your own words and write something about the notion of leadership as exerting influence. Are you comfortable with that? How is it different from telling people what to do? Use content from the rest of the chapter to address that question. How would you characterize your potential as a leader?

ENTRY 6

In light of the material we've discussed in class and that you've read in the text (on roles and leadership, for example), analyze your small-group communication skills. What roles do you typically fill in groups? Are there any skills you'd like to develop further? How often and in what context do you think you will have to work in groups in your professional life?

ENTRY 7

React to our in-class discussion about sexist remarks and gendered references. Is this topic "much ado about nothing"? On what terms and in what ways do you think language influences the way you think and act? Provide some examples. If you marry, will you or your spouse change names?

ENTRY 8

How far have you come in choosing a topic for your informative speech? What sort of feedback did you get from classmates in the class activity Tuesday? Analyze the strengths and weaknesses of the topics you are considering in terms of your qualifications and interest in the topic, the relevance of the topic to the class, and the suitability of the topic for this occasion and setting. (Text material on pp. 265–285 should be used in this entry.)

ENTRY 9

Write me a letter that answers the questions and/or supplies the additional information requested in my letter to you about your first set of log entries.

ENTRY 10

You have been asked to address an audience of inner-city high school students on why they should attend college. What things about this audience would you like to know before you plan the content of your speech? What issues do you think might be important to raise? How likely is this audience to believe your opinions on this topic? Are there things you might be able to do to enhance your credibility?

ENTRY 11

Take and score the communication apprehension quiz. How does this feedback compare with how you feel about doing the speech? What ideas in the text (pp. 373–379) might help you overcome the anxiety you associate with speaking?

ENTRY 12

Take stock of how you are doing in this class so far. How many points do you have now? Revisit your game plan outlined in Entry 1 and discuss any changes you plan to make. Is this course structure and grading system having any impact on your learning? Include some examples to illustrate the impact you have described.

ENTRY 13

(Write this entry during the period after you do your speech.)

So how did it go? Using the critique form, assess your speech. Answer the questions at the bottom of the page. **Submit the completed critique form with this entry.**

ENTRY 14

Describe an experience you've had trying to persuade someone to change his or her mind about something. Were you successful? Analyze your success or failure in terms of the eight principles of persuasive speaking on text pages 417 through 441.

Entry 15

Take and score the Uncritical Inference Test (which I will distribute in class). Report and comment on your score. What do you think an exercise like this is trying to teach you? Is this an important lesson? Why? Why not?

Entry 16

Compare and contrast your analysis of your speech with the feedback provided by your classmates and the teacher. Any noticeable differences? Any feedback from others that strikes you as particularly constructive?

Entry 17

Use the ad you brought to class or pick another one and analyze it in terms of fallacies and propaganda. More important than correctly naming the fallacy or propaganda technique is being able to explain what is wrong with the argument being made. Also write about the ad in terms of the nonverbal messages it portrays. **Include the ad with this entry.**

Entry 18

(Write this entry only if you plan to take Test 2.)

Develop a study game plan for Test 2. If you took Test 1, think about what you learned from that experience. If you didn't, write about the content you expect to see on the exam and how you'll go about preparing yourself. Include in the entry a timeline identifying how much time you'll spend and what you'll do each day leading up to the exam.

Entry 19

Return to text pages 327 through 351 in the chapter on organizing speech material. Prepare a two-page study guide identifying material from the text that you believe will appear on the exam. Describe how you can use the study guide to learn this material.

ENTRY 20

You have your exam back. Did you do better or worse than you expected? If you developed a game plan, analyze how well it worked, including how closely you did or didn't follow it. If you were in a study group, explain how the group efforts dovetailed with your individual preparation. If you took the exam as an individual, were the group scores posted in class higher or lower than you expected? How do you account for this? Next semester, what one thing could you do that would most improve your performance on multiple-choice exams?

ENTRY 21

(To be completed only if you've written Entry 2.)

Return to the assessment of your communication skills offered in Entry 2. How would you describe and assess those skills now? Evaluate any progress you made toward reaching the goal you set for yourself.

ENTRY 22

(Submit this entry on the last day of class in a sealed envelope with your name on the envelope. I will record 10 points upon receiving the envelope. I will read the contents after I have submitted final grades.)

Over the summer a friend e-mails you to say that she has signed up for this class in the fall. She asks you what she needs to do in order to do well in the course. What would you tell her? Telling her to drop the course and get into another section is fine, so long as you tell her why. On the other hand, you might share with her what you would do differently if you were taking the course again. If you've done well in the course, to what would you attribute your success? What important things, if any, have you learned?

RESOURCES THAT DEVELOP LEARNING SKILLS

The resources that follow can be used to help develop students' learning skills. Also included are some brief suggestions as to how they might be used.

Successful Students: Guidelines and Thought for Academic Success A positive and constructive handout that describes good learning behaviors, it might be attached to the course syllabus, distributed when students have demonstrated some less-than-successful behaviors or posted on the course website.

Ten Commandments for Effective Study Skills The style here captivates at the same time that its contents deliver constructive messages about studying.

Discussion Guidelines for Students The author includes these in his syllabus. They offer a detailed description of actions that improve discussion. You might start by having students work in groups to generate their own guidelines and then use these for comparison.

Consider a Study Group Students can be encouraged to form study groups on their own. Here's how one instructor encourages them to do so. Groups can also be formed to review each other's papers or projects.

Group Members' Bill of Rights and Responsibilities There are lots of ways a document like this can be used, starting with simply distributing it to students prior to their participation in a group activity. During their first meeting, they can review and discuss the document. They can revise it so that it directly applies to the activity they will complete together. The importance of the document can be underscored by having students sign and submit the document. Or you might have group members construct their own bill of rights and responsibilities.

Note-Taking Types and Characteristics to Help Students Succeed This concise matrix can be used to make students aware of some of the different methods of taking notes.

SUCCESSFUL STUDENTS: GUIDELINES AND THOUGHTS FOR ACADEMIC SUCCESS

Successful students exhibit a combination of successful attitudes and behaviors as well as intellectual capacity. Successful students:

1. **Are responsible and active.** Successful students get involved in their studies, accept responsibility for their own education, and are active participants in it!
2. **Have educational goals.** Successful students have legitimate goals and are motivated by what those goals represent in terms of career aspirations and life's desires.
3. **Ask questions.** Successful students ask questions to provide the quickest route between ignorance and knowledge.
4. **Learn that a student and a professor make a team.** Most instructors want exactly what you want: they would like for you to learn the material in their respective classes and earn a good grade.
5. **Don't sit in the back.** Successful students minimize classroom distractions that interfere with learning.
6. **Take good notes.** Successful students take notes that are understandable and organized, and they review them often.
7. **Understand that actions affect learning.** Successful students know their personal behavior affects their feelings and emotions, which in turn can affect learning. Act like you're disinterested and you'll become disinterested.
8. **Talk about what they're learning.** Successful students get to know something well enough that they can put it into words.

9. **Don't cram for exams.** Successful students know that divided periods of study are more effective than cram sessions, and they practice it.

10. **Are good time managers.** Successful students do not procrastinate. They have learned that time control is life control and have consciously chosen to be in control of their lives.

Source: from Steven J. Thien and Andy Bulleri, *The Teaching Professor,* 1996, *10*(9), 1–2. Reprinted with permission from Magna Publications.

TEN COMMANDMENTS FOR EFFECTIVE STUDY SKILLS

THOU SHALT BE RESPONSIBLE AND THOU SHALT BE ACTIVE—FOR THERE BE NO OTHER PASSAGE TO ACADEMIC SUCCESS!

Responsibility means control. Your grade in a class is relatively free of any variables other than your own effort. Sure, you may have a lousy professor. It happens. But remember: you are the one who has to live with your grade. It goes on *your* grade report, not your *instructor's.*

If you are seeking a way of increasing learning and improving grades without increasing your study time, active classroom participation is your answer. Look at it this way: classroom time is something to which you are already committed. So you can sit there, assume the "bored student position"—arms crossed, slumped in the chair, eyes at half-mast—and allow yourself an "out-of-body" experience. Or you can maximize your classroom time by actively listening, thinking, questioning, taking notes, and participating totally in the learning experience.

THOU SHALT KNOW WHERE THY "HOT BUTTONS" ARE, AND THOU SHALT PUSH THEM REGULARLY!

The next time you seat yourself in class, ask yourself these questions:

- What am I doing here?
- Why have I chosen to be sitting here now?
- Is there some better place I could be?
- What does my presence here mean to me?

Your responses to these questions represent your educational goals. They are the "hot buttons," and they are without a doubt the most important factors in your success as a college student.

College is not easy. Believe it or not, there will be times when you tire of being a student. And that's when a press or two on the hot buttons can pull you through!

IF THOU HATH QUESTIONS, ASKETH THEM; IF THOU HATH NO QUESTIONS, MAKETH SOME!

Just as a straight line usually indicates the shortest distance between two points, questions generally provide the quickest route between ignorance and knowledge.

In addition to securing the knowledge that you seek, asking questions has at least two other extremely important benefits. The process helps you pay attention to your professor and helps your professor pay attention to you.

THOU SHALT LEARN THAT THOU AND THY PROFESSOR MAKETH A TEAM—AND THOU SHALT BE A TEAM PLAYER!

Most instructors want exactly what you want: they would like for you to learn the material in their respective classes and earn a good grade. After all, successful students reflect well on the efforts of any teaching; if you learned your stuff, the instructor takes some justifiable pride in teaching.

THOU SHALT NOT PARKETH THY BUTT IN THE BACK!

Suppose you pay $50 to buy concert tickets for your favorite musical artist. Do you choose front-row seats or the cheap seats at the rear of the auditorium? Why do some students who spend far more money on a college education than on concerts willingly place themselves in the last row of the classroom? In class, the back row gives invisibility and anonymity, both of which are antithetical to efficient and effective learning.

THOU SHALT NOT WRITE IN THY NOTES WHAT THOU FAILETH TO UNDERSTAND!

Avoid the "what in the hell is that" phenomenon experienced by most college students. This unique reaction occurs when students first review their notes for a major examination. Being unable to read, decipher, or comprehend the mess that passes for notes, students are likely to utter the expression that grants this particular phenomenon its name.

IF THINE INTEREST IN CLASS BE GONE, FAKETH IT!

If you are a good actor, you may even fool yourself into liking the lecture.

How do you fake interest? You simply assume the "interested student position": lean forward, place your feet flat on the floor in front of you, maintain eye contact with your professor, smile or nod occasionally as though you understand and care about what your instructor is saying, take notes, and ask questions.

THOU SHALT KNOW THAT IF SILENCE BE GOLDEN, RECITATION SHALT BE PLATINUM!

Recitation is not only good for checking whether or not you know something; it's perhaps the best method for learning it in the first place. Reciting unquestionably provides the most direct route between short-term and long-term memory.

THOU SHALT KNOWETH THAT *CRAM* IS A FOUR-LETTER WORD!

If there is one thing that study skills specialists agree on, it is that divided periods of study are more efficient and effective than a single period of condensed study. In other words, you will learn more, remember more, and earn a higher grade if you prepare for Friday's examination by studying one hour a night, Monday through Thursday, rather than studying for four hours straight on Thursday evening.

THOU SHALT NOT PROCRASTINATE—AND THOU SHALT BEGINNETH NOT DOING IT RIGHT NOW!

An elemental truth: you will either control time or be controlled by it! There is no middle ground. It's your choice: you can lead or be led, establish control or relinquish control, steer your own course or have it dictated to you.

When I ask students which they prefer—choosing their own path or having it chosen for them—they almost uniformly select the first option. In spite of this response, however, failure to take control of their own time is probably the number-one study skills problem of college students.

So these are the Ten Commandments for Effective Study Skills. They work, but don't take my word for it. Try them! Use them! Make them your own. What have you got to lose, except poor grades and sleepless study nights?

Source: from Larry M. Ludewig, *The Teaching Professor,* 1992, 6(10), 3–4. Reprinted with permission from Magna Publications.

DISCUSSION GUIDELINES FOR STUDENTS

- Try to make comments that connect ideas from the course with phenomena outside the classroom, and between ideas in one part of the course with those in a different part.
- Avoid war stories, rambling speeches heavily punctuated with the word "I," and raw opinions that we could just as easily get from the average patron at the nearest tavern who has never heard of this course and its assigned reading.
- Realize that when our emotions are aroused, our brain wants to take orders from them. It is essential, therefore, to be

willing to disconnect one's brain from one's gut long enough to render due process to ideas, particularly those that are unpopular or personally distasteful. This is an unnatural act and requires courage. You will probably find it easier to join [in] . . . from time to time.

- Understand that the right to have an opinion does not include the right to have it taken seriously by others. Nor is having an opinion necessarily laudable in itself. An opinion is only as good as the evidence, theory, and logic on which it is based.
- Be careful about basing your opinions uncritically on the testimony of experts. Experts are subject to error and bias. They often disagree with other experts. All of this applies to the authors of your texts and your professors.
- Beware of the tendency to view questions in dichotomous terms, such as either-or, all-or-none. The world is a complex, messy place where absolute answers are hard to find, gray is more common than black and white, and contradictory things are often in the same package.
- Appreciate the importance of the distinction between "the truth" and "the truth, the whole truth, and nothing but the truth."
- Value tentativeness. It's OK to admit you're unsure. It's OK to change your mind.

Source: from Howard Gabennesch, *The Teaching Professor*, 1992, *6*(9), 6. Reprinted with permission from Magna Publications.

CONSIDER A STUDY GROUP

Study groups give students the opportunity to discuss course content and assigned reading. They can be especially useful in preparing for exams. Group members can test each other's knowledge and discuss questions or problems they anticipate seeing on the exam. Consider organizing one with a group of your colleagues!

If you do decide to form a study group, the following guidelines outline how those groups will work in this class:

- Groups of four to six students are formed by the mutual agreement of the members.
- To be considered a study group for the class, groups must register with the instructor, providing group member names and student ID numbers.
- Groups may expel a member (say, one who is using the group as opposed to contributing to it) by unanimous vote.
- If group membership falls below four, the group is automatically disbanded, unless they vote in a replacement.
- No students may belong to more than one study group, and no student is required to belong to any study group.
- Groups organize their own activities, deciding what to do at their meetings. The instructor is happy to meet with groups to suggest activities and/or to review proposed study plans. This meeting is optional for the groups.
- Registered groups receive bonus points on all assignments according to the following formula. The bonus is based on the average of all individual grades received by the group members. If the group average is A, all members receive three percentage points; if it's B, two percentage points; and if it's C, one percentage point. If an individual member receives an A, but the group average is C, the member still receives the one-percentage-point bonus.

If you would like to participate in a study group, but don't know students in the class well enough to organize one, please let the instructor know. The instructor will be happy to help students organize groups.

Source: adapted from H. J. Robinson, *The Teaching Professor,* 1991, 5(7), 7. Reprinted with permission from Magna Publications.

GROUP MEMBERS' BILL OF RIGHTS AND RESPONSIBILITIES

- You have the right and responsibility to select meeting times and locations that are convenient for all members.

- You have the right to contribute to the formation of group goals, the dividing of the work among group members, and the setting of deadlines.
- You have the right to expect all group members to do their fair share of the work, and you have the right to confront group members who are not doing their fair share. You have the responsibility to complete the work assigned to you.
- You have the responsibility to be an active participant in the group process. And you have the right to expect active participation from other group members.
- You have the right to expect feedback from the group on work you complete for the group, and you have the responsibility to provide constructive feedback on the work of other group members.
- You have the right to expect group meetings to begin and end promptly and that the group will follow an agenda that outlines the tasks it expects to accomplish during the meeting. You have the responsibility to help the group fulfill these expectations by being at meetings on time and helping the group develop and follow the agenda.
- You have the right to participate in a group that works cooperatively and handles disagreements constructively.
- You have the right to ask group members to limit the amount of time devoted to socialization or the discussion of extraneous topics. You have the responsibility not to engage in excessive socialization or to bring up extraneous topics. You have the responsibility to help the group stay on task.
- You have the right to expect group members to listen to you respectfully and you have the responsibility to listen to all group members respectfully.

Source: adapted from D. G. Longman, *The Teaching Professor,* 1992, 6(7), 5. This version appeared in The Teaching Professor blog, February 8, 2012 (www.facultyfocus.com).

Note-Taking Types and Characteristics to Help Students Succeed

Type	Uses	Benefits	Attentiveness	Lecture rate	Process	Format
Conventional	Traditional method	Convenient for students	Students may lose valuable information when trying to write as much down as possible	Difficult for students to keep up; ideas get lost	Involves listening, large short-term memory, writing down information	Verbatim notes; no indentations; full sentences
Two-column	Summarize key ideas in far left column	Helps with factual details; room for reorganization after class; good for multiple-choice exams	Students may still lose valuable information when trying to write down too much information	Summarization in left column during lecture so ideas lost	Involves listening, large short-term memory, writing down information	Far left column for topics and summaries; right for details, etc.
Outline	Students use to review and find relationships among topics and subtopics	Students include more key ideas, more details and examples; great for preparing for multiple-choice and short-answer exams	Focus on ideas and relationships during lecture, then write down notes	Students capture more ideas	Students write down key ideas and indent under topics to add related materials	Indented topics; Roman numerals, numbers, or bullets used
Concept map	Helps define key ideas and relationships	Students discover more relationships; leads to higher-order thinking; great for preparing for essay exams	Focus on ideas and relationships during lecture, then write down notes	Students capture more ideas	Students write down key ideas and connect them	Key ideas with circles around them connected by lines
Matrix	Helps define key ideas and relationships	Students discover more relationships; leads to higher-order thinking; great for studying for essay exams	Focus on ideas and relationships during lecture, then write down notes	Students capture more ideas	Write topics across the top row and general characteristics down the first column	Table, similar to this one

Source: from Lisa Shibley, *The Teaching Professor,* 1999, *13*(9), 3. Reprinted with permission from Magna Publications.

REFERENCES

Ackerman, D. S., and Gross, B. L. "My Instructor Made Me Do It: Task Characteristics of Procrastination." *Journal of Marketing Education,* 2005, *27*(1), 5–13.

Albanese, M., and Mitchell, S. "Problem-Based Learning: A Review of Literature on Its Outcomes and Implementation Issues." *Academic Medicine,* 1993, *68*(1), 52–81.

Albers, C. "Teaching: From Disappointment to Ecstasy." *Teaching Sociology,* 2009, *37*(July), 269–282.

Allen, J., Fuller, D., and Luckett, M. "Academic Integrity: Behaviors, Rates and Attitudes of Business Students toward Cheating." *Journal of Marketing Education,* 1998, *20*(1), 41–52.

Amstutz, J. "In Defense of Telling Stories." *Teaching Professor,* 1988, *2*(April), 5.

Appleby, D. C. "Faculty and Student Perceptions of Irritating Behaviors in the College Classroom." *Journal of Staff, Program, & Organizational Development,* 1990, *8*(1), 41–46.

Archer, C. C., and Miller, M. K. "Prioritizing Active Learning: An Exploration of Gateway Courses in Political Science." *PS: Political Science and Politics,* 2011, April, 429–434.

Armbruster, P., Patel, M., Johnson, E., and Weiss, M. "Active Learning and Student-Centered Pedagogy Improve Student Attitudes and Performance in Introductory Biology." *Cell Biology Education,* 2009, *8*(Fall), 203–213.

Aronowitz, A. "Paulo Freire's Radical Democratic Humanism." In P. McLaren and P. Leonard (eds.), *Paulo Freire: A Critical Encounter.* New York: Routledge, 1993.

Ayers, W. "Thinking about Teachers and the Curriculum." *Harvard Educational Review,* 1986, *56*(1), 49–51.

Bacon, D. R., and Stewart, K. A. "How Fast Do Students Forget What They Learned in Consumer Behavior? A Longitudinal Study." *Journal of Marketing Education,* 2006, *28,* 181–192.

Baez-Galib, R., Colon-Cruz, H., Resto, W., and Rubin, M. R. "Chem-2-Chem: A One-to-One Supportive Learning Environment for

Chemistry." *Journal of Chemical Education*, 2005, *82*(12), 1859–1863.

Baker, D. F. "Peer Assessment in Small Groups: A Comparison of Methods." *Journal of Management Education*, 2008, *32*(2), 183–209.

Bandura, A. *Self-Efficacy: The Exercise of Control.* New York: Freeman, 1997.

Barkley, E. F. *Student Engagement Techniques: A Handbook for College Faculty.* San Francisco: Jossey-Bass, 2010.

Barr, R. B., and Tagg, J. "From Teaching to Learning: A New Paradigm for Undergraduate Education." *Change*, November–December 1995, pp. 13–25.

Bean, J. C. *Engaging Ideas: The Professor's Guide to Integrating Writing, Critical Thinking, and Active Learning in the Classroom.* (2nd ed.) San Francisco: Jossey-Bass, 2011.

Benjamin, L. T. "Setting Course Goals: Privileges and Responsibilities in a World of Ideas." *Teaching of Psychology*, 2005, *32*(3), 146–149.

Benson, T. A., Cohen, A. L., and Buskist, W. "Rapport: Its Relation to Student Attitudes and Behaviors Toward Teachers and Classes." *Teaching of Psychology*, 2005, *32*(4), 237–239.

Benvenuto, M. "Teaching Is Learning: Maximum Incentive, Minimum Discipline in Student Groups Teaching General Chemistry." *Journal of Chemical Education*, 2001, *78*(2), 194–197.

Biggs, J. *Teaching for Quality Learning at University: What the Student Does.* Buckingham, U.K.: Open University Press, 1999a.

Biggs, J. "What the Student Does: Teaching for Enhanced Learning." *Higher Education Research and Development*, 1999b, *18*(1), 57–75.

Biggs, J., Kember, D., and Leung, D.Y.P. "The Revised Two-Factor Study Process Questionnaire: R-SPQ-2F." *British Journal of Educational Psychology*, 2001, *7*(Part 1), 133–149.

Black, K. A. "What to Do When You Stop Lecturing: Become a Guide and a Resource." *Journal of Chemical Education*, 1993, *70*(2), 140–144.

Blumberg, P. *Developing Learner-Centered Teaching: A Practical Guide for Faculty.* San Francisco: Jossey-Bass, 2009.

Blumberg, P., and Pontiggia, L. "Benchmarking the Degree of Implementation of Learner-Centered Approaches." *Innovative Higher Education*, 2011, *36*(3), 189–202.

Boud, D. (ed.). *Developing Autonomy in Student Learning.* London: Kogan Page, 1981.

Braye, S. "Radical Teaching: An Introduction." *Teaching Professor*, 1995, *9*(October), 1–2.

Brookfield, S. D. *Becoming a Critically Reflective Teacher.* San Francisco: Jossey-Bass, 1995.

Brookfield, S. D. *The Skillful Teacher: On Technique, Trust, and Responsiveness in the Classroom.* (2nd ed.) San Francisco: Jossey-Bass, 2006.

Brown, J.P.P. "Process-Oriented Guided-Inquiry Learning in an Introductory Anatomy and Physiology Course with a Diverse Student Population." *Advances in Physiology Education,* 2010, *34*(3), 150–155.

Brown, P. L., Abell, S. K., Demir, A., and Schmidt, F. J. "College Science Teachers' Views of Classroom Inquiry." *Science Education,* 2006, *90*(5), 784–206.

Brown, S. D. "A Process-Oriented Guided Inquiry Approach to Teaching Medicinal Chemistry." *American Journal of Pharmaceutical Education,* 2010, *74*(7), Article 121.

Bruffee, K. A. *Collaborative Learning: Higher Education, Interdependence, and the Authority of Knowledge.* Baltimore: Johns Hopkins University Press, 1993.

Buchler, J. "Teaching Quantitative Methodology to the Math Adverse." *PS: Political Science and Politics,* 2009, *42*(July), 527–530.

Bunce, D. M. "Teaching Is More Than Lecturing and Learning Is More Than Memorizing." *Journal of Chemical Education,* 2009, *86*(6), 674–680.

Burrowes, P. A. "A Student-Centered Approach to Teaching General Biology That Really Works: Lord's Constructivist Model Put to a Test." *The American Biology Teacher,* 2003, *65*(7), 491–502.

Calder, L. "Uncoverage: Toward a Signature Pedagogy for the History Survey." *The Journal of American History,* 2006, *92*(4), 1358–1370.

Candy, P. C. *Self-Direction for Lifelong Learning.* San Francisco: Jossey-Bass, 1991.

Carvalho, H. "Active Teaching and Learning for a Deeper Understanding of Physiology." *Advances in Physiology Education,* 2009, *33*(2), 132–133.

Centra, J. "Will Teachers Receive Higher Student Evaluations by Giving Higher Grades and Less Course Work?" *Research in Higher Education,* 2003, *44*(5), 495–519.

Chapman, K. J., Davis, R., Toy, D., and Wright, L. "Academic Integrity in the Business School Environment: I'll Get by with a Little Help from My Friends." *Journal of Marketing Education,* 2004, *26*(3), 236–249.

Church, M. A., Elliot, A. J., and Gable, S. L. "Perceptions of Classroom Environment, Achievement Goals, and Achievement Outcomes." *Journal of Educational Psychology,* 2001, *93*(1), 43–54.

Coffman, S. J. "Ten Strategies for Getting Students to Take Responsibility for their Learning." *College Teaching*, 2003, *51*(1), 2–4.

Cooper, M. M., Cox, C. T., Nammouz, M., and Case, E. "An Assessment of Collaborative Groups on Students' Problem-Solving Strategies and Abilities." *Journal of Chemical Education*, 2008, *85*(6), 866–872.

Covington, M. V. *Making the Grade: A Self-Worth Perspective on Motivation and School Reform.* Cambridge: Cambridge University Press, 1992.

Covington, M. V., and Omelich, C. L. "Controversies or Consistencies: A Reply to Brown and Weiner." *Journal of Educational Psychology*, 1984, *76*(1), 159–168.

Cranton, P. *Understanding and Promoting Transformative Learning: A Guide for Educators of Adults.* San Francisco: Jossey-Bass, 2006.

Crisp, B. R. "Is It Worth the Effort? How Feedback Influences Students' Subsequent Submission of Assessable Work." *Assessment and Evaluation in Higher Education*, 2007, *32*(5), 571–581.

Cullen, R., Harris, M., and Reinhold, R. H. *The Learner-Centered Curriculum: Design and Implementation.* San Francisco: Jossey-Bass, 2012.

Dee, K. C. "Student Perceptions of High Course Workloads Are Not Associated with Poor Student Evaluations of Instructor Performance," *Journal of Engineering Education*, 2007, *96*(1), 69–78.

Deeter, L. "Incorporating Student Centered Learning Techniques into an Introductory Plant Identification Course." *NACTA Journal*, 2003, June, 47–52.

Derting, T. L., and Ebert-May, D. "Learner-Centered Inquiry in Undergraduate Biology: Positive Relationships with Long-Term Student Achievement." *Cell Biology Education—Life Sciences Education*, 2010, *9*(Winter), 462–472.

Deslauriers, L., Schelew, E., and Wieman, C. "Improved Learning in a Large-Enrollment Physics Class." *Science*, 2011, *332*(13 May), 862–864.

DiClementi, J. D., and Handelsman, M. M. "Empowering Students: Class-Generated Rules." *Teaching of Psychology*, 2005, *32*(1), 18–21.

Ditzier, M. A., and Ricci, R. W. "Discovery Chemistry: Balancing Creativity and Structure." *Journal of Chemical Education*, 1994, *71*(8), 685–688.

Dobrow, S. R., Smith, W. K., and Posner, M. A. "Managing the Grading Paradox: Leveraging the Power of Choice in the Classroom." *Academy of Management Learning and Education*, 2011, *10*(2), 261–276.

Dochy, F., Segers, M., den Bossche, P. V., and Gijbels, D. "Effects of Problem-Based Learning: A Meta-Analysis." *Learning and Instruction*, 2003, *13*, 533–568.

Duffy, T. M., and Raymer, P. L. "A Practical Guide and a Constructivist Rationale for Inquiry Based Learning." *Educational Technology*, July–August 2010, pp. 3–15.

Eberlein, T., and others. "Pedagogies of Engagement in Science: A Comparison of PBL, POGIL, and PLTL." *Biochemistry and Molecular Biology Education*, 2008, *36*(4), 262–273.

Ebert-May, D., and others. "What We Say Is Not What We Do: Effective Evaluation of Faculty Professional Development Programs." *BioScience*, 2011, *61*(7), 550–558.

Edwards, N. M. "Student Self-Grading in Social Statistics." *College Teaching*, 2007, *55*(2), 72–76.

Ege, S. N., Coppola, B. P., and Lawton, R. G. "The University of Michigan Undergraduate Chemistry Curriculum: 1. Philosophy, Curriculum, and the Nature of Change." *Journal of Chemical Education*, 1996, *74*(1), 74–91.

Eifler, K. "Academic 'Speed-Dating.'" *Teaching Professor*, 2008, (June–July), 3.

Eisner, E. W. "The Art and Craft of Teaching." *Educational Leadership*, January 1983, pp. 5–13.

Ellery, K. "Assessment for Learning: A Case Study Using Feedback Effectively in an Essay-Style Test." *Assessment and Evaluation in Higher Education*, 2008, *33*(4), 421–429.

Entwistle, N. "Taking Stock: An Overview of Key Research Findings." In J. C. Hughes and J. Mighty (eds.), *Taking Stock: Research on Teaching and Learning in Higher Education.* Montreal and Kingston: Queen's Policy Studies, McGill-Queens University Press, 2010.

Erickson, B. E., Peters, C. B., and Strommer, D. W. *Teaching First-Year College Students.* (Revised and expanded edition.) San Francisco: Jossey-Bass, 2006.

Erickson, B. E., and Strommer, D. W. *Teaching College Freshmen.* San Francisco: Jossey-Bass, 1991.

Falchikov, N., and Boud, D. "Student Self-Assessment in Higher Education: A Meta-Analysis." *Review of Higher Education Research*, 1989, *59*(4), 395–430.

Favero, T. G. "Active Review Sessions Can Advance Student Learning." *Advances in Physiology Education*, 2011, *35*(3), 247–248.

Felder, R. M., and Brent, R. "Navigating the Bumpy Road to Student-Centered Instruction." *College Teaching*, 1996, *44*(2), 43–47.

Fink, D. L. *Creating Significant Learning Experiences.* San Francisco: Jossey-Bass, 2003.

Finkel, D. L. *Teaching with Your Mouth Shut.* Portsmouth, N.H.: Boynton/Cook, 2000.

Finkelstein, M. J., Seal, R. K., and Schuster, J. *The New Academic Generation: A Profession in Transformation.* Baltimore: Johns Hopkins University Press, 1998.

Fischer, C. G., and Grant, G. E. "Intellectual Levels in College Classrooms." In C. L. Ellner and C. P. Barnes, *Studies of College Teaching.* Lexington, Mass.: D. C. Heath, 1983.

Fitzgerald, J., and Baird, V. A. "Taking a Step Back: Teaching Critical Thinking by Distinguishing Appropriate Types of Evidence." *PS: Political Science and Politics,* 2011, *44*(July), 619–624.

Flachmann, M. "Teaching in the 21st Century." *Teaching Professor,* 1994, *8*(March), 1–2.

Fosnot, C. T. (ed.). *Constructivism: Theory, Perspectives, and Practice.* New York: Teachers College Press, 1996.

Fox, D. "Personal Theories of Teaching." *Studies in Higher Education,* 1983, *8*(2), 151–163.

Fraser, B. J. *Classroom Environment.* London: Croom Helm, 1986.

Fraser, B. J., Treagust, D. F., and Dennis, N. C. "Development of an Instrument for Assessing Classroom Psychosocial Environment at Universities and Colleges." *Studies in Higher Education,* 1986, *11*(1), 43–53.

Frederick, P. "The Dreaded Discussion: Ten Ways to Start." *Improving College and University Teaching,* 1981, *29*(3), 109–114.

Freeman, S., Haak, D., and Wenderoth, M. P. "Increased Structure Improves Performance in Introductory Biology." *Cell Biology Education—Life Science Education,* 2011, *10*(Summer), 175–186.

Freire, P. *Pedagogy of the Oppressed.* New York: Herder & Herder, 1970.

Freire, P. *Pedagogy of the Oppressed.* (Rev. ed.) New York: Continuum, 1993.

Fritschner, L. M. "Inside the Undergraduate College Classroom: Faculty and Students Differ on the Meaning of Student Participation." *Journal of Higher Education,* 2000, *71*(3), 342–362.

Gardiner, L. F. "Why We Must Change: The Research Evidence." *Thought and Action,* Spring 1998, pp. 71–87.

Garner, M., and Emery, R. A. "A 'Better Mousetrap' in the Quest to Evaluate Instruction." *Teaching Professor,* 1993, *7*(November), 6.

Genereux, R. L., and McLeod, B. A. "Circumstances Surrounding Cheating: A Questionnaire Study of College Students." *Research in Higher Education,* 1995, *36*(6), 687–704.

Gibson, L. "Student-Directed Learning: An Exercise in Student Engagement." *College Teaching*, 2011, *59*(3), 95–101.

Gosser, D. K., Kampmeier, J. A., and Varma-Nelson, P. "Peer-Led Team Learning: 2008 James Flack Norris Award Address." *Journal of Chemical Education*, 2010, *87*(4), 374–380.

Goza, B. K. "Graffiti Needs Assessment: Involving Students in the First Class Session." *Journal of Management Education*, 1993, *17*(1), 99–106.

Green, D. H. "Student-Generated Exams: Testing and Learning." *Journal of Marketing Education*, 1997, *19*(2), 43–53.

Greeson, L. E. "College Classroom Interaction as a Function of Teacher- and Student-Centered Instruction." *Teaching and Teacher Education*, 1988, *4*, 305–315.

Gregory, M. "From Shakespeare on the Page to Shakespeare on the Stage: What I Learned about Teaching in Acting Class." *Pedagogy*, 2006, *6*(2), 309–325.

Grow, G. O. "Teaching Learners to Be Self-Directed." *Adult Education Quarterly*, 1991, *41*(3), 125–149.

Hale, D., and Mullen, L. G. "Designing Process-Oriented Guided-Inquiry Activities: A New Innovation for Marketing Classes." *Marketing Education Review*, 2009, *19*(1), 73–80.

Handelsman, J., and others. "Scientific Teaching." *Science*, 2004, *304*(23 July), 521–522.

Harris, M., and Cullen, R. *Leading the Learner-Centered Campus: An Administrator's Framework for Improving Student Learning Outcomes.* San Francisco: Jossey-Bass, 2010.

Hawk, T. F., and Lyons, P. R. "Please Don't Give Up on Me: When Faculty Fail to Care." *Journal of Management Education*, 2008, *32*(3), 316–338.

Heider, F. *The Psychology of Interpersonal Relations.* New York: Wiley, 1958.

Herreid, C. F. "Case Studies in Science: A Novel Method of Science Education." *Journal of College Science Teaching*, 1994, *23*(4), 221–229.

Herreid, C. F. "Dialogues as Case Studies: A Discussion on Human Cloning." *Journal of College Science Teaching*, 1999, *29*(2), 245–256.

Herreid, C. F. (ed.) *Start with a Story: The Case Study Method of Teaching College Science.* Arlington, Va.: National Science Teachers Association Press, 2007.

Hill, N. K. "Scaling the Heights: The Teacher as Mountaineer." *Chronicle of Higher Education*, June 16, 1980, p. 48.

Hilsen, L. R. "A Helpful Handout: Establishing and Maintaining a Positive Classroom Climate." In K. H. Gillespie (ed.), *A Guide to Faculty Development: Practical Advice, Examples, and Resources.* Bolton, Mass.: Anker, 2002.

Hockings, S. C., DeAngelis, K. J., and Frey, R. F. "Peer-Led Team Learning in General Chemistry: Implementation and Evaluation." *Journal of Chemical Education,* 2008, *85*(7), 990–996.

Hollander, J. A. "Learning to Discuss: Strategies for Improving the Quality of Class Discussion." *Teaching Sociology,* 2002, *30*(3), 317–327.

hooks, b. *Teaching to Transgress: Education as the Practice of Freedom.* New York: Routledge, 1994.

Horton, M., and Freire, P. *We Make the Road by Walking: Conversations on Education and Social Change.* Philadelphia: Temple University Press, 1990.

Howard, J. R. "Just-in-Time Teaching in Sociology or How I Convinced My Students to Actually Read the Assignment." *Teaching Sociology,* 2004, *32*(4), 385–390.

Howard, J. R., and Henney, A. L. "Student Participation and Instructor Gender in the Mixed-Age Classroom." *Journal of Higher Education,* 1998, *69*(4), 384–405.

Howard, J. R., Short, L. B., and Clark, S. M. "Students' Participation in the Mixed-Age College Classroom." *Teaching Sociology,* 1996, *24*(1), 8–24.

Hsiung, C. "The Effectiveness of Cooperative Learning." *Journal of Engineering Education,* 2012, *101*(1), 119–137.

Hudd, S. S. "Syllabus Under Construction: Involving Students in the Creation of Class Assignments." *Teaching Sociology,* 2003, *31*(2), 195–202.

Hudd, S. S., Smart, R. A., and Delohery, A. W. " 'My Understanding Has Grown, My Perspective Has Switched': Linking Informal Writing to Learning Goals." *Teaching Sociology,* 2011, *39*(2), 179–189.

Janick, J. "Crib Sheets." *Teaching Professor,* 1990, *4*(June–July), 2.

Jansen, E. P., and Bruinsma, M. "Explaining Achievement in Higher Education." *Educational Research and Evaluation,* 2005, *11*(3), 235–252.

Johnson, P. E. "Getting Students to Read the Syllabus: Another Approach." *Teaching Professor,* 2000, *14*(March), 1–2.

Kagan, S. "Group Grades Miss the Mark." *Cooperative Learning and College Teaching,* 1995, (*1*), 6–8.

Karabenick, S. A. (ed.). *Strategic Help Seeking: Implications for Learning and Teaching.* Mahwah, N.J.: Erlbaum, 1998.

Kardash, C. M. "Evaluation of an Undergraduate Research Experience: Perceptions of Interns and Their Faculty Mentors." *Journal of Educational Psychology,* 2000, *92*(1), 191–201.

Kardash, C. M., and Wallace, M. L. "The Perceptions of Science Classes Survey: What Undergraduate Science Reform Efforts Really Need to Address." *Journal of Educational Psychology,* 2001, *93*(1), 199–210.

Kearney, P., and Plax, T. G. "Student Resistance to Control." In V. P. Richmond and J. C. McCroskey (eds.), *Power in the Classroom: Communication, Control, and Concern.* Hillsdale, N.J.: Erlbaum, 1992.

Keeley, S. M., Shemberg, K. M., Cowell, B. S., and Zinnbauer, B. J. "Coping with Student Resistance to Critical Thinking: What the Psychotherapy Literature Can Tell Us." *College Teaching,* 1995, *43*(4), 140–145.

Kember, D., and Gow, L. "Orientations to Teaching and Their Effect on the Quality of Student Learning." *Journal of Higher Education,* 1994, *65*(1), 58–74.

Kember, D., and Leung, D.Y.P. "Establishing the Validity and Reliability of Course Evaluation Questionnaires." *Assessment and Evaluation in Higher Education,* 2008, *33*(4), 341–353.

Kiewra, K. A., and others. "Fish Giver or Fishing Teacher? The Lure of Strategy Instruction." *Teaching Professor,* 2001, *15*(February), 4.

King, A. "From Sage on the Stage to Guide on the Side." *College Teaching,* 1993, *41*(1), 30–35.

Kloss, R. J. "A Nudge Is Best: Helping Students through the Perry Scheme of Intellectual Development." *College Teaching,* 1994, *42*(4), 151–158.

Knapp, M. L., and Hall, J. A. *Nonverbal Communication in Human Interaction.* (3rd ed.) New York: Holt, Rinehart and Winston, 1992.

Knapper, C. K., and Cropley, A. J. *Lifelong Learning and Higher Education.* London: Croom Helm, 1985.

Knapper, C. K., and Cropley, A. J. *Lifelong Learning in Higher Education.* (3rd ed.) London: Kogan Page, 2000.

Knight, J. K., and Wood, W. B. "Teaching More by Lecturing Less." *Cell Biology Education,* 2005, *4*(Winter), 298–310.

Kohn, A. *No Contest: The Case Against Competition.* Boston: Houghton Mifflin, 1986.

Krohn, K. R., and others. "Reliability of Students' Self-Recorded Participation in Class Discussion." *Teaching of Psychology,* 2011, *38*(1), 43–45.

Lewis, S. E., and Lewis, J. E. "Departing from Lectures: An Evaluation of a Peer-Led Guided Inquiry Alternative." *Journal of Chemical Education,* 2005, *82*(1), 135–139.

Lyon, D. C., and Lagowski, J. J. "Effectiveness of Facilitating Small-Group Learning in Large Lecture Classes." *Journal of Chemical Education,* 2008, *85*(11), 1571–1576.

Macaskill, A., and Taylor, E. "The Development of a Brief Measure of Learner Autonomy in University Students." *Studies in Higher Education,* 2010, *35*(3), 351–359.

Maharaj, S., and Banta, L. "Using Log Assignments to Foster Learning: Revisiting Writing across the Curriculum." *Journal of Engineering Education,* 2000, *89*(1), 73–77.

Mallinger, M. "Maintaining Control in the Classroom by Giving Up Control." *Journal of Management Education,* 1998, *22*(4), 472–483.

Marini, Z. A. "The Teacher as a Sherpa Guide." *Teaching Professor,* 2000, *14*(April), 5.

Marsh, H. W., and Roche, L. A. "Effects of Grading Lenience and Low Workload on Students' Evaluations of Teaching: Popular Myth, Bias, Validity, or Innocent Bystanders?" *Journal of Educational Psychology,* 2000, *92*(1), 202–228.

Martin, J. H., and others. "Hard but Not Too Hard: Challenging Courses and Engineering Students." *College Teaching,* 2008, *56*(2), 107–113.

Marton, F., Hounsell, D., and Entwistle, N. (eds.). *The Experience of Learning: Implications for Teaching and Studying in Higher Education.* (2nd ed.) Edinburgh: Scottish Academic Press, 1997.

Marton, F., and Saljo, R. "On Qualitative Differences in Learning II: Outcome as a Function of the Learner's Conception of the Task." *British Journal of Educational Psychology,* 1976, *46*(2), 115–127.

Mazur, E. "Farewell, Lecture?" *Science,* 2009, *323*(2 January), 50–51.

McBrayer, D. J. "Tutoring Helps Improve Test Scores." *Teaching Professor,* 2001, *15*(April), 3.

McCreary, C. L., Golde, M. F., and Koeske, R. "Peer Instruction in General Chemistry Laboratory: Assessment of Student Learning." *Journal of Chemical Education,* 2006, *83*(5), 804–810.

McGowan, S., and Lightbody, M. "Enhancing Students' Understanding of Plagiarism within a Discipline Context." *Accounting Education: An International Journal,* 2008, *17*(3), 273–290.

Meyers, S. A. "Do Your Students Care Whether You Care About Them?" *College Teaching,* 2009, *57*(4), 205–210.

Mezirow, J., and Associates. *Learning as Transformation: Critical Perspectives on a Theory in Progress.* San Francisco: Jossey-Bass, 2000.

Michael, J. "Where's the Evidence that Active Learning Works?" *Advances in Physiology Education*, 2006, *30*(4), 159–167.

Mihans, R., Long, D., and Felton, P. "Power and Expertise: Student-Faculty Collaboration in Course Design and the Scholarship of Teaching." *International Journal for the Scholarship of Teaching*, 2008, *2*(2), 1–9.

Minderhout, V., and Loertscher, J. "Lecture-Free Biochemistry: A Process Oriented Guided Inquiry Approach." *Biochemistry and Molecular Biology Education*, 2007, *35*(3), 172–180.

Momsen, J. L., Long, T. M., Wyse, S. A., and Ebert-May, D. "Just the Facts? Introductory Undergraduate Biology Courses Focus on Low-Level Cognitive Skills." *Cell Biology Education—Life Sciences Education*, 2010, *9*(Winter), 435–440.

Mourtos, N. J. "The Nuts and Bolts of Cooperative Learning in Engineering." *Journal of Engineering Education*, 1997, *86*(1), 35–37.

Nash, R. J. "Resist the Pedagogical Far Right." *Inside Higher Education*, September 22, 2009.

Nicol, D. J., and Macfarlane-Dick, D. "Formative Assessment and Self-Regulated Learning: A Model and Seven Principles of Good Feedback Practice." *Studies in Higher Education*, 2006, *31*(2), 199–218.

Nilson, L. B. "Improving Student Peer Feedback." *College Teaching*, 2003, *51*(1), 34–38.

Noel, T. W. "Lessons from the Learning Classroom." *Journal of Management Education*, 2004, *28*(2), 188–206.

Norcross, J. C., Dooley, H. S., and Stevenson, J. F. "Faculty Use and Justification of Extra Credit: No Middle Ground?" *Teaching of Psychology*, 1993, *20*(4), 240–242.

Norcross, J. C., Horrocks, L. J., and Stevenson, J. F. "Of Barfights and Gadflies: Attitudes and Practices Concerning Extra Credit in College Courses." *Teaching of Psychology*, 1989, *16*(4), 199–203.

Nunn, C. E. "Discussion in the College Classroom: Triangulating Observational and Survey Results." *Journal of Higher Education*, 1996, *67*(3), 243–266.

Pandey, C., and Kapitanoff, S. "The Influence of Anxiety and Quality of Interaction on Collaborative Test Performance." *Active Learning in Higher Education*, 2011, *12*(3), 163–174.

Parrott, H. M., and Cherry, E. "Using Structured Reading Groups to Facilitate Deep Learning." *Teaching Sociology*, 2011, *39*(4), 354–370.

Pascarella, E. T., and Terenzini, P. T. *How College Affects Students: Twenty Years of Research, Volume 1.* San Francisco: Jossey-Bass, 1991.

Pascarella, E. T., and Terenzini, P. T. *How College Affects Students: A Third Decade of Research, Volume 2.* San Francisco: Jossey-Bass, 2005.

Perry, R. P., and Magnusson, J-L. "Effective Instruction and Students' Perceptions of Control in the College Classroom: Multiple-Lectures Effects." *Journal of Educational Psychology,* 1987, *79*(4), 453–460.

Phelps, P. H. "Teaching Transformation." *Teaching Professor,* 2008, *22*(December), 2–3.

Pike, D. L. "The Tyranny of Dead Ideas in Teaching and Learning." *The Sociological Quarterly,* 2011, *52,* 1–12.

Pintrich, P. R. "A Motivational Perspective on the Role of Student Motivation in Learning and Teaching Contexts." *Journal of Educational Psychology,* 2003, *95*(4), 667–686.

Pintrich, P. R., Smith, D.A.F., Garcia, T., and McKeachie, W. J. "Reliability and Predictive Validity of the Motivated Strategies for Learning Questionnaire (MLSQ)." *Educational and Psychological Measurement,* 1993, *53*(3), 801–813.

Pollio, H. R., and Beck, H. P. "When the Tail Wags the Dog: Perceptions of Learning and Grade Orientation in and by Contemporary College Students and Faculty." *Journal of Higher Education,* 2000, *71*(1), 84–102.

Pollio, H. R., and Humphreys, W. W. "Grading Students." In J. H. McMillan (ed.), *Assessing Students' Learning.* New Directions for Teaching and Learning, no. 34. San Francisco: Jossey-Bass, 1988.

Power, L. G. "University Students' Perceptions of Plagiarism." *Journal of Higher Education,* 2009, *80*(6), 645–662.

Prince, M. J. "Does Active Learning Work? A Review of the Research." *Journal of Engineering Education,* 2004, *93*(3), 223–231.

Prince, M. J., and Felder, R. M. "Inductive Teaching and Learning Methods: Definitions, Comparisons, and Research Bases." *Journal of Engineering Education,* 2006, *95*(2), 123–138.

Prince, M. J., and Felder, R. M. "The Many Faces of Inductive Teaching Learning." *Journal of College Science Teaching,* 2007, *36*(5), 14–20.

Prosser, M., and Trigwell, K. "Confirmatory Factor Analysis of the Approaches to Teaching Inventory." *British Journal of Educational Psychology,* 2006, *76*(2), 405–419.

Ramsden, P. "Studying Learning: Improving Teaching." In P. Ramsden (ed.), *Improving Learning: New Perspectives.* London: Kogan Page, 1988.

Ramsey, V. J., and Fitzgibbons, D. E. "Being in the Classroom." *Journal of Management Education,* 2005, *29*(2), 333–356.

Roberts, J. C., and Roberts, K. A. "Deep Reading, Cost/Benefit, and the Construction of Meaning: Enhancing Reading Comprehension and Deep Learning in Sociology Courses." *Teaching Sociology,* 2008, *36*(April), 125–140.

Sadler, D. R. "Beyond Feedback: Developing Student Capability in Complex Appraisal." *Assessment and Evaluation in Higher Education,* 2010, *35*(5), 535–550.

Sanger, L. "Individual Knowledge in the Internet Age." *Educause,* March/April 2010, pp. 14–24.

Sarros, J. C., and Densten, I. L. "Undergraduate Student Stress and Coping Strategies." *Higher Education Research and Development,* 1989, *8*(1), 1–13.

Shrock, A. A. "The Sign at the Side of the Door." *Teaching Professor,* 1992, *6*(June–July), 8.

Silverman, R., and Welty, W. M. *Case Studies for Faculty Development.* White Plains, N.Y.: Pace University, 1992.

Singham, M. "Moving away from the Authoritarian Classroom." *Change,* May/June 2005, pp. 51–57.

Singham, M. "Death to the Syllabus." *Liberal Education,* 2007, *93*(4), 52–56.

Sipress, J. M., and Voelker, D. J. "The End of the History Survey Course: The Rise and Fall of the Coverage Model." *The Journal of American History,* 2011, *97*(4), 1050–1066.

Spence, L. "The Teacher of Westwood." *Teaching Professor,* 2010, *24*(November), 3.

Stage, F. K., Muller, P. A., Kinzie, J., and Simmons, A. *Creating Learner Centered Classrooms: What Does Learning Theory Have to Say?* ASHE-ERIC Higher Education Report No. 4. Washington, DC: ERIC Clearinghouse on Higher Education and the Association for the Study of Higher Education, 1998.

Starling, R. "Professor as Student: The View from the Other Side." *College Teaching,* 1987, *35*(1), 3–7.

Straumanis, A. R., and Simons, E. A. "A Multi-Institutional Assessment of the Use of POGIL in Organic Chemistry." In R. S. Moog and J. N. Spencer (eds.), *Process Oriented Guided Inquiry Learning.* New York: Oxford University Press, 2008.

Terenzini, P. T., and others. "Collaborative Learning vs. Lecture/Discussion: Students' Reported Learning Gains." *Journal of Engineering Education,* 2001, *90*(1), 123–129.

Thiel, T., Peterman, S., and Brown, B. "Addressing the Crisis in College Mathematics: Designing Courses for Student Success." *Change,* July–August 2008, pp. 44–49.

Tichenor, L. L. "Student-Designed Physiology Labs." *Journal of College Science Teaching*, December 1996–January 1997, *20*(3), 175–181.

Tien, L. T., Roth, V., and Kampmeier, J. A. "Implementation of a Peer-Led Team Learning Instructional Approach in an Undergraduate Organic Chemistry Course." *Journal of Research in Science Teaching*, 2002, *39*(7), 606–632.

Tomasek, T. "Critical Reading: Using Reading Prompts to Promote Active Engagement with Text." *International Journal of Teaching and Learning in Higher Education*, 2009, *21*(1), 127–132.

Tompkins, J. "Teaching Like It Matters." *Lingua Franca*, August 1991, pp. 24–27.

Trigwell, K. "Teaching and Learning: A Relational View." In J. C. Hughes and J. Mighty (eds.), *Taking Stock: Research on Teaching and Learning in Higher Education*. Montreal and Kingston: Queen's Policy Studies, McGill-Queen's University Press, 2010.

Trigwell, K., Prosser, M., Ramsden, P., and Martin, E. "Improving Student Learning through a Focus on the Teaching Context." In C. Rust (ed.), *Improving Student Learning*. Oxford, U.K.: Oxford Center for Staff and Learning Development, 1999.

Trigwell, K., Prosser, M., and Waterhouse, F. "Relations between Teachers' Approaches to Teaching and Students' Approaches to Learning." *Higher Education*, 1999, *37*(1), 57–70.

Ueckert, C., Adams, A., and Lock, J. "Redesigning a Large-Enrollment Introductory Biology Course." *Cell Biology Education—Life Sciences Education*, 2011, *10*(Summer), 164–174.

Verderber, R. F. *Communicate*. (8th ed.). New York: Wadsworth, 1995.

Vernon, D., and Blake, R. "Does Problem-Based Learning Work? A Meta-Analysis of Evaluative Research." *Academic Medicine*, 1993, *68*(7), 550–563.

Walczyk, J. J., and Ramsey, L. L. "Use of Learner-Centered Instruction in College Science and Mathematics Classrooms." *Journal of Research in Science Teaching*, 2003, *40*(6), 566–584.

Wamser, C. C. "Peer-Led Team Learning in Organic Chemistry: Effects on Student Performance, Success and Persistence in the Course." *Journal of Chemical Education*, 2006, *83*(10), 1562–1566.

Watts, M., and Schaur, G. "Teaching and Assessment Methods in Undergraduate Economics: A Fourth National Quinquennial Survey." *The Journal of Economic Education*, 2011, *42*(3), 294–309.

Weimer, M. "What Should Future Teaching Be Like?" *Teaching Professor*, 1988, *2*(February), 1.

Weimer, M. "Exams: Alternative Ideas and Approaches." *Teaching Professor*, 1989, *3*(October), 3–4.

Weimer, M. *Inspired College Teaching: A Career-Long Resource for Professional Growth.* San Francisco: Jossey-Bass, 2010.

Weiner, B. *An Attributional Theory of Motivation and Emotion.* New York: Springer Verlag, 1986.

Weinstein, C. E., Palmer, D. R., and Hanson, G. R. *Perceptions, Expectations, Emotions, and Knowledge About College.* Clearwater, Fla.: H & H, 1995.

Weinstein, C. E., Schulte, A. C., and Palmer, D. R. *LASSI: Learning and Study Strategies Inventory.* Clearwater, Fla.: H & H, 1987.

Welty, W. M. "Discussion Method Teaching: How to Make It Work." *Change,* July–August 1989, pp. 40–49.

Wiggins, G., and McTighe, J. *Understanding by Design.* (2nd ed.) Upper Saddle River, N.J.: Pearson Education, 2005.

Wilson, J. H. "Predicting Student Attitudes and Grades from Perceptions of Instructors' Attitudes." *Teaching of Psychology,* 2006, *33*(2), 91–95.

Winston, R. B., Jr., and others. "A Measure of College Classroom Climate: The College Classroom Environment Scales." *Journal of College Student Development,* 1994, *35*(1), 11–35.

Woods, D. R. "Participation Is More Than Attendance." *Journal of Engineering Education,* 1996, *85*(3), 177–181.

Yamane, D. "Course Preparation Assignments: A Strategy for Creating Discussion-Based Courses." *Teaching Sociology,* 2006, *34*(July), 236–248.

Zimmerman, B. J. "Self-Regulated Learning and Academic Achievement: An Overview." *Educational Psychologist,* 1990, *25*(1), 3–17.

Zimmerman, B. J. "Becoming a Self-Regulated Learner: An Overview." *Theory into Practice,* 2002, *41*(2), 64–70.

Zimmerman, B. J. "Investigating Self-Regulation and Motivation: Historical Background, Methodological Developments, and Future Prospects." *American Educational Research Journal,* 2008, *45*(1), 166–183.

Zimmerman, B. J., and Martinez Pons, M. "Development of a Structured Interview for Assessing Students' Use of Self-Regulated Learning Strategies." *American Educational Research Journal,* 1986, *23*(3), 614–628.

Zimmerman, B. J., and Martinez Pons, M. "Construct Validation of a Strategy Model for Student Self-Regulated Learning." *Journal of Educational Psychology,* 1988, *80*(3), 284–290.

Name Index

A

Abell, S. K., 65
Ackerman, D. S., 132
Adams, A., 50–51
Albanese, M., 43, 44
Albers, C., 201, 233
Allen, J., 172
Amstutz, J., 69
Appleby, D. C., 160
Archer, C. C., 67–68
Armbruster, D. S., 49
Armbruster, P., 109
Aronowitz, A., 18
Ayers, W., 62

B

Bacon, D. R., 119–120
Baez-Galib, R., 46
Baird, V. A., 229
Baker, D. F., 192, 193
Bandura, A., 17
Barkley, E. F., 160
Barr, R. B., 61
Bean, J. C., 192
Beck, H. P., 171
Benjamin, L. T., 104, 234
Benson, T. A., 155
Benvenuto, M., 82
Biggs, J., 32, 33, 62, 63
Black, K. A., 73–74, 105
Blake, R., 43, 44
Blumberg, P., 230–231, 236
Boud, D., 174
Braye, S., 92
Brent, R., 201
Brookfield, S. D., 6, 238
Brown, B., 52, 106
Brown, J.P.P., 45, 46, 109
Brown, S. D., 45, 65, 109

Bruffee, K. A., 21–22
Buchler, J., 229
Bunce, D. M., 89
Burrowes, P. A., 49–50
Buskist, W., 155

C

Calder, L., 116, 124
Candy, P. C., 34, 125
Carvalho, H., 119
Case, E., 47
Centra, J., 154
Chapman, K. J., 173
Church, M. A., 170
Clask, S. M., 102
Coffman, S. J., 151
Cohen, A. L., 155
Colon-Cruz, H., 46
Cooper, M. M., 47
Coppola, B. P., 24
Covington, M. V., 172
Cowell, B. S., 203
Cox, C. T., 47
Cranton, P., 6, 24
Crisp, B. R., 179
Cropley, A. J., 120
Cullen, R., 231

D

Davis, R., 173
DeAngelis, K. J., 46
Deeter, L., 186–187
Delohery, A. W., 139
Demir, A., 65
den Bossche, P. V., 43, 44
Dennis, N. C., 147–149, 161
Densten, I. L., 176
Derting, T. L., 51, 220, 230
Deslauriers, L., 53

SUBJECT INDEX

"*The Nurture Effect* is a remarkably ambitious book that draws the blue-prints for creating prosocial communities aiming to help people live healthier, value-directed, and enjoyable lives. Biglan explains how people can work together to reduce suffering and improve quality of living for each other, and supports these plans with reliable behavioral research. The science of this book is captivating because Biglan expresses the ideas in an understandable and practical manner. In other words, he simplifies the science of human behavior so you can use it to improve your own community. *The Nurture Effect* hits the ground running with clear, concise, well-stated facts about creating a social context for people to experience a life well-lived. Throughout the book, Biglan expands these ideas into the different branches of community, such as family, schools, work, peer-relations, and discusses how—when approached appropriately—they can make lasting positive contributions to individuals. The perspectives you gain from this book will not only assist you in helping your community to become stronger and healthier, but will also help you as an individual to experience those same positive outcomes."

—**D.J. Moran, PhD**, founder of Pickslyde Consulting and the MidAmerican Psychological Institute

"*The Nurture Effect* is exciting because it is grounded in science but leads us well beyond the fragmented slivers in which scientific findings are often delivered. Anthony Biglan persuades us that rather than focusing on preventing individual problems of family dysfunction, drug addiction, academic failure, child abuse, and even crime, we need to cut to the chase and attend to what all of these have in common. Biglan shows that poverty consistently makes it harder to help, and that nurture is so frequently missing. By integrating findings from the past fifty years in psychology, epidemiology, education, and neuroscience, he pulls out the common threads to show that it is possible to make families, schools, and the larger social context more nurturing, and ultimately to create the nurturing environments so vital to well-being and to preventing widespread harm."

—**Lisbeth B. Schorr**, senior fellow at the Center for the Study of Social Policy, and coauthor of *Within Our Reach*

"This marvelous book integrates the most compelling scientific knowledge about how we can improve the lives of citizens of this country with a bold call to action. Fundamentally, Anthony Biglan—a gifted and experienced behavioral scientist—challenges us to ask, 'What kind of society do we want? How can we use what we know to create such a society?' His central thesis is that widely implementing what we have learned over decades in developing programs that nurture children, adolescents, parents and adults in families, in schools, and in the larger society—which he calls a *revolution in behavioral science*—will make a huge difference.

The book contains highly practical, specific recommendations for families, practitioners, and policy makers. Biglan rightly recognizes that to significantly change society for the better, we must address larger social forces—for example, the negative effects of poverty and economic inequality, or of marketing tobacco and alcohol to youth. Eminently readable, this book comprehensively reviews evidence based on a lifetime of experience as a social scientist, and knits it together with a compelling agenda, that if enacted, could lead to a significant, positive transformation of our country."

> —**William R. Beardslee, MD**, director of the Baer
> Prevention Initiatives at Boston Children's Hospital, and
> Gardner-Monks Professor of child psychiatry at Harvard
> Medical School

"This work is Anthony Biglan's magnum opus. He has pulled together many ideas from multiple disciplinary domains. It is required reading for anyone who is serious about fixing the problems in our education system and alleviating poverty. Anyone who liked David Brooks' *The Social Animal* will also like this. Although Biglan is a self-identified and proud behaviorist, this work shows his openness to other perspectives. I was especially happy to see his new nuanced view of the role of reinforcement in human behavior (pages 28-29). Intrinsic motivation is more powerful in the long term than extrinsic motivation."

> —**Brian R. Flay, DPhil**, professor of social and behavioral
> health sciences at Oregon State University, Corvallis,
> OR, and emeritus distinguished professor of public health
> and psychology at University of Illinois at Chicago,
> Chicago, IL

"The author's engaging writing style enables readers to appreciate the elegance of applying knowledge based on rigorous research to develop and apply evidence-based interventions that prevent problems and promote well-being on a societal scale."

> —**Marion S. Forgatch, PhD**, senior scientist emerita at the Oregon Social Learning Center (OSLC), where she developed and tested programs for families with children at risk or referred for child adjustment problems and substance abuse

"*The Nurture Effect* is one of those rare books that draws from a lifetime of careful scientific study to provide clear prescriptions—in language non-scientists can understand—about how to make our world a better place. Pushing back against contemporary fatalism, Anthony Biglan shows us that we know more than ever about how to promote human flourishing. The problem is that we're not applying this knowledge as we should. *The Nurture Effect* explains how we could change that, and, even more important, how *you* can help make the change happen."

> —**Jacob S. Hacker, PhD**, Stanley B. Resor Professor of political science, director at the Institution for Social and Policy Studies, and coauthor of *Winner-Take-All Politics*

"In *The Nurture Effect*, Anthony Biglan offers a challenge and a road map for making our society more effective and successful. His message is at once simple and overwhelming. There is a science of human behavior, and we need to use it."

> —**Rob Horner, PhD**, endowed professor of special education at the University of Oregon

"Tony Biglan's book puts forth a bold and thought-provoking plan to help every community ensure that our young people grow into caring and productive adults. It's well worth reading."

> —**Senator Merkley**

The
Nurture
Effect

How *the* Science *of* Human Behavior *Can* Improve Our Lives *&* Our World

ANTHONY BIGLAN, PHD

New Harbinger Publications, Inc.

Publisher's Note

This publication is designed to provide accurate and authoritative information in regard to the subject matter covered. It is sold with the understanding that the publisher is not engaged in rendering psychological, financial, legal, or other professional services. If expert assistance or counseling is needed, the services of a competent professional should be sought.

Distributed in Canada by Raincoast Books

Copyright © 2015 by Anthony Biglan
New Harbinger Publications, Inc.
5674 Shattuck Avenue
Oakland, CA 94609
www.newharbinger.com

Cover design by Amy Shoup
Acquired by Catharine Meyers
Edited by Jasmine Star

Library of Congress Cataloging-in-Publication Data on file

Printed in the United States of America

17   16   15

10   9   8   7   6   5   4   3   2   1   First printing

To Georgia. She has restrained my most selfish excesses, put up with my many foibles, and nurtured me and everyone around her.

Contents

PART 4
Evolving the Nurturing Society

Foreword

The Hope of Science and the Science of Hope

Think of this book as a beacon of hope.

The dire statistics and horrific stories that litter our newscasts present the modern world as aimless, chaotic, and lost, going backward in almost every area of social importance. There is an element of truth to that characterization, but there is also a force for good in the modern world that has the potential to reverse all of these trends. What it is and what it says is what this book is about.

We can have a large impact on the prevention and amelioration of abuse, drug problems, violence, mental health problems, and dysfunction in families. As this book shows, we know how to do it, we know what it would cost, and we know how long it would take. We even know the core principles that underlie these successful approaches, so we can narrow our focus to what really matters. We know all these things because modern behavioral and evolutionary science has proven answers that work. The careful, controlled research has been done. The answers are in our hands.

Unfortunately these answers and the foundations they stand on are often invisible to policy makers and to the public at large. Some of this invisibility is unintentional—it is sometimes difficult to separate the wheat from the chaff in scientific knowledge. Some of this invisibility comes because vested interests are threatened. Tobacco companies, for example, thrived on the ignorance and confusion that they themselves fostered.

Beacons are needed in exactly such situations. They cast light so that what was unseen can be seen. They give direction so that instead of wandering aimlessly, we can stay on course during long and difficult journeys. And they allow us to mark and measure whether we are making progress, providing reassurance that every step we take is bringing us closer to our destination.

Tony Biglan brings four decades of experience on the front lines of behavioral science to this far-reaching, carefully argued, and compelling book. A major prevention scientist, Tony knows many of the people who have tested these methods; he himself was involved in key studies, policy innovations, and legal struggles. He tells the stories of knowledge developers and of the people whose lives have been affected, showing in case after case that these methods are powerful tools in the creation of deliberate social change.

Tony is not content merely to list these solutions; he organizes them and shows the core principles by which they operate: increasing nurturance, cooperation, and psychological flexibility, and decreasing coercion and aversive control. He distinguishes empirically between the psychological and social features that are engines of change, and the psychological or social features that come along for the ride. And he nests this knowledge in an examination of what might need to change for us to make better use of it.

Over and over again, the same small set of features have been shown to have profound and lasting effects. Spend a dollar on the Good Behavior Game with children in first or second grade, and save eighty-four dollars in special education, victim, health care, and criminal justice costs over the next few decades. Aggressive boys randomly assigned to play this simple game at age six or seven had two-thirds fewer drug problems as adults!

There initially may be a "too good to be true" reaction to results like this, but Tony takes the time to walk the readers through the research, and its quality and replication. As common themes emerge, unnecessary skepticism gradually washes away and we begin as readers to wake up to an incredible reality. Because of our belief in science and the hope it provides, we as a society have spent billions on research to learn what works in addressing our social and psychological problems. Today we have a mountain of answers that could enormously impact our lives.

Tony provides the means for parents and others to take advantage of what we know right now. At the end of every chapter he provides sections on action implications for particular audiences, and summarizes what has been shown into a manageable set of bulleted takeaway points. He opens the door that policy makers and the public might walk through by listing the policy implications of what we know for the ability to better our children and our society.

As the book progresses, you realize that our failure to work together to ensure that research matters in the creation of a more nurturing society is itself produced by features of our current system. Children are nested within families, who are nested within communities. Communities are nested within political and economic structures. All of this is evolving—but not always positively. Sometimes social evolution is crafted by organized forces linked to economic visions that are producing rapidly increasing economic and health disparities. This wonderful book casts light and provides direction even here. Regular people can play the social evolutionary game too. We can develop our systems toward a purpose if we have the knowledge and foresight needed to do so. This book provides a healthy serving of exactly that knowledge and foresight.

In the end readers will know that together we can create a more nurturing and effective society, step by step. We have the knowledge to do better—much, much better. And ultimately we *will* follow such steps—knowledge of this level of importance does not remain forever unused. But why wait? Why not act now? By bringing together the fruits of behavioral and evolutionary science, the modern world can begin a grand journey, buoyed up not just by the hope of science in the abstract but by the substantive scientific knowledge we already have in hand. We will learn more as we go, but because of the hope that science represents, we as a human community have already funded the knowledge developers who have created this body of work. It is time to use what we have together created. It is time to apply the science of hope.

—Steven C. Hayes
    Foundation Professor and Director of Clinical Training
    University of Nevada
    Author of *Get Out of Your Mind and Into Your Life*

Acknowledgments

If it takes a village to raise a child, it also takes a village to nurture the development and productivity of behavioral scientists. I have been extremely fortunate in that respect. Bob Kohlenberg got me to read B. F. Skinner's work and put me on a path that has guided my entire career. David Kass mentored my budding behaviorism during my internship at the University of Wisconsin.

Then there is the behavioral science community of Eugene, Oregon. Peter Lewinsohn showed me how to develop a research project and get it funded. Jerry Patterson, Tom Dishion, John Reid, Marion Forgatch, and Hill Walker have made such important contributions to science and have continued to inspire me. I thank Kevin Moore, my good friend, whose admiration for my work meant more to me than he realizes.

My many colleagues at Oregon Research Institute (ORI) have nurtured me for thirty-five years. Ed Lichtenstein and Herb Severson collaborated with me on our first project at ORI. Hy Hops, my good friend and amiable colleague, showed me how to have fun and do science at the same time. Then there is Christine Cody. Her skill as an editor has made this a better book, and without her, I would have published many fewer things over the past fifteen years. Sylvia Gillings has taken care of so many aspects of my work, just as she has nurtured everyone else at ORI.

Steve Hayes has had a profound impact. His work has transformed my research and my life, and his friendship has supported and inspired me.

I thank Dennis Embry, my most enthusiastic ally, who leads the way in making the fruits of behavioral science available to everyone.

David Sloan Wilson is leading a worldwide movement to organize the human sciences within an evolutionary framework. He has promoted prevention science and provided critical mentoring for me in writing this book.

My career would not have happened had it not been for funding from the National Institutes of Health, and I thank both the institutes and the people in them who have been so supportive over the years: the National Cancer Institute (especially Cathy Backinger, Bob Vollinger, and Tom Glynn), the National Institute on Drug Abuse (especially Liz Robertson, Zili Sloboda, and Wilson Compton), the National Institute of Mental Health, and the National Institute of Child Health and Human Development.

This book is about creating nurturing environments. I am blessed by a nurturing family. Georgia, my wife of forty years, and I have grown so much closer as we learned to apply the insights that her work and mine have taught us about human behavior. My son Sean has a keen eye for the flaws in an argument, which has sharpened my thinking. Some of the most intellectually stimulating conversations I had as I wrote this book have been with him. I have watched my son Mike and my daughter-in-law Jen nurture their children, Ashlyn and Grayson, as I have written this book. Without them, I would be bereft of examples! I also thank my sisters, Hekate and Kathie. Hekate read so many versions of so many chapters, provided many insights, and always cheered me on. And Kathie has nurtured the ties of family that have kept us connected across many miles and many years.

When I began working with New Harbinger on the editing of this book, I was wary of where they seemed to be trying to take me. No more! This is a far better book thanks to the clear, direct, patient, and richly reinforcing feedback from Jess Beebe, Melissa Valentine, and Nicola Skidmore.

Lastly, humans are not the only species that has nurtured me. As I write this, my cat, Charlie, is sitting in my lap with his head and paws draped over my left arm, purring. Thanks, Charlie!

Introduction:
The Way Forward

After forty years of working on prevention of a wide range of common and costly psychological and behavioral problems, I am convinced we have the knowledge to achieve a healthier, happier, and more prosperous society than has ever been seen in human history.

I have been doing behavioral science research for over four decades. For the past thirty-five, I have been a scientist at Oregon Research Institute, conducting research funded almost entirely by the National Institutes of Health. My research has involved efforts to prevent the psychological and behavioral problems of young people that account for most of society's social and health problems. Perhaps because I have studied so many different problems, I was fortunate to be elected president of the Society for Prevention Research in 2005. That led to a 2007 request from the Institute of Medicine (IOM) to serve on a committee reviewing the progress the United States had made in preventing these problems.

The IOM is part of the National Academy of Sciences, which President Lincoln created to articulate the state of scientific knowledge in every area. As our committee reviewed the huge body of evidence accumulated since the 1994 prevention report, we realized that a far more nurturing society is within reach. As our report stated, "The scientific foundation has been created for the nation to begin to create a society in which young people arrive at adulthood with the skills, interests, assets, and health habits needed to live healthy, happy, and productive lives in caring relationships with others" (IOM and NRC 2009, 387).

As ambitious as this sounds, I believe we can achieve it. While working on the IOM committee, I began to see common threads that ran through all successful prevention programs, policies, and practices. If you look into these programs, you find that all of them make people's environments more nurturing. They encourage families to abandon conflict. Step-by-step, they teach people to support each other's well-being and development. They convince families and schools to abundantly reinforce young people for helping each other and contributing to their schools and communities. They limit opportunities and influences to engage in problem behavior. They encourage us to persevere in pursuing our most cherished values, even while facing significant obstacles, including thoughts and feelings that discourage us from trying. Nurturing environments are key to creating a healthier, happier society.

We can make our environments more nurturing by widely implementing the preventive interventions that research is identifying. But contextually focused behavioral science is also identifying how the larger social context for families and schools must change to fully realize nurturing environments in society. We have evolved a worldwide system of corporate capitalism that has brought us great prosperity and unimagined technological innovations. But it also increases poverty and economic inequality in developed countries and promotes materialistic values and practices that undermine nurturance in families, schools, neighborhoods, and communities. Although the behavioral sciences have not made as much progress on how to reform this larger social system as they have on making families and schools more nurturing, the outline of what is needed is becoming clear.

The tobacco control movement provides a good model for how to achieve massive societal changes. In 1965, over 50 percent of men and 34 percent of women smoked. By 2010, only 23.5 percent of men and 17.9 percent of women were smoking (CDC 2011). These numbers represent one of the twentieth century's most important public health achievements. When public health officials, epidemiologists, and victims of the cigarette industry united to mobilize opposition to the unfettered marketing of a product that was killing four hundred thousand Americans each year, they moved a mountain. They formed a network of government agencies and advocacy organizations that showed the public how harmful cigarettes are. That created a growing movement that convinced most Americans that the cigarette industry had been lying to them. It also mobilized support for policies that encouraged people to quit—or not start—and educated them about the problem. Think of the last few meetings or social events you attended. Was anyone smoking? Forty years ago, such events probably would have taken place in smoke-filled rooms. We have evolved a largely smoke-free society, despite powerful opposition.

Just as we have created a society in which it would be unthinkable to light up a cigarette in the Kennedy Center lobby, we can create a society where it is unthinkable that a child suffers abuse, fails in school, becomes delinquent, or faces teasing and bullying. We could have a society in which diverse people and organizations work together to ensure that families, schools, workplaces, and neighborhoods are nurturing and that our capitalistic system functions to benefit everyone.

Addressing all the problems we confront might seem daunting. Would we need a similar movement for each problem? Largely, we have that now: Mothers Against Drunk Driving combats alcohol problems; the Community Anti-Drug Coalitions of America battle drug abuse; the criminal justice system fights crime; schools foster academic success. However, a broad, science-guided social movement that works to ensure that all facets of society support nurturance is possible.

This book is about how we can create such a movement. Nearly all problems of human behavior stem from our failure to ensure that people live in environments that nurture their well-being. I am confident that, if we marshal the evidence for nurturing environments and use the advocacy techniques that worked so well for the tobacco control movement, we can truly transform society. Not only will we have smoke-free gatherings, we will have communities that see to the well-being of every member. We will have less crime, mental illness, drug abuse, divorce, academic failure, and poverty.

The benefits of this science-based approach to transforming society can extend well beyond prevention of individual psychological and behavioral problems. At this point, we can use a wealth of accumulated knowledge to evolve a society where people cooperate and care for each other. From that fertile soil we can grow a society where businesses, nonprofits, and governments work effectively for the common good. These claims may seem incredible, but that is only because most people—including many behavioral scientists—are unaware of the extraordinary advances of behavioral science.

Evolution takes a long time. Even cultural evolution can go so slowly that it is hard to notice change within a lifetime. This is the case for the behavioral sciences. Fifty years ago, there was not one intervention to treat or prevent a problem of human behavior. But over the ensuing fifty years, behavioral scientists developed numerous programs, policies, and practices to transform families, schools, work organizations, and neighborhoods into nurturing environments that can ensure the successful development of virtually every young person.

Even many people who have made major contributions to this evolution don't realize how comprehensively behavioral science has addressed problems of human behavior. Most scientists work on a fairly narrow range of problems. By concentrating their energies on the myriad details of one specific problem, they advance knowledge by pinpointing its influences or testing refined interventions.

I deeply admire this disciplined approach. I have long felt that I am too undisciplined as a scientist. Those I most admire concentrate on carefully defined and circumscribed problems; I, on the other hand, have worked on a wide variety of problems, and this has limited my contributions in any specific area. Yet my lack of discipline and wide-ranging interests have helped me recognize some basic principles that unite the dramatic advances the behavioral sciences have made in the past fifty years.

In this book, I hope to show you how these principles can guide us toward the kind of society the IOM committee on prevention envisioned. Despite society's countless troubles right now, seeing the tremendous scientific advances we have made in understanding and taking practical steps to nurture human well-being makes me optimistic about our future.

An Overview of the Book

This book has four parts, described below.

A Science Equal to the Challenge of the Human Condition

Part 1 of this book consists solely of chapter 1, which provides an overview of the scientific principles that guide our progress. I don't claim that this is the one true account of behavioral science. Indeed, one of the things emerging from research on human behavior is the recognition that what we say about the world is better thought of as talk that may be useful for some purpose, rather than truth with a capital T. So I ask you to consider this take on the status of the behavioral sciences in terms of its usefulness for advancing the human condition.

Nurturing Well-Being Through Prevention and Treatment

In part 2 of the book, I describe interventions that have been developed to provide treatment or prevention to individuals or families. Chapters 2 through 4 focus on prevention. Prevention science integrates findings from the past fifty years in psychology, epidemiology, education, and neuroscience into a public health approach to ensuring everyone's positive development. Although the field of prevention science has only been around for about twenty years, it has produced a large number of programs, policies, and practices with proven benefit.

Figure 1 is from the Institute of Medicine's report on prevention (IOM and NRC 2009). Each entry refers to one or more programs shown to prevent development of psychological, behavioral, or health problems. Most of the interventions focus on families or schools, since these are the major environments affecting young people's development. Most interventions address multiple problems. For example, the Nurse-Family Partnership (Olds et al. 2003), which provides support to poor single mothers during pregnancy and the first two years of the baby's life, not only prevents child abuse but also improves children's academic performance.

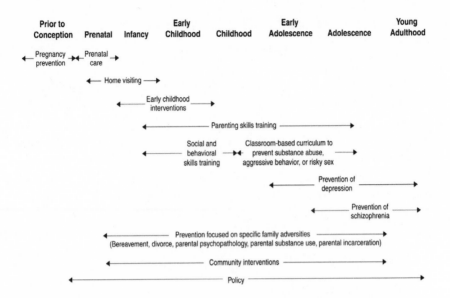

Figure 1. Interventions by developmental phase. (Reprinted with permission from *Preventing Mental, Emotional, and Behavioral Disorders Among Young People: Progress and Possibilities* [2009] by the National Academy of Sciences. Courtesy of the National Academies Press, Washington, DC.)

As you can see, there are effective interventions for every phase of development. In addition, many of these programs produce benefits long after the program's implementation. For example, the Nurse-Family Partnership reduced the number of children arrested for delinquency as adolescents by more than 50 percent (Olds 2007). Finally, most preventive interventions save more money than they cost. For example, the Good Behavior Game, which helps elementary school children develop self-regulation and cooperation skills, saves about eighty-four dollars for every dollar invested in it. It does this because it prevents problems ranging from crime, smoking, and alcohol abuse to anxiety and suicide attempts (Kellam et al. 2008).

The two most important environments for building a highly prosocial society are families and schools. Virtually every problem we seek to prevent emerges because of families and schools that fail to nurture prosocial development. In chapter 2, I describe numerous effective family interventions. In chapter 3, I describe what we have learned about how schools can nurture the social and academic skills of children from preschool through high school. The third major influence on young people's development is their peer group. Chapter 4 describes how peer groups can influence young people in harmful ways and how to prevent this.

However even in a world in which families and schools nurture development, there will be many people who arrive at adulthood with significant problems. Chapter 5 describes the tremendous progress in the treatment of psychological and behavioral problems of adults over the past four decades.

Addressing Well-Being in the Larger Social Context

Truly transforming societies so they ensure nearly everyone's well-being requires a perspective beyond attention to individuals, families, schools, and peer groups. We have to translate this knowledge into benefits for entire populations. Behavioral scientists have now begun to figure out how effective programs can be made more widely available.

Families, schools, and peer groups exist within a larger social environment that affects them in many ways. The larger context for individuals, families, and schools includes corporations, government agencies, and nonprofit organizations, whose practices have enormous impacts on well-being. We need a scientific understanding of these impacts. And we need scientific advances to help us understand how we can evolve organizational practices that are more supportive of well-being.

For this reason, part 3 provides an analysis of the larger social context affecting human well-being. In chapter 6, I present the public health framework, which can guide this analysis. Public health practices evolved out of efforts to deal with physical illness. They are now being applied to behavioral influences on well-being and the factors that affect these behaviors. The public health framework looks at well-being in terms of the incidence and prevalence of behaviors and the actions of groups and organizations. In chapter 6, I use the example of the tobacco control movement to show how a public health approach can advance the goal of making societies more nurturing.

In chapter 7, I describe corporate marketing practices that harm people. These include the marketing of tobacco, alcohol, and unhealthful food. I propose standards for determining when the need to regulate marketing in the interest of public health outweighs the need to limit government interference in marketing.

Chapter 8 addresses the problems of poverty and economic inequality. The United States has the largest proportion of young people being raised in poverty of any economically developed nation. We also have the highest level of economic inequality. These conditions stress millions of families and limit the effectiveness of even the best-designed family interventions. Despite much public discussion to the contrary, poverty and economic inequality are far from inevitable. In chapter 8, I describe how the recent evolution of public policy has contributed to these problems.

Chapter 9 examines the recent evolution of corporate capitalism. Over the past forty years, public policy affecting economic well-being has shifted dramatically away from ensuring that every member of society has at least a basic modicum of material well-being. This is the direct result of well-organized and well-funded advocacy conducted on behalf of some of the wealthiest people and largest corporations in the United States. I analyze this evolution in terms of the economic consequences that have selected corporate lobbying practices and the resulting implications for how we can evolve corporate practices that are more likely to contribute to the evolution of a nurturing society.

Evolving a Nurturing Society

If we can bring to bear everything that the behavioral sciences have taught us over the past fifty years, I believe we can evolve societies that nurture unprecedented levels of well-being. Part 4 of this book consists of two chapters outlining concrete steps we can take to make this a reality. Because caring relationships among people are so important, in chapter 10 I describe the psychological and interpersonal processes that are needed to help people cultivate caring relationships with everyone around them. Building on this, in chapter 11, the final chapter, I envision a social movement that could influence the evolution of society such that our families, schools, neighborhoods, corporations, and governments all become more nurturing.

PART 1

Science Equal to the Challenge of the Human Condition

In this section I provide an overview of the scientific principles that have led to so much progress over the past fifty years. Biological and behavioral sciences are converging on a view of what human beings need to thrive and what leads many people to develop psychological, behavioral, and health problems. Thanks to an explosion of experimental evaluations, we have identified programs, policies, and practices with proven benefit in preventing multiple problems and nurturing successful development.

CHAPTER 1

A Pragmatic Science of Human Behavior

In the past 150 years, science has dramatically transformed a world that was largely unchanged for centuries. In 1850, it took two and a half months to get from New York to San Francisco. Today you can fly there in five and a half hours. It took a month to get a letter from Utah to California in 1850; today you can talk to *and see* almost anyone in the world instantly. In 1854, London was the world's largest and most prosperous city. Its Soho neighborhood suffered a cholera outbreak that killed over six hundred people. Today, we would be shocked to hear that anyone died of cholera in London.

Could the scientific study of human behavior produce similarly remarkable transformations? They are well within reach. Yet because the conflict, abuse, and neglect occurring in so many families have been with us for millennia, they sometimes seem inevitable. In this book, I will describe numerous tested and effective programs that reduce family conflict and abuse and ensure children's successful development. The same is true for schools. Throughout history, a sizable proportion of young people failed to gain the social skills and knowledge necessary to succeed in life. Thanks to careful research on the impact of school environments, we have developed effective approaches to teaching and to nurturing social skills and values that help young people become cooperative and caring people. If these facts conflict with your impression of the state of schools and families, it is because these science-based strategies are not yet widespread enough to produce massive change. But that will happen.

Then there are the so-called mental illnesses. When I began to study psychology in the 1960s, not one treatment procedure reliably alleviated psychological disorders. In chapter 5, I will tell you about dramatic advances in treating all of the most common and costly psychological and behavioral problems.

Historic transformation of societies requires change not only in individuals, families, and schools. Businesses, governments, and nonprofit organizations must be transformed if we are to reduce the stresses these systems now place on so many people. Science has not made as much progress in creating change in the latter systems. But I will show you how the same pragmatic and evolutionary principles that informed the development of effective family, school, and clinical interventions can show us the flaws in our current system and what we can do to make it more conducive to human well-being.

In sum, I hope to show you how we can evolve societies where most people live productive lives in caring relationships with others. Science has altered the physical world beyond anything our great-grandparents could have imagined. Yet those changes generally have not made people happier or better at living together; in many cases, they have produced massive threats to human well-being. But the scientific advances in our practical understanding of human behavior put us in a position to create a world where we have not only previously unimaginable creature comforts, but also the psychological flexibility and loving interpersonal relations that can enable us to evolve societies that nurture human well-being and the ecosystems on which we depend.

Evolution and Pragmatism

In my view, the key feature of the science that has brought all this progress is evolutionary theory (D. S. Wilson et al. 2014). Until Darwin, the primary framework for thinking about causation in science was mechanical. Scientists made tremendous progress in understanding the relations among physical objects by studying the ways those objects influenced each other. Thinking about these relations as one would think about a machine, the focus was on the parts of the world, their relations, and the forces that influence those relations. Our understanding of the physical world has come largely from building and testing models of these mechanical relations—whether the influence of gravity on the motion of planets, or the relations of time and space (Isaacson 2007). The emphasis was on the antecedent conditions that influenced the phenomenon of interest.

Darwin introduced a new model of causation: selection by consequences. He wasn't the first to recognize that species evolved (Menand 2001), but he was the first to see that it was the consequences of the characteristics of species that determined whether a species would survive—and with it, its characteristics. This was a profound development in scientific thinking. Humans readily discern antecedent causes. Indeed, the tendency to see this kind of causation probably evolved out of the fact that antecedent causation is so common and seeing it is vital to surviving. (In fact, we are so inclined to look for antecedent causes of events that there is a Latin phrase for the tendency to misattribute causation due to antecedents: *post hoc, ergo propter hoc*, or "after this, therefore because of this.")

Although the genetic mechanism that underlies species selection was not known in Darwin's time, most thinking about evolution in biology has centered on genetic selection. However, the principle of selection by consequences is also relevant to understanding the development of behavior—the epigenetic process that has only recently been recognized as playing an important role in both biological and behavioral selection, the symbolic process involved in human language, and even the evolution of groups and organizations, such as those involved in capitalism (Jablonka and Lamb 2014; D. S. Wilson et al. 2014). Throughout this book, I will point out how our understanding of human behavior and development is influenced by consequences and how this understanding contributes to our ability to evolve a more nurturing society.

Evolutionary thinking also contributed to the development of the philosophy of pragmatism, which is the other defining feature of the science I want to describe. Unlike mechanical analyses of causation, evolutionary thinking starts with the unique event and its context. Evolutionary biologist David Sloan Wilson (1998) describes how features of the bluegill sunfish differ within a single lake depending on whether they inhabit open-water or shoreline areas. An evolutionary analysis starts by studying the phenomenon of interest and its context and seeks to explain the phenomenon as a function of its context. This is true for behavioral explanations as much as it is for the study of species and genes.

In his Pulitzer Prize–winning book *The Metaphysical Club* (2001), Louis Menand describes how the philosophy of pragmatism grew out of evolutionary thinking and the tragedy of the American Civil War. The death of 600,000 shattered Americans' certainty about their beliefs. A number of prominent thinkers, such as Charles Pierce, Oliver Wendell Holmes, William James, and John Dewey, began to evaluate their ideas not in terms of their correspondence to the world they were said to describe, but in terms of their value in achieving a goal. They focused on the consequences of their ideas in the same way that evolutionary thinking focused on the success of species characteristics in a given environment. In both cases, the question was not whether success would hold in every environment, but whether it worked in the particular environment in question.

Once you start to evaluate your ideas in terms of their workability, you must specify your goals. A variety of pragmatic systems have been developed (Hayes et al. 1993); they differ in terms of the goals they specify. One version of pragmatism is what Steven Hayes (1993) has called *functional contextualism*, in which the goal is to "predict-and-influence" behavior or other phenomena. The phrase is hyphenated to emphasize a focus on scientific analyses pinpointing variables that predict and influence behavior or other phenomena of interest.

This approach to the human sciences guides my thinking. I don't claim that this is the one true way to do science. Indeed, it is not yet the dominant way of thinking about science even in the behavioral sciences, and I can offer no criterion to prove it is better than the mechanistic tradition. Mechanism and functional contextualism are simply different ways of doing science.

I would argue, however, that if you choose to pursue predicting *and influencing* individual behavior or organizational practices, you will be more likely to identify malleable contextual conditions you can use to influence whatever you are studying. And if you are studying a problem like drug abuse, antisocial behavior, depression, or anxiety, your work may contribute to finding more effective ways to prevent or ameliorate that problem.

In sum, I believe that the progress in understanding how to improve the human condition that I report in this book stems largely from pragmatic evolutionary analysis, which has pinpointed critical environmental conditions that select useful or problematic functioning, and has led to increasingly effective interventions as a result.

Humans: The Cooperative Species

This is an exciting time for the human sciences. Biobehavioral sciences are converging on a pragmatic, evolutionary account of the development of individuals and the evolution of societies (D. S. Wilson et al. 2014). We have an increasingly clear understanding of what humans need to thrive and which conditions hamper development. This science has made enormous practical progress on how we can create conditions that nurture human thriving and prevent a gamut of psychological, behavioral, and health problems.

The Evolution of Cooperation

A key insight organizing current thinking is that, among vertebrate organisms, humans are uniquely cooperative. David Sloan Wilson (2007) points out that multicellular organisms arose when they had a survival advantage over individual cells in certain environments. When the environment is favorable to the success of coordinated action among multiple units—be they genes, cells, people, or groups of people—those coordinated entities are likely to survive and reproduce. Conversely, when the environment favors individual units, those units will be selected even at the group's expense.

This view has sweeping implications for life and well-being, whether concerning cancerous cells that reproduce to their benefit while harming the organism; individuals who engage in antisocial behavior to the benefit of the individual and the harm of the group; or corporations that maximize their profits to the disadvantage of the larger society. The challenge for our well-being is to ensure that cells, people, and organizations contribute to the group. Whether that happens is a function of the environment's favorability to the coordinated action of members of the group. Thus, at every level, success and survival require an environment that selects that coordinated action.

Helpful Babies

Humans have evolved levels of cooperation that are unprecedented among primate species. You can see it even in babies. Say you are playing with a baby and begin to put the toys in a box. If you point to one of the toys, the baby is likely to put it in the box (Liebal et al. 2009). If a baby sees one person cooperate with another while a second person does not, the baby will reward the first person but not the second (Hamlin et al. 2011). Human babies are more likely than other primates to follow another's pointing or gaze. Thus, even before adults have socialized them, babies show tendencies to be in sync with the social behavior of others, to infer others' intentions to cooperate, and to prefer cooperation in others.

Prosociality

These wired-in tendencies are foundational for developing prosociality. *Prosociality* refers to a constellation of values, attitudes, and behaviors that benefit individuals and those around them (D. S. Wilson 2007; D. S. Wilson and Csikszentmihalyi 2008). Examples of prosocial behavior include cooperating with others, working for their well-being, sacrificing for them, and fostering self-development. These behaviors are not only "nice"; they are the essential components of the success of groups. Prosocial individuals contribute to others' well-being through kindnesses, productive work, improving their community, and supporting family, friends, and coworkers, as well as creative acts of all kinds, from solving technological problems to composing music or making an entertaining movie.

From an evolutionary perspective this makes great sense. All of these behaviors and values contribute to group survival. Groups full of prosocial, cooperative people can outcompete groups with selfish individuals. Doesn't this capture the problem our societies face? How can we suppress or control the selfish actions of individuals in the interest of the group? Examples abound: An employee steals from the company and the company goes bankrupt. A father demands that family life revolve around his needs to the detriment of his children's development. Isn't this the problem we confront as a nation when, for example, a corporation acts in the interest of its profits but harms others in the process?

Wilson's evolutionary analysis lines up nicely with evidence about the benefits of prosocial behaviors and values for the individual. Prosocial people have more and better friends (K. E. Clark and Ladd 2000) and fewer behavioral problems (Caprara et al. 2000; Kasser and Ryan 1993; Sheldon and Kasser 2008; D. S. Wilson and Csikszentmihalyi 2008). They excel in school (Caprara et al. 2000; Walker and Henderson 2012) and are healthier (Biglan and Hinds 2009; D. S. Wilson 2007; D. S. Wilson and Csikszentmihalyi 2008; D. S. Wilson, O'Brien, and Sesma 2009).

We have been accustomed to thinking that highly skilled people who place great value on supporting those around them are some kind of fortuitous gift to the community. But behavioral science is teaching us how to create environments that foster these qualities. In an effort to promote these qualities, my colleagues and I, working together within the Promise Neighborhoods Research Consortium, have created an overview of the social, emotional, behavioral, cognitive, and health milestones for children at each developmental phase (Komro et al. 2011). These are "marching orders" for any effort to increase the number of young people who develop successfully.

Antisocial Behavior and Related Problems

If prosociality is good for the individual and for the group, why is there so much antisocial behavior and human conflict? One way to understand this is to consider the details about how human groups evolved. Yes, human groups that were good at cooperation were more likely to survive. But one thing they needed to do to survive was defend themselves from competing groups. So we are selected for in-group cooperation and for being quick to aggress against those in other groups.

Additionally, during the evolution of our species, humans have had to cope with periods of great deprivation and threat. During those times, cooperation might not have worked. Survival required being on high alert for danger, perhaps at every moment, and being quick to aggress against those who might be a threat. In addition, reproduction required having babies as early and often as possible. In those times of danger, becoming depressed may have also had advantages, because it reduces the tendency of others to attack or dominate (Biglan 1991).

While humans have the propensity to develop a suite of prosocial behaviors, they are also capable of developing antisocial behavior, engaging in substance abuse, experiencing depression, and bearing children at an early age. These behaviors are detrimental to the people engaging in them and to those around them. Young people who develop aggressive behavior tendencies are likely to develop problems with tobacco, alcohol, and other drug use; to fail academically; to have children at an early age; and to raise children likely to have the same problems (Biglan et al. 2004). Academic failure contributes to poverty and poor health and undermines workforce productivity in ways that harm the entire society.

All of these problems affect people's health. Academic failure, depression, and use of tobacco, alcohol, and other drugs are risk factors for our most common and costly illnesses: cancer and cardiovascular disease (Rozanski, Blumenthal, and Kaplan 1999; Smith and Hart 2002).

I led a review of research on adolescent "problem behavior" during a year at the Center for Advanced Study in the Behavioral Sciences, which is now part of Stanford University. Ted Miller, an economist at the Pacific Institute for Research and Evaluation, analyzed the costs of many of these problems (T. Miller 2004). His estimate of the annual cost of antisocial behavior, substance use, risky sexual behavior, school dropout, and suicide is $608 billion in 2012 dollars. Note this analysis was just for youth problem behavior. Although most of these problems begin when people are adolescents, many continue into adulthood. Indeed, many are lifelong.

In talking about these problematic behaviors, I do not intend to blame those of us who have them. One of my major goals in writing this book is to convince you that these problems stem from our environments. Blaming or stigmatizing struggling people for the problem is neither consistent with the evidence nor likely to prevent or mitigate the problems.

In short, we have ample reason to prevent these problems and promote prosociality. Behavioral science has fortunately pinpointed the kind of environment needed to ensure the development of prosociality and prevent virtually the entire range of common and costly societal problems.

Nurturing Environments

We can boil down what we have learned in the last fifty years to a simple principle: we need to ensure that everyone lives in a nurturing environment. Such a simple statement may seem to fly in the face of the enormous heterogeneity of behavior, genes, and environments. But all evidence points to the fact that people become prosocial members of society when they live in environments that nurture their prosocial skills, interests, and values. Conversely, they develop various patterns of harmful behavior when their environments fail to nurture them in specific ways.

Imagine how this simple summary could organize efforts to improve human well-being. If it is scientifically accurate to say that people thrive and are prosocial amid nurturing environments, then we have a simple, readily understandable, and easily communicated message that could organize us from the level of our individual efforts to make our way in the world to the priorities of nation-states. At every level and in every interaction, we must ask ourselves whether we are contributing to the safety and supportiveness of our environment, both for us and for those around us. Nurturance becomes a standard and a value for our interpersonal interactions and by which to judge our public policies. Do they contribute to safety, comfort, and positive development, or do they stress and threaten people? Imagine what such a standard might imply for policies about incarcerating youth, cutting unemployment insurance, or decreasing subsidies for low-cost housing.

As noted in the introduction, the tobacco control movement is probably the most significant science-driven behavioral change our culture has ever seen. It helped that cigarette smoking is a discrete, easily measurable, and highly harmful behavior. The goal of the tobacco control movement could therefore be stated very simply: "We have to get everyone to stop smoking." Whatever people working on this problem did, they could evaluate it in terms of one simple question: Did the activity reduce smoking?

When it comes to other problems—from crime to drug abuse to depression—it may seem that we need a unique campaign for each problem. For the most part, research and practice have proceeded as if problems like depression and crime have nothing in common and require completely different solutions.

But suppose that the same nonnurturing environment contributes to both of these problems and many others? Suppose that following the simple dictum "Make our environments more nurturing" could guide us in preventing almost every problem we face? If that is true, we can create a unified movement that consolidates everything we have learned about the prevention of each of these problems in a way that unites the forces and resources of all the disparate efforts to alleviate human suffering into one broad, powerful movement. This movement would be clear and simple enough to inspire a dad to find gentler ways of guiding his son, but scientifically sound enough to organize research and public health efforts.

My analysis of the details of tested and effective preventive interventions has convinced me that creating nurturing environments is fundamental to preventing most problems of human behavior and producing the kind of caring and productive people every society values. All successful interventions make environments more nurturing in at least three of four ways:

- Promoting and reinforcing prosocial behavior

- Minimizing socially and biologically toxic conditions

- Monitoring and setting limits on influences and opportunities to engage in problem behavior

- Promoting the mindful, flexible, and pragmatic pursuit of prosocial values

Teach, Promote, and Richly Reinforce Prosociality

If we want a world in which most people are prosocial, we need to create environments where prosociality is taught, promoted, and, most importantly, reinforced. We need parents to help their young children develop the ability to restrain impulsive behavior and cooperate with others. We need schools to teach students how to be respectful and responsible, give them opportunities to be good school citizens, and recognize and reward their contributions to the school. We need communities to recognize citizens' contributions to their communities and hold them up as community models, thus promoting prosociality in others.

Families, schools, and communities can promote prosocial behavior and values through stories, models, and recognition of those who act in prosocial ways. However, we could flood a community with stories and models designed to promote prosociality and yet get very little increase in such behaviors if we don't also richly reinforce those behaviors. What do I mean by "richly" reinforce? I mean that we should be less stingy with praise, appreciation, public recognition, attention, interest, approval, smiling, touching, love, and tangible rewards such as pay. Reinforcement is critical to nurturing human well-being, so I want to emphasize it here.

In my view, the fact that human behavior is selected by its consequences is the most important scientific discovery of the twentieth century. The most prominent advocate of the theory that human behavior is a function of its consequences was B. F. Skinner. In 1953, he published *Science and Human Behavior*, which claimed that human behavior was shaped and maintained by its consequences, just as consequences were known to affect rat and pigeon behavior. Not surprisingly, given our conceit that humans differ from all other animals, this assertion caused quite a stir. At the time, there was not a shred of evidence for the effects of consequences on human behavior. But by the 1960s, psychologists were beginning to publish empirical studies that supported Skinner's assertions. The *Journal of Applied Behavior Analysis* began publication in 1968. Every issue presented evidence that human behavior was affected by its consequences. Alone, such evidence could hardly shake the beliefs of someone who assumed that human behavior involved autonomous individual choice. But within the context of Skinner's fundamental assumption that behavior was selected by its consequences, each new finding cried out for further exploration of this assumption.

Initially, I ardently opposed behaviorism. As a civil libertarian, I saw it as antithetical to allowing people to choose their behavior freely. But just after I got my PhD, Bob Kohlenberg, a colleague at the University of Washington, persuaded me to read Skinner's work. When I read *Science and Human Behavior*, I began to see that Skinner was simply extending evolutionary thinking to behavior. Organisms evolve features that contribute to their survival, and one of those features is the ability to learn new behaviors when they achieve consequences that aid in survival.

I also found inspiration in Skinner's vision of a society in which most people would fully develop their potential and work for the good of others (Skinner 1953). Mining the assumption that all human behavior is selected by its consequences opened up the possibility of achieving that vision. The question of untoward control over people's behavior—such as Huxley depicted in the dystopian *Brave New World* (1932), written as an attack on behaviorism—was really a matter of controlling who would control the reinforcers. As Skinner pointed out in a later book, *Beyond Freedom and Dignity* (1972), most movements to preserve human freedom involve trying to eliminate the use of coercive and punitive means of controlling behavior. These efforts helped evolve more just and beneficial societies. However, an exclusive focus on eliminating coercive control overlooked the fact that many positive reinforcement systems, such as gambling, prostitution, and the marketing of cigarettes, exploit humans.

Ubiquitous Reinforcement

A common misconception about reinforcement is that it is involved in human behavior only when we provide tangible rewards like food or stickers. However, consequences constantly guide our behavior. My friend and colleague Dennis Embry provided one of the best demonstrations of how ubiquitous reinforcement is for human behavior. In 1974, he started graduate school at the University of Kansas Department of Human Development. A number of Skinner's disciples had settled there and were seriously exploring the power of reinforcement. Dennis was working in the laboratory of Frances Horowitz, who was one of the first people in the world to show that newborn infants learned through social reinforcement.

It isn't easy to show scientifically that newborns respond to social reinforcement. Tiny babies have almost no ability to control their movements—except their gaze. The researchers rigged up a special screen on which they could project slides in front of the newborn. Dennis and another grad student were stationed behind a divider panel, observing the baby's eyes. One of them sat on the right of the baby and the other on the left. The baby was propped up in a way that made it easy to look at or away from the screen. There was also an audio speaker underneath the screen. The observers could tell if the baby was looking at the screen from its reflection in the baby's eyes. When the baby's pupils reflected the screen image, the observers pressed a button that turned sounds on or off or changed the screen image. This allowed them to study which consequences reinforced the baby's behavior of looking at the screen. If a baby looked at the screen, the observers changed the image or sound to see whether the change made the baby look at or away from the screen. Dennis says they learned some astounding things. This is how he described it to me:

> Day-old babies quickly learned to look at a target on the screen in order to keep the sound of their mother's voice on the speaker. That is, listening to the sound of Mom's voice was reinforcing compared to any mixture of other women's voices. These day-old babies would look away to switch the sound to their mother's voice, and then look

back at the screen image (same picture) to "turn on" Mom's voice. They kept looking much longer at the image if they could hear Mom's voice; it was number one on the hit parade. As a guy, I was distressed to discover newborns had no preference for Dad's voice.

Little babies did not like to look at frowning faces, angry faces, or disgusted faces; they liked to look at smiling faces. If a sad or mad face came on the screen, the babies quickly learned that they could look away and change the face on the screen to a smiling face. Clearly pleasant faces and Mom's voice were reinforcing what babies looked at.

Over the last fifty years, thousands of researchers have explored the scope and depth of Skinner's assumption that human behavior is selected by its consequences. Behaviorists have studied the effects of all kinds of consequences. One of the most powerful reinforcers is simply human attention. Why? Because it precedes virtually any other reinforcement you might get from another person. From the day we are born to the day we die, virtually anything we get from someone else—food, drink, hugs, touch, help, advice, approval—starts with that person simply giving us attention. We have also learned that many experiences are intrinsically reinforcing. Engaging in physical activity, mastering a skill, playing, and learning something new are all reinforcing.

Although there proved to be fundamental flaws in Skinner's approach to key features of human behavior, the relentless study of environmental influences on behavior has produced a science that has proven its ability to improve human well-being immensely (Biglan 2003). In families, schools, workplaces, recreational facilities, and institutions, we have learned to richly reinforce prosocial behavior.

Resistance to the Use of Reinforcement

Despite overwhelming scientific evidence of the power and importance of reinforcement, people continue to resist its use. For most of my career, this resistance has troubled me. One reason is that I am aware of many programs that use the principle of reinforcement to treat or prevent the problems of childhood and adolescence. Given what I know, rejecting reinforcement-based programs seems as harmful to children as refusing to have them vaccinated.

My belief in the importance of reinforcement is also motivated by the overwhelming evidence that the behavior of all species, including humans, is a function of its consequences. Reinforcement processes are an evolved capacity of organisms, which operate according to the same principles of variation and selection that underpin genetic evolution. Therefore, I find it implausible that reinforcement could be a fundamental influence on all other species but not humans. That strikes me as just another prideful human conceit, like rejecting Copernicus's heliocentricity or Darwin's theory of evolution.

The archenemy of reinforcement is Alfie Kohn. In his book *Punished by Rewards* (1993), he argues that rewards are no different than punishments—that both are means of control that produce only temporary obedience. He claims that rewards are essentially bribes and actually undermine people's motivation.

This argument distresses me for at least two reasons. First, it overlooks overwhelming evidence of the benefits of reinforcement in helping children develop important skills. Second, it discourages parents from getting the help they need. Before behaviorists started using reinforcement techniques to help children develop key skills, most children with developmental disabilities lived short and brutish lives in institutions. Children with aggressive behavior problems—that might improve after five or ten sessions with a psychologist—would develop lifelong patterns of criminal behavior.

Nonetheless, I have recently found myself forming a more nuanced view of the role of reinforcement in human behavior. There are circumstances in which the use of rewards is problematic. Researchers at the University of Rochester (Deci, Koestner, and Ryan 1999) have delineated situations in which rewards for behavior are either ineffective or counterproductive. They found that when rewards influence people to feel they aren't competent or that another person is trying to control them, they may actually undermine motivation.

It took me a long time to get this, but my son Sean taught me a lesson about it. Sean was born six years after his brother Michael. Having an older brother can be a challenge, especially in a family that gets excited about kids learning a lot. If you are five and your brother is eleven, who knows more? Who can shoot baskets better?

Sean was an exceedingly perceptive kid. At an early age, he understood that his dad was a behaviorist who believed that behavior could be shaped by praise and rewards. It took me much longer to understand that when I praised Sean, such as for shooting baskets well, it meant to him that he was not yet sufficiently competent. I fear my theory of reinforcement blinded me to the irritation he felt when I communicated, through attempts to praise him, that he was not yet fully competent.

Similarly, I sometimes see instances in preschool settings, especially for children with developmental disabilities, when the teacher's use of praise in attempts to teach a skill may actually be unpleasant for the child. When praise and other rewards are delivered in a situation where children feel they are being pushed into doing something they don't want to do, words like "Good job!" may be no more reinforcing than statements like "Do what I say!"

Psychologists are slowly converging on a view of child development that integrates the emphasis on children's need for autonomy with the importance of reinforcement. Early childhood educators stress the importance of following the child's lead, and behaviorally oriented psychologists have shown that a parent's or preschool teacher's attention to a child in situations in which the child leads an activity reinforces what the child does (Webster-Stratton 1992).

In sum, I ask you to remain open to the possibility that we could improve human well-being by greatly increasing positive reinforcement for all the prosocial things people do—not simply through extrinsic rewards, which may often be needed, but through all the ways in which we show interest, support, love, and appreciation for what others do. In the process, we will build a society of highly skilled people who are adept at making their way in the world and are strongly motivated to contribute to the well-being of others.

Minimizing Coercion, the Fundamental Process in Human Conflict

Reinforcement works as Skinner said it would. Initial studies on helping families with behavior problems showed that getting parents to reinforce children's appropriate behavior reduced aggressive behavior (for example, Zielberger, Sampen, and Sloane Jr. 1968). But what made children aggressive in the first place? The pursuit of this question led to work that was unprecedented in human history. The direct observation and analysis of the moment-to-moment interactions of family members revealed that coercion is at the root of human conflict. Coercion involves using aversive behavior to influence another's behavior. When you realize how pervasive this process is, you begin to see that reducing coercion is essential to creating a nurturing society.

Jerry Patterson was one of the first psychologists to show that reinforcement affects children's behavior. I describe his seminal contributions to behavioral parenting skills training in chapter 2. But I think his work on coercion was even more important (Patterson 1982). He and his team of researchers were the first to go into homes to observe interactions between aggressive children and their parents and siblings. Observers coded the talk of each person in terms of whether it seemed pleasant or unpleasant and the immediate reaction of others. For the first time, scientists studied in real time the consequences that each person provided to other family members' behavior and the effects of those consequences.

At the time, no one believed that such mundane interactions between parents and children could produce career criminals. But Patterson and his colleagues showed that these seemingly trivial events are the crucible that molds lifelong patterns of aggressive, intimidating, and cruel behavior.

You might think that families would shut down when strangers were sitting in their living rooms, but they didn't. Early in this line of inquiry, researchers discovered that families with aggressive children couldn't fake good behavior—even when instructed to do so. For families with a great deal of conflict, negative reactions to each other are so ingrained that they seem to happen automatically.

Patterson found that families with aggressive children—usually boys—had more conflict and handled conflict differently from other families. One person might tease, criticize, or needle another person. The other person might deal with that by teasing back. Because neither person liked what the other was doing, eventually one of them would escalate, getting angry, shouting, or hitting. That got the other person to back off.

Patterson looked at this in terms of *negative reinforcement*. Rather than a positive event, such as praise or attention reinforcing the behavior, removing an unpleasant or aversive event functioned as the reinforcer. For example, say Timmy teases his older brother Dustin, and Dustin gets mad. He says something like "Fuck you!" Timmy laughs at him and calls him a baby. Dustin hits Timmy, and Timmy runs to his room.

What just happened? Timmy's teasing was aversive to Dustin. An *aversive event* is one a person is motivated to terminate. For example, if you were wired up to a machine that gave you a shock, you would work like hell to get it to stop. If you had a lever that stopped it, you would press it frequently and vigorously. Dustin got irritated because that is how people respond to aversive stimuli. He said, "Fuck you!" because sometimes that had worked to get people to stop teasing. He was pressing a lever that worked for him in the past.

Not this time. Timmy keeps teasing. So Dustin escalates and hits Timmy. This works. Timmy leaves him alone. Dustin is reinforced for hitting because it ends Timmy's teasing. And Timmy is reinforced for running away because it allows him to escape further assault from Dustin. However, each is left feeling angry at the other, which makes another occurrence in this ongoing and increasingly destructive cycle more likely.

Patterson's careful analysis of hundreds of hours of these types of interactions revealed that highly aggressive children live in families where bouts of coercion are common and the only thing that works to terminate them is one person escalating. On average, a deviant child is aversive once every three minutes at home and on the playground. A bout of such conflict occurs about once every sixteen minutes. People in these families have a hair trigger. Each person is skilled in using taunts, threats, anger, and physical aggression to get others to back off. No one is happy, but anger and aggression are what work to get people to stop being aversive.

This pattern has clear evolutionary roots. Organisms under attack are more likely to survive if they fight back. If they are reinforced by signs that their attacker is harmed or by the attack ending, they are more likely to be effective fighters. Followers of Skinner (Azrin, Hutchinson, and McLaughlin 1972) demonstrated this process. They found that monkeys who were shocked would press a lever repeatedly if it gave them an opportunity to attack other monkeys. The monkeys assumed that the shock was due to the other monkeys. After all, monkeys didn't evolve around psychologists, they evolved around other monkeys.

Thanks to our genetically determined tendencies to counteraggress and our propensity to be reinforced when counteraggression harms the attacker or buys even a brief respite from others' aggressive behavior, humans readily fall into patterns of coercive interactions. Patterson and his colleagues followed a sample of aggressive and nonaggressive children into adulthood (Capaldi, Pears, and Kerr 2012). Early on, they found that, thanks to repeated bouts of coercion in their families, aggressive children had a finely honed repertoire of aggressive behavior by the age of five. Unfortunately, they had not learned "nicer" skills like taking turns, obeying adults, inhibiting their first impulse, or using humor to soften family interactions—skills found in the families of nonaggressive children.

The results were disastrous at school. The aggressive children were uncooperative with teachers and therefore did not learn as much. They were irritating to other children, who then avoided them. So they learned fewer of the social graces that emerge in the normal course of interactions with others.

When the aggressive kids in Patterson's study reached middle school, they were falling behind in academics and had few friends. Due to conflict at home, their parents had given up trying to monitor what they did or set limits on their activities, so they were free to roam the neighborhood with other aggressive, rejected kids.

Since Patterson began this work, an enormous body of evidence has accumulated showing that families with high levels of conflict and coercion contribute to all of the common and costly problems of human behavior. Children raised in coercive families are more likely to act aggressively, fail academically, begin smoking, develop drug and alcohol problems, and become delinquent. As adults, they are more likely to battle with their partners, get divorced, and raise children with the same problems (Biglan et al. 2004). These children are also likely to have depression. And due to the stress these young people experience—in their homes and in their often conflictual relations with others—they are more likely to develop cardiovascular disease later in life (Wegman and Stetler 2009).

The work on coercion is an example of an important but subtle shift in how we think about behavior. It is easy to see a child's aggressive behavior. Because it is troubling, we may pay a great deal of attention to it, discuss it, complain about it, punish it, worry about it, and so on. But it is much harder to see the consequences of behavior, let alone to see how consequences select behavior. Until the twentieth century, no one realized that behavior could be selected by its consequences. Getting people to see consequences is itself an important step in the evolution of our culture. Indeed, getting people to see the consequences that influence behavior and to work toward having consequences that shape and maintain the kind of behavior that benefits them and those around them could be one of the most important developments in cultural evolution.

Coercion in Marriage

Patterson's work on coercion pinpointed for the first time the major mechanism of human conflict. Although most of his empirical work focused on aggressive children and their families, he also found coercion at the root of marital discord. A book chapter he wrote with Hyman Hops (Patterson and Hops 1972) proposed that the coercion process underlying parent-child conflict could explain why married couples fight. A host of other researchers have since shown this to be true (for example, Weiss and Perry 2002). Couples who aren't getting along act in angry or quarrelsome ways because this is intermittently successful in getting the other person to stop being aversive.

Troubled couples I have counseled typically have several complaints about each other. He gets angry and irritated when she doesn't discipline their child. She complains that he doesn't help around the house. Both think that if the other would just do what they say, things would improve. But each resists being "pushed around"; and neither is willing to praise, thank, or acknowledge the good things the other does because they think, *I shouldn't have to*, or fear that doing so will excuse their partner's transgressions. So over months and years, couples become locked into using anger—or silence—to get the other person to back off or to punish the other. No one has fun, but each is sometimes reinforced by the brief respites from conflict anger produces. Although anger gets the other person to back off, it never contributes to finding more peaceful and caring ways to interact. Often the process ends in divorce.

Coercion and Depression

You can see how aggressive behavior like teasing, hitting, or getting angry can cause someone else to back off. But you might be surprised to learn that even the behavior involved in depression can get others to stop being aversive. In 1980, I began working with Hyman Hops at the Oregon Research Institute on a study of whether coercive processes were involved in depression. I had been studying depression in work I did with Peter Lewinsohn at the University of Oregon, and I had read Patterson's papers on coercion. I thought coercive processes might be involved in depression, and Hy had the expertise to develop a system for coding the behavioral interactions of couples. We proposed to observe family interactions to study how depressed women and their families interact. We were fortunate to get project funding from the National Institute of Mental Health.

Our study (Biglan, Hops, and Sherman 1988) showed that depressed women's sad and self-critical behavior is reinforced because it gets other family members to reduce their aggressiveness. For example, we did a moment-to-moment analysis of husbands and wives discussing a problem. It showed that when a depressed woman's husband criticized her or complained, he would typically stop if she cried, acted sad, or complained about her inadequacies. No one is having fun, but being sad brings a brief respite from criticism, teasing, or angry behavior.

Nick Allen, an Australian psychologist, has since argued that depression has evolutionary roots (Allen and Badcock 2006). When others are threatening, acting sad may decrease the risk of attack. Moreover, groups that tended to those who were hurt or incapacitated might have had a survival advantage compared with groups that left the weak by the side of the trail.

I hope you can see how important the problem of coercion is. If there is one thing that we can do to significantly reduce the burden to society of all of the common and costly problems of human behavior, it is to help families, schools, workplaces, and communities become less coercive and more nurturing of children's positive social behavior.

As the importance of coercion has become clear, family therapists have focused on helping families replace coercive practices with gentler, more effective means of reducing children's aggressive and uncooperative behavior and worked with parents to increase positively reinforcing interactions with their children. Similarly, couples therapists help couples abandon angry and argumentative ways of trying to get what they want from their partner. They help couples listen to and paraphrase each other, and they aid both partners in letting go of the feeling that they must defend themselves. The agenda shifts to finding mutually satisfying ways to be together. A multitude of studies show that these interventions significantly reduce strife and often reignite the love that couples once had (Shadish and Baldwin 2005). Couples counseling can also reduce depression. When conflict declines, women no longer need to be depressed to survive a day with their spouse (Beach et al. 2009).

Monitor and Limit Influences on Problem Behavior

Another colleague of mine, Ed Fisher, researches health behavior. In conversation, he once observed that people working to help people lose weight sometimes mistakenly believe that successful treatment should get people to the point where they can be in a room full of cream pies and ask for an apple. That ain't gonna happen. In a world full of abundance and enormous freedom, we face constant exposure to temptation. It is unrealistic to think that we can make people resistant to temptations that hundreds of thousands of years of evolution have created. Instead, we need to create environments that minimize these influences.

One of the most important arenas in which we need to do that involves adolescents. In one study (Richardson et al. 1993), researchers looked at what happens when ninth-grade students have no supervision after school. They found that, compared to peers who had a parent at home or attended adult-supervised after-school activities, those who were at home unsupervised were significantly more likely to experiment with drugs, be depressed, and get poor grades. They had even greater problems if they were hanging out with other teens after school. In chapters 2 through 4, I will tell you about programs that help parents, schools, and communities monitor and set limits on what teens are doing while also gradually allowing them to manage their own free time in safe, fun, and productive ways.

Teens also develop problems when they have access to tobacco and alcohol. I bought my first pack of cigarettes when I was fifteen and remained addicted to cigarettes until I was twenty-six. Even though it was illegal to sell cigarettes to those under eighteen, no one gave it a thought. As recently as the 1990s, when colleagues and I were conducting a smoking prevention study in Oregon, we were unable to get police to enforce the laws against selling tobacco to teens—despite research showing that easy access to cigarettes was one of the reasons that so many youth were getting addicted (Biglan 1995). Such sales have greatly diminished thanks to stepped-up enforcement and programs to reward clerks for not selling tobacco to minors.

Youth access to alcohol also poses problems. Laws prohibiting sales of alcohol to minors are seldom enforced. Many adults supply alcohol to young people, calling it a rite of passage. Sadly, more than five thousand people under age twenty-one die each year in alcohol-related car crashes or due to alcohol-fueled violence (National Institute on Alcohol Abuse and Alcoholism 2013).

Then there is marketing. Young people witness a large volume of very effective marketing for tobacco, alcohol, and unhealthful foods (Grube 1995; National Cancer Institute 2008; Nestle 2002). Limiting these influences would reduce youth consumption of these products.

Promote Psychological Flexibility

So far, I have emphasized how our understanding of reinforcement has enormous power in helping create environments that nurture well-being. We can richly reinforce all of the cooperative, prosocial behaviors that benefit individuals and those around them while also making sure that problems don't develop because people are living in environments that are coercive or that entice them to develop costly behaviors. But this is far from the whole story. We also must ensure that people develop a pragmatic and resilient approach to living in a way consistent with their values and unhampered by the rigid influence of language.

Language and the Blessing of Symbolic Processes

Humans have a capacity that separates us from other species: we talk. We use our words to analyze our world and solve problems that other organisms can't solve. We can relate a blueprint to the dimensions of the actual building and transform a vacant lot into a fine house. We can think about how compressing a gas changes its temperature and use that information to invent a heat pump. Our ability to talk about the world and relate our language to things in the world has given us the power to become the planet's dominant species—for better and for worse.

Behavioral scientists have struggled with how to effectively analyze human language capacities. Behaviorists with a Skinnerian orientation insist it can be understood as simply verbal behavior that is shaped by reinforcing consequences, just as any other behavior is. That view led to considerable success in helping children with developmental disabilities learn how to talk. But it fell short of the goal of a comprehensive understanding of human language. Cognitive psychologists insisted that human language and cognitive processes could not be understood in terms of reinforcement processes. In fact, some argued that the influence of cognition on human behavior proved that the laws of learning that had been worked out with animals were irrelevant in accounting for human behavior (Seligman 1970).

Quite recently, however, a convergence has emerged that yields an integrated and powerful understanding of cognitive or language processes. Evidence from both behavioral and cognitive traditions shows that the fundamental feature of human language involves the capacity to arbitrarily relate stimuli and to apply those relational responses, or "frames," to the world in ways that enable effective manipulation of our environments. These relational or symbolic abilities have been shown to arise from the same reinforcement processes involved in learning simpler behaviors, such as walking or imitating others (Törneke 2010). And once a broad repertoire of symbolic processing has been established, it constitutes a distinct process that in numerous situations overrides the immediate effects of the reinforcing contingencies affecting other organisms.

Here is an example: Thanks to thousands of occasions where children get reinforced for following others' requests, instructions, and advice, humans develop a repertoire of rule following that serves them very well. Consider what we teach our children about cleanliness. When my grandkids, Ashlyn and Grayson, were each about two, they enjoyed a book called *Yummy Yucky* (Patricelli 2012). Each page has a picture and a little story about something that is yummy or yucky. "Spaghetti is yummy. Worms are yucky." Thanks to that book, they learned that worms, blue crayons, and many other things don't go in our mouths, while things like blueberries and spaghetti do. The book helped my son Mike and his wife Jen teach their kids how to interact with a whole lot of things—without Ashlyn and Grayson having to eat something that harmed them or having to be punished for doing so. Once they learned the concepts yummy and yucky, they could easily learn about hundreds of additional things if Mike and Jen simply labeled them as "yummy" or "yucky." "Yucky" can even be used to override the naturally reinforcing effects of unhealthful foods. For example, if Jen and Mike told Ashlyn and Grayson that Big Macs were yucky, it could influence them to not want Big Macs.

This kind of symbolic processing has allowed humans to pass a vast body of knowledge from generation to generation without having to expose children directly to all of the things our language symbolizes. For example, you don't have to gain weight and have a heart attack in order to learn that obesity can cause heart attacks.

Thus, human symbolic processing enables us to transcend the limits of having to learn solely through exposure to the direct consequences of our behavior. It enables us to persist even when immediate consequences would not support our behavior. For example, one of the primary motivations for our pursuit of learning comes from our ability to imagine the reinforcement we will achieve if our education leads to a good job or prestigious profession. In short, our symbolic processes have been the force that has enabled us to transform the world.

Mindfulness and the Curse of Literality

There is a dark side to the power of language, however. We have so much experience and success with treating our talk about things as though the words were the things that we often don't notice that the word is not the thing. This is the problem of literality. The same symbolic abilities that enable us to surround ourselves with creature comforts in a warm, well-lit home can make us want to kill ourselves.

Like other organisms, we make avoiding danger our highest priority. It is a simple evolutionary story: organisms that didn't do so simply didn't survive. Kelly Wilson, a friend and colleague who has helped therapists around the world use the principles of symbolic processes in their work, likes to say that it is better to miss lunch than to be lunch. He talks about a bunny rabbit out in a meadow. If that bunny finds some really good veggies and becomes so engrossed in them that she doesn't keep looking around, she is liable to be eaten by a cougar. Only bunnies that learned to eat while keeping a constant eye out for predators remain to inhabit this earth.

But unlike bunnies, we humans can describe the past and possible futures. I can think about how my father died of carotid artery blockage and worry that the same thing might happen to me. You can think about your child at school and worry that he is being picked on by other kids. Although our thoughts about the future can make us thrilled in anticipation of good things to come, we are also prone to crippling visions of bad things that might happen to us, thanks to our evolutionary bias to avoid danger. Then, thanks to our verbal, relational abilities, we can inhabit a terrifying world while sitting in a perfectly safe, quiet room.

In Robert Sapolsky's delightful book *Why Zebra's Don't Get Ulcers* (1994), he talks about what happens when humans think about the dangers they can so readily imagine. A lion chasing a zebra instigates a cascade of hormones that puts the zebra's body into high gear. If the zebra has the good fortune to have an older, slower zebra nearby, it escapes the lion and the process is reversed. Hormones return to normal levels, heart rate slows, blood pressure returns to normal.

But thanks to our minds, humans can be in the presence of threatening stimuli all the time. Did you ever have a conflict with someone and find yourself lying in bed thinking about it? That person isn't in your bed—the person might even be dead—but there you are, still stressing about him.

Sapolsky's book is a compendium of the harm that chronic stress causes: insomnia, colds, irritable bowel syndrome, ulcers, miscarriages, memory impairment, major depression, hypertension, cardiovascular disease, adult-onset diabetes, osteoporosis, immune suppression, and drug addiction. Stress can even stunt children's growth.

Stress also affects our behavior. Stressed people don't make good companions, parents, siblings, doctors, lawyers, or friends. They are more irritable, angry, argumentative, anxious, depressed, and disinterested in others.

Think about how literality can affect whether families and schools richly reinforce cooperation and prosociality or, conversely, descend into conflict and violence. For example, say the mother of a young child has trouble getting him to cooperate. Her own mother often talked about willful children and how kids are born that way. Viewing her son's behavior through this lens, she readily becomes irritated with him. She also overlooks and fails to reinforce times when he is cooperative. Over time, she becomes increasingly punitive. The research I describe in chapter 2 reveals that the boy's behavior can easily be changed by increasing reinforcement for his cooperation, and a good family therapist can help the mother learn this. But it will be hard to do as long as she continues to view her son as willful and incorrigible.

Until very recently, at least in the Western world, the most common answer to the problem of literality has been to try to control or get rid of all the verbal lion attacks. In chapter 5, I describe how research by clinical psychologists is helping people escape the curse of literality. Rather than seeing the world through our thoughts, we can learn to step back, notice that they are thoughts, verbally construct what we want in our lives, and take whatever steps seem likely to move us in valued directions.

This orientation is what many psychologists call *psychological flexibility*. It consists of acting based on chosen values while being in contact with what is happening within us and around us, and not trying to judge, change, or control our present-moment experience. The mother who keeps having the thought that her son is willful can think about what she wants for him and what she wants for her relationship with him. In this context, she can notice her thoughts and her irritation and yet choose to listen to him, notice when he is cooperative, and be attentive to him at those times. In many instances, she may find that when she pays attention to what he is feeling and how he is acting, she can help him become better able to experience strong feelings and, rather than throw a tantrum or act impulsively, do something that is more likely to get reinforced, such as tell his sister that he wants his toy back.

Social environments can undermine psychological flexibility in several ways. Teaching children they shouldn't feel certain ways, such as angry or anxious, can encourage a lifelong pattern of avoidance of such feelings. And in order to successfully avoid such feelings, people need to avoid the situations that bring on those emotions. This might work well in some cases. For example, if you decide that your frequent arguments with your spouse aren't good for you because they often leave you feeling angry, it might contribute to a more loving relationship with your spouse. On the other hand, if you avoid other people because you feel anxious when you are around them, that might prevent you from learning important things or making valuable friends.

Our culture teaches us that it isn't good to have "negative" thoughts and feelings. This is often done in seemingly caring ways, as when someone tries to get you to not feel so bad. But it is also often done quite punitively, with statements like "I'll give you something to cry about." Both approaches reflect avoidance on the part of the other person. People often don't want to feel what they feel when you tell them what you feel, so the message is "Shut up about it."

Thus, one key in promoting psychological flexibility is accepting others' emotions and thoughts so that we don't purposely or inadvertently motivate them to try to control, resist, or deny their experience. A second thing that promotes psychological flexibility is using a detached and even playful way of talking about thoughts (Hayes, Strosahl, and Wilson 1999). Try putting the phrase "I'm having the thought that…" before every thought you state. For example, I might say, "I'm having the thought that I will never finish this book." It puts a little space between me and the thought. It is a thought, not reality. I don't have to act on the thought. It can just be there.

The third thing our environments can do to build psychological flexibility is encourage us to be clear about and keep thinking about what we want in our lives—what we most value—and what we can do that will further our values.

Building a Nurturing Society

In this chapter I have provided an overview of how a science of human behavior and society is helping us to understand what people need to thrive. I don't claim that it is the one true take on this science. Keep in mind that, for a pragmatist, words are not seen as definitive descriptions of the way the world *is*, but as ideas that may be useful. In the remainder of this book, I will describe how this way of thinking about science and humanity could guide us to a more nurturing society.

PART 2

A Wealth of Knowledge About How to Help People Thrive

In this part of the book, I will describe how the scientific principles I described in chapter 1 have helped in the development of interventions that assist families, schools, and peer groups to become environments that nurture human development and well-being. I will also tell you about recent advances in clinical psychology that have made it possible to ameliorate most psychological and behavioral problems—not in every case, certainly, but with a much greater success rate than ever before.

CHAPTER 2

Nurturing Families

Thanks to research over the last fifty years, we now have programs that can help families reduce coercive interactions and become much more successful in reinforcing and guiding young people's development. If we implement these programs widely, we can decrease the number of young people who develop problems like antisocial behavior and drug abuse, reducing incidence to much lower levels. In this chapter, I will describe programs created to help families nurture children's development from the prenatal period through adolescence.

It all started in the 1960s with research on behavioral parenting skills training. Many people contributed to this work, but Jerry Patterson was the first to write a book for parents explaining the principles of reinforcement in ways that could help parents make good use of them. The book, written with Elizabeth Gullion, was *Living with Children* (1968). It described specific things parents could do to teach young children to cooperate with requests, not be aggressive, and follow common routines, such as going to bed at a certain hour.

In 1972, when I was living in Seattle and had just started learning about behavioral approaches, my sister Kathie and her daughter Robyn visited on their way from Los Angeles to Rochester, New York. Kathie had split up with her husband in Southern California two years before and had moved back home to Rochester. Robyn had just spent her kindergarten year living in California with her father and his second wife. Robyn's father had decided that she should return to live in Rochester with Kathie because his new wife and Robyn weren't getting along. Newly freed from an unhappy situation, Robyn was testing all her limits and showing some talent at pressing Kathie's buttons, particularly with bedtime. Kathie and Robyn needed some help.

I knew what a handful Robyn could be. Two years earlier, I had been visiting Kathie at Christmastime in Anaheim. Robyn kept getting out of bed, and nothing could get her back. At one point, she was sitting on the sofa next to me, with a glass of milk in her hand, and I said something snide about her behavior. She calmly looked me straight in the eye and poured the milk on my lap.

During their visit, I gave Kathie a copy of *Living with Children*. In a way I'm sure could have been more considerate of her feelings, I told her the book could help her with Robyn. Desperate for some useful guidance, she devoured the book and told me later that she kept it at her bedside for times when she needed a refresher. Kathie started using rewards for cooperative behavior, including things like going to bed and helping around the house. She also began to use time-outs rather than yelling for misbehavior.

It all worked for Kathie. Robyn became much more cooperative and much less defiant. She became more fun to be around. And contrary to the common criticism of behaviorism at the time, she did not become meek and submissive. The negative behavior she was using to get what she wanted morphed into a charming style of assertiveness and confidence that served her well.

These days, just about every kid who has been in a preschool knows what a time-out is. But in the 1960s, it was a new development. Instead of hitting, yelling, or severely punishing a child, parents would have them sit quietly for several minutes before returning to whatever they had been doing. Millions of people have been able to replace harsh or abusive parenting with this calm, nonviolent approach. It has prevented much child abuse and probably saved some lives.

In his work on using reinforcement with children, Jerry Patterson planted a tree that has grown many branches. The Institute of Medicine report that I helped write (IOM and NRC 2009) sets forth numerous tested and effective family interventions, many with roots in Patterson's work, that provide critical help to families from the prenatal period through adolescence. I am convinced that these programs are the single most important building block for the society we want to create.

Nurturing Development During Pregnancy and the First Two Years of Life

On the night of October 6, 1998, Russell Henderson and Aaron McKinney took Matthew Shepard to a remote area outside Laramie, Wyoming, pistol-whipped him, robbed him, and left him tied to a fence. A cyclist found him eighteen hours later. He died five days afterward, having never regained consciousness.

The nation was shocked. Shepard was gay, and the crime was apparently due to Henderson's and McKinney's hatred of gays. But there was more that didn't make the headlines. Both Henderson and McKinney were addicted to methamphetamine. At the time of the murder, they were drunk and tweaking (coming down from meth), which is when aggressive and impulsive behavior is at its worst.

Hatred of gays and meth addiction may have been the immediate causes of this tragic event, but Henderson and McKinney had been put on the road to this horrific act by their toxic families. As young children, both had endured mistreatment from parents and other adults. One suffered from the effects of fetal alcohol syndrome, the other from disturbed experiences with his mother. One of the killers had been sexually victimized as a seven-year-old and locked in a basement each day as a young child because his mother worked at a low-paying job and couldn't afford child care; the other had been physically abused by his mother's boyfriends and was subsequently removed from the home.

Prenatal alcohol and drug exposure and poor maternal nutrition produce infants whose brain functioning is impaired (Soby 2006). It makes them more irritable and difficult to soothe as infants. For parents who are stressed and unskilled, such infants become aggressive and uncooperative, which leads to poor performance in school and social rejection. Abuse and neglect put infants into a state of constant high arousal that alters normal functioning of stress hormones in ways that keep children hyperaroused and ready to fight or flee (G. E. Miller et al. 2009). They feel as though there is constant danger.

Help for Poor, Single, Teenage Mothers

Suppose we could intervene to help parents who have the kind of problems that Henderson's and McKinney's mothers had. How much trouble could we prevent?

Consider Claire, a sixteen-year-old girl who became pregnant. This isn't an unusual occurrence in the United States, which has the highest rate of teenage pregnancy of any developed country. Like 80 percent of pregnant teenage girls, Claire didn't want a baby. However, she chose not to have an abortion, unlike nearly one-third of pregnant teens (Henshaw 1998).

Claire and her baby face very significant challenges. Her boyfriend became angry when she told him and accused her of trying to get pregnant. They broke up, and although Claire wants him to provide support, she doesn't want to marry him. Her parents are furious, blaming and criticizing her, and in their worry and distress, they are oblivious to the fact that Claire needs caring and support.

Claire is poor and hasn't been doing well in school. She is unlikely to graduate. With Claire unmarried and uneducated, she and her baby will probably face a life of poverty. The Institute of Medicine report I coauthored (IOM and NRC 2009) documents how such poverty makes it much more likely that Claire's baby will be unhealthy and develop costly problems, and will not develop the social and verbal skills needed to succeed in school. In one study of poor teenage mothers, about 35 percent of their children were arrested by age fifteen. Now, with nearly eighty out of every one thousand teenage girls getting pregnant each year (CDC, n.d.), the United States has a bumper crop of children headed for problems that will cost them, their families, and their communities for many years to come.

What Claire needs is someone to help her through the coming months and years. Could a warm supportive person really make a difference? The answer is emphatically yes.

The most comprehensive and well-researched program for women in Claire's situation is called the Nurse-Family Partnership (Olds 2007), created by developmental psychologist David Olds when he was at the University of Rochester. Its benefits are so well established that it inspired the Obama administration to propose putting billions of dollars into implementing it, along with several other carefully researched family support programs.

If Claire had the good fortune to have the Nurse-Family Partnership in her community, a nurse would contact her during her pregnancy. That nurse would befriend her, listen to her concerns, clarify her hopes for herself and her baby, and help her begin to move in a direction she desires. Her newfound mentor would advise her about ways to resolve conflict with her family and boyfriend and begin to get the support she needs from them, or from others if her boyfriend and parents are unwilling to provide it. The nurse would make sure Claire gets the prenatal care necessary to ensure a successful pregnancy. Together, they would develop plans for Claire to get her education. As Claire takes steps on all these fronts, she would find that she has a wise and supportive friend to help her through difficulties and cheer her progress.

Fast-forward a bit, to when Claire has a healthy baby boy. She names him Ethan. Having a first baby is a huge challenge for any family, especially for a single teenager. Fortunately, Claire's nurse would be there when Ethan is born and during his first two years of life. She could reassure Claire about the worries that naturally arise, such as when a baby cries and is difficult to console. In such a situation, it is natural to be frustrated and distressed, especially when you aren't sure you are doing the right thing. Claire's nurse would reassure her that a crying baby is normal and would help her provide the patient, soothing care that is vital to bonding between Claire and her baby. Through patience, practice, and support, Ethan can learn to let Claire comfort him—the first step in his development of emotion regulation.

The benefits of the Nurse-Family Partnership have been documented in three separate randomized trials over the past twenty years. Compared with high-risk mothers who didn't get the program, mothers who did had children who were better adjusted; they also waited longer to have a second child, made more money, and were less likely to abuse their children or be on welfare (Olds, Sadler, and Kitzman 2007).

In David Olds's first study, about 35 percent of the children of high-risk first-time mothers who did not participate in the Nurse-Family Partnership program were arrested by age fifteen (Olds et al. 2003). The children whose mothers participated in the program were arrested less than half as much. That is a lot of crime prevented.

Finally, the Washington State Institute for Public Policy analyzed the costs and benefits of the Nurse-Family Partnership program (Lee et al.

2012). They concluded that for every dollar spent on the program, $3.23 was saved, a 223 percent return on investment.

Nurturing in the First Two Years of Life

The principles guiding the Nurse-Family Partnership are vital for every family during pregnancy and the first two years of life. During pregnancy mothers must provide a nontoxic environment for their baby by eating a diet rich in nutrients (WebMD 2013). And, of course, they shouldn't smoke, drink alcohol, or take drugs. Smoking causes premature birth, miscarriages, low birth weight, increased risk of asthma, impaired cognitive function, and sudden infant death syndrome (Van Meurs 1999). Any alcohol consumption increases the risk of facial deformities, retarded development, brain and neurological problems, low tolerance for frustration, and impaired development of academic skills (American Academy of Child and Adolescent Psychiatry 2011).

It is also important to minimize stress during pregnancy. Stressful events increase a mother's production of cortisol, which can not only influence fetal development but even result in impairment in children's cognitive development as late as age eight (Douglas Mental Health University Institute 2014). In Claire's story, I described above some of the most common stressors—namely, aversive behavior of other people. This is another example of how important it is to create environments that minimize coercion and conflict.

Minimizing coercion continues to be important for both parents and infants during the first two years of a baby's life. Parents can be stressed by the uncertainties of how to care for a newborn and by conflict with and criticism by those around them. As for infants, those who do not receive warm, patient, soothing interactions from their caretakers will fail to develop the healthy attachment they need to gain the capacity to be soothed.

Rather than a harsh and punitive environment, what all family members need is an environment where they are richly reinforced. Parents benefit from having people around who patiently and approvingly help them navigate the first two years of the baby's life. Babies benefit from patient, soothing interactions with lots of stimulation, such as eye contact, talking and cooing, smiling, and cuddling. These interactions reinforce the infant for interacting, smiling, and laughing, and they increase hand-eye coordination, fine and gross motor skills, and emotion regulation skills.

The Critical Role of Emotion Regulation

I want to highlight emotion regulation, because this is a critical skill that everyone needs to develop beginning in infancy. Let's start with crying babies. Evolution has engineered babies to cry because it motivates parents to take care of them and develops their parenting behaviors. Dramatic evidence of this comes from a study of colicky babies done by M. M. de Vries in Africa (1987). Colic involves a pattern of uncontrollable crying that affects from 5 to 25 percent of babies (Roberts, Ostapchuk, and O'Brien 2004). We still don't know exactly why it happens. De Vries rated a large sample of babies on how much they cried uncontrollably. By coincidence, a famine occurred soon after the ratings were completed. When de Vries went back months later, he found that more of the colicky babies had survived. It turns out that there is a strong evolutionary reason why babies cry: in difficult circumstances, those who cry more are more likely to be fed.

So from the very start, infants cry and parents are highly motivated to calm them. In some families, the result can be tragic, as in the case of shaken baby syndrome, which involves brain damage due to shaking an infant. Parents may use this approach because, initially, shaking reinforces the parent by silencing the child. However, it typically results in severe brain damage and often the death of the infant.

Fortunately, in most families parents learn how to calm their infant through patiently soothing, rocking, and talking. A key part of the process involves nurturing infant behavior that is an alternative to crying. This process is fundamental to child development. It creates a bond between parents and children. It also helps children develop the ability to calm themselves and fosters rudimentary behaviors that are alternatives to crying.

Nurturing Young Children

Even if infants are well cared for during the first two years of life, their further development will be hampered if they don't get the nurturance they need. What happens from age two until about age five, when they enter kindergarten, can make the difference between eventually becoming a college-educated professional or a dropout. During these early years, parents can use the hundreds of opportunities that arise each day to help children develop the cognitive, language, and emotion regulation skills that are vital to success as they mature.

The Power of Attuned, Attentive Interactions

You can see the fine-grained details of what young children need by watching how a skilled adult interacts with a young child. Take our granddaughter, Ashlyn, and her interactions with "Grandma Georgie." From the time Ashlyn was a baby, Georgia has been talking to her—nonstop. I sometimes joked that Ashlyn's first full sentence would be "Will someone let five minutes go by without labeling things?" But she hasn't said that yet because Georgia's talk is always in sync with what Ashlyn is interested in. From the start, she would follow Ashlyn's lead. If Ashlyn looked at a cup, Georgia would describe it: "Oh, that is a cup—a green cup." Then she would encourage Ashlyn to hold it, play with it, and drink from it, extending Ashlyn's skill and knowledge about the world around her, but always in keeping with what Ashlyn was interested in at the moment. She never forced Ashlyn to continue with something she had lost interest in.

Georgia also promotes Ashlyn's knowledge about herself. When Ashlyn is upset, Georgia coaches her about her emotions: "Oh you're upset because you bumped your knee. That must hurt!" In the process, Ashlyn learns words to name both her feelings and the things that cause her emotions. By matching the intensity of her feelings to Ashlyn's, Georgia also conveys empathy and caring. In the process, Ashlyn begins to calm down and Georgia can prompt her to engage in problem solving: "Do you want to come and have me put a Band-Aid on it?" This process is vital to helping Ashlyn learn to regulate her emotions. This is crucial, as children with good emotion self-regulation can have emotions without becoming impulsive or aggressive. They also do better in school and at making friends.

One day when Ashlyn was three years old, she fell from a step stool and hit her face. I braced myself for a long episode of screaming and crying. She started to cry and ran to her mom. Jen comforted her briefly, and in about two minutes Ashlyn was back on the step stool helping prepare a meal. I was stunned at how quickly the episode passed and asked Jen about it. She said that whenever Ashlyn fell, she comforted her and then prompted her to get back to whatever she had been doing. She also made sure that Ashlyn's return to action was richly reinforced, perhaps with extra attention to Ashlyn when she went back to whatever she was doing before she got hurt. At three years old, Ashlyn was learning the essentials of self-regulation, persistence, and resilience!

When I think about the complexity and subtlety of the moment-to-moment interactions involved in building Ashlyn's social, emotional, and cognitive skills, I marvel that so many parents raise successful kids. But once you understand the basic principle that a child's skills are nurtured by parents' ongoing patient attention to the child's developing interest in the world and their support of the child's emotion regulation, you have a grasp of the fundamental features of programs that are helping a constantly growing number of parents succeed.

As infants grow into childhood, they continue to develop new ways to restrain the impulse to cry or get angry. Most parents get good at reinforcing behavior that is incompatible with crying. For example, when our grandson, Grayson, was two years old, he developed an ear-piercing scream that he used whenever his big sister took something he was playing with. Thankfully, my son and daughter-in-law have taught him to instead ask Ashlyn to give back the toy—and also taught Ashlyn to do so.

My point here is that young adults' ability to manage their emotions in ways that allow them to negotiate with others without alienating them is the result of literally thousands of interactions that occur on a daily basis throughout childhood. Helping families develop their ability to nurture emotion regulation is vital not only for children's future well-being, but also for the well-being of society. Children who don't develop the ability to regulate their emotions end up on a life path that often includes aggressive social behavior, substance abuse, poor performance in school, and crime.

Nurturing Children's Prosocial Development

Once you understand that behavior is continuously guided by its consequences, you can begin to appreciate how important parents are in nurturing their children's development. Early childhood educators stress the importance of following the child's lead, and behaviorally oriented psychologists have shown that a parent's attention to the child in these situations reinforces each thing the child does. If you have a young child, you know how important your attention is: "Mommy, look at me!" The reason it is so important is that parental attention is the gateway to every other form of reinforcement parents provide: food, comfort, activities, toys, and so on.

The Incredible Years

One behavioral parenting skills program, the Incredible Years, is particularly attuned to the importance of parents following their child's lead in order to develop mutually reinforcing interactions. It was developed over a twenty-five-year period by Carolyn Webster-Stratton, a professor of nursing at the University of Washington. The Incredible Years helps parents become more skilled in nurturing their children's development (Webster-Stratton, Reid, and Stoolmiller 2008). Although she teaches parents to praise children and reward desired behavior with stickers and other treats, she starts by teaching parents to play with their children. Her first goal is to get parents to let the child take the lead.

Why is taking the lead so important? It ensures that parents are developing a pattern of mutually reinforcing interactions that provide lots of positive attention as children explore their surroundings. In these interactions, parents extend their children's knowledge: "Yes, that's a *red* fire engine."

Think about how these interactions build the cooperation and self-regulation of a child. In ten minutes of playing together, a parent and child might each cooperate with the other a dozen times: "Do you want the yellow block?" "No, give me the green block." Likewise, the parent can repeatedly and gently guide the child to try again when something doesn't happen the way the child wanted it to. These are opportunities to build the child's emotion regulation and persistence.

To teach parents to follow their child's lead, the Incredible Years uses videos that illustrate better and worse ways to handle situations. In one, a mother is asked to play tic-tac-toe with her three-year-old son. They have a big board on which to put three-inch-high X's and O's. The child has never seen the board before and clearly knows nothing about tic-tac-toe. The mother places an X on the board and tells her son to put an O on the board. Instead, he puts it on his ear. She corrects him by telling him, "No, it goes here on the board." Within a few minutes, this cute little boy has completely lost interest in the game. He gets out of his chair, walks over to some cabinets, and tries to open them. His mom's efforts to get him to come back and sit down are fruitless.

Adults are quick to tell children what to do and correct them when they are "wrong." They focus on the situation from their perspective and fail to see it from the child's viewpoint. Often when children don't do what they are asked, parents get angry because they think their child understands what they want and is being willful.

However, parents usually overestimate what children understand and are capable of doing. The Incredible Years gets parents to follow their children's lead so that they are in sync with what the child is interested in and can do. This reduces instances of parents telling their children what to do and prevents children from losing interest in being with Mom or Dad. When a parent connects with what the child cares about, they develop mutually reinforcing interactions. In this program, a mom like the one in the tic-tac-toe video would learn to notice what the child is looking at and doing. She would be encouraged to do things that hold her child's interest. She might put an O on her ear. She might lay the X's and O's on the table and see if her son wants to arrange them. She might tell him the names of these objects and see if he can name them. If he can, she might ask him to give her an O.

By helping parents follow their children's lead, the Incredible Years helps parents create interactions that are much more mutually reinforcing. Too often, parents' interactions with their children include criticism, cajoling, pleading, and anger. By instead following the child's lead, parents can reinforce child behaviors such as talking to the parents, engaging in fine and gross motor activities, cooperating, and persisting in challenging activities. Parental patience, attention, and warmth are reinforced by the child's cooperative behavior—and by all of the cute, warm ways young children behave when they are enjoying an activity.

Think about how these interactions build a relationship of mutual respect and caring. As your child gets older and spends more time out in the world, you are going to need him to tell you what is going on in his life in school and with friends if you are going to prevent problems and encourage good choices. How likely is it that he will tell you what is happening in his life at age ten or fifteen if he doesn't enjoy talking with you at age four?

Carolyn Webster-Stratton's Incredible Years is one of the most carefully researched parenting programs. Over a twenty-year period, she has evaluated it in a series of randomized trials. She and her colleagues did six such evaluations (for example, Webster-Stratton and Herman 2008; Webster-Stratton, Reid, and Stoolmiller 2008), and at least five others have been done (for example, Barrera et al. 2002). Results of those studies consistently show that the program helps parents be more warm and reinforcing and less critical and commanding. They learn techniques for setting limits on problem behavior without resorting to spanking or other harsh methods of discipline. The result is that even children who are aggressive and uncooperative become more loving and cooperative. The program also reduces parental depression.

Communities that want to improve the well-being of their children and families would do well to invest in the Incredible Years. The Washington State Institute for Public Policy analyzed the cost-benefit ratio of the Incredible Years (Aos et al. 2011). The program costs about $2,000 to deliver to a family, but its benefits per family were estimated to be more than $3,000 due to outcomes like reduced health care costs and increased educational attainment. Other benefits included nearly $2,500 in reduced costs to taxpayers (for example, on special education and criminal justice) and about $2,700 in benefits to others. Ultimately, for every dollar spent on the Incredible Years, there was a return of $4.20!

Promoting Young Children's Verbal Development

In helping young children develop prosocial skills, it is highly important to nurture their verbal knowledge about their world and themselves. A child's verbal and cognitive skills are the result of literally thousands of interactions between parents and child. In the 1980s, psychologists Betty Hart and Todd Risley did a study of children's language learning that was a real sleeper. Only in the past ten years have behavioral scientists begun to realize how important their study is. They went into the homes of forty-two families once a month for two and a half years, beginning when the children were seven to twelve months old. They discovered an enormous variability in how much parents talked to their children. Thanks to observing in the home and diligently counting how much was said to each child, they estimated that, in the first three years of the children's lives, parents who were professionals spoke about thirty million words to their child, while working-class parents spoke about twenty million, and parents on welfare spoke only about ten million. The amount and quality of parents' talk with their children during those first three years was strongly related to children's IQ scores at age three and their language skills when in the third grade. It shouldn't be surprising that the families' social class predicted children's language skills in third grade, but this study showed that how much parents talked with their children was an even stronger predictor of children's skill than their parents' social class (Hart and Risley 1995).

More recently, Susan Landry and her colleagues at the University of Texas Health Science Center have created Play and Learning Strategies, a program that helps children develop their cognitive and verbal skills (Landry et al. 2008; Landry et al. 2012). It teaches parents specific skills for interacting with infants and young children to promote child well-being and stimulate early language development.

Thriving in Childhood

If young children don't have the kind of nurturing family I've been describing, they may have significant behavior problems by the time they reach kindergarten. As described in chapter 1, if parents are harsh and inconsistent in how they deal with unwanted behavior, they and their child are likely to develop a growing repertoire of angry, cruel, and even dangerous ways of trying to control each other. Yet even in later childhood it is not too late to help children get on a path toward prosociality. Thanks to research on family interventions over the last thirty years, we can help families replace coercive interactions with warm, patient, and much more effective means of helping children develop the prosocial values, capacity for emotion regulation, and motor, verbal, and social skills they need to thrive.

Achieving Peace in a Family

To give you a feel for how much a family can benefit, here is a description of a case that was provided to me by Kevin Moore, a good friend and a highly experienced behavioral family therapist, who was trained by Jerry Patterson and his colleagues.

Jane was a mother at her wits' end. She had two boys, Mike, age ten, from her first marriage, and Kurt, age six, from her second marriage. Mike had always been a shy and quiet boy who was easy to parent, whereas Kurt was very difficult. He had colic as an infant and was hard to soothe. He yelled so much that he developed nodules on his vocal cords.

Jane said that she was increasingly worried about Kurt and his constant escalation of aggressive behavior. He had started breaking and throwing things when he was upset and saying he hated his parents and brother. He was frequently angry and his anger often escalated into rage.

Jane was also concerned about how often she and her husband were resorting to hitting him. His father was quite stern. When Kurt's behavior became severe, his dad spanked him or slapped his hand. Because Kurt was so unpleasant, Jane found that she was spending less and less time with him and that she seldom had positive interactions with him. But her deepest fear was that she was developing a dislike of him. She was ashamed and scared about such thoughts and feelings. She cried throughout the first two therapy sessions about how this situation was ruining all the relationships in the family.

Kurt's dad refused to come in for family therapy, but he did agree to not use corporal punishment for ten weeks and to not undermine the therapeutic approach Jane was going to try. I began by teaching Jane about the coercive cycle the family was locked into. I explained that corporal punishment wasn't likely to solve the problem because it left Kurt angry at everyone, and because no parent would be willing to use it every time a boy like Kurt misbehaved. As an alternative to hitting Kurt, I taught Jane to use time-outs.

Jane and her husband had tried time-outs, but they hadn't been doing it correctly. They would yell at Kurt while he was in time-out and keep him in it for long periods of time. (Five minutes is plenty of time for a six-year-old.) They often ended the time-out with a long lecture about Kurt's behavior, which simply got him worked up again.

I then showed Jane how to increase positive reinforcement for Kurt when he did what he was asked. Rather than let him watch TV and play video games whenever he liked, Jane made access to these activities contingent on doing what he was asked. I made sure that Jane's requests were clear and unambiguous, for example, "Please come to the table" as opposed to "Dinner is ready."

I also helped Jane set aside a special time with Kurt each day, when she would read stories to him or play a game of his choice for ten minutes no matter how the day had gone. As treatment progressed, Kurt was eventually able to earn ten-minute increments of this special time for specific targeted behaviors, like picking up his toys. This helped Jane get better at defining and reinforcing the specific behaviors that Kurt needed to learn to take care of himself, cooperate, and get along with others.

It worked. By the end of treatment Jane's daily phone reports about Kurt's behavior indicated a big drop in Kurt's problem behaviors, with an incidence similar to that in families with nonaggressive children. Jane also said that Kurt's dad had committed to never using corporal punishment again and that he was now using time-outs appropriately. In addition, she said that her special time together with Kurt was the highlight of her day and that he had softened and was more cooperative. Similarly, his dad was spending more time with Kurt.

Notice how Kevin helped Jane and her family replace coercive methods of trying to control Kurt's behavior with much greater use of positive reinforcement. When Jane had to deal with misbehavior, she used time-outs instead of corporal punishment. In essence, rewards became a prosthetic device to get warm interactions going. Instead of Kurt behaving coercively to get his parents to do what he wanted (which also motivated them to be more punishing), Jane used higher rates of positive reinforcement to foster Kurt's more positive behaviors and get the family out of the coercion trap. Also notice how, contrary to Alfie Kohn's criticism of rewards described in chapter 1, rewards worked very well in establishing positive interactions between Kurt and his mother. Rather than Kurt losing interest in what he did with his mom, they developed a loving, special time that became the high point of each day. The reinforcement provided by Jane's loving interactions with Kurt became a major motivator for him.

Oregon Parent Management Training Goes to Norway

Over the past thirty years, the empirical evidence supporting behavioral parenting skills training programs has mounted. As a result, they are being implemented around the world. For example, the Norwegian government asked Terje Ogden at the University of Oslo to find effective programs for families with aggressive children. His search led him to Parent Management Training–the Oregon Model (PMTO), a version of behavioral parenting skills training developed by Marion Forgatch and Jerry Patterson at Oregon Social Learning Center.

At Ogden's invitation, Forgatch and her colleagues trained family therapists in each of the seven regions of Norway in how to provide PMTO (Patterson, Forgatch, and DeGarmo 2010). They even did a randomized trial to test the effectiveness of the program when done by Norwegians. Their results confirmed its benefit for reducing family coercion, increasing warm and positively reinforcing relationships among family members, and reducing children's aggressive and uncooperative behavior. The program is now in use throughout Norway. More recently, Forgatch has been implementing PMTO programs in the Netherlands, Michigan, Kansas, and New York City.

The benefits of PMTO are clear (Forgatch et al. 2009; Wachlarowicz et al. 2012). A remarkably thorough and careful analysis of its benefits using nine years of data from a randomized controlled trial of the program with divorcing mothers (Patterson, Forgatch, and DeGarmo 2010) showed that it significantly reduced families' use of coercive parenting techniques, such as explosive anger, nagging, and authoritarian discipline. These changes, in turn, led to reductions in delinquency, improvements in the families' standard of living, and even reductions in the chances that the mother would be arrested. PMTO also increased *positive parenting*, which involves reinforcing children's successes and showing affection, respect, empathy, and interest. Improvements in positive parenting during the year in which families participated in the program reduced parents' use of coercive techniques and led to steady improvements in positive parenting over the next three years. These improvements contributed to less delinquency among the children over the next nine years.

PMTO is instrumental in improving all relationships in the family. In one randomized evaluation of PMTO for families in which the mother had just remarried (Bullard et al. 2010), the program not only reduced parents' use of coercive discipline, increased their use of positive practices, and reduced children's behavior problems, but also improved the parents' marital relationships.

Keeping Early Adolescents Out of Trouble

Early adolescence generally refers to ages eleven through fourteen, when most young people go through puberty. Developmental psychologists have shown that this is a time when impulsive, risk-taking behavior increases, which is in keeping with findings that the regions of the brain that control impulsive behavior are not fully developed at this age (Blakemore and Choudhury 2006). In most of the United States, this is when young people transition from elementary to middle school.

All of these changes can make this a difficult period. Adolescents have to cope with newly developed sexual urges and often have to navigate major upheavals in their relations with peers. In research I conducted with colleagues, among a large, representative sample of Oregon adolescents, we found that early adolescents experience higher levels of exposure to bullying and harassment than older adolescents and are more likely to report suicide attempts (Boles, Biglan, and Smolkowski 2006).

In early adolescence, young people begin to experiment with risky behaviors, including delinquency and using tobacco, alcohol, and other drugs. These problems are especially likely among those who are aggressive, who have increasing problems keeping up in school, and who often experience social rejection from peers. These troubled young people tend to join up to form deviant peer groups. One study (Dishion et al. 1996) found that these deviant peer groups are the "training ground" in which most forms of adolescent problem behavior are learned.

Unfortunately, both the physical development of young people at this age and the transition to the less sheltered environment of middle school give many parents the sense that their kids don't need as much guidance as they did when they were younger. And children in coercive families may be particularly skilled in punishing their parents' attempts to guide them, often resulting in these kids being free to roam the neighborhood and hang out with whomever they want.

Thus, nurturance is as important in early adolescence as in earlier stages of a child's development, though the details are a bit different at this stage. Families still need to minimize coercive interactions that involve criticism, yelling, and harsh punishment. Such interactions diminish parents' ability to influence early adolescents, especially in limiting their involvement in risky behavior outside the home. And reinforcement is just as important as it was when the child was younger. Parents' warm involvement with the child maintains their influence, and because it maintains communication, it enables parents to better understand what is going on in parts of the child's life that they can't directly observe. Limiting early adolescents' opportunities to engage in problem behavior becomes particularly important at this time, when such opportunities escalate.

Finally, psychological flexibility is important. Recall that psychological flexibility involves pursuing our values even when our thoughts and feelings seem to function as obstacles to such actions. For the parents of early adolescents, this often means noticing worrisome, negative thoughts they have about their children without succumbing to those thoughts. For example, a father may have the thought that his daughter isn't doing her schoolwork, but rather than nagging her about it and communicating that he doesn't think she is a good student, it may be more useful to redouble his efforts to be positively involved with her. If this seems a bit preachy, I assure you that I wish I'd had this advice when my boys were in early adolescence.

The Family Check-Up

One of the most efficient and effective interventions for families with young teens is the Family Check-Up. It was developed by Tom Dishion, Kate Kavanagh, and Beth Stormshak at Oregon Social Learning Center and, later, at the University of Oregon. They originally created a twelve-session program for groups of parents, which was beneficial in improving parents' effectiveness (Dishion and Andrews 1995). In an independent evaluation of the program, my colleagues and I found that it improved parents' ability to discuss problems with their children, reduced their tendency to overreact punitively or to be lax in their discipline, and improved their feelings toward their children (Irvine et al. 1999). The result was a reduction in antisocial behavior among children whose parents were in the program.

Despite the program's benefits, it proved difficult to get parents to attend twelve sessions. Moreover, the intervention was expensive to provide and reached only a fraction of the parents who might benefit from it. For these reasons, Dishion, Kavanagh, and Stormshak developed a brief, three-session checkup to help individual families. In addition, it was designed to be nonstigmatizing and could be used by any family, regardless of whether they were having problems. Parents didn't have to be incompetent or admit to being incompetent to get assistance. After all, even healthy people get a checkup.

This streamlined version of the Family Check-Up was offered to all parents with children in a series of middle schools in Oregon. A trained parent consultant worked with school administrators to make parents aware of the program. In the first session, the parent consultant befriended the family and began to learn about how parents were handling common problems and what their concerns were. The second session was a home visit during which the consultant made a video of the parents discussing common issues with their middle school student. In the third session, parents got feedback that emphasized the good things they were doing and received suggestions for how they could improve their handling of issues they had expressed concern about. If parents felt the need for additional assistance, they were offered two or three more sessions that focused on how to use reinforcement to promote positive behavior, how to monitor the child's behavior and set limits, and how to improve family communication and problem solving (Dishion et al. 2002).

One of the most common issues for families involves monitoring and setting limits on activities that could cause young teens to get into difficulties. During this stage of development, young adolescents begin to spend more time with peers. In a series of studies, Dishion and his colleagues showed that when parents failed to monitor what their young teen was doing, the youngster was much more likely to get involved in delinquency and substance use (Dishion, Nelson, and Bullock 2004). For this reason, parent consultants encourage parents to monitor where and how their children spent their time after school, and if and when they completed their schoolwork. Parents were encouraged to increase their use of rewards for desired behavior. Often this simply amounted to requiring that their kids do chores and schoolwork before watching TV or playing video games.

Dishion and his colleagues evaluated the program in a randomized trial in three Oregon middle schools and demonstrated its efficacy for a large and ethnically diverse sample of sixth-grade children (Dishion, Nelson, and Bullock 2004). The program significantly increased parents' monitoring and reduced family conflict. When these young people were eighteen, the program—which was delivered only in middle school—helped prevent them from using alcohol, tobacco, or marijuana and made it much less likely they had been arrested (Connell et al. 2007). Another study (Connell and Dishion 2006) found that the program prevented depression in a subgroup of high-risk middle-schoolers. Finally, a study of a subsample of children whose parents were not monitoring their children's activities at the beginning of the study found that the Family Check-Up significantly improved parents' monitoring and that those improvements helped prevent their children from using substances (Dishion, Nelson, and Kavanagh 2003).

Helping Delinquent Adolescents

The family interventions I've been describing show how valuable effective behavioral programs can be in preventing young people from developing common problems. Our society's failure to provide such programs allows a significant number of young people to end up with the kinds of problems that Matthew Shepard's assailants, Russell Henderson and Aaron McKinney, had.

But it is never too late. Using the same principles that underlie all of the programs I've described so far, family researchers have developed interventions that can help families even when an adolescent is already involved in problem behavior. Here too the basic principles of nurturance apply:

- Minimize conflict and coercion

- Teach, promote, and richly reinforce prosocial behavior

- Limit influences and opportunities for problem behavior

- Promote the psychologically flexible pursuit of important values

Two of the best programs for families with troubled adolescents are Multidimensional Treatment Foster Care, which was developed by Patti Chamberlain at Oregon Social Learning Center (Chamberlain 2003; Fisher and Chamberlain 2000), and Multisystemic Therapy (MST; Henggeler et al. 2009), developed by Scott Henggeler at the Family Services Research Center at the Medical University of South Carolina. Both programs have been evaluated in randomized controlled trials, which showed that they significantly reduce further delinquent behavior and do so at considerable savings to taxpayers and crime victims. Indeed for every dollar spent on Multidimensional Treatment Foster Care, more than five dollars is saved in taxpayer, victim, and health care costs (Aos et al. 2011). For Multisystemic Therapy, the benefit is about four dollars for every dollar spent on the program (Aos et al. 2011).

One of the most skilled, passionate, and caring practitioners of Multisystemic Therapy is Philippe Cunningham. I met Philippe when I organized a symposium on family interventions at a meeting of the Association for Behavior Analysis. I'd learned about Multisystemic Therapy a year earlier when I attended a presentation by Scott Henggeler, the developer of the program. Scott couldn't be on my symposium but said Philippe would be great. Scott had emphasized how hard their family therapists worked to establish trust and rapport with families. He told me a story about one of their therapists paying a first visit to a very poor backwoods family whose son had been repeatedly arrested. When the therapist went into the home, the house reeked with an almost unbearable odor. The therapist's first act was to get under the house, where he discovered a dead and rotting possum, which he removed and buried. I told that same story when I introduced Philippe at the symposium. He then told us that he was that therapist.

The work of Philippe and his colleagues illustrates an important general principle: In order to help threatened, angry people, you have to care for them. This is such a contrast to how society in general tends to blame and punish people for their misdeeds and the misdeeds of their children. A public official faced with the horrendous acts of Russell Henderson and Aaron McKinney would think twice about expressing any sympathy for their families. Yet as a practical matter, the most effective way to help such families change is to find ways to befriend them.

Still, doing so can be challenging. In a family where conflict and child abuse are rife, how do you think parents would react to someone knocking on their door and saying he was there to do something about their delinquent child? In Multisystemic Therapy, the therapist's first priority is to get around parents' anger, hostility, and fear and to establish at least a glimmer of trust. In one case, therapists were trying to meet with a family that lived in a rural home at the end of a long gravel driveway. Every time they drove up to the house, the family took off through the back door and fled into the woods. Family members could hear their car coming up the road. Pragmatists that these therapists were, they decided to park out on the highway, walk up the side of the driveway, and knock on the door. When the family answered their knock on the door, the therapists offered them a plate of cookies. Fear transformed into trust, and they started working together.

Philippe, who is African-American, tells the story of a hostile white father in rural South Carolina whose son had been arrested. Philippe told the father that he could help him with his son's behavior. The man said, "No nigger gonna help me with my family." Philippe's immediate reply was "Black folks been helping white folks for hundreds of years."

Both of these programs—Multisystemic Therapy and Multidimensional Treatment Foster Care—work by implementing the four basic principles of nurturance. They greatly increase reinforcement of young people for doing the things they need to do. For example, Multidimensional Treatment Foster Care provides foster parents with training and supervision in implementing a contingency management system where the youth earns rewards for doing chores, attending school, doing homework, and being home on time. Both programs help families replace punitive, angry methods of trying to deal with youth misbehavior with consistent use of more mild consequences, such as the loss of points or assignment of a chore. In addition, they help families do a better job of monitoring what teens are doing to keep them from hanging out with teens who are involved in drug use or delinquency.

Both programs also encourage a flexible, pragmatic approach to parenting. Parents are asked to accept that parenting can be challenging and think about their values for seeing their adolescent develop successfully. Philippe once described a mother he worked with who was addicted to drugs and neglecting her child. He got her to agree to shoot up only after she had put her child to bed. This might not strike you as the ideal situation, but it was an arrangement that improved the child's well-being while also prompting the mother's first step toward becoming more nurturing.

Action Implications

We still have things to learn about how to help families be more nurturing. We need to reduce children's exposure to biological toxins, especially lead (Binns, Campbell, and Brown 2006), and to reduce their consumption of processed foods (Nestle 2002) and foods high in omega-6 fatty acids, which promote obesity, aggression, and depression (Hibbeln et al. 2006). We also need to do more to incorporate principles of psychological flexibility into work with families (Jones, Whittingham, and Coyne, forthcoming).

But we do know enough that if we can make existing programs widely available, we can help millions of families throughout the world. The result will be fewer families breaking up, less child abuse, fewer children who fail in school, and less crime and drug abuse. Many more children will become caring, creative, and productive members of society. Here are specific things that parents, policy makers, and citizens can do to translate all that we have learned into nurturing environments for more young people.

For Parents

- Carolyn Webster-Stratton's book *The Incredible Years* (1992) provides a great deal of helpful guidance about parenting.

- Some of the early behavioral work with children used rather authoritarian language that suggested parents should establish "command compliance." However, research is very clear in showing that it is essential to follow the child's lead, in the way Georgia does with Ashlyn.

  - If your children are young, get down on the floor and play with them. Let them take the lead. These are opportunities to build warm and cooperative relationships. Every interaction is an opportunity to teach them about their world. Give your children many choices so you build their skills at managing their own behavior.

- For older children, notice whether you listen to them or tend to lead the conversation, telling them what you think they should do and believe. Trust that they have the right instincts and, through patient, empathic listening, notice how frequently they arrive at conclusions similar to your own.

- Richly reinforce the development of your child's skills, using reinforcers beyond stickers, treats, and praise. Those can be valuable, especially when children have trouble learning a new behavior. But nearly every interaction between adults and children provides consequences for children's behavior. Your attention, your listening, your interest in them, your time spent playing with them—all are vital to their development. Although some behaviorists suggest providing four positive reactions to children for every negative reaction, that seems stingy to me. If you count simply listening to them or playing with them as positives, shouldn't we do much more than that? Keep in mind that simply telling a child to do something he wasn't already doing (such as "Pick up your toys" or "Time to go to bed") is negative for most children most of the time. How would you feel if your coworkers or friends criticized you or demanded something of you once for every four times they listened to you or praised you?

- Structure, monitor, and set limits. You can prevent much problem behavior by proactively arranging for and richly reinforcing alternative positive behaviors:

  - Give choices wherever possible. It is so much more effective to say, "Would you like to walk to the car or have me carry you to the car?" than "I want you to get in the car."

  - Keep track of what your children are doing and guide them away from risky situations and activities.

  - Use consistent, mild negative consequences when all else fails. Learn how to give simple, brief time-outs rather than getting angry, criticizing, or scolding. You needn't lecture your children about what they did wrong or what they should do next time.

For Policy Makers

- Require the use of evidence-based programs. I hope I have convinced you to explore the tested and effective programs that can significantly reduce the level of psychological and behavioral problems that are so costly to communities, state, and nation. The Institute of Medicine report on prevention, *Preventing Mental, Emotional, and Behavioral Disorders Among Young People: Progress and Possibilities* (IOM and NRC 2009), describes numerous evidence-based programs.

- Investigate the cost-benefit ratio of interventions. Most of these programs save much more money than they cost. *Return on Investment: Evidence-Based Options to Improve Statewide Outcomes* (Aos et al. 2011) carefully analyzes the costs and benefits of many programs and indicates that most offer a significant return on investment.

For Citizens

- Advocate for evidence-based programs. A large constituency isn't yet lobbying for prevention. If you want to see your city have much less crime, drug abuse, teen pregnancy, and academic failure, you can advocate that policy makers learn about the evidence-based family programs that can be made available to those who need them.

CHAPTER 3

Nurturing Schools

I still remember the day I took my son Michael to his first day of first grade. I had a feeling of helplessness. If kids picked on him or his teacher disliked him, what could I do? Would I even know about it?

Imagine that you have done a great job in the first years of your child's life and have a healthy, socially skilled, and highly verbal child. But then you must send her to school. Her fate is no longer in your hands alone. If her school is highly punitive, if it allows children to bully one another, or if its teachers are incompetent, this could scar your child for life.

Fortunately, schools are getting better. That might come as a surprise, given repeated reports about children in the United States lagging behind children in other countries in math and science, and considering the amount of bullying and violence we hear about in US schools. But I am convinced that educational researchers' progress in understanding how schools can become more nurturing and how to teach effectively is beginning to spread into schools throughout the country. In this chapter, I will tell you about research-based methods for teaching positive social behavior and academic skills that schools across the country are adopting.

Nurturing Prosocial Behavior

The principles underlying how schools can help children and adolescents develop positive social behavior are the same as those for families. Schools need to minimize coercive and punitive interactions. They must teach, promote, and richly reinforce prosocial behavior. They also need to monitor students' behavior so they can tell what is working to encourage prosocial and academic behavior and modify what isn't.

Minimizing Coercion

When behaviorists began to observe how students and teachers interact in classrooms, they discovered that teachers paid more attention to problem students than to others. It is natural for a teacher to tell a student who gets out of his seat to sit down. The student often complies, so the teacher is reinforced when the student stops his disruptive behavior.

Unfortunately, what also happens is that the teacher's attention reinforces the student's unwanted behavior. As a result, the student gets out of his seat more often. As his misbehavior increases, the teacher gets increasingly frustrated and angry—and so does the student. This is the same kind of coercive process that Jerry Patterson discovered in families (Patterson 1982), as discussed in chapter 2.

Skilled teachers have learned to reinforce desired behavior more than disruptive behavior. They do it by praising, paying attention to, and rewarding cooperative and on-task behavior and ignoring minor disruptions. In the absence of this kind of skilled teaching, high levels of conflict can develop. Humans are quick to learn to punish each other because, as Patterson showed, when you do something aversive to someone who is annoying you, the other person often stops. That immediately reinforces whatever you did to get the person to stop, but in the long run it isn't effective in reducing unwanted behavior. Rather, it evolves into an increasingly punitive environment.

Left unmanaged, schools can become like prisons, where everyone is on guard and angry. An example is the Birmingham, Alabama, school district, which authorized police to use pepper spray in schools. By some reports, more than one hundred students have been pepper-sprayed. In one incident, a girl who was four months pregnant was arguing with a boy who was harassing her. As they were beginning to go their own ways, a police officer handcuffed her and told her to calm down. When she said she was calm, he pepper-sprayed her, causing her to throw up.

Escalating punishment is usually counterproductive. Roy Mayer, a school psychologist at California State University, provided dramatic evidence of this (Mayer 1995). He showed that schools with lots of rules and punishment have *higher* levels of misbehavior and vandalism. As is the case for so many other problems in society, our natural penchant for punishing each other is neither effective nor consistent with humane values.

Promoting Prosocial Behavior

One of the greatest problems educational researchers have faced is how to help teachers move from escalating punishment to using positive reinforcement to nurture prosocial behavior. Over the past five decades, significant progress has taken place. Three good examples of it are the Good Behavior Game, Positive Behavioral Intervention and Support, and the Positive Action program.

The Good Behavior Game

One of the most important developments in using reinforcement to promote cooperation and self-regulation began with Muriel Saunders, a fourth-grade teacher in Kansas in the 1960s, who was at her wits' end due to students' disruptive behavior. Prevention scientist Dennis Embry, who knew Muriel when he was at the University of Kansas, shared her story with me:

> Muriel taught in a small town of less than four thousand souls: Baldwin, Kansas. The other fourth-grade teachers had skimmed off all the "good" kids, leaving her the challenge of a lifetime. Fortunately for her, her students, and the world, she succeeded in creating a strategy that is bringing extraordinary benefits to students throughout the world.
>
> Muriel's story begins in the mid-1960s, when she got a teaching job while her husband was going to graduate school in nearby Lawrence, Kansas, the home of the world-famous Department of Human Development at the University of Kansas. By Thanksgiving, Muriel had become so frustrated with her classroom that she was ready to quit on the spot. But she decided to give it one more go after

talking to her husband's doctoral advisor, Dr. Montrose Wolf. One of Dr. Wolf's other graduate students was Harriet Barrish, who was very interested in studying the impact of behavioral psychology in the classroom, so she joined their cramped but urgent meeting.

Dr. Wolf, always searching for solutions, asked if the class ever behaved better. Muriel initially said no. After a bit of probing, Dr. Wolf asked her if there might be some task or activity in which their behavior was better. "Ah," pondered Muriel, "they do act better and get rather excited when we have a team spelling bee." Dr. Wolf nodded and then said, "Well, perhaps you could make a team contest for being good?"

So they did. They created multiple teams of students. Each team could win a reward for working cooperatively for brief periods of time. Rewards were as simple and inexpensive as an extra five minutes of recess. It was also a soft competition; all teams could win. As teams got better, the length of time the game was played was extended.

In order to evaluate whether the game—now known as the Good Behavior Game—made a difference, Harriet Barrish organized an experiment (Barrish, Saunders, and Wolf 1969). She trained observers to sit in the classroom during math and reading and record all the things that would drive a teacher crazy and disrupt learning, such as students getting out of their seats and talking during lessons.

As you can see from figure 2, prior to their introduction to the game, students were getting out of their seats and talking disruptively most of the time. Then they implemented the Good Behavior Game during the students' math period but not during reading. As you can see, there was a dramatic reduction in the kids' disruptive behavior. When they stopped playing the game in math (indicated by "Rev." in the figure), disruptions skyrocketed. Then they implemented the game during both reading and math, and disruption virtually ended. (You can read a thorough account of the study online; refer to Barrish, Saunders, and Wolf 1969 in the References section for details.)

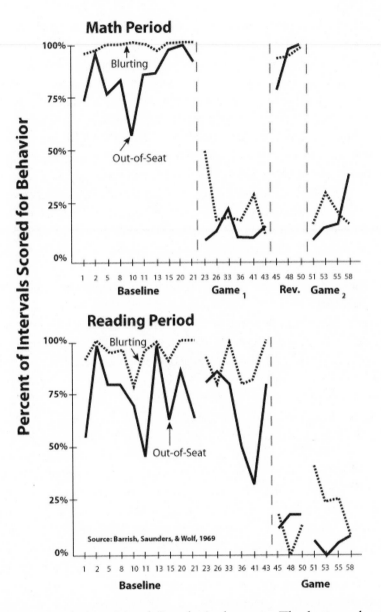

Figure 2. Graph from Muriel Saunders's classroom. The horizontal axis indicates minutes of class time. (Reprinted with permission from H. S. Barrish, M. Saunders, and M. M. Wolf. 1969. "Good Behavior Game: Effects of Individual Contingencies for Group Consequences on Disruptive Behavior in a Classroom. *Journal of Applied Behavior Analysis* 2: 119–124.)

Since the invention of the Good Behavior Game, more than fifty studies around the world have evaluated it (for example, Ialongo et al. 1999; Leflot et al. 2013). These studies showed that, in all kinds of classroom settings, the game motivated children to work together cooperatively and reduced student behaviors that disrupted learning and distressed teachers. But could such a simple game have any lasting benefit?

Shep Kellam, a psychiatrist at Johns Hopkins University, thought it could. He was looking for a way to improve children's social competence and thought it was possible to prevent even fairly serious problems by simply making sure that children develop the ability to cooperate with teachers and get along with their peers. When one of his behavior analyst colleagues brought the Good Behavior Game to his attention, he thought it might be just what he needed. Twenty years later, it is clear that it succeeded beyond his wildest dreams.

Shep Kellam is one of the more interesting characters I've met in my journeys and one of the few psychiatrists in the prevention science community. Thanks to that and the fact that he has been prominent for a long time, he has played a major role in getting prevention science the research support required to show its value. Like Skinnerian behaviorism, the field of prevention science has succeeded because a small number of people were inspired by a vision of what the field could do, long before there was any evidence to confirm that vision.

Kellam's first major contribution was the Woodlawn Study (C. H. Brown, Adams, and Kellam 1981; Kellam et al. 1983), which focused on the Woodlawn neighborhood just south of the University of Chicago. In 1966, he began studying a group of African-American children to see if he could figure out what influenced some children to develop psychological and behavioral problems, such as depression, drug abuse, and criminal activities, and what protected others from the same fate. Studies like this are commonplace now and have revealed an enormous amount about what leads young people to develop these problems. But when the Woodlawn Study began, there was virtually no precedent for the idea that you can learn what influences problem development through a *longitudinal study*—research that assesses people multiple times over the course of years. Kellam and his team of researchers recruited 1,242 African-American families of first-grade students. The families agreed to let them assess these children repeatedly, and Shep Kellam and his wife, Peg Ensminger, ultimately followed these young people to age thirty-two. They found that aggressive children were more likely to use drugs by adulthood, and that low family socioeconomic status and loss of interest in school were associated with substance abuse (Fothergill et al. 2008).

By the time Kellam moved to Johns Hopkins in 1982, he was already famous (well, as famous goes among behavioral scientists). Perhaps for this reason, and because of what he had learned from working with the famed community organizer Saul Alinsky, he was able to get an incredible level of cooperation from the Baltimore school system for testing the impact of the Good Behavior Game on the development of elementary school students. He wanted to see if it could prevent kids from developing academic, social, and behavioral problems; and to do that, he needed to conduct a randomized controlled trial.

Kellam convinced the school district to randomly assign first- and second-grade teachers to classrooms, and then randomly assign classrooms to one of three conditions: using the Good Behavior Game, following a curriculum called mastery learning (an evidence-based teaching strategy), or not receiving a special intervention. This randomization meant that kids who got the Good Behavior Game were pretty much the same as the kids who didn't. Because of randomization, any differences between the groups—whether one, five, or even fifteen years later—was very likely to be due to the Good Behavior Game.

What Kellam and his colleagues found was extraordinary. During the year of the intervention, he had observers go into classrooms and code what they saw. In the Good Behavior Game classrooms, students were on task and cooperative. In the control classrooms (both mastery learning and no special intervention), some skilled teachers had classes that were on task and working well. But most classrooms in the control condition were scenes of chaos. Children were wandering around the room and not paying much attention to the teacher. Very little learning was taking place.

Kellam and his crew followed the kids into sixth grade to see if there were any lasting effects of the game. He found that those who had played the Good Behavior Game in first or second grade were much less likely to face arrest or become smokers (Kellam et al. 1998).

Then, through extraordinary efforts of his research team, they followed these children into adulthood (Kellam et al. 2008). What they discovered may be the single most impressive finding in the annals of prevention science. The kids who had played the game—only for one year, in either the first or second grade—were less likely to be addicted to drugs or suicidal and had committed fewer crimes. An independent analysis of the economic benefit of this intervention indicated that for every dollar spent on the Good Behavior Game, about eighty-four dollars could be saved through reduced special education, victim, health care, and criminal justice costs (Aos et al. 2012; WSIPP 2014).

Think about the lives that this simple game changed. Among the boys who were aggressive in first grade and did not play the Good Behavior Game, 83 percent were addicted to drugs as adults. But among the aggressive boys who played the Good Behavior Game, only 29 percent had drug addiction problems. Given that drug addicts are more likely to die prematurely (Nyhlén et al. 2011), we can safely say that this simple game saved lives.

Positive Behavioral Intervention and Support

Other heroes of prevention science are also working in schools. Education researchers Rob Horner and George Sugai developed a school-wide system for supporting students' positive behavior, called Positive Behavioral Intervention and Support (PBIS), and it is bringing peace and a nurturing environment to schools around the world. At last count, more than fifteen thousand schools nationwide have implemented the program.

Horner and Sugai both initially worked with severely developmentally delayed young people with serious behavior problems, including very destructive behavior. Their approach usually involved setting up a program to increase reinforcement for desirable behavior and curtail it for problem behavior. But before you can curtail reinforcement for a problem behavior, you have to figure out what the reinforcers are. To do this, they developed a functional behavioral assessment to determine the purposes of specific problem behaviors.

The two most important consequences of problem behavior are escaping from an unpleasant task and getting attention from teachers or other students. If a student becomes angry and disrespectful during a lesson, it may be because she can't do the work; and in the past, angry reactions have typically gotten her sent to the office, allowing her to escape from the task. If the student doesn't have the skills to do the work, it will do little good to increase rewards for doing it. Thus, one of the key ways to prevent the development of behavior problems in schools is make sure instruction is effective.

If attention from teachers or other students seems to reinforce a student's misbehavior, the remedy is to reduce attention for misbehavior and increase attention for desired behavior. That might involve increased attention and praise when the student works appropriately. It could also include a system for providing daily reports to parents about their child's successes so that both parents and teachers can reward these efforts.

Horner and Sugai found that their programs usually worked in the short run. However, it was difficult to maintain the benefits. Moreover, concentrating efforts on the kids who were most out of control didn't prevent other kids, who were getting less attention, from developing problems. They realized they needed a school-wide system.

Influenced by Roy Mayer's (1995) finding that slow escalation of rules and punishment for violations as a response to student misbehavior only further motivated student rebellion, they sought to help schools reduce the number of rules and increase positive reinforcement for following rules. To this end, a team of PBIS teachers developed a small set of simple rules for the school, such as "Be respectful," "Be safe," and "Be responsible." Staff members then taught what these rules meant in every venue in the school. For example, being respectful in a classroom meant listening to what the teacher was saying and treating other students courteously.

The resulting PBIS systems have been evaluated in randomized trials in which some schools engage in PBIS, while others didn't. In Maryland, where PBIS is in the process of being implemented in every school, a study by Catherine Bradshaw and her colleagues (2009) found that elementary schools that had already introduced PBIS had fewer suspensions and discipline referrals than those that hadn't. In Illinois, another randomized trial showed that students in elementary schools that implemented PBIS had better academic performance than students in other schools (Horner et al. 2009).

PBIS is an effective system for reducing harassment and bullying. One report (Sugai, Horner, and Algozzine 2011) describes how the system helps create an environment that promotes positive social behavior among students and provides extra positive behavioral support for students who engage in bullying or harassment. In an early evaluation of this system that I was involved in (Metzler et al. 2001), we found that implementing PBIS in a middle school significantly reduced male students' discipline referrals for harassment and increased the proportion of students who said they felt safe in school.

Positive Action

The proliferation of randomized controlled trials of interventions in schools has proved threatening to people who have unevaluated programs. I often hear comments like "I know our program works. We don't have the money to do the research on it, but I'm sure it works." Many researchers, including me, have been skeptical. After all, we are committed to the proposition that science is essential to improving human well-being. The feeling among many researchers is that much of what is being done in the way of school or family interventions hasn't been evaluated, and that some of what has been evaluated has turned out to be useless or even harmful. Meanwhile, over the last thirty years or so researchers have been conduct-ing randomized controlled trials that have identified more effective inter-ventions. Researchers have often seethed at practitioners' resistance to adopting evidence-based interventions, and frequently haven't been very sympathetic or polite toward those who aren't researchers but are sincerely trying to make a difference in people's lives.

One prevention program specialist I know found a unique solution to this problem: she married a researcher. Carol Allred developed a school-wide program called Positive Action in the 1980s and 1990s. She devel-oped curricula for classrooms, materials for parents, a counselor program, and a community program, all designed to help schools and communities replace punitive practices with a culture that promotes positive actions on the part of children and the adults around them. Then, in 1998, she attended the Society for Prevention Research meeting in Park City, Utah, where she met Brian Flay, one of the most prominent methodologists in the behavioral sciences. They fell in love with each other, and Brian fell in love with Carol's program. He was convinced that it was a great program, although it lacked studies to prove it. So he did what any good methodolo-gist would do: he evaluated it.

Brian and his colleagues conducted two randomized trials of Positive Action in elementary and middle school grades; a third trial was done independently of his work. In all three trials, Positive Action had a beneficial effect in reducing the decline in prosocial behavior that is frequently found across the elementary school years (Washburn et al. 2011). PA has also proven beneficial in preventing the development of problems as diverse as substance use, disruptive behavior, bullying, violence, and delinquency (Beets et al. 2009; Lewis et al. 2012; Lewis, Schure et al. 2013), as well as depression (Lewis, DuBois et al. 2013). Additional analyses have shown that Positive Action prevents these problems because it nurtures prosocial norms and behavior (Lewis et al. 2012; Snyder et al. 2013).

Many educators resist implementing programs that are focused on improving social behavior because they feel they must concentrate on enhancing academic achievement. But this is a false choice. Children's interest and ability to learn is enhanced in an environment where they feel safe, have cooperative peers, and receive a lot of positive reinforcement. In the case of Positive Action, evaluations show that schools that implement the program have improved school climate (Snyder et al. 2012) and do better academically. In the randomized trial in Hawaii, Positive Action significantly improved reading and math performance compared with schools that didn't get the program (Snyder et al. 2010). Beneficial effects on reading and math achievement were also found in the randomized trial that was done in Chicago (Bavarian et al. 2013).

Monitoring Behavior

It is easy to see the value of replacing coercive interactions with systems that teach and reinforce prosocial behavior. What may be less obvious is that effective programs include systems for monitoring their impact on students' behavior. For example, in the Good Behavior Game teachers count the number of disruptions and use this information to tell if the game is having its expected effect. Likewise, Positive Behavioral Intervention and Support utilizes a web-based system for recording discipline problems in every venue of the school. This helps staff identify places where extra attention is needed. In order to be sure programs are nurturing desired behavior, they must include a means of measuring their effectiveness.

Creating Schools That Nurture Prosocial Behavior

With their development of the Positive Action program, Allred and Flay provide a particularly striking example of how scientists and practitioners are working together to encourage the nurturance of prosocial behavior. But there are many others. Just as fights among people in different subfields of the behavioral sciences are diminishing, the split between researchers and practitioners is closing as evidence about what young people need becomes more definitive. A growing community of educators, family practitioners, and researchers is coming together to spread positive methods for nurturing students' prosocial behavior. To me, this is one of the most encouraging developments in education in the last fifty years.

The programs I have described are important early steps in the evolution of a more caring and effective culture. Like the family programs I described in chapter 2, they replace coercive and punitive ways of trying to control young people's behavior with more effective, proactive methods of structuring environments to teach and reinforce prosocial behavior and critical academic skills, and they minimize situations that encourage problem behavior. The number of schools that have implemented PBIS (fifteen thousand) is far fewer than the number of schools in the United States (over one hundred thousand), but it is the beginning of a movement that is gaining momentum as evidence for the benefit of these more nurturing strategies accumulates and becomes more widely understood.

Much more publicity goes to dramatic and rare events like school shootings—which, by the way, happen more frequently in states with more punitive schools (Arcus 2002). But slowly and quietly, positive methods like the Good Behavior Game, Positive Action, and Positive Behavioral Intervention and Support are taking hold throughout the country. As they spread and replace punitive practices, we can be confident that more students will learn to cooperate, restrain impulsive behavior, and regulate their emotions. Fewer children will face bullying and harassment. Given the results of the Good Behavior Game in Baltimore, it is likely that as these methods spread, rates of crime, depression, drug abuse, and academic failure will decline dramatically.

Teaching Children Well: The Importance of an Evidence-Based Approach

Even the most socially skilled, prosocial young people will fail to become productive adults if they aren't taught well. Moreover, as noted above, deficits in a student's academic skills can be at the root of behavior problems. If we are going to construct a society in which everyone is both productive and caring, we need schools that make sure that every student learns and loves to learn.

However, year after year, American students do poorly in comparison to students in many other countries. The Trends in International Mathematics and Science Study assesses math and science skills among fourth- and eighth-grade students around the world. In 2007, US eighth-graders did worse in math than students in Taipei, Hong Kong, Japan, Korea, and Singapore (Gonzales et al. 2008). American fourth-graders also did poorly in math compared with students in eight other countries, including the Russian Federation. US eighth-graders did worse in science than those in eight other countries, including Hungary, the Czech Republic, Slovenia, and the Russian Federation.

It isn't that all schools in the United States are doing a poor job. In more affluent communities and neighborhoods, students are doing just as well as the top students in Singapore, the world leader in math and science. Rather, the problem lies in America's failure to ensure high-quality education in high-poverty schools. The US Department of Education reported that nine-year-olds in high-poverty schools are more than three grade levels behind students in low-poverty schools in reading and more than two grade levels behind in math (Perie, Moran, and Lutkus 2005).

These disparities parallel racial and ethnic differences in academic achievement. Black and Hispanic students, on average, do significantly less well than white students (National Center for Education Statistics 2014). Of course, there is a correlation between poverty and ethnicity. I think it is more important to focus on poverty than on race or ethnicity for two reasons. First, focusing on race or ethnicity tends to be stigmatizing and divisive. Second, poverty is something we can change. I will discuss this further in chapter 8. Here, I want to tell you about teaching methods that can overcome the educational disadvantages that face so many children living in poverty.

Conflicting Visions

Although I have done only one study evaluating a curricular intervention (Gunn et al. 2000), I have followed developments in education closely. To me, the progress in education research is another facet of the behavioral revolution that began with Skinner's insistence that human behavior is a function of the environment and that by creating the right kind of environments we can build a better society. However, progress in the improvement of teaching has been slow, owing to the just-mentioned lack of commitment to experimental evaluations and to the dominance of the philosophy of discovery learning.

Discovery Learning

The main idea of discovery learning is highly plausible: children learn best when we let them determine their own pace of learning, deciding when they want to learn new things. Educators who favor this approach argue that children who are systematically taken through a structured curriculum that organizes what is to be learned in the most efficient sequence are being regimented, and that such regimentation will kill their love of learning.

This vision fits with some of the experience that most of us had in school. Weren't there many times when you were bored to tears in school? Wouldn't it have been great if most of your learning had involved the excited pursuit of new knowledge, without being told what to study or when? Indeed, schools such as Sudbury Valley School in Massachusetts allow students to determine what they want to learn and when they want to learn it, and a study of these schools (Gray 2013) documented the considerable success of their (mostly middle-class) students.

But there have also been some significant disasters, such as the whole-language movement. According to the whole-language philosophy, phonics instruction, in which children learn how to sound out words, is unnecessary. Instead, whole-language proponents believe children can learn to read by figuring out the meaning of words from their context. Given that you have gotten this far in my book, you are already a competent reader. But see if you can infer the missing words in the following sentence: "The _____ came running up to the door, _____ all the way."

Absent any empirical evidence of the effectiveness of the whole-language approach, its advocates convinced the state of California to abandon phonics instruction and embrace whole language. The number of children who couldn't read soared. Bonnie Grossen, a friend of mine who is an expert in the direct instruction methods I describe below, spent a couple of years helping the Sacramento school system provide remedial reading instruction in middle schools because so few of the children could read well. More generally, reviews and meta-analyses of the effects of discovery learning do not support its efficacy (Alfieri et al. 2011), particularly for children in need of special education (Fuchs et al. 2008).

Direct Instruction

Unfortunately, as mentioned, many educators are not yet convinced that they should pay attention to empirical research. Therefore, discovery learning advocates have been able to convince them that structured, direct teaching of skills and concepts undermines children's ability to think and that children hate it. That was certainly not our experience when both of our sons learned to read and developed terrific math skills thanks to direct instruction. I would love to take all the credit for this—that it was all the encouragement we provided, or perhaps our "superior genes." But the main reason for their success was the system of direct instruction that my wife, Georgia, had become skilled in.

By the time Michael was four, Georgia had taught him to count and do simple arithmetic. Georgia had received training in direct instruction (DI), a systematic method of developing and delivering curricula. She had a workbook for DI arithmetic at home and introduced Michael to it, and the next thing we knew, he was working through it by himself. We would get up in the morning and find him at the kitchen table doing arithmetic. He loved it!

We were extremely fortunate that the best first-grade teacher in the district, Pat Holland, taught at Parker Elementary School, just down the hill from our house. During teacher introductions at our first parent meeting, a loud whoop went up when Pat was introduced. When Michael started first grade, Pat quickly realized how advanced he was in math and got him into third-grade math. The head start he got in math carried him a long way. He was the mental math champion of Lane County in third grade and the city champion in fifth grade. By the time he finished high school, he had completed two years of college math. He then went to the University of Chicago, where he majored in economics and carried a 3.9 average in this math-heavy field. (Our son Sean showed similar gifts in math and finished a couple of years of college math while still in high school.)

Direct instruction is the brainchild of Siegfried Engelmann, Wesley Becker, and Doug Carnine, initially at the University of Illinois around the time I was a graduate student in psychology there. I can remember seeing Engelmann on the TV news fervently insisting that directly teaching poor preschool children what they needed to know could erase their academic disadvantages.

Engelmann developed his teaching methods by constantly testing everything he did to see if children were learning what was being taught. He discovered that children learned and remembered material best if they had frequent opportunities to give correct answers. A well-designed lesson can be highly reinforcing, not because students are getting rewards, but simply because they are frequently able to demonstrate their knowledge. DI often involves children learning in small groups where the group responds more than ten times per minute. This ensures that the teacher knows whether students are mastering the material so they can go back and work on things the children haven't learned well.

Direct instruction lessons are scripted, giving teachers little leeway in what they teach. This is one reason many teachers have resisted DI, complaining that it is too regimented and that children will be bored or stifled. But that is not the case. When DI is done properly, children enjoy lessons because they experience so much success in learning. And DI is very successful, especially in aiding the success of children who would otherwise fail.

What many teachers don't understand is that the scripting is done to ensure that concepts are taught as efficiently and effectively as possible, not as a way to constrain teachers. If you already understand a concept, you might not see how easily a child who doesn't understand it can be confused by a poorly constructed teaching sequence.

Take the word "under." You can try to teach a child who doesn't understand "under" by showing him a pencil under a table and saying, "The pencil is *under* the table." But without any negative examples— examples of what is not "under"—a child can be quite confused. Maybe "under" means pencils are in some way connected with tables; if you were to put the pencil above the table, the child may say that the pencil is under the table.

A DI sequence includes both negative examples and positive examples. Holding the pencil above the table, you would say, "The pencil is *not under* the table." And to be sure that the child doesn't infer that "under" is about pencils below tables, these irrelevant features of the concept are eliminated in other examples: "The ball is *under* the blanket." "The shoe is *not under* the bed." By carefully sequencing positive and negative examples of concepts, DI ensures efficient instruction.

Research clearly indicates that DI methods are more effective than most other teaching techniques (Adams and Engelmann 1996). Beginning in the 1970s, DI methods were compared to numerous other methods of teaching, and DI outperformed all other approaches—including a discovery learning approach where students selected the tasks they wanted to engage in (Stebbins et al. 1977). DI even improved self-esteem more than a strategy that directly focused on increasing self-esteem. It turns out that children have higher self-esteem when they are experiencing the intrinsic reinforcement of learning new things, whereas trying to raise their self-esteem artificially in the absence of genuine success is useless.

As you might imagine, there have been plenty of examples of the power of evidence-based approaches to instruction. For example, Wesley Elementary School in Houston, Texas, consists almost entirely of poor minority students. Yet by implementing direct instruction, the school has virtually every child reading and doing math at grade level (Carter 2000).

The Emerging Consilience

Biologist E. O. Wilson (1998) has popularized the concept of *consilience*—the idea that evidence from different areas of science can converge in a unified understanding of a phenomenon. I see that happening in education.

For most of my career, the two visions of how children learn described above have been in conflict. I've been frustrated by resistance to the proven teaching methods that have arisen from the behaviorist tradition. I've seen firsthand how powerful these methods are and how our failure to use them has greatly harmed millions of American children. At the same time, I've come to see the wisdom of paying close attention to what children are interested in and following their lead. Too often, behavioral approaches to teaching have focused so much on teaching a skill that they ignore the fact that the child has lost interest in the learning task. Fortunately, it seems that people from each of these two camps are becoming a little less strident and finding ways to work together to improve the effectiveness of teaching methods.

What is emerging is an approach to education that is clear about the core knowledge and skills that children need to learn, that is accountable for achieving good outcomes for all children, and that intensely engages children while allowing them a sense of authenticity. The battles are receding between those who have labeled any highly structured effort to teach children as "drill and kill" and those who have been dismissive of children's need for choice and autonomy. Increasingly, teaching practices have their basis in empirical evidence showing that carefully designed instructional sequences can help at-risk children learn at a level they never could have achieved by waiting until they discovered what they needed to know. That said, there is also a wealth of evidence that children learn best when they have considerable choice and autonomy.

Research in middle schools also demonstrates the importance of engaging students in meaningful learning in contexts that richly reinforce their efforts. When schools are highly competitive, it undermines learning for its own sake. There is considerable evidence that early adolescents need a caring and noncompetitive learning environment that emphasizes mastery of school tasks over academic competition and where they feel highly regarded by teachers. In schools that emphasize competition as opposed to self-development, students are more likely to be depressed and angry, have lower self-esteem, value education less, and have lower grades (Roeser and Eccles 1998).

Achieving Effective Reform in Schools

Fortunately, due to growing consilience concerning educational methods, schools are increasingly becoming places that nurture both the social and the academic development of students through efficient and engaging instructional practices, minimization of punishment and situations that elicit problem behavior, respect for students' autonomy, and lots of reinforcement, both explicit and intrinsic.

Progress on this problem has begun to occur, prompted by a surprising source—the George W. Bush administration. Although the Bush administration ignored scientific evidence in many areas, it did more to bring science into education than any previous administration. Unlike the National Institutes of Health, which had been funding high-quality scientific research in the biological and behavioral sciences for many years, the Department of Education didn't previously have a strong commitment to funding rigorous research or using scientific evidence to guide the choice of teaching practices.

But under the Bush administration, the Department of Education created the Institute of Education Sciences, which funds careful experimental evaluations of teaching methods, as well as studies that shed light on how to get schools to adopt effective methods. The department's What Works Clearinghouse identifies teaching methods that have been proven more effective through randomized controlled trials and promotes the use of these methods. As effective teaching practices become more widely used, we can expect to see many more poor and minority children succeed in school.

One of the most important developments in this regard has been the creation of Common Core State Standards by the Council of Chief State School Officers and the National Governors Association Center for Best Practices. These standards define the key skills and knowledge that students need to have in mathematics, English language arts, history, and social studies. Forty-five states have adopted these standards, and they are collaborating on a set of common assessments that will measure how well students are doing on the skills and knowledge that are vital to their success and the well-being of their communities.

Some educators continue to be concerned that standardized testing will constrain what teachers teach and students learn—that we will "teach to the test." There are certainly reasons to be cautious about testing. In Atlanta, when incentives were placed on teachers to increase student performance, some teachers simply cheated (Copeland 2013).

However, do you doubt that it is a good thing if every child learns to read and do math? I think about the Bethel School District here in Eugene, Oregon, where over the past eight years the district has steadily increased the proportion of students who are performing at grade level and a decreased the disparity between performance of white and Hispanic children. I am confident that, given a choice, the families of at-risk children would choose to have their children be at or above grade level. But if the district had chosen not to measure students' performance, parents wouldn't even know whether their children were progressing.

At the same time, we should not lose sight of the fact that there is much more to human beings than test scores. I hope that, as schools improve, we get better at recognizing the valuable diversity among young people and the fact that they have skills, interests, values, and potential that standardized tests don't capture. Nurturing their development in these areas may prove as important to society as their scores on achievement tests.

Action Implications

I have briefly outlined key research-based teaching strategies that have proven benefit in helping children learn efficiently and develop self-regulation, social skills, and cooperativeness. Science shows that schools can be much more effective at helping our children achieve the social and academic skills they need. The next step is for these beneficial practices to be more widely adopted.

For Parents

- If you have a child who is four or five and interested in learning to read, I recommend using *Teach Your Child to Read in 100 Easy Lessons* (Engelmann, Haddox, and Bruner 1983). Georgia and I taught both of our sons to read with this book and our son Mike did the same with his daughter, Ashlyn.

- Be sure your child's school monitors your child's academic progress, and advocate for adjustments to teaching methods when warranted.

- If phonics-based methods aren't being used to teach reading, advocate for using phonics.

- If your child isn't at grade level in any subject, ask the school how it plans to remedy the situation.

- Make sure your child's school is implementing some form of school-wide positive behavioral support, such as Positive Behavioral Intervention and Support, Positive Action, or the Good Behavior Game. (You can learn more about the Good Behavior Game at http://www.goodbehaviorgame.org.)

- Use the principles outlined in this chapter to support your child's scholastic success:

  - Monitor and guide your child's progress in school.

  - Each day, ask your child about what is happening in school and listen to your child's reply.

  - Make sure your child does all assigned homework. Early on, establish routine times for doing homework. For example, you might require your child to do homework before enjoying "screen time."

  - If your child is having trouble with other students, bring it to the attention of teachers or other school officials and ask them what they will do to remedy the situation.

  - Reinforce your child's academic progress. For children who aren't doing well, it will be helpful to set up a system of rewards. For others, it may be enough to show interest in the child's work and your appreciation and pride in successes along the way.

- Establish a good relationship with your child's teachers.

  - Find, recognize, and express appreciation for the things teachers do for your child.

  - When you have a concern, be sure to raise it with the teacher, but do it with respect, care, and openness to the teacher's input.

- Consult the What Works Clearinghouse at http://www.ies.ed.gov /ncee/wwc for reliable information about effective teaching methods.

For Educators

- Make schools more nurturing by adopting one of the many evidence-based programs that have shown their benefit in enhancing self-regulation, cooperation, and prosociality.

- Use behavioral principles to shape behavior:

    - Reduce the use of punishment.

    - Teach a small number of clear rules and richly reinforce students for following them.

    - Richly reinforce positive behavior through recognition, rewards, and support of students' autonomy.

- Adopt evidence-based teaching methods. These include not only research-based instructional methods, but "response-to-intervention" methods in which frequent monitoring of children's progress guides adjustments in instructional methods in light of their success.

- Ensure that every child is reading at grade level by the end of third grade.

For Citizens

- Ask educators and policy makers whether they are monitoring the use of punishment and the incidence of bullying in schools.

- Advocate that educators and policy makers ensure implementation of evidence-based programs and practices, particularly in reducing punishment and bullying. Consult the What Works Clearinghouse.

- Recognize, praise, approve, and elect those who adopt these practices.

For Policy Makers

- Require that all schools monitor the extent of punishment (including detention, suspension, and expulsion) and bullying to ensure that both remain at a minimum.

- Require the implementation of evidence-based programs and practices shown to minimize punishment and conflict and promote prosocial behavior.

- Require the use of evidence-based teaching methods. Consult the What Works Clearinghouse.

- Require ongoing monitoring of students' academic progress—not just annual assessments, but response-to-intervention techniques that monitor learning progress at least weekly—and adjust teaching methods in response.

CHAPTER 4

Peers and Problems

Nurturing schools are vital to young people's prosocial development. However, as children reach adolescence they are developmentally more inclined to seek reinforcement from peers than from adults. So peer groups are the natural next topic in our exploration of how we can build a society that nurtures prosociality.

Deviancy Training

"So what would you do if your girlfriend got pregnant? Shoot her?"

"No, punch her in the stomach, real hard."

This conversation occurred in an observation room at Oregon Social Learning Center. Tom Dishion and his colleagues were trying to learn more about why some kids become delinquent. He and many other behavioral scientists knew that most adolescents who get in trouble do so with other adolescents. Delinquency is a group enterprise. But Dishion took the research a step further. He wanted to see if he could actually observe the social influence processes that motivate kids to defy adult expectations and engage in criminal acts. So he asked young men who were participating in a longitudinal study of delinquency to bring a friend into the lab and have a series of brief conversations about things like planning an activity or solving a problem with a parent or friend.

What he found was startling. The conversations these young men had about deviant activities provided direct and strong reinforcement of deviant behavior. Even though these thirteen- and fourteen-year-old boys knew their conversations were being observed and recorded, some of them talked quite freely about committing crimes, getting drunk, taking drugs, and victimizing girls. Even more surprising was the fact that the amount of this kind of talk predicted whether individuals engaged in delinquent behavior well into adulthood (Dishion et al. 1996).

You might think this occurred simply because adolescents who are already involved in problem behavior tend to talk more often about deviance. Maybe this topic was a by-product of their delinquent lifestyle and didn't influence their delinquent behavior. But that was not the case. It is true that young people's levels of problem behavior predict their future problem behavior. However, even when Dishion's team controlled statistically for the influence of prior deviant behavior, the level of deviancy talk in these thirty-minute videotaped discussions predicted adult antisocial behavior two years later (Dishion et al. 1996). The conversations escalated their deviant behavior.

Why would deviant talk lead to deviant behavior? And why did some kids talk about deviance while others didn't? The answer Dishion reached is the most interesting thing about his research, and it lines up with the information I've outlined about social interactions in families and schools: if you want to understand why people do things, look for the reinforcers. Dishion and his colleagues (1996) coded not only the deviant talk of these kids, but also the reactions of their friends. He simply coded deviant and nondeviant talk and two possible reactions to each statement: pause or laugh. They found that the more laughs a boy got for what he said, the more he talked about that topic. In pairs where most of the laughs followed deviant talk, there was a great increase in the deviant talk. In statistical terms, 84 percent of the variance in deviant talk related to the rate of laughter for deviant talk. That is huge.

Even more interesting was the fact that the rate of reinforcement for deviant talk strongly predicted later delinquency (Dishion et al. 1996). Boys whose friends approved of their talk of delinquent and violent acts were more likely to engage in these acts. Dishion called interactions like this "deviancy training." In subsequent research he showed that simply letting at-risk kids get together raised the level of their misbehavior (Dishion and Andrews 1995). Those findings led to a series of conferences that alerted policy makers to the harmful effects of bringing at-risk youth together in schools and in the juvenile justice system (Dodge, Dishion, and Lansford 2006).

Think back to what I've said about the lives of aggressive and defiant children. Jerry Patterson's research in families showed that these kids get little reinforcement for cooperative, prosocial behavior (Patterson, Reid, and Dishion 1992). Their families use mostly aversive behavior to control each other. Each family member's aggressive behavior is honed by its effect in getting others to back off, to stop being aversive. These kids don't get much love and approval and don't have much fun.

They don't get much love in school either. Teachers give them attention for their aggressive and uncooperative behavior, but it is mostly negative attention ("Sit down!"). Because these kids haven't developed skills for playing cooperatively with peers, their peers often reject them (Patterson, Reid, and Dishion 1992). And thanks to their inability to do what teachers want, they don't learn as much and eventually fall behind (DeBaryshe, Patterson, and Capaldi 1993).

By sixth or seventh grade, these kids feel isolated and rejected. They are often depressed. They also become increasingly resentful of constant efforts to get them to do the "right" thing. Then they meet other kids with the same background. It's magic! As Dishion's work shows, they finally find friends after enduring years of rejection by other, less aggressive kids. At last they have someone who approves of all the deviant things they want to talk about.

A colleague of Dishion's, Deborah Capaldi, studies violence between men and women. She wondered if the deviancy training that Dishion discovered influenced how boys treat girls. When the boys in Dishion's study were seventeen or eighteen years old, the researchers invited them back to have another conversation with a friend. One thing they asked them to talk about was what they liked and disliked about girls they knew. They coded these conversations in terms of how often they talked in hostile ways about girls. (The example at the beginning of this chapter comes from one of those conversations.) When the young men were twenty to twenty-three years old, Capaldi got data from them and their girlfriends or wives about how often the men were physically violent. Sure enough, those who had talked approvingly about violence toward women years earlier were, in fact, more aggressive toward their partners (Capaldi et al. 2001).

A further analysis of the interactions of these boys when they were sixteen or seventeen (Van Ryzin and Dishion 2013) revealed that the men who were most violent at twenty-two or twenty-three were the ones who not only had received reinforcement for talk of deviant behavior, but also had a friend or friends with whom they had coercive interactions. In addition to assessing the deviancy training I described above, this study coded how much the two friends were coercive toward each other. In this case, coercion was defined as engaging in dominant or dismissive behavior, using profanity, and being abusive to the other person. Even when the researchers controlled statistically for the teens' antisocial behavior as children and the quality of parental discipline, those who talked about deviance the most and were coercive toward their friend were most likely to engage in violence as adults.

This study makes me realize that although it remains very difficult to predict whether a given individual is going to be violent, the violence of many young men is hardly unique or unpredictable. It emerges from highly coercive environments that put young men on a trajectory toward violence in later life. Although we can't predict and prevent every act of violence in society, we can use what we know to make sure that many fewer young men become violent.

The Pathway to Deviance

The accumulated research on families, schools, and peer groups tells a compelling story about how communities produce troubled youth. Young people whose social environments fail to reinforce prosocial behavior go on to commit crimes, mistreat others, fail in school, and become addicted to tobacco, alcohol, and other drugs. They often lead lives marked by poverty, depression, and repeated failure in social relations. Once you understand this process—and all the tools we have available to prevent it—the prescription for a more successful society becomes clear.

Dishion's recent work provides a good example of how children become teens with multiple problems. In one study (Dishion, Ha, and Véronneau 2012), he followed a sample of 998 kids from ages eleven through twenty-four. His team looked at the quality of the kids' environment when they were eleven through thirteen and its influence on their subsequent development. They found strong evidence of harm from stressful environments. Young people were more likely to get involved with deviant peers by age fourteen if they came from poor families, were disliked by other children, and lived in a family with high levels of conflict, where parents weren't supportive and didn't set limits on their involvement with deviant peers.

The dry statistics of Dishion's analysis of deviant peer development tell a precise and compelling story of why youth grow up to cause trouble for themselves and those around them. The 998 children in this study lived in Portland, Oregon. Dishion first met them when they were in sixth grade, mostly age eleven. His study showed that many of them came from families that were stressed due to poverty. That meant they often didn't have enough to eat, wore shabbier clothing than other children, had vehicles that broke down, had to move due to evictions, or lived in cars or homeless shelters. Their poverty was one reason that other kids rejected them. Kids, especially in middle school, are very sensitive to status and readily tease and bully others in an effort to establish that they have higher status (Rusby et al. 2005). Dishion's study tells us that, in 1998, sixth- and seventh-graders in Portland were getting teased and bullied. Some children woke up every morning dreading going to school.

Due to the stresses they experience, poor families are less likely to be warm and loving and more likely to have conflict and coercion. Thus, many of the poor children who were living through the hell of peer harassment at school probably didn't have help from their family in coping with it. This is understandable when you consider the standpoint of these parents. People who are trying to cope with the threat of unemployment, homelessness, or discrimination may find it hard to support their children in many ways. Learning that their child is being harassed may simply further threaten and stress them. They may feel powerless to do anything about it. Their reaction may be to blame the child, which simply adds family difficulties to the stress the child is experiencing at school. So it's likely that, in 1998, many of the children in Dishion's study experienced threats and slights at school and anger, criticism, and abuse at home.

By 2001, a group of fourteen-year-olds in Dishion's sample who were angry, hurt, frightened, and rejected began to cluster together, or self-organize. The social influence process that Dishion documented in his earlier study began. Kids whose parents paid little attention to what they were doing or whom they were hanging out with got together to talk about and do the things that we call "delinquent acts" and they call "fun!" Virtually all delinquent acts are committed by two or more young people acting together, with the kids richly reinforcing each other's behavior.

By the time these kids were sixteen and seventeen, many were using drugs, stealing, getting into fights, and having sex. In 2001, Portland had more than three thousand violent crimes and more than twenty-eight thousand property crimes. The kids in Dishion's study committed some of those crimes.

Between 2009 and 2011, Dishion and his colleagues assessed these young people at ages twenty-two through twenty-four. They found that young people who had highly stressful and uncaring lives at ages eleven or twelve were much more likely to have had children by their early twenties. This line of research shows a clear path from stress during early adolescence to friendships with other rejected kids at age fourteen to sexual promiscuity at age sixteen or seventeen to early reproduction.

The Source of the Problem: Nonnurturing Environments

In our punitive and disapproving society, in which we customarily hold people personally responsible for what they do and punish them for transgressions, it is easy to fall into a stance of blaming these kids for how they turned out. But if anything deserves blame, it is their environments—though, truth be told, blaming is a worthless activity.

Can we blame their parents? In most cases, they presumably did some things they shouldn't have done and failed to do some things that they should have done. But Dishion's later study (Dishion, Ha, and Véronneau 2012) shows that the "guilty" parents probably were themselves the victims of similar environments. After all, how do people become poverty-stricken, stressed, aggressive, nonnurturing parents? They typically grow up in environments that are coercive and rejecting, get into trouble, fail in school, and have children early. (Dishion views this dynamic too from an evolutionary perspective. In a threatening world, it may be prudent to have children early, since you might not survive to have them later.)

Only when we transform young people's family and school environments to minimize coercion, teach and richly reinforce prosocial behavior, and stave off the development of deviant peer groups will we end this intergenerational propagation of poverty, academic failure, delinquency, and teenage pregnancy. As I hope I have convinced you in earlier chapters, the means for doing so lie within our grasp.

Not Every Troubled Teen Becomes a Delinquent

In writing about youth with multiple problems, I sometimes worry that I will promote negative and unsympathetic views of young people that will increase support for punitive approaches to dealing with them. I hope I have conveyed that it isn't their fault that they are having these problems. Rather, their environments created their problems. Moreover, it is possible to intervene at any point along their life course to reduce the problems they're facing and prevent future ones.

I didn't have to go far to find an example of a young person who reversed course in this way. Tom Dishion once led the kind of life he often describes in his research. He and his friends experimented with many behaviors, including drug use. When he was in high school he was arrested at school for possession of marijuana. That resulted in his transfer to an alternative high school. There he saw firsthand how schools and programs for troubled youth brought delinquent kids together, creating a context in which they further reinforced each other's problem behavior. He and his friends were on their way to a life of failure.

However, sometimes it just takes a little nurturance to steer a kid in a different direction. When Tom's older brother moved to Santa Barbara, Tom moved there as well. He found an apartment and attended the city college, where he discovered a group of young people who were enthusiastic about learning. That started him down the road to becoming, in my estimation, one of the most innovative and productive behavioral scientists I know. All it took was a nurturing social environment.

Preventing Deviant Peer Influences

The frequently repeated tragedy of young people joining a deviant peer group and developing multiple problems can be prevented. When children are young, they can learn the social and self-regulatory skills they need so that their peers don't reject them. And even when kids are having problems as they enter adolescence, we can prevent them from traveling down a troubled pathway by monitoring their peer associations and limiting their opportunities to get involved in peer groups that reinforce problem behavior.

Establish Good Peer Relations at an Early Age

A toddler who doesn't get his way is likely to cry. A toddler who has a toy grabbed away from him by another child is liable to hit or push the other child. But it is probably a safe bet that last time someone was rude to you, you didn't cry or hit him. One of the most important skills young children must develop is emotion regulation: the ability to control emotions and restrain themselves from impulsively attacking others. This is a basic building block of a civil society. Fortunately, we have learned a lot about how to help young children develop this skill.

One of the most basic methods is what psychologist John Gottman (1997) calls *emotion coaching*. In chapter 4, I described how my wife, Georgia, talks to our granddaughter, Ashlyn, about her emotions when she seems upset. It is a technique that Georgia's preschool adopted based on Gottman's writing. When a child becomes distressed, adults approach her sympathetically and try to match the type and intensity of the child's emotion empathically: "Oh, you are angry!" By labeling the emotion, they help the child learn to understand her emotions in the same way they might help a child to learn to name colors. They also say something about the situation that apparently evoked the emotion so the child learns to understand what evokes her emotions: "He took your toy." This empathic approach helps children begin to calm down. Then adults can suggest ways of resolving the situation: "Why don't you tell him that you didn't like how he took your toy and that you want to play with it? Then he can have a turn after you."

This whole approach is a departure from traditional behavioral strategies that sought to avoid reinforcing children's negative emotions. The fear was that children would use these emotions to get what they wanted and escape from the demands of adults. But I have repeatedly seen Grandma Georgie stick with whatever request she is making of Ashlyn while also showing great empathy for the frustration Ashlyn feels at having to, for example, stop an activity she is enjoying. By doing this and giving Ashlyn choices within the context of the request (for example, "Do you want to put on the green socks or the pink ones?"), many struggles are avoided. Instead, cooperation begins to grow.

Prevention scientists Mark Greenberg and Celene Domitrovich have developed a systematic program for teaching these emotion regulations skills in preschools and elementary schools: Promoting Alternative

Thinking Strategies (PATHS). It is designed to teach children directly about each emotion and appropriate ways to express it. Children learn to understand the emotions others are feeling by taking the other person's perspective. That initially involves seeing what the other sees. As their sophistication grows, they develop the ability to infer what someone else is feeling. PATHS also helps children learn to use problem solving in emotionally difficult situations so they can better resolve conflict with other children. In addition, it directly teaches and reinforces basic skills such as sharing and cooperating. The program is in widespread use in schools, and randomized experimental evaluations show that it improves children's social competence, reduces social withdrawal, and prevents the development of aggressive social behavior, anxiety, and depression (Domitrovich, Cortes, and Greenberg 2007; Kam, Greenberg, and Kusché 2004).

Monitor and Set Limits with Adolescents

As children move into adolescence, they seek much more autonomy. At this stage, parents must achieve a delicate balance between granting adolescents autonomy and making sure they don't get into situations where problematic or even dangerous behavior could occur. To establish a strong foundation for navigating this period, it is helpful if parents have already established effective, regular communication with their children about what they are doing each day and have nurtured their children's prosocial values and academic interests. This makes it likely that their children are involved with other teens who are enthusiastic about school and not into risk taking. Yet even these parents must be watchful for situations that could encourage experimentation with problem behavior. An example would be the findings of Jean Richardson and her colleagues (1993). They discovered that ninth-grade students who were at home unsupervised by a parent were significantly more likely to experiment with drugs, be depressed, and get poor grades. Such kids had even greater problems if they were hanging out with other teens after school.

This is why every effective parenting program for families with teenagers focuses on getting parents to monitor what their teenager is doing when they aren't around and establishing rules to make sure the teenager engages in appropriate activities when not under adult supervision. Programs such as the Family Check-Up (Dishion, Nelson, and Kavanagh

2003) encourage parents to talk with their teens each day about what they have been doing and to make and enforce rules about the time teens need to be home, where they can go when they are out, and whom they can be with. In this way, a program like the Family Check-Up can prevent teen delinquency, drug use, and declining grades for as long as five years after families participate in the program.

Do Not Congregate Troubled Youth!

Despite all the evidence about how peers influence each other's deviant behavior, our society routinely deals with delinquency by bringing troubled youth together. Tom Dishion found this out the hard way. He did a randomized trial of the impact of a parenting intervention (an early version of the Family Check-Up) versus a program to teach kids good self-management and study skills (Dishion and Andrews 1995). He randomly assigned families of at-risk youth to either participate in the parenting intervention or not, and randomly assigned the youths to participate or not participate in the self-management program. He expected that the best outcomes would be for those who received both programs.

The parenting program worked as expected, but to Dishion's surprise, the self-management program led to *increases* in youth smoking. When he coded videotapes of the interactions of youth in self-management training groups, he discovered that those who were talking about deviant activities were most likely to get others' attention. This was exactly the process he showed in the research I described earlier in this chapter (Dishion et al. 1996): peer social approval reinforces deviant behavior.

Additional evidence has accumulated that raises serious questions about many of the things our society does in efforts to deal with at-risk or delinquent youth. We routinely put students who are doing less well academically on a different academic track than those who are doing well. In the process, we stigmatize them and bring them together, where they become friends and have little contact with students who embrace prosocial norms and behaviors. If at-risk kids have trouble in school, they are often transferred to alternative schools where the student body consists almost entirely of kids who experiment with drugs and other forms of risk taking. If they are arrested, they are locked up with other problem youth or treated in groups of adjudicated youth.

We need to change all of these practices. Of course, the best way to do so would be to intervene earlier with the approaches I described in chapters 2 and 3. This would allow families and schools to do what is necessary to prevent problems from developing in the first place.

Create Numerous Opportunities for Prosocial Activities

Most American communities don't have enough opportunities for youth to recreate in safe settings that support positive social behavior. This deficit was brought home to me when I attended a conference on mental health in Helsinki, Finland, several years ago. My colleague Hendricks Brown and I bought a basketball and went to a nearby park to play. We had been there maybe half an hour when suddenly several hundred teens showed up with a number of adults. They proceeded to play basketball and many other games. I didn't see a single instance of conflict. Unfortunately, I have never seen anything like that in a US community.

Offering numerous opportunities for young people to play a greater role in civic life and governance is another way that we can enhance prosocial development and prevent problems. Starting in preschool, children can be given meaningful roles in their school—roles that give them responsibility and pride. Examples include setting up equipment for an assembly, taking roll, or photographing prosocial activities. Evidence indicates that assuming such roles increases young people's prosocial behavior (Embry and Biglan 2008).

Action Implications

Research clearly shows that we need to cultivate prosocial peer relationships among youth to prevent deviant behavior and nurture their development. If left to their own devices, young people who are at risk for problems typically reinforce each other's deviant tendencies. Thus, families and schools need to be sensitive to the importance of peer relationships in young people's development. And while peer influences are especially important in adolescence, ensuring that adolescents have friends who support their positive social development ideally begins in early childhood, when children learn to regulate their emotions and cooperate with others.

For Parents

- Monitor your children's activities by talking to them about what they are doing in school and with friends. If you establish routine conversations with them when they're young, they will continue to tell you what is going on in their lives. This also creates numerous opportunities for you to show your appreciation and approval of the good things they do, and to guide them away from risky activities and toward prosocial choices.

- If you haven't established good communication with your children before adolescence, it is still possible to monitor and set limits on what they are doing. Tom Dishion and Kate Kavanagh's book *Intervening in Adolescent Problem Behavior: A Family-Centered Approach* (2003) offers guidance to parents of adolescents that you may find helpful.

- Set limits on your teenagers' opportunities to hang out with youth who get into trouble. If they are home alone after school, make sure they don't have friends over. As they get older and you become more confident that they will engage in safe, productive, or enjoyable activities alone with friends, you can gradually grant them more autonomy. Establish a routine in which they use after-school time to do their homework, household tasks, or solitary recreational activities. Be sure to show great interest and approval for the positive things they do after school.

For Schools

- Reduce or eliminate the practice of putting students into tracks based on their academic performance because this congregates and stigmatizes at-risk students and contributes to problem development.

- Implement evidence-based, school-wide systems of positive behavioral support to reduce social rejection of students by other students. (Chapter 3 describes several such programs.)

For Policy Makers

- Eliminate practices that congregate at-risk youth, such as incarceration and group treatment of those who are delinquent.

- Eliminate academic tracking in schools.

- Increase the availability of settings and activities that provide opportunities for young people to engage in prosocial behavior, such as participation in community betterment and social and recreational activities, as well as recognition for prosocial activities within the community.

CHAPTER 5

The Behavioral Revolution in Clinical Psychology

Chapters 2 through 4 largely focused on applying behavioral principles to nurturing children and adolescents. But what about the psychological and behavioral problems of adults? Can the principles of behaviorism be used to develop effective treatments for problems such as anxiety and depression among adults? They can, as a quick review of the history of behavior therapy reveals.

Although clinical psychology was practiced as early as the end of the nineteenth century, this work—treating people for psychological problems—began in earnest the 1940s. At first, Freudian theory dominated the work. Neuroses were seen as being due to deep-seated, unconscious problems that could be treated only through years of daily psychoanalysis. There was no empirical basis for this treatment. Nor was there a tradition of empirically evaluating the effectiveness of treatments.

That began to change in the 1950s, when psychiatrist Joseph Wolpe reported on a new technique for treating phobias, which he called systematic desensitization. Up to that point, people crippled by fear of specific stimuli, such as spiders (arachnophobia) or public places (agoraphobia), only had the option of a long course of psychoanalysis—if they could afford it.

Wolpe believed that phobias arose because of a conditioning history in which the thing a person feared had repeatedly been paired with high levels of anxiety. He believed he could decondition the fear by pairing the presence of the feared stimulus with relaxation. His method involved creating a hierarchy of situations ranging from mildly distressing (such as seeing a spider across the room) to highly distressing (such as holding a spider in one's hand). Using a deep muscle relaxation technique that Edmund Jacobson (1938) had developed, he taught clients to relax deeply. Then he had them imagine feared situations while remaining relaxed, starting with the least fear-arousing situations.

Wolpe used this technique with a large number of clients and kept a careful record of his results. His publication of *Psychotherapy by Reciprocal Inhibition* (1958) led to the first randomized experimental evaluation of a clinical intervention when Gordon Paul, a psychologist at the University of Illinois, evaluated the effects of systematic desensitization for treating anxiety associated with public speaking (Paul 1966). What followed was an explosion of research on the treatment of phobias and other anxieties. This work, combined with the advances made by psychologists who were applying Skinner's principles, marked the beginning of the development of behavior therapy. The two distinctive features of behavior therapy were its application of behavioral principles to the study of human behavior, and its insistence on empirically evaluating the impact and effectiveness of treatment procedures derived from these principles.

My Own Journey

I began my career as a social psychologist. However, by the time I got my doctorate in 1971, I was disillusioned. Social psychology had become boring to me. A new generation of social psychologists that craved the prestige of "real sciences" like physics had banished the practical and socially relevant aspects of social psychology from the field. Doing research that smacked of anything applied had become verboten. Prestige went to those who conducted obscure and clever studies of "nonobvious" phenomena. If something was obvious, such as prejudice or conflict, it was regarded as too trivial. This didn't appeal to me. Whenever I tried to read the latest "hot" study in the *Journal of Personality and Social Psychology*, I fell asleep.

Meanwhile, because of the Vietnam War, the sizzling sixties had turned into the radical seventies, with talk of free love and socialist revolution. I was living in Seattle and still studying social psychology at the University of Washington, a hotbed of radical activity. I was more committed than ever to changing the world, but social psychology and its fascination with fame and prestige no longer seemed a good vehicle for accomplishing that task.

I decided to get retreaded as a clinical psychologist. It was the time of the counterculture movement, with its emphasis on personal growth, mind expansion, and consciousness raising. I was a child of the times. I began to embrace the personal growth movement, along with free love and revolution. I found it exhilarating to get inside people's heads, advise them, and guide them on their journeys.

Ned Wagner, the head of the clinical psychology program at "U Dub," agreed to give me a year of postdoctoral training in clinical psychology if I would teach a course on social psychology. He gave me an office across from Bob Kohlenberg, and eventually Bob introduced me to B. F. Skinner's work in behaviorism. By the time I finished my clinical training and got an internship at the University of Wisconsin Psychiatry Department, I was engrossed in the developing field of behavior therapy. By the end of my Wisconsin internship, I'd read virtually all of the extant works on behaviorism, behavior therapy, and the philosophy of science that underpins them.

Establishing the Behavior Change Center

By 1977, I had cofounded a storefront clinic in Springfield, Oregon, with three friends from the University of Oregon: Jane Ganter, the administrative assistant at the University of Oregon Psychology Clinic; Nancy Hawkins, a psychologist trained at the university; and David Campbell, the director of the Psychology Clinic.

We called our new clinic the Behavior Change Center. It was the first behavior therapy clinic in Oregon. As of 1975, behavior therapy researchers had accumulated enough knowledge that we could offer behavioral therapy to the public. We saw adults with depression or anxiety, families that were having problems with their children, and people who wanted help with specific behaviors, such as smoking, procrastinating, or literally pulling their hair out, which is known as trichotillomania.

For that time, we were pretty good at what we did. We helped people develop goals about what they wanted in their lives, and we used their sessions to help them take specific steps in the direction of their goals. Unlike traditional therapies, with their focus on treating deep-seated, underlying neuroses through extensive talk therapy, we simply helped people change behaviors they wanted to change, and we tried to do it in as few sessions as possible at as low a cost as possible. Initially, we charged seven dollars for fifteen minutes.

In people's first session, we asked them to tell us what would be different if, six months from that day, they looked back and could say, "Things are much better." Most people said they wanted to feel less anxious or less depressed, and many said they wanted to improve their relationships with others.

Our focus was always on what people could do in specific situations that came up in the daily course of their lives. I liked to say, "You could have a wonderful time in our sessions, but it wouldn't mean much if things 'out there' were still a problem. We need to use our sessions to plan the steps you can take to move in the direction you want to go out there." As a result, we focused on helping people try new behaviors in the daily situations that challenged them. We taught people who had problems with anxiety how to relax in practice sessions. But rather than simply have them practice once a day, we had them do "comfort checks" five times a day to get good at relaxing in all circumstances of their daily lives.

Although we based our approach on behavioral theory, our fundamental commitment was to use empirically based practices. One set of findings that informed our work but didn't come from behavior theory involved the way in which therapists interact with clients. Carl Rogers, who had developed what he called client-centered therapy, argued that therapists were most effective when they provided empathy, genuineness, and warmth to clients (1951). A review of evidence supporting this approach (Truax and Carkuff 1967) convinced my colleagues and me that we could more effectively help people if we were genuinely warm and empathic. This wasn't hard to do. After all, we were in this line of work because we wanted to help people.

Learning to Take the Long View

Peter Lewinsohn, who had developed a behavioral approach to treating depression at the University of Oregon, suggested I read a book by Alan Lakein called *How to Get Control of Your Time and Your Life* (1973). I did and found it very helpful in my own life and began using it with clients. Following Lakein's approach, I asked people to brainstorm the things they wished to achieve in life at three different times: their whole lives, the next five years, and if they had only six months to live. I then had them pick the most important ones from each period and ultimately boil them down to five or so things they most wanted to focus on.

Lakein argued that the day-to-day demands we all encounter typically crowd out attention to important things that might take hundreds or even thousands of little steps to achieve. This insight was one of the most important things I ever learned. I made a list of my major goals using Lakein's approach, then reviewed and revised it annually. At the beginning of each week, I chose some concrete things I could do that week to move forward on important goals, and then I made a task list for each day.

People who are struggling with anxiety and depression—and in truth, I was one of them—can get so focused on how they are feeling that they become stuck. They make not feeling bad the central theme of their lives, thinking they can't move on with their lives until their emotional problems end. Lakein's approach of setting goals and breaking them down into small steps did a great deal to help people begin to move out of their depression or anxiety.

It certainly worked for me. I have used variations on this approach to organize my work throughout my career. It not only guided me to get projects done but also helped me calm down. I eventually got to the point where, if I woke up on a Monday morning sky-high with anxiety and worry about all the things I needed to do, I could simply make my list for the week and the day and calm down. I didn't need to worry about all the things I had to do: I only needed to do the things on that day's list. In fact, I often told my clients, "Rather than having to worry about what you need to do, you can have your list worry for you."

This system worked quite well for most of our clients at the Behavior Change Center. They learned to relax in common stressful situations and began to accomplish things that moved them out of the miasma of depression and anxiety. In six to ten sessions, most clients began to feel better and do the things that moved them toward a more satisfying life.

However, some clients didn't improve. With them, it seemed that everything I suggested only amplified their feelings of anxiety, worry, and depression. Typically, they were people who had already been through a lot of therapy. While I was increasingly confident that the behavioral approach was helping many people, it was clear that there was still much to learn.

The Schism in Behavior Therapy

One thing missing from early behavior therapy was an effective analysis of cognition and verbal behavior. Although Skinner had inspired a generation of psychologists to consider the possibility that people's behavior is influenced by its consequences, virtually all of the research involved directly observable behavior. What people were thinking and feeling hardly entered into the early research. This produced a schism within the behavior therapy movement. A number of prominent people began to advocate for *cognitive* behavioral therapy.

It was undeniable. People talk and think, and what they say and think has enormous influence on what they do. For Skinner, however, the ultimate causes of behavior were found in the environment. He labeled explanations in terms of thoughts and feelings as "mentalism."

For centuries, the standard way of explaining what people did was to point to their desires, intentions, beliefs, and feelings, which were said to be the causes of their behavior. This was the so-called doctrine of autonomous man. In this view, people, not their environment, determined their behavior. Skinner saw this way of thinking as the biggest obstacle to a science of human behavior. If people continued to believe that the causes of our behavior are inside us in the form of wants, wishes, and so on, we would never examine how the environment affects behavior. Only when people stopped being satisfied with mentalistic explanations would they be willing to explore environmental influences on behavior.

In addition, the cognitive movement stemmed from resistance to the notion that people's behavior was determined by their environments. As with prior paradigmatic revolutions in science (Kuhn 1970), the behaviorist revolution was threatening to those who held the view that humans had a privileged place in the universe. Humanity's fall from its pedestal had begun with Copernicus, who argued that the earth was not the center of the universe, and Galileo, who ended up under house arrest for agreeing with him. Darwin's assertion that humans were just another species that had evolved as the result of the same processes that produced every other species was another blow to our primacy. Now Skinner was saying that even our understanding that we freely choose our behavior was mistaken, claiming instead that our behavior was shaped by the same laws that accounted for the behavior of pigeons and rats. I found his line of thinking quite compelling. In particular, if humans evolved according to the same processes as all other species, and if resistance to prior Copernican revolutions had been due to the conceit of humans, why should it be any different for human behavior?

But it didn't help that Skinner had a penchant for putting his claims in strident terms. Perhaps as a result, his critics tended to attack in rather nasty ways. Among the most prominent of those critics was Albert Bandura, who published papers and books attacking the view that human behavior was shaped by the environment. Using pejorative terms, he wrote about "odious imagery, including salivating dogs, puppetry, and animalistic manipulation" (1974, 859) and a wholly robotic view of humans.

I never quite understood why Bandura felt salivating dogs were odious, but he certainly found an eager audience within the behavior therapy movement. Many people who would laugh at any rejection of Darwinian evolution were relieved to encounter a view that preserved the autonomy of humans, and they latched on to it.

For my part, I felt quite threatened by these developments. Most of the people who embraced the cognitive movement hadn't read Skinner, but they were comfortable being dismissive of his theories. On more than one occasion, I encountered sneers from other psychologists. I felt a bit like a persecuted minority.

Research with children, especially children with developmental disabilities, continued to make use of behavioral consequences. But cognitive behavioral therapy largely dominated research with adult humans. Peter Lewinsohn's behavioral approach to depression prompted people to increase reinforcing activities (Lewinsohn 1975). But according to the cognitivists, "depressogenic" thoughts caused depression. Therefore, their treatment approaches emphasized getting people to modify dysfunctional beliefs and distorted thinking. Twenty years later, Lewinsohn's approach was vindicated. Studies that compared the cognitive components of depression treatment with components that prompted people to get active showed that the activation component was what made a difference (N. S. Jacobson et al. 1996).

At the Behavior Change Center I tried to help my clients modify their dysfunctional beliefs, but I was never very good at it. I couldn't deny that people's thoughts influenced their behavior. However, in my view, a different underlying process was at work—one in which thoughts, including private thoughts, were a form of verbal behavior. After all, when I encouraged clients to identify what they most wanted to accomplish in life and make to-do lists to help achieve their long-term goals, I was helping them make choices and influence their subsequent behavior. And Skinner had convinced me that the functional influence our plans have on subsequent behavior is due to a long history of getting reinforcement for doing what we say we will do and getting punishment when we fail to do so.

Furthermore, I could see the consequences at play in my clinical work. As a therapist, my social support, encouragement, and attention were consequences that helped people establish their ability to make a plan and carry it out. If that was successful, my clients would continue to engage in sequences of planning and doing because of positive consequences in their lives. Meanwhile, ample empirical justification for this view was emerging. Research with children included the "say-do" literature, which showed that children learned to do what they said they would do thanks to reinforcement for doing so (Ballard 1983).

Psychological Flexibility and the Third Wave of Behavior Therapy

In 1986, I received a book chapter from a psychologist by the name of Steven Hayes. I had never heard of Hayes, and to this day, neither he nor I know why he sent me the chapter. The chapter was titled "A Contextual Approach to Therapeutic Change" (Hayes 1987). When I read it, I realized that Hayes was describing all of the clients I had been unable to help: people who were so locked into their struggle with anxiety or depression that they couldn't escape.

Hayes argued that the cognitive behavioral therapy approach to controlling unwanted thoughts was counterproductive. Efforts to control troublesome thoughts, rather than getting rid of them, actually amplified them (Hayes 1987). This resonated with my experience with clients who didn't benefit from relaxation training. Although they practiced a procedure that worked for many other people, it just seemed to heighten their anxiety.

For example, I sometimes worked with people suffering from panic attacks, most of whom had gradually limited their lives by avoiding new situations that seemed to trigger panic. If they experienced panic attacks in movie theaters, they stopped going to movies. If they became anxious driving on bridges, they stopped driving across them. They were acutely aware of their bodily sensations and monitored them to detect whether panic was arising. Their philosophy was that they could proceed with their lives only after getting rid of these terrible feelings and thoughts. Then they could see a movie, drive to work, or go shopping.

Hayes described a new method of helping people change their orientation toward frightening thoughts and feelings. Rather than supporting people in efforts to get rid of such experiences, he encouraged them to be willing to have those experiences—to let go of efforts to control them. He called this approach comprehensive distancing. Using metaphors and experiential exercises, he helped clients step back from thoughts and feelings they had been attempting to control and start doing the things they had been avoiding.

He also developed methods, including the use of metaphors, for helping people see that the things they had been doing to feel good were actually part of the problem. In one such metaphor, he asked clients to imagine that they have fallen into a hole. They discover that they have a shovel, and being highly motivated to get out of the hole, they use the only tool they have available to try to get out. The only problem is, shovels are for digging, and that just makes holes bigger. Then he posed a question: Hadn't the client been digging for many years to avoid this terrible anxiety, depression, or panic? Perhaps the first thing to do is to put down the shovel and stop trying to dig yourself out of the hole. Hayes described impressive successes with this approach, although he had not yet tested the intervention in randomized trials.

A Contextual Account of Human Behavior

To me, the most exciting thing about Steve Hayes's approach was that it was completely consistent with Skinner's orientation. Hayes too had embraced the Skinnerian idea that the environment shapes human behavior. For Skinnerians, people's thoughts and feelings are not causes of behavior—they are simply other behaviors.

The practical goal of this approach is to be able to predict and influence behavior. It is undoubtedly true that my thinking can influence other things I do. I make a plan, and then I follow it. I remember something I said I would do, and then I do it. But what about all the times my thoughts don't result in action? For example, among procrastinators, simply saying they are going to do something may almost guarantee that they don't do it. We can't simply assume that thoughts cause other actions. We need to understand why they sometimes influence other actions and sometimes don't.

The answer is to look to the environmental context that influences not only what we think and what we do, but also the relationship between our thoughts and our actions. In my work with clients at the Behavior Change Center, I helped people strengthen the relationship between their plans and their actions by supportively reinforcing this consistency—for example, by discussing how they had done on following through with the plans we made in the previous session. The same process is involved when a parent praises a child for doing what she said she would do or admonishes her for not doing so.

The problem with traditional cognitive behavioral therapy is that it doesn't consider how the context affects the relationship between thoughts and other actions. It just tries to help people get rid of thoughts that seem to cause problematic actions or obstruct effective action. In Hayes's approach, on the other hand, the goal is to change the context that maintains the power of words over action. Rather than help people get rid of problematic thoughts, his approach focuses on loosening the relationships between thought and actions that cause people trouble. People don't need to get rid of these thoughts; they need to get to a point where they can be less influenced by them so they can consciously choose a course of action and follow through.

As I got to know Steve and studied his improvements to Skinner's behaviorism, I realized that his contextual approach was not just generating powerful new methods to help people with their psychological problems, but also providing a general account of how the environment shapes all aspects of human behavior. This includes not simply people's thoughts and feelings, but the relationships between their thoughts and feelings and the rest of their behavior. His approach has since been developed and elaborated on by a large and growing number of behavioral scientists around the world, and it is proving to have profound implications for what it means to be human and how we can build a more caring and effective society that nurtures everyone's well-being.

Acceptance and Commitment Therapy

Hayes's treatment approach came to be known as acceptance and commitment therapy, or ACT (said as one word). It involves helping people develop more of the psychological flexibility I described in chapter 1. Russ Harris, one of the most prolific writers about ACT, suggests that we think of psychological flexibility as involving three things: making room for our thoughts and feelings without judging or struggling with them, being in the present moment, and doing what matters most to us (2009a).

Treating Schizophrenia with ACT

As of this writing, more than eighty randomized trials have shown the benefit of ACT with problems as diverse as schizophrenia, epilepsy, depression, and quitting smoking. To give you a feel for it, I will tell you about Patty Bach's work with people with schizophrenia (Bach and Hayes 2002).

Schizophrenia is the most damaging and difficult mental illness. It usually strikes in late adolescence or early adulthood and involves becoming overwhelmed by hallucinations or delusions. Patients have sometimes described it as a descent into hell. Hospitalization and heavy medication are typical treatments. But while this helps people gain some control over their bizarre experiences, they usually don't resume a "normal" life. Bach, a clinical psychologist in Chicago, told me the story of one woman's descent into hell, which I'll summarize here.

Emma was a thirty-year-old white woman whose early life held great promise. She was a bright, attractive teenager and an outstanding student in high school. In college she met a guy she really cared for, and soon they married. She seemed to be headed toward a wonderful life.

She had her first psychotic episode while still in college. She began withdrawing from her husband, family, and friends. She started skipping classes frequently because she believed other students were talking about her. Then she became convinced that one of her professors was delivering messages to her through his lectures and stopped attending his class altogether. Her husband took her to the emergency room after an episode in which she accused him of trying to harm her, called his parents, and told them they had raised a monster. She was treated with antipsychotic medication and released after a four-week hospitalization. Her husband tried to be supportive, but it was difficult. He hadn't bargained on having a schizo-phrenic wife and living with constant fear about what she might do, and they eventually divorced. He remarried but continued to provide financial and social support. Eventually, however, he moved away.

For a while Emma coped reasonably well. She didn't return to college but did occasionally hold down a job—usually until she quit due to some suspicion about her employer or coworkers. She received treatment at a community mental health center and took her medication most of the time. She had some money from a trust fund, which covered her basic costs of living. But when the money in the trust fund ran out, she began to deteriorate.

In a conversation one day, her landlady mentioned that her husband had been sick but she had taken care of him. Emma somehow concluded that her landlady had murdered her husband, and this developed into an unyielding delusion that occupied most of Emma's life. She reported it to the police, but they did nothing about it. She began interpreting every-thing her landlady did as a threat directed at her. Emma began posting signs that said things like "Murderer!" She was eventually evicted and moved into a nearby hotel. In her continuing efforts to get someone to do something about this "murder," she contacted the FBI, the police, and the circuit court. At some point she stopped getting treatment and quit taking her medication. She was eventually homeless and living on the street.

Emma came to Bach's attention when she was arrested for harassing personnel at a courthouse where she was trying to get someone to do something about the "murder." Realizing that she was paranoid, the police brought her to the psychiatric hospital where Bach worked. At this point, a typical outcome would be: Emma gets back on her meds, damping down her paranoid delusions, but no one is able to talk her out of the delusions. She is unable to hold a job, and will cycle in and out of mental hospitals for the rest of her life.

Schizophrenia is like a huge boulder. It often seems as if there is no way to move it. However, scientific breakthroughs often involve finding a lever and a fulcrum that no one has seen before. When these forces align prop-erly, even big boulders can be moved with ease. That is what happened for Emma, because Bach had received ACT training from Steve Hayes.

To see how ACT exerts a different and more effective force on schizo-phrenia, we need first to take a deeper look at this devastating illness.

Imagine that one day you have a hallucination. You are quite frightened, both by what you hallucinated and by the fact that you had a hallucination. You know this is very bad. Perhaps you tell a loved one, who also becomes frightened. You don't want this, and neither does your loved one. You consult a psychiatrist, who joins you in trying to make sure that these things don't happen. Your psychiatrist puts you on medication. Now your life has become about not having any more hallucinations. That is the absolute imperative, so you're constantly alert to the possibility that you might be having one.

Delusions are a bit different; unlike a hallucination, the individual experiencing a delusion is not aware that the delusion isn't real. Emma's life became focused on dealing with the "murder," and because there had been no murder, everyone tried to get her to give up her delusion. But that just made her even more dedicated to getting people to understand and take action. For Emma, the defining issue in her life was this "murder," and little else was going to happen in her life until it was dealt with.

Bach focused on helping Emma take a different tack: beginning to move forward in other areas of her life anyway. Rather than trying to talk Emma out of her delusion, Bach guided Emma in exploring her values. What was important to her? What did she want her life to be about? She said she wanted a job and wanted to work with developmentally delayed children. She even named specific agencies she wanted to work for. As a result, she focused on how to get a job.

Emma never gave up her delusion, even after she was back on her medications. But in their work on values, Bach and Emma clarified that, for Emma, justice was an important value. Emma was able to come to the resolution that she had done her part to try to see that justice was served. The cost for her had been high, and it was time for her to move on. So she stopped talking about her landlady and began to focus on other things.

Emma was in the hospital for four months. Toward the end of that time she got day passes to apply for jobs. Bach and her colleagues helped Emma practice for job interviews and other social interactions. She got a job in a health care setting as a janitor. Bach's team arranged for Emma to live in a residential facility, and Emma developed a plan to get her own apartment eventually. The last time Bach saw Emma, she was moving forward in her life.

If you don't know much about schizophrenia, this may seem like a sad story. Compared to how Emma was doing before she began to have delusions, working as a janitor and living in a residential facility may not seem like much of a life. But compared to the way many people with schizophrenia live—with a constant focus on delusions or hallucinations, in and out of hospitals, and living on the street—it is actually quite a bit. Emma had begun to focus on things that she valued and worked toward making her life about those things. As a result, her delusions were no longer torturing her.

A Randomized Trial of ACT for Schizophrenia

Bach was one of Steve Hayes's graduate students when she came up with the idea of trying ACT for people with schizophrenia. ACT had proven effective for depression, anxiety, and a number of other problems, and she wondered whether it might be useful for this intractable psychiatric problem. Based on initial work with a few patients at a Reno psychiatric hospital, she began to think it could.

She and Hayes decided to test this in a randomized controlled trial. They identified eighty people who were hospitalized with a psychotic disorder and randomly assigned them to get treatment-as-usual or treatment-as-usual augmented with ACT. The ACT intervention consisted of four sessions with Bach, each forty-five to fifty minutes long.

In the first session, Bach encouraged patients to talk about how they had been trying to deal with their symptoms. They usually described continual efforts to suppress or control problematic thoughts. She then tried to help them adopt a new perspective: that instead of struggling with these thoughts, they could simply notice and accept them without doing anything about them. To do this she used a classic ACT intervention: taking their mind for a walk (Hayes, Strosahl, and Wilson 1999).

In this intervention, Bach would ask a patient to walk around the hospital as she walked just behind him, talking to him as if she were his mind. She provided a running commentary on whatever the patient encountered, evaluating, analyzing, predicting, and recommending various actions. Prior to beginning the exercise, she asked the patient to just notice what his "mind" was saying without acting on it and to behave however he chose, without regard to what his mind said. The purpose was to give these patients some experience with not taking their thoughts literally or needing to do anything about them. ACT therapists call this process *defusion*, in a reference to not being fused with thoughts. From a defused stance, you don't see the world through your thoughts; you see that you are having thoughts.

In the second session, Bach worked on helping patients accept their symptoms even if they didn't like them. She did this using another classic ACT intervention, the polygraph metaphor (Hayes, Strosahl, and Wilson 1999). It is typically presented along these lines:

> *Imagine that you're hooked to a very high-quality polygraph. It can detect the slightest increase in any type of fear or arousal. It has meters that show different aspects of arousal, such as heart rate, breathing, sweating, and blood pressure. So if you get upset, I'll know about it! Your job is to stay calm. In fact, it is essential that you stay calm. Think of it as a matter of life or death. In fact, just to make sure you're motivated, I'm going to put a gun to your head and pull the trigger if any of these meters move. Do you think you can stay calm?*

This metaphor is designed to help people *experience* the paradox that focusing on not having unwanted feelings actually makes them worse. In terms of Bach's study, the patients clearly couldn't control the unpleasant thoughts and feelings their schizophrenia generated, so it was important to help them understand that trying to control those thoughts and feelings actually makes them more intense and frequent.

In the third session, Bach talked to patients about their valued goals and questioned whether their efforts to control their symptoms were working to get them what they valued. Many patients said they wanted to live independently. Then Bach asked them to look at how they'd tried to control their symptoms. For example, yelling at voices or using illicit drugs might stop some symptoms for a while, but these behaviors could be a barrier to living independently. In ACT, clients aren't cast as being right or wrong for trying these things; rather, the point is to determine what works.

The fourth session in the experimental intervention took place upon a patient's discharge from the hospital. In that session, Bach reviewed what they had covered in the previous three sessions.

The results of this intervention were some of the best ever seen in research on the treatment of schizophrenia. Four months after patients left the hospital, 40 percent of those who received treatment as usual had been rehospitalized, as opposed to only 20 percent of the patients who received the additional ACT intervention.

In addition, those who received ACT and were rehospitalized stayed out significantly longer than those in the other group. You might think this occurred because those who received ACT had fewer symptoms. However, one of the most surprising things about the study is that the people who received ACT reported *more* symptoms. But ACT had helped many of them develop a new relationship to those symptoms. Instead of fighting to control symptoms, they had become more accepting of them. Those who received ACT and were rehospitalized tended to be people who continued to deny their symptoms. Apparently, they had not benefited from ACT in the sense that they were continuing to struggle to control their symptoms.

Perhaps most significantly, all of this was achieved with less than four hours of treatment. Most of the people in this study had already undergone countless hours of other forms of treatment without the same beneficial effects. These results are not a fluke. A second study, done by different people, produced similar results (Gaudiano and Herbert 2006).

A Universal Approach

Bach's success is an especially striking example of the strides that behavioral scientists have made in helping people change their behavior. But there are many other success stories. ACT practitioners have shown the value of this approach for a surprisingly diverse number of problems. Tobias Lundgren and JoAnne Dahl applied these principles to treating people with severe epilepsy (Lundgren et al. 2008). They helped patients practically eliminate their seizures—not by trying to stop the seizures, but by helping patients accept what they didn't seem able to change and start living in the service of their values.

Several ACT researchers have achieved dramatic improvements in helping people quit smoking (for example, Bricker et al. 2010). Instead of supporting smokers' beliefs that they could stop smoking only if they didn't have cravings, they helped them accept their cravings while choosing to act in the service of their value of living longer. Barbara Kohlenberg is a clinical psychologist who has done some of the research on smoking cessation using an ACT approach. She told me that many of these ex-smokers reported that they also started using ACT principles to change many other aspects of their lives.

Other studies have shown the value of ACT for treating depression, anxiety, drug addiction, chronic pain, and obesity. It is also useful in helping diabetics keep their disease under control. In addition, it is proving helpful in reducing prejudicial thinking, preventing burnout in work settings, and decreasing stigmatizing attitudes that health care providers sometimes have toward patients. (For a thorough, searchable listing of empirical studies into the effectiveness of ACT, visit http://www.context ualscience.org/publications.)

ACT has changed my life and the lives of many others. It has helped me to become more patient, empathetic, and caring. It has made me less materialistic. It has helped me cope more effectively with the stresses I now realize are simply a part of life.

Implications of the Progress in Clinical Psychology

The progress made in clinical psychology in the past fifty years is unprecedented in human history. This doesn't mean we have the ability to "cure" every psychological or behavioral problem. Indeed, the ACT work indicates that rather than getting rid of all of the difficult and unpleasant things involved in the human experience (which the word "cure" implies), our well-being improves when we learn to live flexibly despite, and *with*, these difficulties. This means accepting our emotional and cognitive reactions to our experience while continuing to live in alignment with our values.

These developments in clinical psychology have important implications for how we can build a better world. We need not wait until people develop psychological and behavioral problems such as depression, aggression, or drug abuse. Instead, we can foster psychological flexibility and a commitment to acting on values within families, schools, workplaces, and communities. In the process, we can significantly reduce human suffering and help make our world the best it can be.

B. F. Skinner argued that science tends to develop by focusing on the places where it can gain traction, moving on to more complex problems only after work with simpler problems has provided tools to help us tackle more intractable ones. In part 2 of this book, I hope I've shown you how much we have learned about human behavior and how much we can use this science to help people live more productive and caring lives.

Yet to enhance human well-being on a broad scale, we must use what we know about individual behavior to build the more nurturing larger social system we need. These problems have seemed insurmountable. However, in part 3 of the book, I will explore how we can apply what we have learned in studying the behavior of individuals to large organizations and cultural practices. By employing the same contextualist principles of prediction and influence to society on a broader scale, we can achieve transformations unlike any previously seen in human history.

Action Implications

The progress made in clinical psychology has important implications for how all of us can live our lives more effectively. It also has implications for public policy.

For Everyone

- Cultivate psychological flexibility, perhaps using one or more of the many recent ACT books for the general public:

  - To develop more psychological flexibility, *The Happiness Trap* (Harris 2007)

  - For overcoming psychological problems in general, *Get Out of Your Mind and Into Your Life* (Hayes 2005)

  - For depression, *The Mindfulness and Acceptance Workbook for Depression* (Robinson and Strosahl 2008)

  - For anxiety, *Acceptance and Commitment Therapy for Anxiety Disorders* (Eifert and Forsyth 2005)

  - For strengthening partner relationships, *ACT on Love* (Harris 2009b)

For Policy Makers

- Make evidence-based clinical interventions available to all who need them. Although I think ACT has made advances over cognitive behavioral therapy, I don't suggest that CBT is ineffective. The Evidence-Based Behavioral Practice website (http://www.ebbp.org/index.html) provides extensive information about the efficacy of CBT for many psychological problems. Similarly, the website of the Association for Contextual Behavioral Science (http://www.contextualscience.org) provides information about the efficacy of ACT.

- Fund further research on clinical interventions. Much progress has occurred in research on clinical treatments for psychological and behavioral problems. One of the most important areas of future research will be to investigate how clinical interventions can be available to more people through online programs and smartphone apps.

PART 3

The Larger Social Context Affecting Well-Being

I hope I've convinced you that advances in behavioral science make it possible to help families and schools become more nurturing. However, this still needs to be translated into approaches that can benefit entire populations. Evolving a society in which virtually every family and school is nurturing is partly a matter of making effective programs available to all families and schools that need them. But it also requires that we change the larger social system within which families and schools exist.

Families and schools exist within communities. Mass media and the state of the economy affect those communities; public policies may either support or stress them. Families and schools also exist within a network of for-profit, nonprofit, and government organizations that can have a huge influence on their functioning and the well-being of individuals. To realize the vision of a society that nurtures the well-being of every member, behavioral science needs to understand these larger social systems and their effect on families, schools, and individuals. It must provide principles to guide the evolution of larger social systems so their practices benefit everyone.

In this part of the book, I'll explore how the public health framework can guide such efforts, describing the major, society-wide factors that undermine well-being and showing how we can understand most of these factors in terms of the influence of recent developments in the evolution of corporate capitalism. Then, in part 4, I'll describe a strategy for evolving a system, based on the public health framework, that restrains capitalism's worst excesses while maintaining its many benefits.

CHAPTER 6

From People to Populations

The public health framework organizes how we can translate recent advances in prevention and treatment into widespread benefits. By applying the principles of this framework not just to physical health, but also to the gamut of physical, psychological, and behavioral problems that plague us, we can evolve societies that nurture everyone.

The goal of public health is to increase the incidence and prevalence of well-being in entire populations. It has five key practices:

- Targeting the incidence and prevalence of specific indicators of well-being

- Making use of epidemiological evidence to identify the major risk factors that contribute to the targeted aspect of well-being

- Setting up a surveillance system to monitor the incidence and prevalence of the target problem

- Pragmatically implementing programs, policies, and practices that can diminish the incidence or prevalence of the targeted problem

- Establishing an effective advocacy system to effect the changes in norms, policies, and practices required for population-wide improvements in well-being

We can use these principles to create a comprehensive public health movement that will evolve a society that nurtures the well-being of every person. The tobacco control movement is a great example of what we can accomplish. If you are under forty, you may not be aware that in the 1960s more than half of US men and about 35 percent of US women smoked

(CDC 2011). People smoked everywhere. In 1963, I was an orderly in the Emergency Department at Strong Memorial Hospital in Rochester, New York; we and our patients regularly smoked in the ER.

In this chapter, I describe the key features of an effective public health effort, provide examples of these efforts drawn from the tobacco control movement, and show how public health principles could be applied to increasing the prevalence of a nurturing environment in families and schools. I believe this could be the most significant intentional cultural change humans have yet achieved.

Targeting Incidence and Prevalence

Public health practice evolved from sometimes desperate efforts to control epidemics. One of the first and most disastrous was the bubonic plague. It arrived in Europe in 1347 when Genoese sailors arrived in Sicily from the Crimea. Many were already sick. They—or the fleas on the rats that accompanied them—proceeded to infect all of Europe, killing as many as twenty-four million people. That was one-third of the population.

More localized epidemics continued to erupt over the next three centuries.

It wasn't hard to define success in dealing with these terrifying epidemics. Authorities needed to reduce the *incidence* of a disease (the rate of occurrence of new cases) and thereby reduce its *prevalence* (the proportion of the population with the disease).

Although public health developed as a way to control infectious diseases, its practices are relevant to addressing anything that affects human well-being, including behaviors and environmental conditions. Public health agencies now monitor the incidence and prevalence of most diseases. And as they identify factors, such as smoking, that cause disease, they develop systems for monitoring the incidence and prevalence of those factors.

Unfortunately, the typical approach is to treat each problem as though it is unrelated to other problems. As a result, we pay little attention to environmental conditions that contribute to multiple problems. One of the most important things we could do to accelerate the improvement of human well-being would be to shift our focus from individual problems to the prevalence of environments that contribute to most of our problems.

Epidemiology

Epidemiology is the study of the patterns and causes of diseases in populations. Once reducing the incidence and prevalence of a disease is established as a public health goal, epidemiologists try to figure out what is causing the disease.

A classic example of this process was the discovery that contaminated water causes cholera. In *The Ghost Map* (2006), Stephen Johnson tells the story of John Snow, a London surgeon who developed the theory that contaminated water, not bad air, caused cholera. On four occasions between 1831 and 1854, there were outbreaks of cholera in London. On August 31, 1854, an outbreak began in the Soho area. By September 10, it had killed five hundred people. In an exhausting process, Snow and a local pastor interviewed the surviving victims of this outbreak and found that most lived in proximity to a pump at the corner of Broad and Cambridge Streets. Those living closer to another pump in the neighborhood had a much lower incidence of the disease. Snow convinced the Board of Guardians of St. James Parish, which controlled the pump, to remove the pump handle. When they did, the outbreak of cholera ended. (One building in the neighborhood—a brewery—had no cholera deaths. Guess what they were drinking.)

The episode stands as the first clear victory for the fundamental elements of public health. Careful observation led to a hypothesis about a risk factor for disease. Removal of that risk factor—the water—ended the epidemic.

Once a risk factor for a disease is identified, it becomes a target of public health efforts. Once we learned that cigarette smoking caused lung cancer, it became imperative to reduce the prevalence of smoking. That in turn led to identifying and targeting the prevalence of major influences on smoking behavior, such as the marketing of cigarettes to young people.

This way of thinking can be extended to any problem that confronts humans. Consider how it applies to nurturing environments. There is clear evidence that diverse psychological, behavioral, and health problems result from family and school environments that fail to nurture prosocial development (Biglan et al. 2012). This is ample justification for establishing a society-wide goal of increasing the prevalence of nurturing families and schools.

Embracing such a goal could help organize and integrate the disparate efforts of health care providers, educators, researchers, and policy makers, who are often working on individual problems, such as crime, drug abuse, or academic failure, but are not taking into account the fact that all of these problems stem from the same nonnurturing environments.

Once you embrace the goal of increasing the prevalence of nurturing families and schools, the natural next question is which factors can help effect these outcomes. In the following chapters, I describe how poverty and many corporate practices directly affect the development of youth and the quality of family life and school environments. In chapter 7, I describe corporate marketing practices that have a deleterious effect on well-being and suggest ways that these harmful influences can be reduced. In chapter 8, I describe how poverty and economic inequality in the United States increase the stress that families experience. I also describe the public policies that have contributed to the huge economic disparities that have arisen over the past forty years. In chapter 9, I trace these policies to the recent evolution of capitalism, wherein advocacy for such policies has emerged from their benefits to the economic well-being of the wealthiest among us. This analysis has direct implications for how we might reverse these harmful trends.

Good Surveillance

Public health practitioners refer to monitoring a disease as *surveillance*. People unfamiliar with that use of the term sometimes comment that it has a creepy connotation of spying on people. But this is good surveillance. It helps us know if we are reaching our goals for improving health and well-being.

You cannot know whether you are making progress in combating a disease or problem behavior unless you carefully measure its incidence and prevalence in the population. The practice of counting the number of people who contract a disease dates back to the monitoring of plague epidemics in the sixteenth century, when each summer the plague descended upon the cities of Italy. These days, all infectious diseases are routinely monitored.

Now the practice is slowly being extended to monitoring psychological and behavioral problems. The National Institute on Drug Abuse funds

Monitoring the Future, a system for assessing drug use and related behaviors in a representative sample of students throughout the country annually. It provides invaluable information about rates of alcohol consumption, adolescent smoking, and illicit drug use. In the 1990s, when data showed that adolescent cigarette smoking was increasing, Monitoring the Future triggered successful efforts to combat the rise (Johnston et al. 2013).

The tobacco control movement has been shaped and guided by evidence about how its actions and policies affect smoking prevalence. When policy initiatives such as ensuring clean indoor air proved helpful in motivating people to quit smoking, advocacy for such policies accelerated. Similar monitoring of psychological problems has lagged behind. For example, we still have no system to monitor rates of depression and anxiety among adults.

Ultimately, a surveillance system suited to creating a culture of nurturance would extend beyond monitoring problems. As almost all psychological, behavioral, and health problems are influenced by environments that either do or do not nurture healthy, prosocial development, we should be monitoring the quality of our environments. I would start with families and schools, and eventually move to tracking the quality of workplaces and public spaces.

A system for monitoring the prevalence of nurturing families and schools can be built on existing systems that monitor youth and adult well-being, such as Monitoring the Future and the Center for Disease Control's Youth Risk Behavior Surveillance System (Eaton et al. 2012). We could begin by monitoring nurturance in families through adolescent surveys. The Behavioral Risk Factor Surveillance System (Li et al. 2011), which assesses a wide range of health conditions and behaviors, obtains data on health and well-being from representative adult samples. However, although conflict-filled stressful environments are a major contributor to most psychological, behavioral, and health problems, the Behavioral Risk Factor Surveillance System obtains no data on conflict in homes.

Most surveillance systems provide good estimates of the rates of problems at the state level but do not have large enough samples to provide estimates at the community level. However, some communities are beginning to get data at this level (Mrazek, Biglan, and Hawkins 2005). Ultimately, every community should have accurate and timely data on the proportion of families and schools that are nurturing.

Now let me address a "Yes, but…" you may be having—namely that it is inconceivable that we would ever devote the resources needed to accomplish such surveillance. I've even heard such skepticism from people who conduct Monitoring the Future and the Youth Risk Behavior Surveillance System. Yet consider this: every mass-produced product you purchase is manufactured in a system that carefully monitors the quality of each item produced. The quality assurance procedures that have evolved in manufacturing over the past fifty years have increased the quality and durability of material goods enormously. For example, my son Mike still drives a Toyota Camry we purchased in 1994. In the 1960s it was rare if a car lasted more than five years.

Given this level of care in monitoring the quality of manufactured goods, surely it makes sense to be just as vigilant about the development and well-being of our fellow humans. And in the unlikely event that you have no interest in the well-being of young people, you should still value a system that monitors family and school nurturance. The benefits may reduce the taxes you pay and the chances that you or a loved one will be harmed due to failure to provide nurturing environments.

Programs, Policies, and Practices

Public health researchers and practitioners are pragmatic. They will implement any intervention that seems likely to promote a desired outcome in a population, and they will evaluate its impact in terms of creating the desired change, as measured by the surveillance system. There are three main routes to delivering such interventions: programs, policies, and practices.

Programs

I've already described many family and school programs that can improve these two environments and promote prosocial development. The family programs were developed mostly for delivery to individual families or small groups of families. However, as we adopt the goal of increasing the prevalence of nurturing families, we need to find more efficient methods to ensure that we reach every family that would benefit.

One of the first people to embrace the goal of affecting an entire population of families was Matt Sanders, a New Zealander who is now at the University of Queensland in Brisbane, Australia. Like me, Sanders has a background in behavior analysis. He began developing behavioral interventions for families in the late 1970s and has an especially pragmatic approach. Early on, he realized that intensive home-based coaching of parents could be effective but wouldn't reach many parents. Then he visited the Stanford Heart Disease Prevention Program and was impressed by their effort to reach the entire population in several California communities. This inspired him to spend the next ten years developing the interventions that now comprise his multilevel program, the Triple P–Positive Parenting Program. It makes use of mass media, offers ninety-minute seminars for parents, and provides parents with tip sheets for specific problems, such as getting a young child to go to sleep at night. It also provides more intensive support for families that need it.

Sanders also teamed up with Ron Prinz, from the Psychology Department at the University of South Carolina, to see if they could affect the prevalence of behavioral problems among children in an entire population. They randomly assigned eighteen South Carolina counties to either offer or not offer Triple P. In the nine counties that offered the program, they trained about six hundred people who were likely to be in contact with parents of young children and therefore in a position to give parents advice about common behavioral problems, if the parents wanted advice. They trained preschool staff, child care providers, health care workers, and providers of mental health and social services.

At the time of the study, child maltreatment had been increasing throughout South Carolina. However, in the counties with the Triple P program, rates of child maltreatment did not rise, and further, they were significantly lower than in the control counties (Prinz et al. 2009). The intervention also significantly reduced foster care placements, which often result after abuse is detected. The Washington State Institute for Public Policy independently determined that the intervention produced a $6.06 return on each investment dollar (Lee et al. 2012).

The era of developing and evaluating family interventions seems to be winding down, having resulted in a substantial number of family interventions that have proven benefit. Research and practice are now turning to the question of how to reach families with brief, efficient, and effective programs that prevent or ameliorate the most common relationship problems they encounter.

There are also impressive examples of community-wide interventions to implement family and school-based interventions in entire communities. David Hawkins and Rico Catalano, at the Social Development Research Group at the University of Washington, created Communities That Care, a program that helps communities identify and address major risk factors for youth. In a randomized trial, the program helped communities significantly reduce usage of tobacco, alcohol, and other drugs, as well as delinquency (Hawkins et al. 2014). Prevention scientists Richard Spoth of Iowa State University and Mark Greenberg of Pennsylvania State University have teamed up to test a community intervention that provides both a family intervention and a school-based intervention. Their randomized trial showed that the intervention helped communities reduce substance use (Spoth et al. 2013).

Policies

In this book, I use the term *policies* to refer to laws and regulations that affect health or behavior, or conditions that affect either one (Wagenaar and Burris 2013). Examples include taxation of harmful products, prohibitions on marketing harmful products, and requirements to provide incentives for desirable behavior.

At the outset of the tobacco control movement, many of us hoped we could develop effective cessation and prevention programs that would reduce the prevalence of smoking. But despite all the work I've done on smoking prevention (for example, Biglan et al. 2000), I have to confess that policies, public advocacy, and education have been far more important than programs in reducing smoking.

Researchers with a public health orientation often argue that policies are the most efficient way of affecting entire populations. For example, Harold Holder, who worked at the Center for Advanced Study in the Behavioral Sciences as I did, often said something along the lines of "You wouldn't have to reach every parent with a program if you had policies that directly affected adolescent drinking." He pointed out that simply raising the price of alcohol has helped to reduce youth use, alcohol-related car crashes, and the development of alcoholism (Biglan et al. 2004).

Fortunately, there is no need to choose between policies and programs. No single intervention can be entirely successful, so we should take public health victories wherever we can get them.

Since working with Harold, I've had the pleasure of working with Kelli Komro, another advocate of policy interventions. She and her husband, Alex Wagenaar, who are at the University of Florida, collect policy studies the way some people collect baseball cards. Komro worked with me and twenty other behavioral scientists on the Promise Neighborhood Research Consortium, leading our efforts to identify evidence-based policies that are beneficial for child and adolescent development. The consortium's website (http://www.promiseneighborhoods.org) lists more than fifty such policies.

One example of an effective and beneficial evidence-based policy is taxation of alcoholic beverages. Komro's review concluded that doubling the tax on alcoholic beverages could produce all of the following benefits:

- A 35 percent reduction in alcohol-related morbidity and mortality

- An 11 percent reduction in traffic crash deaths

- A 6 percent reduction in sexually transmitted diseases

- A 2 percent reduction in violence

- A 17 percent reduction in beer consumption

- A 25 percent reduction in wine consumption

- A 25 percent reduction in distilled spirits consumption

Recently Alex Wagenaar and Scott Burris edited an excellent book on policies, titled *Public Health Law Research: Theory and Methods* (2013). It provides numerous examples of policies that are benefiting public health, along with information about how the impact of policies can be evaluated. We also have to be concerned with policies that harm well-being. In chapter 8, I'll describe how numerous policy changes in the United States over the past thirty years have harmed families and young people.

Practices

In addition to developing programs and policies, behaviorists and other interventionists have come up with a large number of simple techniques for influencing behavior. These are valuable resources for anyone engaged in efforts to help people develop their skills. In earlier chapters, I've mentioned Dennis Embry and his work in developing the Good Behavior Game. A voracious reader, he has been tracking the development of simple behavior-influencing techniques for many years and has identified more than fifty techniques proven to affect one or more behaviors of children, youth, or adults. He calls the individual techniques *kernels* (Embry and Biglan 2008).

Many kernels involve providing reinforcement for behavior you want to increase. Examples include praise notes, which teachers can write to students and students can write to each other, and "the mystery motivator" or "prize bowl," where people draw prizes of varying values for behaviors as diverse as completing homework or having drug-free urinalysis results.

Kernels exert their effects in different ways. Examples of kernels that reduce reinforcement for a problem behavior or increase the cost of such behavior include time-outs and higher taxes on cigarettes or alcohol. Other kernels affect behavior through *antecedent stimulation*, meaning establishing a signal that elicits a desired behavior. For example, you can establish nonverbal transition cues that guide students from one activity to another. Many teachers establish a cue such as flipping the lights on and off or raising a hand to signal that it is time for the class to pay attention to the teacher. This might seem trivial, but studies have shown that orderly transitions from one classroom activity to another can free up a week or more of instructional time across a school year.

Some kernels affect behavior by changing the way people think about things. For example, when people make a public commitment, it is more likely they will do what they said they would do. This is because we all have a history of reinforcement for doing what we said we would do, along with a history of social disapproval when we failed to follow through. Finally, some kernels affect well-being by affecting physiology. For example, considerable recent evidence indicates that supplementing diets with omega-3 fatty acids can reduce aggression, violence, depression, bipolar disorder, postpartum depression, and borderline personality disorder (Embry and Biglan 2008).

People like kernels because they are simple, easy-to-implement practices that usually produce immediate results. Parents, teachers, child care workers, and managers can use these positive techniques to nurture prosocial behavior in others and replace nagging, criticism, and cajoling. Spreading awareness of these techniques and promoting their use is another way we can help entire populations become more nurturing.

Advocacy

Returning to the tobacco control movement: As evidence about the harm of smoking grew, it mobilized people who had been harmed by smoking to create advocacy organizations that supported further investigation of the health consequences of smoking and the factors that influence smoking. In what I like to call a virtuous cycle, researchers learned more and more about the harm of smoking, advocates spread the word about these detrimental effects, and this generated further support for research and advocacy about the harm of smoking and ways to reduce smoking.

Surgeon General reports, National Cancer Institute monographs, and Institute of Medicine reports systematically marshaled evidence about specific aspects of the smoking problem to generate support for antismoking policies. For example, a series of Surgeon General reports documented how cigarettes cause heart disease, strokes, aneurysms, chronic obstructive lung disease, asthma, low birth weights of babies, premature births, sudden infant death syndrome, and most kinds of cancer (US Department of Health and Human Services 1980, 1981, 1982, 1983, 1984, 1988, 1989). A Surgeon General report on the effects of secondhand smoke showed that as many as fifty thousand people a year die due to exposure to other people's cigarettes (US Department of Health and Human Services 1986). That enlisted support among nonsmokers for restricting smoking and getting smokers to quit. Another report showed that tobacco is an addictive product, which undermined tobacco industry arguments that smoking was simply a lifestyle choice (US Department of Health and Human Services 1988).

The tobacco control movement has been enormously creative in finding ways to persuade people that cigarette smoking should be treated as an epidemic. To dramatically illustrate how many people cigarettes kill each year, we often say that it is as if two Boeing 747s crashed every day of the year, killing everyone on board. If two 747s crashed today, the FAA would probably ground all other 747s until it had thoroughly investigated the problem and determined the cause. Can you imagine such carnage going on for a week without government taking action?

A similar effort could convince millions of Americans that their well-being and the well-being of the nation depend on making families, schools, workplaces, neighborhoods, and communities more nurturing. Non-nurturing environments contribute directly to most of the psychological, behavioral, and health problems of society. We need to find creative ways to communicate evidence of this via many avenues, from government reports and news stories to blogs and social networks to entertainment media.

Action Implications

I envision—and hope you can envision—a society-wide movement working to increase the prevalence of nurturing environments. I think we should start with a focus on families and schools because they are the most important environments for youth, and because most psychological, health, and behavioral problems begin in childhood or adolescence.

For Policy Makers

- Create an umbrella organization focused on nurturing families—a coalition of advocacy organizations and foundations dedicated to alleviating one or more of the most common and costly psychological, behavioral, or health problems.

- Produce Institute of Medicine or Surgeon General reports on how to ensure that families and schools are nurturing.

    - In the report on families, merge all of the evidence on the detrimental impact of family dysfunction on all aspects of well-being. Describe the policies, programs, and practices now available to reduce the prevalence of dysfunctional families, thereby contributing to preventing an entire range of psychological, behavioral, and health problems. This would provide an agenda for future research and policy making.

- In the report on schools, review the evidence regarding how conflicts between students and adult-to-student punitiveness both contribute to academic failure and the development of psychological, behavioral, and health problems. Review the evidence supporting specific policies, programs, and practices to reduce these conditions. Also call for the research and policy making needed to increase the prevalence of nurturing schools.

- Create policies that target increasing the prevalence of nurturing families and schools, such as the following:

  - Assessing the prevalence of nurturing environments in both families and schools

  - Making evidence-based family interventions available to families that need them

- Requiring schools to monitor levels of punishment and student conflict, and requiring them to implement evidence-based social behavior programs to address these problems

- Adopt policies that reduce stress on families and schools. (See chapter 8 for details.)

For People Working on Family Support

- Create a unified profession that unites all the disparate professions and organizations that work to improve family functioning.

- Instead of relying on agencies that only detect and intervene in cases of child abuse, build a system that, like Triple P, attempts to reach every family with as much or as little help as they need to deal with common problems in child rearing. The resulting agency or network of agencies should have the responsibility to contact parents and support their success from before the birth of their first child through their children's adolescence.

For Educators

- Identify and implement one or more of the evidence-based programs that have proven benefit in reducing conflict and punitiveness and promoting prosocial behavior.

- Join and support the Association for Positive Behavior Support, which is already advancing nurturing practices in our schools.

For Parents and Other Community Members

- Examine your own environments. Consider your immediate and extended family, your workplace, your circle of friends, your neighborhood, the organizations you belong to, and the civic activities you are involved in.

  - For each environment, ask yourself how nurturing it is. Are people kind and caring, or do they tend to be critical and argumentative?

  - Think about your own behavior in each environment. Do you add to conflict and discomfort, or do you model and reinforce kind and caring behavior?

  - Are there small things you can do to make these environments more nurturing?

  - Notice any tendencies you may have to blame others for things they do that increase your stress or that of other people. You may be correct about that, but you can choose to step back from such thoughts and find ways to act that, over time, can move you and those around you toward more compassionate behavior.

- Join organizations that support policies and programs to increase nurturance in families and schools.

- Advocate that your elected officials implement family support policies and programs.

- Inquire about whether your child's school is implementing evidence-based programs to prevent conflict and bullying.

CHAPTER 7

Harmful Corporate Marketing Practices

Imagine, if you will, that you raise your children carefully, using all of the love, patience, and skills described in part 2 of this book. Would you be satisfied if your kids got a good education, got married, had kids, had a good job, and then died of a smoking-related illness at age forty-five? Of course not.

Successful nurturance includes protecting our children from everything that could damage their health and well-being throughout life. One of the influences that is most important yet also most difficult to control is the marketing of harmful products. If you've ever been in a supermarket with a young child, you've probably had the experience of your child demanding candy at the checkout counter and getting upset when it wasn't forthcoming. Of course, stores put candy there because they know how little kids work—and because they know how hesitant most parents are to refuse and risk a tantrum.

Even the most competent and motivated parents are challenged to protect their children from the risks modern marketing poses to healthy child development. For example, John Pierce and his colleagues at the University of California, San Diego, studied a group of 894 early adolescents whose parents used effective parenting practices: they were warm, they monitored their kids' activities, and they did a good job of setting limits. Yet even among these well-parented teens, those who were interested in and liked cigarette ads were more likely to start smoking over the next three years (Pierce et al. 2002).

In this chapter, I describe some of the most harmful marketing practices, along with the behavioral principles that underlie successful marketing, and propose guidelines for restricting marketing practices that undermine efforts to nurture children's healthy development.

Marketing

Products are marketed by associating the product or brand with things the consumer desires. Through advertising, promotions, store displays, distribution of branded paraphernalia, and placement of products in the media, marketers try to get potential consumers to feel that the product will give them something they'd rather have than their money. It might be something tangible, like the ability to cut grass; or it could be emotional, like the feeling you get when you wear new clothes and someone compliments you on them. This is not to say that marketing is inherently evil. It actually has many benefits, including telling us about things that genuinely improve our lives. But sometimes it can cause great harm.

Marketing Cigarettes to Teens

I began to realize the importance of corporate practices on well-being when the US Department of Justice asked me to study the tobacco industry's youth marketing. Before I was finished, I had read more than twenty thousand pages of tobacco company documents and reviewed thousands of cigarette ads. As I studied the documents, I began to see how the tobacco companies were systematically recruiting young people to become addicted to cigarettes.

And for good reason. Numerous documents showed that tobacco companies had carefully analyzed the cigarette market and knew that very few people would start smoking after their teen years. In the ninety-six pages of testimony I submitted regarding the tobacco company R. J. Reynolds, I cited numerous documents showing that the company understood that recruiting underage teens to smoke was vital in maintaining their market share. In a memo to Reynolds executives, an R. J. Reynolds employee, Dianne Burrows, nicely summarized the situation: "*Younger adult smokers have been the critical factor in the growth and decline of every major brand and company over the last fifty years. They will continue to be just as important to brands/companies in the future* for two simple reasons: The renewal of the market stems almost entirely from eighteen-year-old smokers. No more than 5 percent of smokers start after age twenty-four. The brand loyalty of eighteen-year-old smokers far outweighs any tendency to switch with age" (Biglan 2004, p. 292; emphasis in the original). (Other documents showed that "eighteen-year-old smokers" was in fact code for those under eighteen. It came into use after tobacco companies stopped talking openly about those under eighteen due to concerns about accusations they were marketing to underage teens.)

Over at Philip Morris, the analysis was pretty much the same. As one executive put it, "It is during the teenage years that the initial brand choice is made: At least part of the success of Marlboro Red during its most rapid growth period was because it became *the* brand of choice among teenagers who then stuck with it as they grew older" (Biglan 2004, Demonstrative 8, p. 3).

The resulting marketing has had devastating consequences. John Pierce, Betsy Gilpin, and Won Choi (1999) calculated that Marlboro's marketing between 1988 and 1998 would eventually lead to deaths of 300,000 young people who became addicted as teens. Camel marketing eventually contributed to the deaths of even more young people—520,000—thanks to the success of the Joe Camel campaign, which Philip Morris implemented during this period.

The best available estimates are that smoking currently kills about 400,000 smokers in the United States each year, along with about 50,000 people who don't smoke but are exposed to others' smoke (CDC 2008).

If smoking kills, then anything that induces people to smoke makes a direct contribution to death and is itself a killer. Tobacco industry marketing should be treated in the same way we treat the cause of an infectious disease.

The Behavioral Processes Involved in Marketing

In chapter 1, I described human verbal relational abilities. This capacity has a great deal to do with why marketing can be so effective. Human valuing of things is a function of the relational networks in which those things are embedded. In marketing cigarettes to young people, corporations utilize this by starting with some things young people already value and associating them with the product to be sold. Through brand identities, logos, and repeated messages, consumers come to associate valued outcomes with the product. If a company can get the consumer to relate the brand to valued outcomes, they can make having that product highly reinforcing.

Consider the red chevron on Marlboro packs of cigarettes. What kinds of things do young people value that the company could get them to relate to the Marlboro brand? The most basic and important thing for most adolescents is social acceptance. Therefore, it isn't surprising that adolescents who are having trouble academically or experiencing social rejection are particularly likely to be susceptible to advertising that suggests they will be accepted by their peers if they smoke a particular brand of cigarette (Forrester et al. 2007; National Cancer Institute 2008). My review of hundreds of Marlboro ads showed that they routinely associated the brand with popularity. They also associated it with things related to popularity, such as being rugged and physically attractive, being tough, being an independent adult, or being someone that people admire. Many young people—especially those most likely to take up smoking—crave excitement and taking risks. Thus, many Marlboro ads associate the brand with bronco busting and auto racing (National Cancer Institute 2008).

So why do young people take up smoking despite the evidence that it is harmful? One thing to consider is that not all young people are susceptible to tobacco advertising. The susceptible kids are those struggling for social acceptance and excitement. For these kids, the risk of getting a disease many years later is much less important than getting a chance to gain social acceptance in the short term. And for many, the risk associated with smoking may actually make smoking more attractive. This is why, in my most recent work on smoking prevention programs, we have almost entirely abandoned associating smoking with health risks. Instead, we associate *not* smoking with social acceptance, fun, and excitement (Gordon, Biglan, and Smolkowski 2008).

In sum, marketers can make it reinforcing to buy and use a harmful product simply by getting people to relate the brand to things that are already important reinforcers for them. The brand and logo of the product can come to have powerful evocative effects, thanks being associated with multiple images of things the person already values.

Seeing the Harmfulness of Cigarette Advertising

Tobacco industry practices have directly harmed public health in several other ways. As concerns mounted about the dangers of smoking, the industry developed so-called low-tar and low-nicotine cigarettes and marketed them as safer alternatives to regular cigarettes. They did this to persuade smokers to switch to "light" cigarettes rather than stop smoking. However, their own research showed that these cigarettes were not safer.

When concerns were raised that cigarette marketing was enticing young people to smoke, the industry's public relations arm, the Tobacco Institute, created a program supposedly aimed at preventing smoking among youth. But the review of their programs that I did for the Department of Justice showed that it was designed to create the impression that the companies didn't want youth to smoke and that youth smoking was due to lax parenting (Biglan 2004). Internal documents of the Tobacco Institute showed that it typically announced these programs in state capitals and briefed editorial boards and legislators on them. These contacts and their effectiveness in deterring legislation that would restrict tobacco marketing carefully monitored legislative action and reported to the industry. However, I could find no evidence that the industry ever tested whether the programs reached parents or had any impact on smoking among young people.

In a landmark decision in 2006, in *United States v. Philip Morris et al.,* Judge Gladys Kessler found that the tobacco industry knew that cigarettes caused cancer, hid these facts from the public, marketed to youth, and marketed so-called low-tar and low-nicotine cigarettes to prevent people from quitting, even though they knew that these cigarettes were not safer. For the first time, an industry was found culpable for marketing that influenced people to engage in unhealthy behavior.

Marketing Alcohol to Adolescents

Your efforts to raise healthy, successful young people would come to a tragic end if your teen died or received grave injuries in an alcohol-related car crash. According to the Centers for Disease Control and Prevention, in 2010 about 2,700 teens age sixteen to nineteen died in car crashes and

282,000 sustained injuries (CDC 2012). About a quarter of the car crashes are alcohol related, and alcohol marketing plays a significant role in the problem of youth drinking.

When Judge Kessler ruled the tobacco industry was to blame for people becoming addicted to cigarettes and remaining addicted, the implications of this ruling were immediately obvious to the alcohol industry. Therefore, if you search the bottom of most TV ads for alcoholic beverages these days, you'll find a statement like, "Drink Responsibly." If the tobacco industry could be held accountable for the death and disease of young people who were addicted due to cigarette advertising, might the alcohol industry also be liable if it could be shown that their marketing influences young people to drink as minors or to drink to excess? The evidence is mounting that this is the case, although it isn't yet as solid as it is for tobacco marketing.

Alcohol use contributes to death in a variety of ways. In the United States, it accounts for 41 percent of all traffic fatalities—more than seventeen thousand deaths annually (National Highway Traffic Safety Administration 2008). It also contributes to deaths through drowning, falls, hypothermia, burns, suicides, and homicides (CDC 2013). One analysis, carried out by the Bureau of Justice Statistics (Greenfeld 1998), estimated that 40 percent of all crime is committed under the influence of alcohol. Alcohol use, however, is not invariably harmful as tobacco use is. It is a part of most cultures, contributes to social relations, and, in moderation, may have some health benefits.

On the other hand, binge drinking—defined as having five or more drinks at a time—is a major problem, especially among young people. Binge drinkers have more alcohol-related car crashes and are more likely to become alcoholics (CDC 2013). The Harvard School of Public Health College Alcohol Study, which looked at 120 college campuses, found that 44 percent of students reported binge drinking (Wechsler and Nelson 2008). Nearly 20 percent reported such episodes more than once every two weeks. Students on campuses with high rates of binge drinking reported more assaults and unwanted sexual advances. Binge drinking is also a problem among high school students. In Oregon, we found that 10 percent of eighth-graders and 25 percent of eleventh-graders reported binge drinking in the last thirty days (Boles, Biglan, and Smolkowski 2006).

My friend and colleague Joel Grube has summarized evidence on the impact of alcohol advertising. Although the alcohol industry pledged that it wouldn't advertise on TV shows or in magazines where more than 30 percent of the audience is teens, that standard is functionally meaningless because their ads still reach most youth. You see, the industry concentrates its marketing in venues chosen to reach the 30 percent maximum, rather than selecting those likely to reach very few young people. The average teen sees about 245 alcohol ads on TV each year, and the 30 percent who view the most see as many as 780 per year. As a result, young people actually encounter 45 percent more ads for beer and 65 percent more ads for alcopops, or coolers, than adults do. By the way, if you aren't a teen, you may not know that alcopops are alcoholic beverages that are sweetened to make them appealing to those who aren't accustomed to drinking.

(Lest you think that all this concern about alcohol comes from a bunch of prissy teetotalers, each year Joel Grube sends me a fine bottle of California wine. If the California Golden Bears ever beat the Oregon Ducks in football, I will send him an even finer bottle of Oregon wine.)

Although alcohol marketers will tell you that their advertising targets only adults, the evidence shows otherwise. Youth who see more alcohol ads know more about alcohol and are more familiar with brands (Pechmann et al. 2011). And some experiments have shown that when young people see ads for alcohol, they become more interested in drinking (Grube, Madden, and Friese 1996). Finally, some studies, but not all, have shown that communities with more alcohol advertising have more young people who drink and more alcohol-related motor vehicle fatalities (Grube and Nygaard 2005).

Marketing Junk Food

Now the food industry also has reason to worry. The US obesity rate has been steadily increasing, and evidence is mounting that food marketing is one reason.

The definition of obesity is a body mass index (BMI) of 30 or more. BMI is a calculation based on height and weight; for example, an adult who is five foot nine and weighs 203 pounds would have a BMI of 30; for the average person of that height, this would be at least 35 pounds overweight. Figure 3, which comes from the CDC Behavioral Risk Factor Surveillance System, shows the rate of obesity for US states in 1990, 2000, and 2010. In most states for which there was data, less than 15 percent of the adult population was obese in 1990. In 2010, just twenty years later, over 20 percent of adults were obese in every state; in twelve states, more than 30 percent were obese (CDC 2014).

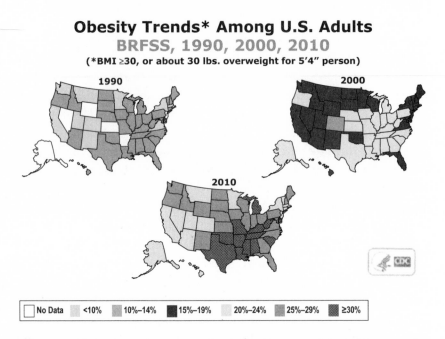

Figure 3. Obesity trends among US adults. (Reprinted from "Overweight and Obesity: Adult Obesity Facts," an Internet-based fact sheet by the CDC, available at http://www.cdc.gov/obesity/data/adult.html.)

In her book *Food Politics* (2002), Marion Nestle (no relation to the food company) has described the role of food processing and marketing in increasing obesity. Food companies spend more than $11 billion annually on advertising, and the foods most heavily marketed are those that are most profitable. Unfortunately, many are high in fat or calories and have little nutritional value.

Television ads for food and beverages on Saturday morning children's shows more than tripled between 1987 and 1994, and by the end of that period, about 57 percent of the ads were for foods of little nutritional value, such as sweetened breakfast cereals and candy. More recently, a study looked at what percentage of TV food ads in 2003 and 2004 targeted to children were for foods high in fat, sugar, or sodium (L. M. Powell et al. 2007). Among two- to eleven-year-olds, 97.8 percent of ads were for such foods, and among twelve- to seventeen-year-olds, 89.4 percent of ads were for such foods.

TV viewing is associated with obesity in children (Dennison, Erb, and Jenkins 2002). Although inactivity is certainly one reason for this link, exposure to ads for fattening foods is another (Borzekowski and Robinson 2001; Dixon et al. 2007). Both broadcasters and the food industry put the onus for this problem on parents, saying that parents need to guide their children. This is the same argument that the tobacco companies make. It may work to prevent unwanted restrictions on broadcasters and advertisers, but as a practical matter, childhood obesity will remain a problem as long as marketing unhealthful foods to children continues.

In 2006, the Institute of Medicine reviewed 123 empirical studies of the influence of food and beverage marketing on the diets and health of children and adolescents (IOM Committee on Food Marketing and the Diets of Children and Youth 2006). Studies involving children ages two to eleven led an Institute of Medicine committee to conclude that there is strong evidence that TV ads influence children's food and beverage preferences and moderate evidence that it affects their beliefs about food and beverages. The committee concluded that food marketing influences children to prefer and request unhealthful foods. The evidence regarding the influence of television marketing on teens was less clear, partly because there have been fewer studies. The committee concluded that exposure to television advertising is associated with childhood obesity. However, despite the fact that the committee reviewed experimental studies showing the causal effect of advertising on children's food preferences, it was unwilling to state conclusively that exposure to food advertising caused childhood obesity.

Even if we reach every family and school with information about the things they need to do to encourage healthful eating and exercise patterns among children, this won't be enough to address the problem of obesity (or drinking and smoking) among young people. We have to reduce the effects of marketing.

Free Speech and Corporate Marketing

Any proposal to restrict marketing by these industries must contend with long-standing principles of free speech. In the United States, we have constitutional protections of speech that extend even to "commercial speech," such as advertising. Restrictions on such speech start us down a slippery slope that could result in substantial governmental suppression of any speech the current government doesn't like.

In the United States, the current constitutional principles regulating commercial speech were articulated in a 1980 US Supreme Court case, *Central Hudson Gas & Electric Corp. v. Public Service Commission*, which established criteria for allowing government regulation of commercial speech. Truthful advertising for legal products is protected. Any restriction must advance a substantial interest of the government, and there must be clear evidence that the regulation serves that interest. Finally, the regulation should be narrowly tailored to restrict only the problematic speech.

This issue has been litigated regarding cigarette advertising. In 2001, the US Supreme Court overturned Massachusetts regulations that prohibited cigarette advertising within one thousand feet of schools (Koh 2002). Massachusetts had enacted the regulations based on evidence that cigarette advertisements appeared more often in areas that reached children than in others. That fact concurs with much other evidence that the tobacco industry has targeted young people (Biglan 2004). However, the court ruled that, although the ban advanced a legitimate state interest—preventing youth smoking—and the restriction would advance that interest, such advertising was truthful and for a lawful purpose. The court concluded that the ban was not narrowly tailored, as it would prohibit most current tobacco advertising in Massachusetts.

Apparently, both sides in the case agreed that the cigarette advertising was truthful and for a legal purpose. I think they were mistaken. The legal analysis in this case points to the need to bring the law into line with what the behavioral sciences have learned about human behavior.

The courts considered the advertising truthful in the sense that it accurately indicated the brand being sold and its price. However, that analysis fails to consider the functional effects of cigarette advertising. Research conducted both by the tobacco industry and by public health researchers shows that advertising for cigarette brands that are popular among youth influences many young people to believe that those who smoke certain brand will be seen as popular, tough, exciting, adventurous, and so on. My testimony in *United States v. Philip Morris et al.* cited nine studies that showed this (Biglan 2004). For example, one study (Pechmann and Knight 2002) found that when ninth-graders were exposed to cigarette advertising, they rated smokers more positively on adjectives such as "fun," "well liked," "sexy," "desirable to date," "successful," "smart," "intelligent," and "cool." In other words, the ads influenced these adolescents to view smokers more favorably. Other studies show that when adolescents view smokers more favorably, they are more likely to take up smoking.

The tobacco companies' own research also shows that their advertising conveys positive images of smokers. For example, one extensive study of the Marlboro image indicated that the brand evoked the following images and concepts: all-American; hardworking and trustworthy; rugged individualism; and being a man's man, as defined by being experienced, sure of oneself, confident, in charge, self-sufficient, down to earth, and cool and calm (Biglan 2004). Cigarette advertising convinces vulnerable adolescents that they can achieve this desired image by smoking a brand popular among youth. And so they smoke.

So is cigarette advertising truthful? In a sense, it is. Many adolescents come to see the Marlboro smoker as tough and popular. So there is some truth to their notion that if they smoke Marlboros, they will appear this way to their peers. Yet this is a Faustian bargain for which adolescents are ill informed. They get an image that may contribute to their social acceptance, and the tobacco company gets an addicted smoker. As one R. J. Reynolds executive put it, "Attract a smoker at the earliest opportunity and let brand loyalty turn that smoker into a valuable asset" (Biglan 2004, 290).

But from another perspective, the advertising is deceptive. It portrays smoking as an activity that will lead to substantial social benefit and says nothing about the fact that an adolescent who takes up smoking will have a difficult and expensive addiction and a one-in-three chance of dying of a smoking-related illness. The law needs to catch up with the behavioral sciences and look at not simply what an ad says but how it functions. Cigarette advertising functions to get young people to take up smoking and to keep current smokers from quitting. As a result, it currently contributes to 450,000 deaths in the United States each year.

Targeting marketing practices because of their impact on public health will seem controversial to many. And any industry worth its salt will try to keep it controversial by sowing doubts about the evidence and arguing that encroachment on their marketing practices unduly restricts freedom of speech. As long as influential citizens can be convinced that altering marketing to improve public health is a radical and unwarranted idea, harmful marketing will continue.

This situation may seem disheartening. But recall the evolution of sanitary practices. It was once nobody's business what people did with their sewage. When it became clear that raw sewage was killing people, standards changed. A similar process is underway for marketing practices that endanger health. If the legal system can stop your neighbor from doing as he pleases with his sewage, why should we not have a legal system that prohibits marketing that systemically contributes to death? The day will come when we will look back and marvel that we ever allowed the cigarette, alcohol, or food industries to market in ways that contribute to disease and death.

Guidelines for Restrictions of Marketing Practices

I am well aware that legal regulation of marketing runs the risk of excessive government control of free speech. If the principle is simply that the government can prohibit advertising that contributes to harm to people in any way, where might we end up? Would we prohibit ads for high-fat food? How about peanuts, which can cause deadly allergic reactions in some people? Reclining chairs encourage inactivity. Perhaps recliner ads should target only those who already exercise. Libertarian op-ed writers could have a field day with this issue.

Epidemiological research can provide guidance. Public health targets disease, health behaviors, and risk factors based on their demonstrated harm to human well-being. Public health officials have the power to restrict or limit practices that contribute to significant disease, injury, or death. For example, they can recall tainted products, quarantine infected people, and prohibit the marketing of dangerous drugs. However, our society has not given the government a blank check to prohibit anything deemed harmful by some passion of the moment.

As applied to marketing tobacco, alcohol, and unhealthful foods, particularly to young people, limitations must be based on clear and convincing empirical evidence that advertising influences a substantial number of people to engage in a behavior that results in death for a significant number of them. And to be clear and convincing, at least some of the evidence would need to be experimental. That is, it would need to show that advertising is a direct influence on the behavior when other sources of influence are controlled.

As an example of how this comes about, in five studies on the effects of cigarette advertising on youth that I reviewed in *United States v. Philip Morris et al.* (Biglan 2004), adolescents were randomly assigned to see or not see the ads, and their attitudes and intentions to smoke were subsequently measured. By randomly assigning adolescents to these two conditions, the studies controlled for other possible explanations of the link between exposure to ads and smoking, such as the possibility that adolescents who were already interested in smoking were more likely to look at the ads. These experiments showed that exposure to the ads significantly increased positive attitudes toward smoking and toward those who smoked the brand advertised, and increased intentions to smoke. Numerous studies have shown that these attitudes and intentions do influence young people to start smoking.

Then there is the question of how to define a "substantial number" of people and a "significant number" of deaths. One way to think about this is in terms of what we would deem substantial or significant in other parallel situations. Research by Betsy Gilpin and colleagues (1999) estimated that about 2,933 people under the age of twenty-one become regular smokers each day. Estimates in the CDC's *Morbidity and Mortality Weekly Report* indicate that about one-third of young people who begin smoking will eventually die of a smoking-related illness (US Department of Health and Human Services 2014). So every day, cigarette advertising lures nearly one thousand people to an early death. We currently prohibit food production practices that have far less serious outcomes. For example, the CDC has mounted a major effort to combat contamination of food by *E. coli*, which kills about sixty people a year (Rangel et al. 2005).

In my view, there currently isn't sufficient *experimental* evidence showing that specific practices in marketing alcohol and food contribute to ill health, injury, and death, although considerable correlational evidence shows that they do. Therefore, experimental studies are needed to determine whether exposure to ads for alcoholic beverages or unhealthful foods increases young people's motivation to drink or to eat those foods. A series of studies showing this would be sufficient reason to restrict such advertising.

Once you begin to consider marketing in terms of its impact on public health, you may wonder whether other corporate practices are also damaging to health and well-being. I am convinced that corporate advocacy for certain economic policies contributes to poverty and economic inequality, which cause substantial harm to well-being. Therefore, in the next chapter, I'll describe how poverty and inequality harm well-being. Then, in chapter 9, I'll analyze how the evolution of economic policies has created the huge income disparities evident in the United States and examine the role that corporate advocacy has played in this evolution.

Action Implications

Research on the impact of cigarette, alcohol, and food advertising could better inform policy makers, parents, and citizens in general. By preventing young people from exposure to harmful advertising, we can significantly reduce the risks to their health.

For Policy Makers

- Fund further research on the impact of food and alcohol marketing practices to obtain experimental evidence on the harm to public health from certain marketing practices.

- Enact laws that establish standards for assessing whether marketing practices are harmful to health, replacing the standard established in *Central Hudson Gas & Electric Corp. v. Public Service Commission* with one that assesses not simply the literal truth of an ad but also the functional effects of ads on unhealthful behavior.

For Parents

- Limit your child's exposure to advertising for tobacco, alcohol, and unhealthful food—if you can. I wish I could provide tips on how to inoculate children against the effects of such advertising. Unfortunately, research has not found media literacy training to reduce the persuasive influence of such advertising. However, I strongly recommend that you take advantage of new technologies that can help reduce children's exposure to TV ads. For example, you might record a show your child watches and fast-forward through the advertisements.

For Citizens

- Support legislation to fund research on the impact of marketing on the well-being of young people, and legislation to limit children's exposure to advertising for tobacco, alcoholic beverages, and unhealthful foods.

CHAPTER 8

Poverty and Economic Inequality

In previous chapters, I've described the nurturing conditions that are important for young people to thrive. Children need warm, patient, attentive, and skilled parents and teachers who provide instruction and reinforcement for all the diverse behaviors and values they need to become productive and caring members of society. They need parents and teachers who minimize punitive, critical, and demeaning behavior toward them and limit their opportunities to engage in dangerous or counterproductive behavior. Ultimately, they must be able to flexibly pursue their values, even when doing so requires considerable persistence and the acceptance of strong negative feelings.

Poverty is a major obstacle to creating these nurturing conditions. I hope I have demonstrated the effectiveness of interventions to improve young peoples' chances in life. Although these interventions can benefit children in poor families and neighborhoods, poverty makes it harder for these programs to help. If we can reduce poverty and economic inequality, we will produce benefits for poor families even if we never reach them with interventions.

Imagining Being Poor

When we hear about the misfortunes of others, it is a natural, psychologically protective mechanism to think of reasons why similar misfortunes couldn't happen to us. See if that process isn't operating as you read this chapter. Watch for thoughts like *It couldn't happen to me.*

Consider a study done in 2007, before the 2009 recession (Himmelstein et al. 2009). It found that medical problems led to 62 percent of bankruptcies. Among people filing for medically caused bankruptcies, 75 percent had health insurance, and most were well educated and owned homes. This study indicates that even if you are middle-class, should you suffer a heart attack or stroke, between the cost of medical care and an inability to work, you could quickly lose your life savings and your home.

What would it be like to be poor? The official poverty level for a family of four is $23,050. Perhaps you earn more than that, or you're a student with good prospects for making more than that in the near future. Imagine living for just one month on a little less than $2,000. If you lived alone you could probably afford an apartment and enough to eat. But what if you were supporting three others? The federal minimum wage is $7.25 an hour. If you worked full-time at that wage, you would earn about $14,500 a year: not enough to afford an apartment almost anywhere in the country.

The Damage Done by Poverty

Psychologist Lisa Goodman and her colleagues at Boston University (2013) summarized the consequences of poverty that make it so stressful. There are the challenges of securing food and housing. Imagine that you haven't yet figured out where you're going to sleep tonight. Poverty is also stigmatizing. If you were poor, there is a good chance that people would apply negative labels to you, such as "unmotivated," "uneducated," "unpleasant," "dirty," "angry," "stupid," "criminal," "violent," "immoral," "alcoholic," and "abusive." As you might imagine, people who have thoughts like this about you wouldn't be very warm or respectful. As a result, you would have many stressful interactions. You would also have very little power. If you felt that a merchant, professional, or bureaucrat had treated you unfairly, how likely is it that you could prevail in a dispute?

Poverty is especially harmful to children, affecting most aspects of their development and making them generally less healthy (McLoyd 1998). They may have lower birth weights, potentially resulting in a variety of conditions affecting cognitive development. Poor children are more likely to be exposed to lead, which affects neurological functioning and reduces school achievement. They often face dangers and victimization in their neighborhoods, stigmatizing attitudes from teachers and other adults, frequent moves or changes to living situation, and homelessness. Such experiences make children hypervigilant and prone to aggression and depression.

Poverty is most harmful to young children. They develop fewer cognitive and verbal skills than other children and are more likely to fail in school. In chapter 2, I described a study that showed that parents on welfare, compared to families of professionals, speak as many as twenty million fewer words to their children during their first three years of life (Hart and Risley 1995). Poor parents don't read to their children as much or teach them as many of the rudimentary facts they need in order to be ready for school—for example, colors, shapes, and the names for common objects. These differences arise partly because poorer families have fewer toys and books, and partly because many poor parents simply have less time to interact with their children due to working two jobs or being a single parent. You might think that some of these effects of poverty arise simply because poor parents are less well educated; but some studies have controlled statistically for parents' education and found that, given two families where parents have the same level of education, the family in greater poverty is more likely to have children who fail in school (McLoyd 1998).

Poverty undermines children's development because it hampers effective parenting (McLoyd 1998). Poor adults have many more stressful life experiences, such as layoffs, evictions, forced moves, conflicts with neighbors, and hostile and discriminatory behavior from others. As a result, they experience more anxiety and depression. Poorer parents are also more likely to be sick, not only because of poorer health habits and inadequate health care, but also because poverty is a physical stressor. Of course, physically ill parents are less able to care for their children and more likely to sink deeper into poverty. So it shouldn't come as a surprise that poor parents are less involved with their children, less positive, more critical and angry, and more punitive.

To see how financial stress affects parenting, imagine two days you might have in your life. On one day, you have just lost your job. On the other, you got a raise. On which day would you take some time to play with your kids? On which would you be short-tempered and unwilling to do anything with them?

The farm crisis of the 1980s provides a dramatic example of the impact of economic hardship on families. During the 1970s, the prices of US corn and soybeans soared largely because of Soviet purchases of these commodities. This led to increases in the value of farmland and more borrowing against the value of that land—factors involved in a classic economic bubble. When prices dropped in the 1980s, the bubble burst and suddenly many farmers were deeply in debt. People who had seen their incomes growing were losing their farms. The results were devastating for many families. A nine-county area in southern Iowa had a 10 percent increase in child abuse. Divorce and alcohol abuse soared. In Hills, Iowa, a farmer killed his banker, his neighbor, his wife, and then himself (Manning 2008).

Rand Conger was a scientist at Iowa State University when he studied a sample of families during this period. He documented how economic hardship had a cascading effect on family well-being (Conger and Conger 2008). Parental stress and depression increased, as did marital conflict. As a result, parents were increasingly hostile and coercive toward their children. This made their children more anxious, depressed, and aggressive. Parents didn't do as good a job of setting limits on their adolescents' behavior, and delinquency increased as a result.

I have only recently encountered research on the impact of poverty on physical illness. In a briefing paper from the National Center on Health Statistics (Fryar, Chen, and Li 2012), researchers reported that among those whose income was 130 percent of the poverty level or less, more than 60 percent had at least one of three risk factors for cardiovascular disease (high cholesterol, high blood pressure, or smoking), while among more affluent Americans, fewer than 40 percent had at least one risk factor.

I was particularly disturbed to discover that children raised in poverty have a significantly greater risk of heart disease *as adults* (Galobardes, Lynch, and Smith 2004, 2008). Even if people escape from poverty, as adults they still have a 20 to 40 percent greater risk of heart disease. One study (G. E. Miller et al. 2009) looked into the mechanisms leading to this situation and found that because poverty increases stressful interactions among family members, it permanently alters the stress reactions of young people in ways that lead to inflammatory processes. However, it need not be this way. The same researchers also found that poverty didn't raise the risk of cardiovascular disease for people who were raised in poverty but had nurturing mothers (G. E. Miller et al. 2011).

Poverty is, of course, not just a problem for children. A Gallup study of 288,000 adults found that those who were poor had significantly higher rates of depression (30.9 percent versus 15.8 percent), as well as higher rates of asthma, obesity, diabetes, high blood pressure, and heart attacks (A. Brown 2012).

Sadly, the United States is a world leader in raising poor children. More than 20 percent of our children live in poverty. Of the thirty developed countries tracked by the Organisation for Economic Co-operation and Development, only three (Poland, Turkey, and Mexico) have higher child poverty rates than those in the US.

American policies that maintain such high levels of family poverty are typically advocated on the theory that social welfare programs undermine individual initiative and take money away from individuals and companies that would spend the money more wisely on business investments. But the empirical facts have brought us beyond the point where such general theories should determine public policy. Poor families cost society. As outlined above, they have higher health care costs due to higher rates of obesity, diabetes, cardiovascular disease, and cancer, and they are more likely to have children who fail academically, become delinquents, and have higher rates of depression.

The US obsession with limiting government spending is myopic. At the same time that we are limiting social welfare costs, we are incurring huge costs in medical care, criminal justice, productivity, and quality of life. The situation is contrary to both sound values and good sense.

Finally, poverty simply isn't good for the economy. People with minimal income cannot fully participate in the economy because they don't have sufficient resources to buy the goods and services they need to be fully productive (Whiting 2004). If even half of the families living in poverty were better off, how many more customers would American business have?

The Damage Done by Economic Inequality

It isn't difficult to see that poverty is extremely damaging—not just for the poor, but also for our society. However, a related but less obvious problem is economic inequality, which exerts ill effects that appear to be distinct from those of poverty. UK epidemiologist Richard Wilkinson has taken the lead in looking at this (1992). He and his colleague Kate Pickett reviewed 155 studies of the relationship between economic disparity and health and found that in countries where the lowest proportion of the country's total income went to the poorest 70 percent of families, life expectancy was significantly lower. As indicated in figure 4, the United States did not fare well in comparison to most other countries.

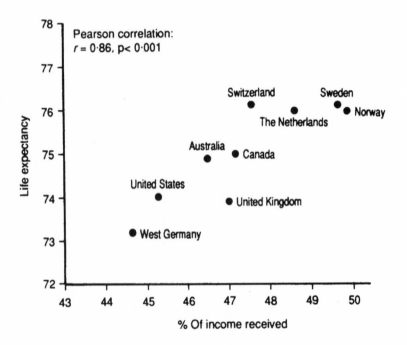

Figure 4. Relation between life expectancy at birth (male and female combined) and percentage of total post-tax and benefit income received by the least-well-off 70 percent of families in 1981. (Reprinted with permission from R. G. Wilkinson. 1992. "Income Distribution and Life Expectancy." *British Medical Journal* 304: 165–168.)

Along similar lines, the US death rate is significantly higher in states where the least-well-off 50 percent have a smaller share of total income (Ross et al. 2000), as indicated in figure 5. This isn't the case in Canadian provinces.

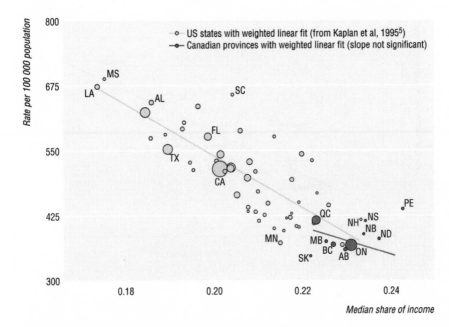

Figure 5. Mortality in working-age men by proportion of income earned by the less-well-off 50 percent of households in US states (1990) and Canadian provinces (1991). (Reprinted with permission from N. A. Ross, M. C. Wolfson, J. R. Dunn, J.-M. Berthelot, G. A. Kaplan, and J. W. Lynch. 2000. "Relation Between Income Inequality and Mortality in Canada and in the United States: Cross-Sectional Assessment Using Census Data and Vital Statistics." *British Medical Journal* 320: 898–902.)

Higher death rates are not the only consequence of inequality. Figure 6 shows the relationship between economic inequality and a host of social and health problems, including mental illness, life expectancy, obesity, children's educational performance, teenage births, homicides, imprisonment rates, social mobility, and level of trust. As you can see, the United States has the highest rate of inequality as measured by the ratio of the income of the top 20 percent of earners to that of the bottom 20 percent.

There is clearly a strong relationship between economic inequality and these diverse social problems.

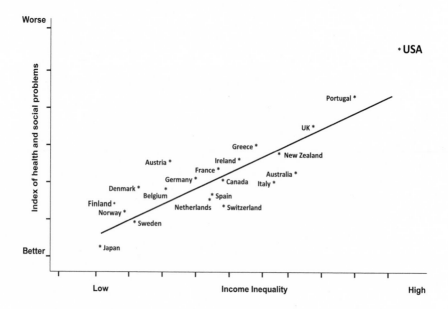

Figure 6. Health and social problems are closely related to inequality in rich countries. (Reprinted with permission from R. Wilkinson and K. Pickett. 2009. *The Spirit Level: Why Greater Equality Makes Societies Stronger.* London: Bloomsbury Press.)

Although health is worse and death rates higher for poorer people than for those who are better off, even wealthier people suffer ill effects from living in unequal societies. Figure 7 shows the rates of various diseases in England and the United States. For each group of three bars, the one on the right represents the group with the highest income, while the one on the left represents those with the lowest income. As expected, disease rates are higher for poorer people. But notice that rates of disease are consistently higher in the United States than in England, where there is less economic inequality—though England is still one of the three countries with the greatest economic inequality.

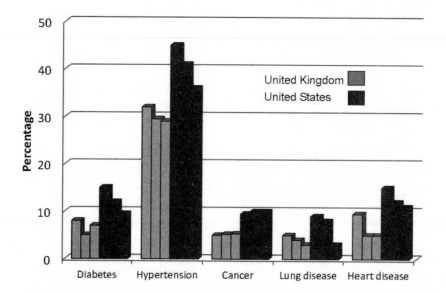

Figure 7. Rates of serious disease in England and United States. (Reprinted with permission from R. Wilkinson and K. Pickett. 2009. *The Spirit Level: Why Greater Equality Makes Societies Stronger.* London: Bloomsbury Press.)

Why would this be? Richard Wilkinson and Kate Pickett (2009) suggest that in societies where social status is important, people measure status by comparing what they have with what others have. They point out that countries with greater economic inequality have higher rates of advertising, which increases people's desire to have things that others don't have. Moreover, countries with greater economic inequality also have more people with materialistic values (Kasser 2011). In essence, people are competing to be richer than those around them.

This is a losing battle. Say you make having a nice car a measure of your worth. You'll start paying attention to cars. You'll soon know the prices of various models and which are deemed better. You can work hard and get yourself a Lexus—well, not the LX at $82,000, but the GX at $49,000. In this scenario, you have spent a bunch of money to enhance your feeling of self-worth, and yet you still don't have the highest-status vehicle. If we measure our worth by money and possessions, we will always be able to find someone who has more. And because we live in a country with greater economic inequality, most of us will always be surrounded by people who are wealthier (unless you are Bill Gates or Warren Buffett). If wealth is your measure of your status, having less than others becomes a source of stress.

The Benefits of Improving Families' Economic Well-Being

Reducing families' economic stress could greatly improve young people's well-being. One study estimated that a $1,000 increase in annual family income would produce a 2.1 percent increase in math scores and a 3.6 percent increase in reading scores (Dahl and Lochner 2012). This effect is probably due to families that are better off having more books and intellectually stimulating toys, as well as more time for interactions between parents and children. If these differences seem small, consider what $10,000 could achieve.

Jane Costello and her colleagues at Duke University provided a dramatic example of the benefits of increasing family income. I got to know Costello when we were serving on an Institute of Medicine committee on prevention. She is one of the most careful researchers looking into what influences the development of mental disorders. She spearheaded the Great Smoky Mountain Study, which focused on what influences children to develop mental disorders (Costello et al. 2003). Her team recruited 1,420 families in western North Carolina and, for each, interviewed a child and a parent every year for eight years.

Their sample included 350 families from the Eastern Band of Cherokee Indians, who lived in two of the counties in North Carolina. The study began in 1993. In 1996, the tribe opened a casino. As a result, every tribal member started receiving payments, including the children, whose money went into trust funds. By 2001, each tribe member was receiving $6,000 annually. In addition, the casino and hotel hired numerous workers, many of whom were members of the tribe.

This was a great natural experiment. Costello and her colleagues could look at the effect of this sudden increase in wealth on the psychological and behavioral problems of the children whose families were lifted out of poverty. Before the casino opened, the poorer children had higher rates of psychiatric symptoms than more well-off children. After the casino opened, the Cherokee children who were lifted out of poverty had no more symptoms than the kids who hadn't been poor initially. Reducing poverty had a direct impact on children's well-being.

In sum, our society's callous disregard for the harm that poverty does to the environments in which families find themselves guarantees a steady stream of poorly raised children—young people who will face challenges in learning and who are less likely to become productive members of society. Instead, they are likely to develop the problems that burden our entire society today—increased crime, drug abuse, unwanted pregnancies, and yet another generation of children who will face the same difficulties. Reducing the number of children who are raised in poverty has clear benefits—not just for them, but for everyone.

Policies That Have Increased Poverty and Economic Inequality

If you are under forty and grew up in the United States, you may never have lived in a country that made reducing poverty a high priority. But there was a time when the most prominent US political leaders made this a high priority—and the majority of Americans supported them. The most passionate and inspiring leader of that era was Robert F. Kennedy. I recall a visit he made to Mississippi in 1967 to call attention to the fact that children were going hungry. It was described in the article "With RFK in the Delta," in the journal *American Heritage* (Carr 2002). The writer of that article, John Carr, was a reporter for the only liberal paper in Mississippi at the time. He describes how Kennedy led reporters to a village of very poor black sharecroppers, where, thanks to recent reductions in pay, many children were malnourished (2002, 93):

The first house we walked into had a refrigerator in a big room. Kennedy opened it. The only item inside was a jar of peanut butter. There was no bread. We walked outside, and he held out his hand to a bunch of young, filthy, ragged but thrilled kids. In a minute or two he was stopped by a short, aging, very heavy black woman in old, baggy clothes. I regret to say that I'd become inured to poverty by a childhood and young adulthood in the Delta, but this poor woman was in awful shape even for Mississippi.

She thanked Senator Kennedy for coming to see them and said that she was too old to be helped by any new program but she hoped the children might be. Kennedy, moved, softly asked her how old she was. "I'm thirty-three," she said. Both he and I recoiled.

When Robert Kennedy ran for president in 1968, I became president of Students for Robert Kennedy at the University of Illinois. It was a time of great hope and inspiration. We were determined to change the terrible conditions less fortunate people faced. If someone had told me then that poverty would be a significant problem in the United States in 2012, I would have dismissed the idea and considered that person to be out of touch with the direction the nation was clearly headed.

But I would have been wrong. Figure 8 shows US Census Bureau data on the rates of poverty in three different age groups: those under eighteen, those eighteen to sixty-four, and those sixty-five and older (DeNavas-Walt, Proctor, and Smith 2010). As you can see, poverty rates declined dramatically between 1959 and about 1970. Then they continued to decline among older Americans, while climbing slightly among eighteen- to sixty-four-year-olds and increasing rather substantially among those under eighteen. In addition, the more recent rates are distinctly higher for young people. And, as I said earlier, the United States has one of the highest child poverty rates among developed countries.

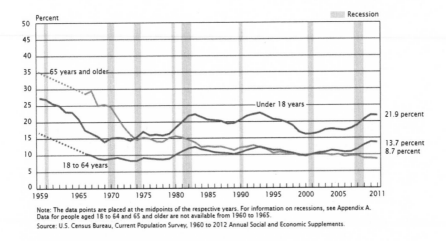

Note: The data points are placed at the midpoints of the respective years. For information on recessions, see Appendix A. Data for people aged 18 to 64 and 65 and older are not available from 1960 to 1965.
Source: U.S. Census Bureau, Current Population Survey, 1960 to 2012 Annual Social and Economic Supplements.

Figure 8. Poverty rates (by percentage) for various age groups in the United States. (Reprinted from DeNavas-Walt, C., B. D. Proctor, and J. C. Smith. 2010. *Income, Poverty, and Health Insurance Coverage in the United States: 2009.* Washington, DC: US Government Printing Office.)

Nor has American society reduced economic inequality. In fact, inequality has steadily climbed. According to the Congressional Budget Office (2011), after-tax income of the top 1 percent of earners increased more than 250 percent between 1979 and 2007, while it increased less than 20 percent for the poorest 20 percent of the population. According to economist Andrew Leigh (2009), the share of total income that goes to the top 1 percent of earners in the United States rose from 8 percent in 1973 to 1975 to nearly 16 percent in 1998 to 2000. By 2007, the Working Group on Extreme Inequality reported that the richest 10 percent of Americans own more than 70 percent of the nation's wealth, with the top 1 percent owning 34 percent of the wealth. In contrast, the bottom 50 percent hold only 2.5 percent of the wealth.

Political scientists Jacob Hacker and Paul Pierson (2010a) have detailed the policy changes over the past forty years that have produced the current situation, wherein the level of inequality in the United States is greater than at any time since 1928. A sizable portion of the disparity resulted from reductions in taxes on the wealthiest. Between 1970 and 2000, the top 0.1 percent of earners increased their share of total national after-tax income from 1.2 percent to 7.3 percent. Had federal policy not reduced their taxation, their share would have increased to only 4.5 percent (Hacker and Pierson 2010a). Other changes in tax policy that have disproportionately benefited the very richest Americans include reductions in the estate tax, changes in the alternative minimum tax, and reduction in the number of IRS audits of the highest earners.

Failure to change outdated policies, including tax policies, has also contributed to the disparity. For example, as unregulated hedge fund activity has expanded, the incomes of hedge fund managers have exploded, with the top twenty-five averaging $600 million *in income* in 2006. Yet due to the way laws were written before hedge funds became a significant activity, these managers are able to treat their income as capital gains and pay income tax at a rate of just 15 percent.

Economic disparity also grew because political leaders failed to update policies in keeping with changes in the economy. Here are some of the most noteworthy examples:

- Failure to index the minimum wage to inflation

- Failure to update or enforce laws regulating the formation of unions

- Failure to adopt health care reforms that could have dealt with the increasing costs of health care for individuals and companies

- Failure to regulate the compensation of CEOs, who, in the United States, earn more than twice the average of their peers in other developed nations

- Failure to regulate new financial instruments, such as derivatives

- Failure to prevent the erosion of company-provided pension plans

Clearly, poverty and economic inequality have grown in the United States over the past forty years in part because public policy has favored these changes. For me, the natural next question is why policies have changed so dramatically in favor of the wealthiest while undermining the well-being of the middle class. These changes must be understood within the broader context of the recent evolution of corporate capitalism, the topic of the next chapter.

Action Implications

If you think the situation is hopeless, you may find the ACT perspective described in chapter 5 helpful. After all, why do we feel distressed about these facts and want to turn away from them? It is because facing them puts us in contact with others' distress and the threat that we too could experience these terrible life outcomes. ACT encourages us to accept these feelings and see that they will not harm us. Indeed, these feelings reflect our empathy for others. If we take action to try to change this situation, that is an example of living and affirming our values, regardless of how much progress we make.

So for anyone who wishes to take action against poverty and economic inequality, the first step is to accept difficult feelings about the situation, rather than struggling with them. The second step is to identify concrete actions we can take to move our society in directions we value.

For Policy Makers

- Request that the Institute of Medicine or the Surgeon General create a report that articulates the epidemiological evidence on the harm of poverty, and that identifies policies that increase or decrease poverty and economic inequality. Such a report would make reducing poverty and economic inequality clear public policy goals. If we are serious about having a society that ensures everyone's well-being, we need to think about these issues in the same way that we think about harmful infectious agents.

- Enact laws that require economic policies to be evaluated in terms of their impact on poverty and inequality. Because poverty and economic inequality are so harmful to well-being, we need to create a system for routinely evaluating how any proposed policies affect them. This would be analogous to policies that require environmental impact analyses before major infrastructure projects can be implemented.

For Citizens

- Campaign for political leaders who will support policies that reduce poverty and economic inequality. It isn't enough to vote for such leaders; we need to work to get them elected in order to create the society we want.

- Join (or create) and generously support organizations aimed at working in favor of policies needed to reduce poverty and inequality.

CHAPTER 9

The Recent Evolution of Corporate Capitalism

If we truly want to ensure the well-being of everyone, we can't stop at providing strong family, school, and community interventions. We also must be concerned about economic policy.

A profound example comes from a study that examined the impact of the 2008 recession on US suicides (Reeves et al. 2012). The suicide rate increased four times faster between 2008 and 2010 than it had in the eight previous years. The researchers estimated that the increase led to an additional 1,500 suicides. Because the recession occurred because of public policies, including banking deregulation and failure to regulate financial vehicles such as credit default swaps (McLean and Nocera 2010), it appears that economic policy had a direct impact on how many people killed themselves. And while suicide is a devastating and tragic outcome, it is only one way in which the recession harmed well-being.

I am sure no one involved in these policies set out to cause suicides. But once we know that a public policy does harm, we need to factor that knowledge into our policy making. First, however, we need to understand what drives policy making.

A Contextual Approach to Policy Making

It might seem that studying the influences on policy making requires entirely new conceptual tools. And in terms of both science and practical action, we know far less about how to influence corporate practices that affect policy making than we do about influencing the behavior of individuals. However, the behavioral science revolution is lapping at the door to this problem. Thanks to David Sloan Wilson's leadership, an increasing number of scientists working in diverse areas of the human sciences are coming to see that their efforts are best organized within an evolutionary framework. B. F. Skinner's notion that behavior is selected by its consequences is simply the application of evolutionary thinking to the evolution of behavior, rather than to organisms.

That same principle of selection by consequences is useful for understanding corporate behavior. Corporate practices are selected and maintained by their consequences in the same way that the behavior of individuals is selected by reinforcing consequences (Biglan and Cody 2013). For both people and corporations, the ultimate consequence is survival. People and corporations don't survive if they don't achieve outcomes that enable them to survive. In a capitalist system, a corporation's survival is a matter of achieving profits.

Let's revisit what I said about the development of the behavioral science revolution in the 1960s and 1970s. Initially, there was virtually no evidence that reinforcing consequences shapes human behavior. But a small group of scientists felt compelled to explore this possibility based on strong evidence from animal studies indicating that consequences affect animal behavior. In addition, evolutionary theory led early behaviorists to doubt that humans were somehow exempt from the effects of reinforcement. What ensued was an incredible accumulation of evidence and practical strategies for influencing behavior.

I believe we are at a similar place with respect to the behavior of organizations. Evolutionary principles suggest that it is extremely likely that organizational practices are selected by their material consequences. Indeed, David Sloan Wilson and his colleagues have enumerated many examples of the selection of group practices from realms as diverse as eusocial insects, such as bees and ants, to the Good Behavior Game to the evolution of religions (D. S. Wilson 2003, 2007).

Just as a person will continue to engage in a behavior that has had favorable consequences, a corporation will continue and expand a practice that results in revenue growth. For example, consider the marketing practices of the tobacco industry discussed previously. That industry innovated in the marketing of cigarettes, and when they found a campaign that worked, they continued it and then refined it. When a campaign failed, they abandoned it and tried something else.

Unfortunately, the fundamental role of selection by consequences is obscured by myriad other ways of thinking about corporations and their practices. I submit that analyzing and testing the impact of consequences on corporate practices would give policy makers and citizens the tools they need to influence the further evolution of corporate practices (Biglan 2009, 2011; Biglan and Cody 2013). Therefore, in this chapter, I provide a brief history of the evolution of corporate practices relevant to the developments I described in chapters 7 and 8. I hope to convince you that both harmful marketing practices and economic policies have evolved as a function of the completely understandable efforts of corporations and wealthy individuals to maximize their gains.

The Powell Memo

Jacob Hacker, a political scientist at Yale, and Paul Pierson, a political scientist at the University of California Berkeley, recently provided a thorough analysis of the political and policy developments that increased poverty and inequality in the United States over the last forty years (Hacker and Pierson 2010a). They credit a 1971 memo from Lewis F. Powell for inspiring a massive redesign of corporate America's advocacy for business-friendly policies. Powell wrote the memo for his friend and neighbor Eugene Sydnor, Jr., the chairman of the US Chamber of Commerce Education Committee. The memo, dated August 23, 1971, argued that there was a growing attack on the free enterprise system (1971, 2–3):

> The most disquieting voices joining the chorus of criticism come from perfectly respectable elements of society: from the college campus, the pulpit, the media, the intellectual and literary journals, the arts and sciences, and from politicians. In most of these groups the movement against the system is participated in only by minorities. Yet, these often are the most articulate, the most vocal, the most prolific in their writing and speaking.
>
> Moreover, much of the media—for varying motives and in varying degrees—either voluntarily accord unique publicity to these

"attackers," or at least allow them to exploit the media for their purposes. This is especially true of television, which now plays such a predominant role in shaping the thinking, attitudes, and emotions of our people.

The business community's concerns were well justified. During the 1960s and early 1970s, many people were highly suspicious of business. Young people were loath to pursue careers in business, and the public strongly favored policies that were hostile to business. Powell was simply describing, in a dispassionate way, some of the reasons that business was viewed so negatively.

Powell said that the business community's response to the problem involved "appeasement, ineptitude, and ignoring the problem" (1971, 8). Rather than each company simply pursuing its own business interests, Powell argued that companies needed to be "equally concerned with protecting and preserving the system itself" (10). He called for an effort to accrue political power through "united action and national organizations [that would engage in] careful long-range planning and implementation [and] consistency of action over an indefinite period of years, [with a] scale of financing available only through joint effort" (11).

In the memo Powell proposed specific steps the business community could take. The first was to increase support on college campuses for conservative intellectual efforts. He argued that top colleges were producing graduates who held strong antibusiness views and were moving into influential roles in the media. If the business community could strengthen support for conservative points of view on college campuses, they could create a cadre of well-trained advocates of conservative viewpoints who would increase public support for conservative values when they graduated and moved into leadership positions in society.

Second, Powell recommended creation of a group of "eminent scholars, writers, and speakers, who will do the thinking, the analysis, the writing, and the speaking" (21), as well as personnel "who are thoroughly familiar with the media, and how most effectively to communicate with the public" (21). Third, he recommended that conservative scholars be encouraged to publish in scholarly journals, popular magazines, and books. Fourth, he proposed that businesses be encouraged to devote some of their advertising budgets to advocacy of the free enterprise system, rather than simply promotion of their products or company. Fifth, he urged more vigorous pursuit of political power (25–26):

> Business must learn the lesson, long ago learned by Labor and other self-interest groups. This is the lesson that political power is necessary; that such power must be assiduously cultivated; and that when necessary, it must be used aggressively and with determination—without embarrassment and without the reluctance which has been so characteristic of American business.

The sixth thing Powell advocated was to develop organizations that would litigate on behalf of the interests of conservatives. He cited the American Civil Liberties Union as a model for well-organized efforts to influence judicial decisions on behalf of a point of view. Seventh, he suggested that the business community help stockholders organize and advocate for the free enterprise system.

Powell noted that the strategy he outlined would require substantial investment from the business community. The money was forthcoming. Through their foundations, a number of very wealthy individuals and families have funded the development of a network of organizations that support all of the conservative efforts that Powell proposed. These backers include Richard Mellon Scaife, the Coors family, Smith Richardson, and John Merrill Olin. Lewis Lapham, writing in *Harper's* in 2004, estimated that the resulting foundations were worth about two billion dollars. He cited Rob Stein as estimating that these foundations had contributed more than three billion dollars to conservative advocacy efforts over the previous three decades.

All of the things Powell advocated are now in place. A system of scholarships supports conservative scholars at America's elite universities. Lapham estimated that scholarships amounting to $39 million were available to support conservative students in 2001, $16 million of that at Harvard, Yale, and the University of Chicago. There is financial support for writing, publishing, and promoting books, magazine articles, op-ed pieces, and scholarly articles that advocate conservative viewpoints. A network of think tanks supports conservative scholarship and advocacy and produces reports, newsletters, briefing papers, and op-ed pieces that dominate public discussion. The network includes the Heritage

Foundation, the American Enterprise Institute, the Cato Institute, the Hoover Institution, the Hudson Institute, the Manhattan Institute for Policy Research, Citizens for a Sound Economy, the National Center for Policy Analysis, the Competitive Enterprise Institute, the Free Congress Foundation, and the Business Roundtable. Lapham estimated that the 2001 annual budgets of the major think tanks totaled $136 million. These organizations supply a steady stream of conservative opinion leaders who regularly appear on television news and talk shows. This system of organizations exerts considerable influence on public opinion, making it more favorable to the needs and interests of business.

Leftist discussions of the Powell memo often characterize it as sinister. But, in truth, it is a fairly balanced and dispassionate analysis of the reasons why, in 1971, public support for policies favoring business was at a low point (15):

> Few things are more sanctified in American life than academic freedom. It would be fatal to attack this as a principle. But if academic freedom is to retain the qualities of "openness," "fairness," and "balance"—which are essential to its intellectual significance— there is a great opportunity for constructive action. The thrust of such action must be to restore the qualities just mentioned to the academic communities.

Powell simply laid out the avenues that are available in a free society to promote policies favorable to business. These interests had huge amounts of money available to them, but the basic principles they employed are applicable to any group's efforts to influence public policy making.

The results of these efforts have been remarkable. Compare the political landscape of 1964 with that of 2014. In 1964, both the federal government and public opinion were decidedly liberal. Lyndon Johnson won the election with 61 percent of the vote. Democrats picked up two Senate seats and thirty-six House seats and had a two-thirds majority in both houses of Congress. Indeed, from 1933, at the height of the great depression, through 1995, a period of sixty-two years, the Democrats controlled the House of Representatives for all but two years. For fourteen of the eighteen years after 1995, the Republicans were in control. In 2014 Republicans controlled the House of Representatives, with 233 Republicans to 199 Democrats. They also controlled 45 Senate seats. Although the latter isn't a majority, it is sufficient to allow them to block legislation and appointments by threatening filibusters.

There have also been huge changes in the nature of public discussion and in public policy making since 1964. Whereas the majority of Democrats considered themselves liberals in 1964, only about one-third of Democrats do so now, and the term "liberal" has become an epithet. The Republicans in leadership positions are all conservatives, and the party is far more conservative than it was in 1964. Furthermore, a Democrat, Bill Clinton—whose policies included welfare reform, balancing the budget, and reducing the federal workforce by about 350,000—declared in his 1996 State of the Union address that the era of big government is over. Finally, government regulation of business has dwindled significantly since the 1960s.

In sum, recognizing that generalized advocacy for conservative points of view would serve their interests, a number of wealthy people invested in creating an infrastructure to influence public opinion and policy making. As the benefits of these efforts became noticeable, increasing amounts of money flowed to the network of organizations working for conservative causes. Major financial instruments such as derivatives were completely unregulated, and as a result, we experienced the worst economic downturn since the great depression (McLean and Nocera 2010).

If the evolution of these corporate and business practices was due to the economic consequences to the individuals and organizations that engaged in them, we should find that businesses benefit from the changes in policy. And indeed they did. As discussed in chapter 8, between 1970 and 2000 the top 0.1 percent of earners increased their share of total national after-tax income from 1.2 to 7.3 percent (Hacker and Pierson 2010a). Moreover, in 1980, chief executives of American corporations made forty-two times what the average blue-collar worker earned. They now make 331 times what the average blue-collar worker earns (Dill 2014).

Capitalism from an Evolutionary Perspective

The changes I've documented are among the most important cultural events of the last forty years. Understanding how and why practices and policies evolved in this way could help us influence the further evolution of policy making and politics in directions that will benefit more people.

You might think of capitalism as evolution on steroids. Just as the behavior of individuals is selected by the consequences of that behavior, the practices of corporations and other businesses are selected in a process that is finely tuned by the marketplace. Quarterly profits quickly reveal whether a company is succeeding. Profitable activities are expanded both through the influx of funds to the company and as other companies adopt a successful company's profitable practices. Variation is assured due to new people entering the marketplace and the continuous invention of new products and services.

These factors result in selection of organizations that are increasingly skilled at discerning what will enhance their profits. The contingencies select *any* practice that contributes to profits, regardless of whether it is beneficial more broadly. Improving products and services is certainly a critical practice, and it is generally beneficial. However, many other practices are detrimental. These include the marketing practices I described in chapter 7, as well as lobbying for favorable government policies or contracts, minimizing costs of labor and materials, and undermining the success of competitors. Indeed, over the past one hundred years, all of these practices have been refined by their economic contingencies.

Marketing and lobbying deserve particular attention in relation to our concern for nurturing human well-being. Since the early 1900s, marketing has expanded enormously thanks to its contribution to profits. In the tobacco industry—a leading innovator in advertising over the last century—advertising has been critical to the expansion of markets. Few women smoked before Lucky Strike began its "Reach for a Lucky Instead of a Sweet" campaign in the mid-1920s.

Lobbying has greatly expanded in the past twenty years, particularly because it has proven increasingly profitable to invest in getting government to change policies and contract with private companies for work the government traditionally conducted. In 2009, registered lobbyists reported spending nearly $3.5 billion, a record amount (Hacker and Pierson 2010b).

Just as marketing and lobbying practices of individual corporations have evolved, a cooperative network of business and advocacy organizations has evolved over the last forty years. This network has been shaped and maintained by its economic consequences, including increased profits, increased political influence that helps maintain profitability, and increased income for the people who lead these organizations.

In essence, the network of business and advocacy organizations has changed the public perception of the value of government, regulation, and redistribution policies. Effective advocacy for business-friendly beliefs and policies led to deregulation of corporate practices. As government regulation of unsafe, unhealthy, or economically disastrous practices has declined, practices have increasingly been determined by the marketplace, which selects whatever works to increase short-term profits. Throughout, general well-being has steadily receded as a value that influences policy making.

I want to stress that this is not a critique of capitalism per se. The benefits of the evolutionary process that is capitalism are evident in all of the products and services that have evolved in the last two hundred years, including the computer on which I am writing this book. However, we need to evolve a system that retains the benefits of capitalism while also restraining its worst excesses.

Increasing Materialism

Substantial changes in the goals and values of Americans have accompanied changes in the political and economic structure of US society. For the past four decades, the Higher Education Research Institute has been surveying incoming freshmen at 1,201 colleges and universities (Astin 2002). These surveys show that the percentage of freshmen who said that being very well-off financially was essential or very important hovered around 40 percent in the late 1960s and early 1970s and then rose steadily to more than 70 percent by the mid-1980s, remaining at that level ever since. In the 1960s, more than 80 percent said that developing a meaningful life philosophy was important, and that number declined steadily until the mid-1980s, at which point it leveled off in the 40 to 50 percent range (Astin 2002).

Jean Twenge, a social psychologist at San Diego State University, has worked with colleagues around the country to analyze changes in the values and aspirations of high school and college students across the years (Twenge 2009; Twenge and Campbell 2008). Her analysis of data from

Monitoring the Future, an annual survey of high school students, found sizable increases in the proportion of youth who say that money is important, buying things you don't need is okay, and doing your own thing is a good idea. Twenge also studied the extent of narcissism, or inflated self-absorption, among college students across the country and found that between 1985 and 2006 the level of narcissism increased significantly (Twenge and Campbell 2009; Twenge and Foster 2010; Twenge et al. 2008).

Other researchers who analyzed data from Monitoring the Future (Wray-Lake, Flanagan, and Osgood 2010) found that the proportion of youth who said that wealth was important rose from 45 percent in 1976 to 63 percent by 2005. In addition, the percent of young people who said that most people can be trusted dropped from 31.5 percent in 1976 to 19.7 percent in 2001.

Is Materialism Beneficial?

Given the unquestionable benefits that capitalism has provided in improved technology, transportation, health, and wealth, it might seem good that people are becoming more materialistic. The more people desire material goods, the harder they will work for them, and the more productive society will be.

However, research on materialism shows that there is a decidedly dark side to pursuing this value. Tim Kasser, a social psychologist at Knox College in Illinois, has been studying materialism for the past twenty years. He and his colleagues have identified two clusters of goals: one involving being popular, financially successful, and attractive, and the other centering around having satisfying relationships with others, improving the world through selfless action, and accepting oneself. In a series of studies (for example, Kasser 2004; Schmuck, Kasser, and Ryan 2000), Kasser and his colleagues found that people tend to endorse one or the other cluster, rather than both. So some people are motivated to have fame and fortune, while others want to make their lives about self-development, caring relationships, and helping their community.

It turns out that people who endorse materialistic goals aren't very happy. In fact, they have many problems (Kasser and Ryan 1993, 1996). College students who endorse materialistic values are more likely to be depressed and anxious and less satisfied with their lives. They report more unpleasant emotions, fewer pleasant emotions, and more physical symptoms and drug and alcohol use. Adolescents who aspire to be rich are more aggressive and uncooperative. Parents with a strong focus on having money and status are less warm and more controlling toward their children. People with materialistic goals are less empathetic, less cooperative, and more greedy when playing a game that involves the sharing of resources. Not surprisingly, they are also more likely to live an environmentally damaging lifestyle.

Given all these downsides, why do people embrace materialism? One answer lies in a study involving three experiments that exposed people to various kinds of threats; in it, Kasser found that threat increases people's materialistic tendencies (Sheldon and Kasser 2008). In the first experiment, half of the subjects were asked to briefly describe their emotions in response to the thought of their own death and to briefly describe what they imagine will happen to them after death. The other subjects answered similar questions about their experience of listening to music. The people who thought about their death were significantly more likely to endorse goals about being rich and famous.

In the second experiment, Kasser's team simply asked people to imagine that a year later they would be either employed and financially secure or unemployed and on shaky ground financially. Those who imagined being insecure endorsed materialistic goals more strongly. The third and final experiment found that people were more likely to endorse materialistic values when they were asked to think about someone "who clearly likes you, tends to be very evaluative of you, and seems to accept you only to the extent that you live up to certain standards of performance" (Sheldon and Kasser 2008, 42).

If you think about this from an evolutionary perspective, it makes sense that when people feel threatened, they focus on having the material and social resources they need to survive. These are the reinforcers they need and seek. Thinking about your own death or financial insecurity naturally focuses the mind on having safety and security. This may be one reason why poorer people are more likely to endorse materialistic values. Similarly, thinking about people who only like you if you measure up to their standards makes the possibility of being rejected more salient, which will probably increase your desire to be accepted.

You may be entertaining the possibility that, for all its harm to individuals, maybe this is just a cost we must endure to have a society with high levels of material well-being. Yet here too, Kasser has found just the opposite, using data on the values of people in twenty different countries (Grouzet et al. 2005; Kasser 2011; Schmuck, Kasser, and Ryan 2000). The countries differed in how much people endorsed values having to do with harmony and egalitarianism versus mastery of the environment and hierarchical relations among people. As it turned out, the more a country's population valued harmony and egalitarianism, the greater the well-being of the country's children, as measured by a UNICEF index of forty indicators of well-being. In addition, the countries that endorsed harmony and egalitarianism had more generous parental leave policies and lower carbon dioxide emissions. The strongest relationships, however, had to do with the amount of advertising to children. Countries that endorsed mastery and hierarchical relationships had much more advertising targeting children. I suspect that this is because advertising increases not only people's desire for material goods, but also their concern about whether they have high social status.

Evolution in the Wrong Direction

Evidence seems to be converging that, for at least the past fifty years, cultural evolution in the United States has been taking us where we don't want to go. As detailed in earlier chapters, research by economists, sociologists, and psychologists indicates that more children are being raised in poverty, and that poverty contributes to family conflict. Psychologists, including Jerry Patterson, have shown that the moment-to-moment interactions within stressed families are marked by conflict and coercion that put children on the road to aggressive social behavior, crime, drug abuse, academic failure, and early childbearing (Biglan et al. 2004). Neuroscientists have delineated the physiological processes that underpin the effects of conflict and threat and wire people to be biased toward aggression, materialism, and all of the just-mentioned problems (Bardo, Fishbein, and Milich 2011). Research by social psychologists, including Tim Kasser, suggests that threatening conditions in families and schools tilt people toward the endorsement of self-aggrandizing, materialistic values (Sheldon and Kasser 2008). These values, in turn, contribute to societies that place a high premium on materialism, do a poorer job of ensuring children's well-being, and fail to sustain the environment. Thus, we have a classic vicious cycle in which harsh, nonnurturing conditions produce a large number of threatened, self-focused, materialistic people who support policies that maintain these harsh and nonnurturing environments.

It is virtually impossible to say whether conservative advocacy influenced the increase in materialism, whether materialism increased support for conservative policy, or whether each increased the other. What is clear, however, is that over the past fifty years, the United States has become a more ideologically conservative, more materialistic, and less trusting place—and a nation that is not providing the material support for families or the programs, practices, and policies that behavioral science shows can improve the well-being of most Americans.

Changing the Consequences for Corporate Practices

If a corporate practice is shown to have a negative impact on well-being and our goal is to improve individuals' well-being, it makes sense to establish a goal of ending or limiting that practice. Yet on a practical level, what do we know about changing the practices of corporations? To some extent, contingency management of corporate behavior is already in place to accomplish this, but not as much as it should be, given the central role of consequences. For example, we can make harmful practices less desirable by taxing them or levying fines on them. The government could fine cigarette companies for every smoker under the age of twenty-one who became addicted to their brand. Or there could be a fine for every alcohol-related car crash among those under twenty-one, levied against the company that produced the beverage involved in the crash. Product liability lawsuits can also produce negative consequences for companies, although the National Restaurant Association has been able to encourage several state legislatures to pass what are deemed "commonsense consumption" laws, which prevent individuals from pursuing obesity-related litigation (Strom 2011).

However, a thorough analysis of selection by consequences suggests more innovative strategies, in particular, using positive consequences to shift corporate practices. Positive strategies could reduce corporate resistance to efforts to change harmful practices. For example, given the growing evidence for the value of foods high in omega-3 fatty acids, food companies could receive tax incentives for marketing such foods. If we want an industry to agree to change a practice, it may initially be more effective to make it profitable to adopt the new practice than to punish the industry for a problematic practice. We could then slowly withdraw incentives for the change once it has been widely enough adopted. Among the many merits of this approach is that it takes into account that corporations are currently very skilled at influencing policy making, and that they are much more likely to fight policies that punish certain practices than policies that offer remuneration for favorable practices.

The Critical Role of Advocacy Organizations

The major obstacle to altering any of these contingencies is, of course, the power of companies to control public opinion and influence government regulatory practices. The most promising strategy I can see for countering the influence of entrenched and powerful organizations is to strengthen the practices of organizations working for change. I've already described how a system of tobacco control organizations evolved and became more effective in influencing the culture of tobacco use. Similar systems are evolving with respect to alcohol problems, although they are only beginning to address marketing practices.

Mothers Against Drunk Driving (MADD) provides an excellent example of what we can accomplish. Thanks to MADD, the rate of drunk driving and alcohol-related car crashes has declined substantially. Since 1980, when MADD was founded, the number of alcohol-related motor vehicle deaths declined by 53 percent, with as many as 150,000 deaths being prevented by reductions in drunk driving (National Transportation Safety Board 2013).

MADD was created by Candy Lightner, whose thirteen-year-old daughter was killed by a hit-and-run drunk driver. Prior to MADD, drunk driving wasn't seen as harmful in quite the way it is today. Then MADD mobilized thousands of victims of drunk driving and the families of victims to form hundreds of chapters around the country, all demanding stronger laws against drunk driving. They were extremely effective. For example, in 1984 the drinking age was raised to twenty-one in all states. Studies have shown that this significantly reduced alcohol consumption by young people and, with it, alcohol-related car crashes (Wagenaar and Toomey 2002). In essence, MADD created a virtuous cycle in which advocacy influenced both the adoption of stronger laws against drunk driving and people's beliefs about the appropriateness of drunk driving. As the public heard about the changes in laws and about people being prosecuted for drunk driving, they became more likely to disapprove of drunk driving and less likely to do it themselves.

A Comprehensive Strategy

The work of the tobacco- and alcohol-control organizations demonstrates that specific corporate policies can be shifted by changing the consequences of corporate behavior. Unfortunately, the influence of corporations on public policy, and thereby human well-being, as described earlier in this chapter, calls for more comprehensive efforts to reform capitalism. We need to evolve a network of advocacy organizations that promote policies, norms, and practices that will enhance well-being.

We also need an umbrella organization that can lead and coordinate the efforts of this network of organizations. Most nonprofit organizations currently working to increase human well-being focus on a narrow range of problems, and concentrate on the major influences on those problems; in doing so they fail to focus on fundamental underlying conditions that affect most problems of human behavior. For example, Mothers Against Drunk Driving has done an excellent job of getting policies enacted that reduce drunk driving. However, to my knowledge they haven't done anything to address family conflict or poverty, both of which contribute to the development of alcoholism.

An umbrella organization could support the efforts of all the individual organizations by coordinating joint action when doing so is likely to be helpful. Perhaps more importantly, it could advocate for changes that would affect fundamental conditions in ways that increase nurturance of and in families, schools, workplaces, and communities, thereby addressing virtually all of the psychological, behavioral, and health problems that are so costly to our society.

One of the obstacles to creating such umbrella advocacy organizations involves the limits on what nonprofit organizations can do. Despite the fact that nonprofit organizations and foundations have evolved to provide benefits to society that neither for-profit companies nor government provide, current regulations limit their ability to work for changes in public policies that are critical to reducing poverty and economic inequality or to moderating other harmful corporate practices.

We need to develop a model policy for the creation of a new type of advocacy organization that is chartered to advocate for those policies, programs, and practices that have been empirically proven to increase human well-being. Such a policy would identify a set of health, behavioral, and economic outcomes that have been shown to increase the prevalence of well-being in the general population. Under this policy, nonprofit organizations would be able to specify one or more of these outcomes to target. Harking back to the early days of capitalism, when corporations were chartered by governments for a fixed time and a fixed purpose, these corporations would be chartered by the government and required to specify a plan of action over a fixed time—say, ten years—and that plan would have to be deemed likely to advance beneficial policies and practices by a panel of experts. The plan would also need to include evaluation of its impact, with renewal of the organization's charter depending on evidence of success.

For example, if an umbrella advocacy organization seeks to create a network of supportive organizations, it could test its strategy for doing so by applying that strategy to successive sets of organizations, measuring how many join the effort at each stage and refining its approach with each iteration. If a policy to restrict a marketing practice is adopted, its impact can be evaluated by assessing its success in achieving the intended outcome. Only through empirical evaluation can we effectively strengthen advocacy organizations and influence problematic organizational practices.

Action Implications

The major policies that will affect whether families and schools are nurturing include those that target the redistribution of wealth, those with a focus on providing programs that support nurturing environments in families and schools, and those that restrain corporations from engaging in financial and other practices that harm individuals, the entire economy, or the environment. Both policy makers and individuals can play a role in enacting such policies.

For Policy Makers

- Develop a model policy for the creation of a new type of advocacy organization that is chartered to promote policies, programs, and practices that have been empirically proven to improve human well-being.

- Require these advocacy organizations to conduct empirical evaluations of their effectiveness in order to retain their charter.

- Fund further research on the impacts of marketing practices on child and adolescent health and well-being.

For Citizens

- Make a list of two or three changes that you would like to see in your community. Then identify one or two local, state, or national organizations that you think are making a difference or could do so. Join those organizations. Support them and advocate that they take helpful actions.

- Join and support organizations that work on one or a few societal problems or on the reform of corporate capitalist practices.

PART 4

Evolving the Nurturing Society

Can we translate all that we have learned about human behavior in the past forty years into truly revolutionary changes in society? I think we can.

In part 2 of this book, I enumerated how much we have learned about how to help families and schools nurture the successful development of children and adolescents and the powerful methods that have been created to help adults with psychological and behavioral problems. In part 3, I described the changes we need in the larger social system of corporate capitalism in order to fully realize the well-being of every member of society.

Here, in the final part of the book, I pull all of this together to describe how we can use our accumulated scientific knowledge about human behavior to produce improvements in human well-being that go beyond anything ever achieved in human history. If that seems like hyperbole, remember how long it took to communicate with someone on the other side of the world in 1850—before science created telephone networks and the Internet.

In chapter 10, I discuss how and why achieving caring relationships is foundational for progress in every facet of society, from families to corporate boardrooms. Then in chapter 11, I envision the movement we can create to make nurturing environments a reality throughout society.

CHAPTER 10

In Caring Relationships with Others

As I mentioned in chapter 1, the Institute of Medicine's report on prevention envisioned a society that we could achieve in which virtually all young people "arrive at adulthood with the skills, interests, assets, and health habits needed to live healthy, happy, and productive lives in caring relationships with others" (IOM and NRC 2009, 387). Imagine what it would be like if we put all of our energies into building caring relationships among people. Suppose we let instructional practices in schools stay as they are, didn't work on changing policies that affect economic well-being, and didn't directly work on reducing global warming; rather, we concentrated solely on cultivating a society in which the highest value and most important priority was that people care for each other. Suppose we were to achieve a society in which, in every contact, we first paid attention to how the other person was doing, and when we saw situations that could harm others' well-being, we worked to alter those situations. What would it be like if, each day, we got up and tried to contribute to the comfort, safety, skill, and success of those around us?

I am convinced that caring relationships are the fundamental building blocks for creating the nurturing environments that are vital to everyone's well-being, and thus achieving the larger goals to which we aspire. In part 2, I focused on relationships in families, schools, and young people's peer groups. As the programs, policies, and practices I described become more widely available, our young people will increasingly go out into the world with the values and skills needed to live in caring relationships with others. However, it is much more likely that we will support this trend if caring relationships become foundational—not only to families and schools, but to all other relationships in society.

Imagine that Fortune 500 companies supported policies that enhanced the nurturance of families and schools because the executive leadership of these companies embraced the value of caring relationships. Would the materialism that so distorts our values and policy making recede? Would everyone insist on economic policies that ensured all members of society had their basic material needs met? How much more likely is it that young people's caring would be nurtured if people throughout society—from grocers, policemen, and physicians to religious leaders, coaches, businesspeople, and neighbors—all embraced and acted on the value of caring for others?

If the well-being of others were at the forefront of our daily thinking, might we also be more likely to work for policies to reduce climate change and other environmental problems? And while successful pursuit of caring relationships might not result in the lion lying down with the lamb, if it became a worldwide feature of human relationships, it would certainly make war a bit less likely.

As a reminder of what I mean by "caring," a good approximation is provided by the four features of nurturing I described in chapter 1: In caring relationships, we minimize toxic conditions, from coercive behavior to biological toxins such as cigarette smoke. We richly reinforce other people's prosocial behavior. We limit negative influences and opportunities. And we promote psychological flexibility.

I'll elaborate on psychological flexibility later in this chapter. But I'd like to begin by exploring the opposite of caring relationships—namely, coercive relationships. Understanding how and why coercive relationships arise illuminates what is needed to cultivate caring relationships.

Coercion: The Main Obstacle to Caring

In chapter 1, I argued that coercion—the use of aversive behavior in an attempt to terminate someone else's aversive behavior—is the fundamental process driving human conflict. There is no shortage of types of conflict and coercion: war, genocide, murder, harassment, bullying, cheating, child abuse, marital conflict, discriminatory behavior; the list goes on. All of this cruelty is rooted in the kind of moment-to-moment coercive interactions I described in chapter 1. Humans are finely tuned to learn strategies that reduce others' aversive behavior, and we readily learn to counteraggress to get immediate relief.

Unless we are fortunate to have people around us who patiently ignore our most irritating behaviors and richly reinforce our prosocial behavior, we end up living in a world where people use aversive means to ward off others' aversive behavior. Conflict-ridden families, schools, and communities are crucibles that create a constant stream of threatened, hostile, and aggressive children and send them out into the world as adults. These damaged people often raise their own children using the same coercive practices their parents used on them. Blaming them simply adds more aversives into the mix. It is also unfair. Recent research on epigenetics shows that being raised in a threatening environment can wire people to have a heightened sensitivity to threat and more aggressive reactions to others—traits they pass on to their children (Jablonka and Raz 2009).

The Evolutionary Roots of Coercion

Unfortunately, just as our inherited preference for high-fat foods and sugar leads to heart disease and diabetes in the modern era, inherited tendencies for dealing with aversives don't serve us well in the modern world. Evolutionarily speaking, organisms that were quick to respond to threat were a bit more likely to survive, and we therefore inherited a propensity to counterattack. While this may often produce short-term gain, it causes us to live in a world filled with people who have a hair-trigger response to anyone else's threatening behavior. In fact, the hair trigger is itself a biologically created bias toward seeing others' behavior as threatening.

One of the biggest dangers to humans is other humans, and not just because other humans may harm or attack us. There is also the threat that our own group may exclude us. Unlike cougars, humans are ill equipped to survive on their own. Thus, even a frown of disapproval constitutes a threatening stimulus.

As humans evolved, being quick and effective in attacking those who threatened us had great survival value. We have gotten very good at counteraggression thanks to our capacity to be reinforced by anything that terminates others' aversive or threatening behavior or by signs that those who are threatening us are harmed or frightened. Combined, our sensitivity to threat and the success of coercive behaviors in producing immediate, albeit temporary, cessation of others' aversive behavior have led to humans developing coercive relationships quite readily.

As I recounted in chapters 1 through 3, reducing coercive relations in families and schools is critical to nurturing the development of prosocial behavior and preventing patterns of problematic behavior. But reducing or eliminating coercion is also critical in most every human relationship. A physician who is quick to be defensive or irritable with a patient may keep that patient from complaining, but this isn't good for either the patient or the physician. Coercion may help a husband in getting his wife to not complain about his behavior, but it is likely to contribute to constant or escalating conflict and, ultimately, the dissolution of the relationship. A prison guard using coercive tactics to keep a prisoner "in line" may further motivate him to be angry and aggressive. Coworkers may coercively damp down each other's aversive behavior, but it may come at the cost of effective cooperation. A coach may think he is teaching his players to be "tough," but his constant criticism will turn many young people away from sports entirely.

Human verbal relational abilities further extend our tendency to develop and maintain coercive relationships. We can remember being slighted by someone years ago. We can anticipate future harm and may treat others badly simply because we think they intend to harm us.

Our social, cooperative tendencies and our language abilities are intertwined in ways that further support coercive interactions. In work organizations, I've often observed a tendency for two people who are in conflict to recruit social support for their own sides of the argument. We are naturally avoidant of confrontation. If someone isn't treating us well, we fear (often with good reason) that confronting the person will simply bring on more aversive behavior. As a result, we often tell a friend, who naturally will listen sympathetically and probably try to help us feel better about it. Unfortunately, this often leads to mutually hostile cliques, because it is highly likely that the other person also has friends in whom she confides.

In the projects I have directed, my policy regarding hostility between coworkers has always been to bring the two people together to discuss their concerns. Boy, do people resist such conversations. But my experience has virtually always been that people get along better if they talk to each other directly in a context of organizational norms that favor cooperation and respect.

The Physiological Costs of Coercion

Robert Sapolsky's book *Why Zebra's Don't Get Ulcers* (1994) explains the physiology involved in interpersonal conflict. Say your toddler gets upset because her brother hit her. This stressor causes her hypothalamus to release corticotropin-releasing hormone, which stimulates the anterior pituitary to release adrenocorticotropic hormone, which in turn stimulates the adrenal gland to release cortisol. This cascade of hormones raises blood pressure, heart rate, and blood glucose and mobilizes the child to either fight or flee—even though neither option may be the best in this circumstance. She cries and screams, which sets off the same cascade of stress responses in *you*, mobilizing you to fight or flee, neither of which is the best move for you or your family.

In his book, Sapolsky reveals how chronic stress reactions contribute to a wide range of physical illnesses, including insomnia, colds, irritable bowel syndrome, ulcers, miscarriages, memory impairment, major depression, hypertension, cardiovascular disease, adult-onset diabetes, osteoporosis, immune suppression, drug addiction, and stunted growth.

The most important stressor we humans typically face comes in the form of coercive interactions with other humans. For example, one study (Eaker et al. 2007) found that married women who self-silenced during conflict, keeping their feelings to themselves, had four times the likelihood of dying than women who didn't self-silence, even when other risk factors, such as blood pressure, body mass index, cigarette smoking, diabetes, and cholesterol levels were controlled statistically.

The implication is clear: if you want to keep your stress-response system from being chronically aroused, it will be helpful if the people around you aren't coercive. When I do workshops with teachers, I point out that it is in their own interest that everyone around them be safe and calm. I might say, "Imagine that one of your students runs into a street gang that threatens him, and arrives at school shaking and upset, but can't explain what happened. How would you like to have twenty-five kids coming in like that every day? It is in your interest—as well as theirs—that their relationships and environments help them be more calm."

The Imperative of Reducing Coercion

There is a simple message in all of the evidence outlined above and in earlier chapters: we need to reduce coercion in *all* of our environments—not just homes and schools, but workplaces and neighborhoods. Parents who feel coerced at work or in a conflict with a neighbor typically coerce their children. Children who are coerced usually pick on each other and act defiantly toward teachers. Coworkers who feel threatened are likely to act in angry and uncaring ways toward each other, often escalating the threatening behavior of those around them. It doesn't take much. One study of young adults showed that their brain functions were harmed even if the only form of abuse their parents subjected them to was verbal (Choi et al. 2009).

We need to replace all of this coercive behavior with behavior that calms, supports, and teaches—the kind of behavior that helps others thrive. Imagine that policy makers, teachers, parents, the grocer down the street—everybody—began to understand that people are harmed by the stressful things that happen to them. That aggressive driver you flipped off the other day got angrier. He went home and yelled at his kid. His kid acted out in school the next day, so his father grounded him for a week. And because that acting out took the form of bullying, the coercion spread, like a disease, to another child and another family. It goes on and on.

Stressing other people makes it more likely that they will be aggressive to you and everyone else. And so we keep conflict going. Unfortunately, due to the American predilection for punishment, the natural answer to this is typically to punish people for being so aggressive. Yet that's just more of the same.

If we could get everyone to begin by thinking about reducing everyone's stress, maybe we would live in a world where school board members say, "Maybe we should think about how much we're punishing kids in school. And are we mostly punishing teachers when kids do poorly? Does that work?" Maybe we could get people in the criminal justice system to look at current practices in terms of how much we punish and stress people and see that this makes them *less* able to reform their ways. Maybe we could get companies to consider whether the stress they expose their workers to undermines productivity and increases health care costs (as, indeed, it does).

If people in public health, psychology, medicine, sociology, and neuro-science joined together to underscore the message that coercion is the culprit underlying most of society's problems, we might get policy makers, health care practitioners, parents, teachers, and supervisors to look for ways to reduce coercive interactions and find better ways to motivate people. But where do we start? How do we influence the entire population to abandon coercive behavior and adopt more nurturing ways? How do we get governments to make human nurturance a goal of public policy? The public health perspective teaches us that we take gains wherever we can find them. We can build from the bottom up by implementing good family and school interventions in individual communities. But we can also work from the top down, creating public policies that require and fund the dissemination of nurturing programs and policies to ameliorate poverty and coercive practices.

Cultivating Forbearance and Forgiveness

The world has struggled with how to deal with others' aversive behavior for centuries. The fundamental problem is to get people to not respond to others' aversive behavior with their own aversive behavior because, more likely than not, doing so will simply perpetuate coercion and conflict. Instead, we need to cultivate forbearance and forgiveness as cardinal features of our culture. We look with wonder at examples of such behavior:

- When Charles C. Roberts stormed an Amish school house and killed five young schoolgirls before he killed himself, the Amish community expressed its forgiveness by attending his funeral and raising money for Roberts's widow and three small children. Those three small children must live out their lives knowing that their father committed a horrendous act. They will face difficulties in any case. But which will be better for them: knowing that the families of their father's victims hate them, or knowing that those families have forgiven their father and care for them?

- When Mohandas Gandhi vowed to fast until all violence between Hindus and Muslims ended, a Hindu man came to him and confessed that he had killed a Muslim boy as revenge for the killing of his son. He implored Gandhi to end his fast because he didn't want to have Gandhi's death on his soul. Gandhi told him that he could atone for his sin by finding a Muslim child whose parents had been killed in the religious riots and raising that child as a Muslim (Gandhi 1998).

- In Matthew 5:38, Jesus says, "You have heard that it was said, 'An eye for an eye, and a tooth for a tooth.' But I tell you, do not resist an evil person. If someone strikes you on the right cheek, turn to him the other also. And if someone wants to sue you and take your tunic, let him have your cloak as well. If someone forces you to go one mile, go with him two miles. Give to the one who asks you, and do not turn away from the one who wants to borrow from you."

- During Martin Luther King's nonviolent movement to end segregation, civil rights activists subjected themselves to violent attacks. In so doing, they inspired the sympathy and support of enough Americans that segregation ended.

- In South Africa under Nelson Mandela's leadership, a Truth and Reconciliation Commission was created to address the many wrongs that had been done during apartheid. The commission invited victims of apartheid to give statements about their experiences. Perpetrators of violence were also invited to give testimony and could request amnesty from both civil and criminal prosecution. The process is generally credited with having prevented a great deal of retaliatory violence.

- A mother patiently changes the dirty diaper of a crying child.

I hope you see how this last example resembles the others. In every instance, the key is that people choose not to retaliate or otherwise respond with aversive behavior. In doing so, they make it a little more likely that peaceful behavior will replace aggressive or unpleasant behavior. When they succeed, they build the capacity of others to react to stressful situations calmly and perhaps even warmly.

You might be inclined to respond to this line of thinking by saying, "Yes, we know all this. It is all in the teachings of people like Gandhi,

Jesus, Martin Luther King, and many others." That is quite true. It is no accident that each of these leaders had an impact on millions of people. However, I'm also offering something I believe to be new and I hope helpful: that the behavioral sciences have developed systematic ways to aid people in controlling threatening or antisocial behavior without acting in ways that simply provoke further aggression.

Only when we spread these practices throughout society and reduce the number of people who arrive at adulthood with coercive repertoires will we achieve the kind of peaceful society that Jesus, Gandhi, and Martin Luther King envisioned. Spreading warm, supportive, caring interpersonal relations requires that people have skills for dealing with others' aversive behavior without further escalating it.

My admittedly behavioristic shorthand label for the skill we need is "stepping over the aversives of others." It might also be called forbearance, which means "patient self-control," "restraint," or "tolerance." Every one of the effective parenting programs developed over the past forty years helps parents get better at stepping over the aversive things that children naturally do: An infant cries and a mother who might otherwise respond abusively or neglectfully receives encouragement from a skilled nurse to step over this aversive behavior. The nurse teaches her to hold the infant and rock him, talking soothingly. The nurse makes it clear that the mother's frustration and distress are natural and understandable (which is an example of the nurse stepping over the distressed behavior of the mother). The nurse commiserates with the mother while also modeling more patient—and more effective—ways of soothing the child.

In numerous family interventions, parents learn a variety of strategies for helping children develop the self-care skills and routines they need to get through the day. These may include praising and rewarding what the child does, or simply doing things together. In essence, parents get a lot better at responding not with anger or impatience but rather with support, interest, and calm, patient guidance, and they thereby help their children develop an ever-expanding set of skills, interests, and, most importantly, the ability to regulate their own emotions and restrain angry or impulsive behavior. In short, parents learn to ignore the milder forms of their children's aversive behavior and simply do what it takes to comfort and soothe their children and guide them in developing new skills.

203

The same is true for couples who aren't getting along. Psychologists such as Bob Weiss and John Gottman have carefully observed the interactions of couples in conflict, who often escalate aversive behavior because it may make their spouse stop doing something aversive. Effective couples therapy helps both partners replace cycles of criticism, blaming, anger, and cold silence with forbearance, patience, and positive activities. It doesn't work in every case, but it does save many marriages.

Stepping over aversives is also useful in helping people who are depressed. Research I conducted with Hy Hops and Linda Sherman showed that depressed mothers got some respite from the aversive behavior of their family members by being sad and self-critical (Biglan 1991). When mothers acted this way, their husbands and children were just a little bit less likely to be angry or critical. No one was having fun, but the mothers occasionally avoided negativity from other family members. Based on that finding, other researchers tested whether reducing conflict between depressed women and their spouses would reduce their depression (Beach, Fincham, and Katz 1998). It did.

So what we need to do is to build people's repertoires of forbearance, forgiveness, empathy, and compassion. This will undoubtedly be a bootstrap affair. But every time we influence someone to replace coercive reactions with behavior that calms and supports others, we have one more person who is cultivating these same nurturing reactions in those around them. And a good place to start in this quest is with children.

Helping Children Develop Empathy

How do we cultivate the skills and values that people need to deal with others' distressing behavior patiently and effectively? If you look at how young children learn to be empathetic, you can see the key skills they need. The first skill is simply having an awareness of their own emotional reactions. In the Early Education Program in Lane County, Oregon—directed by my wife, Georgia—staff members use distressing experiences to do emotion coaching.

Imagine that four-year-old Carlos opens the lunch his mom prepared for him and starts to cry. One of the adults joins him and talks empathically about how Carlos is feeling: "Oh, are you feeling really sad?" In doing so, the teacher is helping Carlos learn the names for his feelings. When asked why he is upset, Carlos says that his mother promised to put a cookie in his lunch, but there isn't one. His teacher might commiserate with him, acknowledging that this would make her sad too and showing, through her tone of voice and facial expression, that she feels sad about his predicament. In addition to helping Carlos develop the ability to describe what he is feeling, their interaction helps him understand that feelings result from things that happen to us. And as he calms down and receives comfort from a caring adult, he is learning to accept and move through his emotions—a small step in the development of emotion regulation.

But empathy also requires being able to see things from someone else's perspective. If I am going to experience caring and concern about how you are feeling, I first have to know *what* you are feeling. Research on perspective taking suggests that young children learn that others see things from a different perspective—literally. As they become more adept at realizing that what others see isn't what they see, they become better able to discern the emotions that others are feeling.

A good illustration of this process is a test that three-year-olds usually fail but five-year-olds easily pass. A three-year-old watches a video of an adult putting a pencil in a green box while a child named Charlie watches. After Charlie leaves the room, the adult moves the pencil from the green box to a red box. When a three-year-old is asked what box Charlie will look in to find the pencil, she or he will say the red box. But in the same situation, a five-year-old will correctly say the green box. The three-year-old has not yet learned to see things from Charlie's perspective.

If children are able to notice and describe their own emotions and can take the perspective of another child, they may then be able to understand the emotions another child is feeling. Suppose Ryan notices that Kaitlin is upset and learns that her mother didn't put a treat in her lunch as Kaitlin had expected. Because of his earlier experience, Ryan may then understand and even experience some of the emotion that Kaitlin is feeling.

These experiences form the foundation for empathy—the ability to perceive and experience what another person is thinking or feeling—as well as loving-kindness, understood in traditions like Buddhism as the expression of love through goodwill and kind acts. But by themselves, such experiences don't guarantee development of the loving-kindness we need to build in our society. For example, a child who perceives that another child is upset about her lunch might use that as an occasion to tease the other child. To build a compassionate and caring society, we need to promote, teach, and richly reinforce loving-kindness.

I recently attended the fifth birthday party for our granddaughter, Ashlyn. At one point, as she and her friends were playing, one of girls, Sara, left the group and sat alone at a table crying. She was very sad. I didn't know why. A few minutes later, Ashlyn came over and, in the sweetest way, rubbed Sara's head and said something soothing. Sara clearly felt better.

I later learned that Sara was the only one of the girls who had not yet turned five, and she was upset and feeling excluded. I also learned that Ashlyn's mother, Jen, prompted Ashlyn to comfort Sara.

You might think that doesn't count as a genuine instance of compassion, since Ashlyn had to be prompted. But that is how these vital repertoires are built. This episode was just a step on the road to building the behaviors and values of compassion and caring.

I know how carefully Jen and Mike have worked to help Ashlyn learn to be considerate of the feelings of her brother and her friends. They interrupt aversive interactions and prompt more positive ways of relating. They richly reinforce instances when Ashlyn is considerate of others. Sometimes they prompt these reactions, but over time, Ashlyn increasingly often acts this way on her own. All of this was facilitated by a lot of labeling and describing the behaviors that count as patient or compassionate: "That was sweet," "You're being so considerate," "You're being really patient."

By cultivating patient, nurturing family and school environments, we can help young children learn to understand and regulate their own emotions, understand the emotions of others, and react to others' distress with empathy and caring. We help them go from automatic distressed and angry reactions to more patient, empathic, and skilled ways of dealing with the distressed and distressing behavior of others. In the process, we help them cultivate a value of nurturing themselves and others.

Helping Adults Develop Empathy

Even if we make great progress in increasing the number of families and schools that help children cultivate these nurturing skills, we will have to do the same for many adults. Recent research on mindfulness interventions offers insight into how adults can be aided in developing these skills and the inclination to use them. It seems that as people become more mindful, they also become more empathic and compassionate. For example, a review of research on the impact of mindfulness training on health care providers showed that mindfulness helped them create a more caring environment, increased their capacity for empathy and appreciation of others, and assisted them in becoming less reactive or defensive in their relationships (Escuriex and Labbé 2011).

Due to the quality of the studies they reviewed (most were not randomized trials), I am hesitant to make great claims based on their findings. However, based on the research I've reviewed and my own experience in working with clients from an ACT perspective, I am inclined to believe that when people become more psychologically flexible, as described in chapter 5, they also tend to become more empathic and less likely to respond to angry or aggressive people with their own anger and aggression. It seems that as people become better able to step back from their thoughts and feelings in a mindful way and be explicit about the values they want in their relationships, they aren't as quick to react negatively and are better able to act in pragmatic ways that strengthen relationships with others.

Why would psychological flexibility help people become more patient, empathic, and compassionate? It probably helps in four ways. First, it involves a mindful way of being in the world—simply being more attentive to what is going on around you in the present moment. If you actively attend to another person, you are more likely to notice how the person feels and discern what she might be thinking.

Second, psychological flexibility involves the ability to take another's perspective. If you become better at noticing what is happening in the present moment, you can also get good at noticing that *you* are noticing all these things. There is a part of us that simply observes but is none of the things we observe. It is what ACT therapists call the *observer self*. It is a safe perspective from which to observe your own thoughts and feelings and those of other people.

Third, if you get good at noticing that the things you see are not the *you* that is seeing, you become better able to experience others' emotions without becoming overwhelmed by them (Atkins 2014). From this perspective, you can experience others' distress without needing to avoid it or to deny that it is important.

Fourth, psychological flexibility involves being clear about our values and having a focus on behaving in ways that are consistent with those values.

In my view, such psychological flexibility is critical to creating a society that nurtures everyone. Think about the troubling people you see in your community. For example, when you see someone begging on a street corner or hear of a person arrested for assault, you may react with irritation, revulsion, or fear. That is understandable. I don't ask you to suppress those reactions. And research shows that it doesn't work to suppress them anyway. Instead, merely think about what that person's life has been like. More than likely, their environment failed to nurture the skills they needed. As children, they probably didn't learn emotion regulation and other self-regulation skills because they lived in stressful environments, and therefore struggled in school and had ongoing stressful experiences with family, teachers, and peers. Now, as adults, they continue to have daily experiences of rejection, derision, and threat.

So while accepting the fact that we are frustrated by many of the troubled people we see around us, we can also invest in making our communities places with far fewer troubled people. I am convinced that most of us value being part of a community that sees to the successful development and well-being of everyone. We all want communities with less crime, drug abuse, and welfare dependency. If we can convince more people that such communities are not only possible but also in everyone's interest, we can bring together the public and private resources to make it a reality.

We need a lot more research on this problem. Even if ACT interventions make individuals more empathic and forgiving, we have a long way to go in translating that approach into strategies that significantly increase the prevalence of caring and compassion in entire societies.

Action Implications

Hopefully I've convinced you that cultivating forbearance, forgiveness, and compassion is fundamental to achieving a nurturing society. Here are some effective actions that can advance these skills and values, whether undertaken individually or in organizations. After all, every organization is a place where people may either experience great conflict or enjoy the support and approval of those around them. And given all of the evidence that positive interpersonal relations benefit both individuals and organizations by increasing effectiveness and reducing stress and stress-related problems, public policies are also essential to promoting nurturing human relationships.

For Everyone

- See if, a few times each day, you can notice whether those around you seem comfortable, involved, and thriving, or tense, threatened, and fearful. Then look for ways to support those who seem troubled. Simply paying attention to people and expressing an interest can make a difference.

- When dealing with people who often act in angry and aggressive ways, try to put yourself in their shoes and see why they might feel threatened. Patient, warm reactions to their irritable behavior could set the stage for changing your relationship with such people. Of course, you will have to accept—but not believe or act on—all the thoughts you will experience about feeling threatened by them or needing to retaliate.

- My friends Peter and Susan Glaser have written a book that is helpful for developing the skills needed to deal effectively with people who are prone to anger and argument: *Be Quiet, Be Heard* (Glaser, Glaser, and Matthews 2006), which offers specific techniques for receiving criticism and raising difficult issues with others while also reducing conflict.

- Another valuable resource is the website of a good friend, Doug Carmine. It's called Feed Kindness: The Ultimate Win-Win (http://www.feedkindness.com). It is a gold mine of ideas, examples, evidence, and resources for adding kindness to the world.

For Organizations

- Systematically assess the quality of interpersonal relations within the organization. If conflict is common, initiate a program to help members adopt more nurturing and less conflictual ways of communicating. An example of such an approach is the Glasers' BreakThrough Conflict program (http://www.theglasers.com/breakthrough-conflict.html).

- Just increasing fun in the workplace can be beneficial. A recent meta-analysis of studies showed that in workplaces with greater humor, employees have higher levels of job satisfaction, better work performance, and less burnout and turnover (Mesmer-Magnus, Glew, and Viswesvaran 2012).

For Policy Makers

- Fund research on how coercive interpersonal relationships can be reduced in families, schools, workplaces, and communities. How can dispute resolution become more effective? What kinds of interventions can reduce conflict in key relationships, and how can those interventions be made widely available?

- Through Surgeon General and Institute of Medicine reports, organize and effectively communicate strategies for reducing coercion and conflict, as well as the evidence about the importance of doing so.

- Increase the availability of effective dispute resolution, including for divorce. Develop legal procedures that provide incentives for parties to enter dispute resolution. Psychologist Irwin Sandler's work on divorce adjustment provides an excellent model of how to proceed (Sandler, Tein, and West 1994; Tein et al. 2004).

For the Entertainment Industry

- Just as the entertainment industry has changed our culture with respect to race relations, smoking, and alcohol use, it could influence all of us to embrace and build values of empathy, compassion, and forgiveness. Compelling movies, television shows, and songs can serve as models for how to respond to people's aversive behavior with forbearance and skill.

CHAPTER 11

Evolving the Society We Want

It is 2042. My grandson Grayson is thirty-one. He sits with his wife, Fatima, and their sleeping newborn, listening to the president's State of the Union address. President Maria Barrera says that she is happy to report that the state of the union is strong. The human well-being index shows that virtually every indicator of psychological, social, and physical health has continued the steady improvement that began around 2020. The index, which has become as closely watched as the unemployment rate and the gross domestic product, shows that the percentage of children living in poverty—a leading indicator of problems in years to come—has reached its lowest level ever. She attributes this to a combination of factors: a steady increase in minimum wage, greater use of the earned income tax credit, programs that help the diminishing number of at-risk mothers get education and employment, and the generally robust economy. Crime, drug abuse, and academic failure have continued their historic decline.

On the downside, she reports that obesity continues to be a stubborn problem, with research over the past three decades indicating that epigenetic processes can pass on metabolic stinginess that is difficult to reverse. However, the food marketing practices that were a major contributor to the explosion of obesity in the 1990s have ended, thanks to policies and regulations outlawing the marketing of unhealthful foods and providing incentives for marketing healthier ones.

President Barrera credits much of the nation's progress to strong bipartisan support for policies that have funded effective family and school programs. She mentions that the well-being index includes a measure of citizens' participation in civic affairs, added because of evidence that participation is a leading indicator of community well-being and people's life satisfaction—more powerful than winning the lottery. After the dark days of the first twenty years of the century, partisan warfare subsided when a new generation of Americans banded together via the Internet to advocate for positive political action and policies. Rather than attacking the media conglomerates and politicians who were using divisive methods to keep their constituency angry at the "other side," this new breed of civic advocates uses humor and warmth to show that public discourse can be more civil, respectful, and focused on everyone's well-being.

It is hard to make contact with dry statistics, but these statistics mean that a little girl in Louisville, Kentucky, whose mother died in a tragic accident, has a network of family, friends, and organizations making sure that she is cared for and gets what she needs to blossom into a successful young woman. It means that across the nation, fewer children are teased, abused, or neglected. The heartening statistics President Barrera shares wouldn't exist without the many warm and generous people who made the well-being of others a higher priority than their own financial success: a grandfather who chose to build a play structure for his grandchildren rather than sit at home watching golf on TV, a stranger who intervened in a thoughtful way to help a single mother find a job when she was laid off, a high school football star who made it a point to be friends with one of the school's most rejected kids, a multimillionaire who lobbied to have his taxes raised to ensure that teachers wouldn't be laid off.

Is such a scenario possible? I think something of this sort is not only possible, but inevitable. I cannot look at the progress made in public health in the past five hundred years and in behavioral science in the past fifty years without feeling optimistic that all nations will focus increasingly on improving the well-being of their citizens. They will be guided by the knowledge that the most meaningful measure of well-being is not wealth, but life satisfaction. They will use and promote the growing number of programs, policies, and practices that clearly achieve better outcomes.

But optimism is not a substitute for action. So in this chapter, I'll discuss how we might evolve toward the world described above—the world I want my grandson to live in.

A Compelling Vision

We need a simple, unifying, and emotionally evocative vision of the kind of world we can create. The best description I've been able to come up with for this world is "nurturing environments." The quality of human life, perhaps even the survival of life as we know it, depends on finding ways to make everyone's environment more nurturing—less coercive and more caring, supportive of human development, and focused on doing what works.

I am acutely aware of my limitations as a creative persuasion artist. And after spending hundreds of hours studying cigarette marketing campaigns on which tobacco companies spent hundreds of millions of dollars, I know how important money is in developing an effective, persuasive campaign and reaching millions of people. Yet even with millions of dollars and highly skilled marketers, the folks at R. J. Reynolds spent two decades tearing their hair out while trying to come up with a campaign that could wrest market share from the Marlboro Man.

When Reynolds came up with the Joe Camel campaign, they finally began to capture some of the youth market away from Marlboro. In fact, Joe Camel had such a tremendous impact that Philip Morris was alarmed. They commissioned focus groups to see if they could pinpoint what was working for Camel. The report on this study, titled "The Viability of the Marlboro Man Among the 18–24 Segment," concluded, "Marlboro should act to minimize the effectiveness of Camel's appeal to the values of the 18–24 segment... Belonging is important to the 18–24 segment." It recommended that they "broaden the advertising to make [the Marlboro man]... less aloof, less severe and tough, more accessible" (Biglan 2004, Demonstrative 11, 7). Philip Morris responded by creating an ad that proved effective in focus groups. It showed two cowboys petting two puppies. So when it comes to persuasion, remember the puppies!

One of the other expert witnesses in *United States v. Philip Morris et al.* was Paul Slovic, a psychologist who studies human decision making. He described the basic principle that explains why puppies work. He calls it the "affect heuristic." A *heuristic* is anything that aids efficient decision making. Slovic's research (2000) shows that people are much more likely to make choices based on how something makes them feel than on any sort of rationale or reasoning process. Kids start smoking Camel because Joe is having fun. Camel equals fun! Got 'em!

In the end, the compelling vision we need to build must have all the emotional appeal of the best marketing. I've mentioned the goal of the Institute of Medicine report on prevention: "a society in which young people arrive at adulthood with the skills, interests, assets, and health habits needed to live healthy, happy, and productive lives in caring relationships with others" (IOM and NRC 2009, 387). I've described how such a society can be achieved by creating nurturing environments. In advertising terms, "nurturing environments" is the brand. Its value for target audience members is built by getting them to associate it with all the things they already value and with preventing things they fear or dislike.

Thus, we need emotionally evocative messages that associate nurturing environments with kindness, innovation, academic success, health, and prosperity, along with messages underscoring that nurturing environments are the key to preventing crime, academic failure, alcohol abuse and alcohol-related problems, tobacco use, drug abuse, teenage pregnancy, marital discord, child abuse, poverty, depression, anxiety, and schizophrenia. We also need to tailor these messages to specific target audiences. Everyone will benefit from hearing about how promoting nurturing environments can help them and those around them, especially when the details of these messages are targeted to specific groups, such as parents, youth, policy makers, law enforcement personnel, health care providers, and educators.

If I had a budget of several million dollars and one year of uninterrupted time, I could hire a top-notch advertising agency to come up with a better term than "nurturing environments." I could create media communications that motivate people to really want nurturing environments. Give me a hundred million dollars, and I could reach millions of people with effective messages. That isn't a lot of money, especially in comparison to statistics indicating that the cigarette industry spent $12.49 billion on advertising in 2006 (T. T. Clark et al. 2011).

The vision we create must also be compelling to the scientific community, so it must be empirically sound. I submit that this book presents the evidence supporting the value of creating nurturing environments, along with a great deal of information on how to achieve such environments.

Creative Epidemiology

In chapter 6, I described how creative the tobacco control movement has been in reducing tobacco use. It dramatically illustrated the magnitude of the problem by comparing the epidemic of smoking-related deaths to two Boeing 747s crashing every day of the year. This movement led to the production of Surgeon General and Institute of Medicine reports and National Cancer Institute monographs that marshaled the evidence in support of specific policy changes, such as clean indoor air laws.

A similar effort can convince millions of Americans that their well-being and the well-being of the nation depend on making families, schools, workplaces, neighborhoods, and communities more nurturing. Imagine a Surgeon General report titled *The Importance of Nurturing Environments for Mental, Behavioral, and Physical Health*. Such a report would bring together all of the evidence regarding the wide range of problems that stem from conflict and coercion in families, schools, workplaces, and neighborhoods. It would document how all of these environments could be guided to become more nurturing, and how such a transformation would vastly enhance human well-being.

Imagine news stories with headlines like "Study Finds Children Do Better in Nurturing Families and Schools." Over time, people would begin to ask themselves whether the environments around them were nurturing. Parents might begin to spend more time just playing with their children. Teachers might increase their efforts to help students become more psychologically flexible. Midlevel managers who read about the importance of nurturing environments and their key features might ask whether their workplace could become more nurturing. A community might determine whether it is preventing family conflict by providing evidence-based family support programs. Prison wardens might join the fledgling effort to replace extreme isolation with effective rehabilitation practices.

Current advocacy for public health focuses mostly on single problems: driving under the influence, drug abuse, obesity, cigarette smoking, academic failure, child abuse, depression, lack of exercise, and so on. Yet the same basic environmental conditions affect every one of these problems. As suggested in chapter 6, rather than focusing on preventing individual problems, we need to cut to the chase and attend to how nonreinforcing, neglectful, and conflict-filled environments contribute to all of these problems—and how interventions that make these environments more nurturing can alleviate all of these problems.

Disseminating Evidence-Based Programs, Policies, and Practices

The spread of good interventions, including several described in chapter 2, is well underway. I mentioned how Marion Forgatch has helped the nation of Norway implement the behavioral parenting skills program she helped develop throughout the country. She is also implementing it in Michigan, Kansas, Denmark, and the Netherlands. Likewise, Patti Chamberlain, who developed Multidimensional Treatment Foster Care for adolescents and young children, has created a center that is working with states around the nation to implement her approach to foster care in child protective services agencies. And Tom Dishion and Beth Stormshak are training people in the implementation of their Family Check-Up in middle schools and preschools. In addition, Matt Sanders's Triple P program, the system described in chapter 6 for getting parenting skills information to parents throughout a community, is in place in more than twenty countries.

In chapter 6, I also talked about how Dennis Embry created a version of the Good Behavior Game designed to make it easier to train large numbers of teachers. He is currently supporting implementation of the Good Behavior Game in classrooms in thirty-eight US states as well as throughout the Canadian province of Manitoba, with more than 8,000 teachers using it and at least 105,000 students impacted. In addition, he is helping people all around North America implement kernels—those simple techniques for influencing behavior described in chapter 6. These approaches help parents, teachers, and other behavior change agents nurture prosocial behavior and prevent problems from developing.

Programs are not the only evidence-based approaches to increasing nurturance. In chapter 6, I mentioned the work of Alex Wagenaar and Kelli Komro at the University of Florida. They have identified more than fifty evidence-based policies that can contribute to human well-being (Komro et al. 2013). As just one example, here are details on some alcohol-related policies with proven benefit: Increasing the tax on alcoholic beverages leads to reductions in alcohol consumption, alcohol-related morbidity and mortality, motor vehicle deaths, sexually transmitted disease, and violent crime (Chaloupka, Grossman, and Saffer 2002). Likewise, limiting the density of alcohol outlets leads to large and significant reductions in alcohol consumption and interpersonal violence (Campbell et al. 2009).

And reducing the hours in which alcohol may be sold leads to reductions in alcohol consumption and related harm, such as violence (Popova et al. 2009). Clearly, all of these reductions in problematic outcomes would greatly contribute to our environments becoming more nurturing.

The Need for More Research

The cliché "More research is needed" has adorned many a master's thesis. One year it was the slogan on our Oregon Research Institute T-shirt. So even if I've convinced you that behavioral science research has made enormous progress in understanding human behavior and taking practical action to improve it, think of how much more progress we can make if we continue to expand this research. We will undoubtedly produce more numerous and effective interventions for families, schools, and communities. And increasingly, research is turning to the problem of how to ensure that interventions are widely and effectively implemented.

Research that strengthens the case for nurturing environments will also be important. Studies that document the common pathway from family conflict and other forms of threat to multiple psychological, behavioral, and health problems will bring policy makers and citizens together around the goal of making our families, schools, communities, and workplaces more nurturing. Such research will create a context for more effective, creative epidemiology and advocacy and generate support for the adoption of evidence-based programs and policies.

Most of the funding for the prevention research I've described has come from the National Institutes of Health (NIH), the bulk of it from the National Institute on Drug Abuse (NIDA). The prevention research branch at NIDA has funded many family and school interventions that have proven effective in preventing not just drug abuse, but all of the most common and costly psychological and behavioral problems. NIDA could have insisted on funding only research narrowly focused on drug abuse, but to their credit, they acted on evidence that drug abuse results from stressful life conditions that can precede the start of drug use by many years. As a result, NIDA has funded research on all risk factors that lead to drug abuse.

Unfortunately, funding for the NIH is dwindling. Despite the fact that, for many years, the NIH has been the most important source of funding for health research worldwide, during the last three years its budget has declined. And thanks to sequestration in fiscal year 2013, its budget decreased by two billion dollars, resulting in a failure to fund 640 projects, many of which involved prevention research. Given the history of the NIH in funding projects that lead to improved health and well-being, this is a tragic development.

Obviously, I am a biased reporter on this; my income for the past thirty years has come almost entirely from NIH funding. But hopefully I've demonstrated how much our society has gained by spending on behavioral science research—which, by the way, has been just a tiny fraction of NIH expenditures.

The Importance of Promoting Psychological Flexibility

Research on psychological flexibility can contribute to making American society more nurturing. If you aren't immersed in this research, that may seem unlikely to you. But I've seen profound changes in the way we deal with so-called mental illness. Already, more than seventy randomized controlled trials have shown the benefit of ACT for virtually every type of psychological or behavioral problem, and for many physical illnesses and health-related behaviors. This research shows that the fundamentals of acting effectively in the world involve being willing to have whatever thoughts and feelings arise without trying to avoid them, and being able to look *at* our private experience instead of letting it be a lens that colors whatever is there to be seen. This approach to life involves taking whatever actions can further our goals and values in a particular situation. I believe ACT has illuminated a way of being in the world that can serve not simply as a way for troubled people to overcome specific problems but also as a cultural innovation that contributes to everyone's well-being.

This assertion is admittedly speculative, and I am acutely aware of the risk that you may dismiss my assertions as the ramblings of a cultist. After all, I am suggesting that incremental behavioral science has produced a qualitatively different view of human functioning. My view grows out of the empirical evidence for ACT and my own observations of what happens to people (myself included) when they become more psychologically flexible. I am convinced that learning to accept our thoughts and feelings in a nonjudgmental way is an act of self-compassion and the first step toward reducing conflict and coercion among people.

Let me give you an example of how this orientation has reduced conflict in my life. One day I was supposed to give our cat Ginger a shot of insulin in the morning. I forgot to do it. My wife, Georgia, who is in charge of cat care, was not pleased. She is as nurturing to cats as to humans, and she does whatever they need. She did not seem angry, however. After all, she is nurturing toward me too. That evening she prepared Ginger's food and syringe of insulin, then handed them to me. She was "making" me do it. I felt humiliated and angry at being told what to do—and because I felt guilty for not having done what I was supposed to. Fuming, I went upstairs to give Ginger her shot.

In the past, this event might have led to a couple of days of not speaking to each other—not saying anything about it, but being sour and noncommunicative, both of us knowing what it was about, and each punishing the other. But on my way upstairs, I found myself accepting that I felt angry and humiliated and that I had made a mistake. What do I mean by "accepted"? I mean my emotions were just there. They could be there, and I didn't need to do anything about them. Rather than being within the humiliation and anger, I sort of stepped back and looked at them. As I did, my emotional experience got smaller. I wasn't struggling to get rid of it or to justify my mistake, so I didn't need to be angry at Georgia or blame her for my humiliation. Through this process, I realized that I wanted to have the kind of warm, cuddly evening that we so often have these days. So I went downstairs and had such an evening. (Georgia has also gotten good at letting thoughts and feelings be there without having to do something about them, so she too could let it go and move on.)

I see this process at work in all of the examples I gave in chapter 10 of people choosing to act in loving ways. The Amish families that forgave the family of Charles Roberts, who killed five Amish girls, were able to do this not because they had no anger, but because they were willing to have the anger and still act on their value of forgiveness. Gandhi must have felt great frustration that the Hindu man beseeching him had killed a Muslim child while Gandhi was in the process of starving himself to death to stop the killing. But he forgave the man and offered him a way out of his pain. When Christ counseled that we should turn the other cheek, he did not suggest we wouldn't feel anger. The civil rights workers who were willing to risk their lives and in some cases die for their cause certainly felt fear. However, they chose to accept their fear and take actions that they believed would arouse the conscience of the majority of Americans. We view these acts as heroic precisely because people were willing to have thoughts and feelings that conflicted with the actions they took.

ACT-based interventions ask people to think deeply about their most important values and envision what they want their life to be about. Sometimes practitioners ask their clients to imagine what might be on their tombstones if they lived up to their own highest ideals. In ACT workshops with Oregon teachers (Hinds et al. 2011), no one suggests what values the teachers should have. Yet all across the state, in both rural and urban settings, teachers usually list the same values: respect, integrity, caring, honesty, family, acceptance, forgiveness, tolerance, faith, fun, trust, kindness, friendship, exercise, and laughter. After teachers have identified their values, we help them take steps to make these values a bigger part of their lives. For example, they might set a specific goal for increasing the respect they get and the respect they give. One teacher decided she would try to listen more attentively to students when they talked to her. She decided that at least once a week for each class, she would take time between periods to talk to the students she had challenging relationships with, asking them about what was happening in their lives. She found that these students became softer and less confrontational.

What would happen if values became a much bigger part of our private lives and our public discourse? Suppose that creative epidemiology could encourage people to focus on valued living and become more psychologically flexible. A movement to nurture psychological flexibility could influence society at every level, including entertainment and the media, the same way that messages about not smoking helped shrink the culture of smoking. If this movement joined with religions that teach turning the other cheek, it might ignite an effort to bring public discussion of our most important problems back to a pragmatic focus on improving everyone's well-being. This kind of social evolution won't come from attacking the "other side"; instead, we need to take actions that model a third way: pragmatic problem solving.

Creating a New Breed of Advocacy Organizations

Social movements depend on advocacy organizations that can mobilize millions of people to take the actions needed for meaningful change. To create the kind of society I envision, we need two significant developments. The first is the creation of organizations that advocate for nurturing families, schools, workplaces, and communities. As mentioned earlier in this chapter, numerous advocacy organizations are already working on specific problems, such as driving under the influence, tobacco control, crime reduction, prevention of child abuse, poverty reduction, getting people to exercise more or eat better, preventing racial discrimination, reducing academic failure, and so on. Name a problem, and there is an organization working on it.

Yet all of these problems are rooted in a failure to ensure that families, schools, workplaces, and communities are nurturing and promote kind, caring, productive, enthusiastic, and conscientious behavior. If we can get all of these advocacy organizations to cooperate in promoting this central message and advocating for policies, programs, and practices that increase nurturance, we can significantly reduce all of the problems they target.

The second thing we need is to strengthen foundations, nonprofits, and advocacy organizations that are working for the common good. Current law places considerable restrictions on what these organizations can do to advocate for policies and practices that would promote nurturing environments. At the same time, the power of for-profit corporations to advocate for policies that benefit business—but may not benefit the common good—has become virtually unlimited, thanks to recent Supreme Court decisions such as *Citizens United v. Federal Election Commission*, which held that the First Amendment prohibits the government from restricting political independent expenditures by corporations, associations, or labor unions, and *McCutcheon v. Federal Election Commission*, which struck down political donor limits. The Alliance for Justice, an association of more than one hundred organizations working on progressive causes, is looking into ways to increase the ability of nonprofit organizations to work for the common good. We need more organizations like the Alliance for Justice.

Evolving a More Beneficial Form of Capitalism

I've already described the marketing, lobbying, and advocacy practices of corporations that harm human well-being. Failing to limit these practices will impair our ability to improve well-being. To address these harmful practices, we need to change the contingencies that select and maintain them. To some extent, increased regulation and increased penalties for harmful actions can help achieve this (perhaps through litigation, as in the case of *United States v. Philip Morris et al.*). Actions of this sort will become more common if we achieve policies that strengthen nonprofit advocacy organizations. However, fundamental changes in the culture of the for-profit world will also be necessary.

One encouraging development is the creation of benefit corporations. Under existing law, a corporation risks a lawsuit by shareholders if it does anything that diminishes profits—even if that action may be beneficial to the community at large. However, a benefit corporation can pursue a general public benefit (Hanson Bridgett LLP 2012). A nonprofit organization (B Lab) is tracking the spread of this innovation. Twenty-six states have adopted laws allowing the creation of such corporations, and there are now more than one thousand of these corporations operating worldwide.

From an evolutionary perspective, we can influence corporate behavior by increasing the negative consequences for harmful corporate actions and the positive consequences for beneficial actions. The straightforward application of this kind of contingency management has been far too long in coming, but it is likely to grow.

The problem, however, is that many corporate leaders who make the pursuit of profit their highest value will work assiduously to prevent passage of any laws that might impinge on profitability. A two-pronged approach can address this problem. One aspect is to advocate for specific contingencies that will curtail harmful actions. The other is to try to change the values of the for-profit corporate world.

Georgia and I once dined at the Four Seasons Restaurant in New York. I noticed that Domaine Drouhin, an Oregon Pinot Noir, was on the menu for $200 per bottle. (We didn't buy one.) I find it hard to believe that anyone can detect a difference in quality between a $100 bottle of wine and a $200 bottle. Perhaps I am just unsophisticated. It seems more likely, however, that being able to go into an upscale restaurant and order a $200 bottle of wine is about status. People living in the moneyed culture of Wall Street are motivated to go for bigger bonuses, and to create investment instruments that net their companies a great deal of money but produce a bubble that eventually results in a recession. Do their actions improve the quality of Americans' lives? Obviously not—even though they pay millions to media pundits to convince Americans otherwise.

We might also consider whether their actions improve even their own lives. Tim Kasser's research on materialistic goals (Kasser and Ryan 1993, 1996; Kasser et al. 2007) suggests that the pursuit of more pay and bigger bonuses doesn't make people happier. After all, seated at the table next to you at the Four Seasons is someone richer than you who just bought a $300 bottle of wine.

If we can create a cultural movement to promote nurturing environments and prosocial values, we may be able to influence many corporate leaders to abandon practices that are harmful to the greater good. I recently got encouraging words in this regard from Dennis Tirch, an ACT therapist who emphasizes the cultivation of self-compassion for clients who are having stress-related problems (see Tirch 2012). He told me that he has treated a number of hedge fund managers in his practice, and that as they become more self-compassionate, they also become more motivated to contribute to the well-being of others.

Changing Popular Culture

Changing popular culture may be the biggest challenge we face. We need entertainment that promotes nurturing environments: movies, TV shows, social media, and so on that model, reward, and recognize the things people do to protect, teach, care for, and forgive others. Violence and conflict currently dominate entertainment, and media corporations deny that this affects behavior, despite solid evidence to the contrary. For example, one study measured the TV viewing habits of children when they were six to ten years old and then assessed their aggressive behavior fifteen years later (Huesmann, Lagerspetz, and Eron 1984). Young people who had watched more violence on TV as children were more likely to be aggressive as adults. These relationships were true even when the researchers controlled statistically for children's socioeconomic status and intellectual ability and the behavior of their parents.

As the diversity of media expands, it becomes ever more difficult to prevent young people from being exposed to images and entertainment that promote conflict, distrust, and aggression. It will be a tall order to change this aspect of our culture. The First Amendment makes legal restrictions on what can be shown difficult to achieve in the United States. But substantial changes in media depictions of cigarette smoking have emerged, thanks to relentless advocacy by tobacco prevention advocates, including Jim Sargent and Stan Glantz. Sargent's research showed an association between kids watching movies that depict heroes smoking and subsequently taking up smoking themselves (Sargent et al. 2002). Stan Glantz (2003) successfully advocated for putting R ratings on movies that depict smoking, and this policy has been beneficial. Creative epidemiological approaches to the media's promotion of nonnurturing behavior could have a similar impact.

Empowering Dramatic Cultural Change

In the mid-nineteenth century, London was the largest and richest city in the world. Yet sewage flowed freely in the streets and into the Thames, fouling the drinking water and causing hundreds of deaths due to cholera. Thanks to scientific research, we now know that contaminated water causes cholera, and we would be shocked to hear of anyone allowing sewage to flow into the street. Our culture has changed.

Scientific evidence regarding the harm that coercive, nonnurturing environments do to human beings is just as strong as that for the harm of contaminated water. We have the capability to help families, schools, workplaces, and communities become more nurturing. At the same time, efforts like the tobacco control movement are teaching us how we can change harmful practices throughout a culture. Making our environments more nurturing is a bigger challenge than reducing tobacco use, but we can do it.

Creating and communicating a compelling vision of the society we could have if we promote nurturing environments can organize everything that must be done. Using creative epidemiology, we can educate citizens about the critical importance of reducing conflict and increasing nurturance. Continued research can expand our understanding of the harm caused by nonnurturing environments and strengthen interventions to support increased nurturance. Continued dissemination of evidence-based programs, policies, and practices will increase the prevalence of nurturing environments. Increased promotion of psychological flexibility through clinical interventions, workshops, and the media will accelerate these trends. Creating and strengthening advocacy organizations will generate support for this movement and empower all of the other approaches. Influencing the corporate world to embrace values that promote nurturing environments will moderate their harmful practices and align corporations with other efforts to promote nurturance. If we can influence popular culture, at least in part, to promote prosocial, nurturing values, we very well may be able to make nurturance an explicit norm for most members of society.

The work that remains is to apply the vast body of knowledge and research methods that has accumulated—to not just disseminate the programs, policies, and practices that are currently available, but to innovate and strengthen them and improve our ability to affect entire populations. We must also use the same principles of selection by consequences that have proved so fruitful in helping people lead more productive and caring lives. We can change the consequences for business, government entities, and nonprofit organizations so that their values and actions will better serve the well-being of everyone.

Taken together, all of these approaches will promote the greater good, creating the world that we and our children deserve. I hope you'll join me in working toward realizing this vision.

Afterword

Evolving the Future

A number of years ago, I received an e-mail from someone named Tony Biglan, who introduced himself as president of the Society for Prevention Research. He invited me to attend a symposium on prevention research from an evolutionary perspective that he was organizing for the society's next annual meeting.

I had never heard of Tony or the Society for Prevention Research, but I was happy to accept his invitation because I had just started to use my evolutionary expertise in a practical way to improve the quality of life in my city of Binghamton, New York. I outlined my new project, which I called the Binghamton Neighborhood Project, to Tony in my reply to his e-mail. Within seconds I had a return reply:

"Oh boy. You need me. This is what I do."

Indeed it was. Over the ensuing weeks and months, I was amazed and delighted to discover that Tony and his colleagues were already doing what I aspired to do: accomplish positive change in real-world settings. Some of their change methods worked at the individual level. If your view of psychotherapy is to spend years on a couch talking about your childhood, think again. I discovered that there are therapeutic methods that can be taught on the basis of reading a single book or attending a single three-hour session. Some of the change methods worked at the level of small groups. One of these was the Good Behavior Game, which provides lifelong benefits when played in the first and second grades. Perhaps most amazingly, some of the change methods worked at the level of large populations, such as a program that reduced cigarette sales to minors in the states of Wyoming and Wisconsin and another program implemented at a countywide scale in South Carolina that reduced the rate of child maltreatment. In a world of problems that seem to defy solutions, I felt that I had stumbled across a secret society of benign wizards.

Many practical change methods are poorly validated, which makes it difficult to know whether, how, or why they work. But Tony and his colleagues were also wizards at assessment. The gold standard of assessment is the randomized controlled trial, in which the individuals or groups that undergo the change method are randomly drawn from a larger pool, creating a comparison group that is similar in every other way. For example, in the South Carolina study (headed by Ron Prinz), eighteen counties were selected that were roughly comparable in size and demographics. Of these, nine were randomly selected to receive the treatment, and their child maltreatment statistics were compared to the other nine counties. Why weren't the results of such a high-quality study front page news?

I was so impressed by what I discovered that I began to wonder what I had to contribute with my own nascent efforts. I needn't have worried. Tony and his colleagues—especially Steven C. Hayes and Dennis Embry— were as eager to "discover" me as I was to "discover" them. The very fact that their work was largely unknown was a problem that I was in a position to help solve.

In my book *Evolution for Everyone*, I write that the Ivory Tower would be more aptly named the Ivory Archipelago—many islands of thought with little communication among islands. The world of public policy and practical change efforts suffers from the same problem. A change method that works arises and spreads within a given island but goes no further unless "discovered" by some brave wayfarer from another island. Evolutionary theory can transform the Ivory Archipelago into the *United* Ivory Archipelago by providing a unifying theoretical framework. This unification took place in the biological sciences during the twentieth century (and continues), and it is in the process of taking place for the human-related academic disciplines. It can also work its magic for the world of public policy and practical change efforts. Tony, Steve, and Dennis sensed this possibility, which made them as excited to work with me as I was to work with them.

I tell the story of teaming up with Tony, Steve, and Dennis for a general audience in my book *The Neighborhood Project*. We outline our vision for a professional audience in an article titled "Evolving the Future: Toward a Science of Intentional Change," which is published with peer commentaries and our reply in the journal *Behavioral and Brain Sciences*. Now Tony has outlined the vision in his own words in *The Nurture Effect* with great wisdom, experience, and humanity.

I think of what Tony and the rest of us are trying to accomplish in historic terms. Historians will look back upon the twenty-first century as a period of synthesis for human-related knowledge, similar to the synthesis of biological knowledge that took place during the twentieth century. With understanding comes the capacity to improve. There is no doubt that the synthesis is taking place, but *how fast* is less certain—and speed is of the essence, because the need to solve our most pressing problems won't wait. The more people who read *The Nurture Effect* and absorb its meaning, the faster the world will become a better place.

—David Sloan Wilson
   President, Evolution Institute
   SUNY Distinguished Professor of Biology and Anthropology
   Binghamton University

References

Adams, G. L., and S. Engelmann. 1996. *Research on Direct Instruction: 25 Years Beyond DISTAR*. Seattle: Educational Achievement Systems.

Alfieri, L., P. J. Brooks, N. J. Aldrich, and H. R. Tenenbaum. 2011. Does discovery-based instruction enhance learning? *Journal of Educational Psychology* 103: 1–18.

Allen, N. B., and P. B. T. Badcock. 2006. Darwinian models of depression: A review of evolutionary accounts of mood and mood disorders. *Progress in Neuro-Psychopharmacology and Biological Psychiatry* 30: 815–826.

American Academy of Child and Adolescent Psychiatry. 2011. Drinking alcohol in pregnancy. *Facts for Families*, number 93. Available at http://www.aacap .org/App_Themes/AACAP/docs/facts_for_families/93_drinking_alcohol_ in_pregnancy_fetal_alcohol_effects.pdf. Accessed May 14, 2014.

Aos, S., S. Lee, E. Drake, A. Pennucci, M. Miller, L. Anderson, and M. Burley. 2012. *Return on Investment: Evidence-Based Options to Improve Statewide Outcomes*. Olympia: Washington State Institute for Public Policy.

Aos, S., S. Lee, E. Drake, A. Pennucci, T. Klima, M. Miller, L. Anderson, J. Mayfield, and M. Burley. 2011. *Return on Investment: Evidence-Based Options to Improve Statewide Outcomes*. Olympia: Washington State Institute for Public Policy.

Arcus, D. 2002. School shooting fatalities and school corporal punishment: A look at the states. *Aggressive Behavior* 28: 173–183.

Astin, A. W. 2002. *The American Freshman: Thirty-Five Year Trends, 1966–2001*. Los Angeles: Higher Education Research Institute.

Atkins, P. W. B. 2014. Empathy, self-other differentiation, and mindfulness. In *Organizing Through Empathy*, edited by K. Pavlovich and K. Krahnke. New York: Routledge.

Azrin, N. H., R. R. Hutchinson, and R. McLaughlin, R. 1972. The opportunity for aggression as an operant reinforcer during aversive stimulation. In *The Experimental Analysis of Social Behavior*, edited by R. E. Ulrich and P. T. Mountjoy. New York: Appleton-Century-Crofts.

Bach, P., and S. C. Hayes. 2002. The use of acceptance and commitment therapy to prevent the rehospitalization of psychotic patients: A randomized controlled trial. *Journal of Consulting and Clinical Psychology* 70: 1129–1139.

Ballard, K. D. 1983. Teaching children to do what they say they will do: A review of research with suggested applications for exceptional children. *Exceptional Child* 30: 119–125.

Bandura, A. 1974. Behavior theory and models of man. *American Psychologist* 29, 859–869.

Bardo, M. T., D. H. Fishbein, and R. Milich. 2011. *Inhibitory Control and Drug Abuse Prevention*. New York: Springer.

Barrera, M., Jr., A. Biglan, T. K. Taylor, B. K. Gunn, K. Smolkowski, C. Black, D. F. Ary, and R. C. Fowler. 2002. Early elementary school intervention to reduce conduct problems: A randomized trial with Hispanic and non-Hispanic children. *Prevention Science* 3: 83–94.

Barrish, H. H., M. Saunders, and M. M. Wolf. 1969. Good behavior game: Effects of individual contingencies for group consequences on disruptive behavior in a classroom. *Journal of Applied Behavior Analysis* 2: 119–124. Available at http://www.ncbi.nlm.nih.gov/pmc/articles/PMC1311049/?tool=pubmed . Accessed May 14, 2014.

Bavarian, N., K. M. Lewis, D. L. DuBois, A. Acock, S. Vuchinich, N. Silverthorn, et al. 2013. Using social-emotional and character development to improve academic outcomes: A matched-pair, cluster-randomized controlled trial in low-income, urban schools. *Journal of School Health* 83: 771–779.

Beach, S. R. H., F. D. Fincham, and J. Katz. 1998. Marital therapy in the treatment of depression: Toward a third generation of therapy and research. *Clinical Psychology Review* 18: 635–661.

Beach, S., R. H. Jones, D. J. Franklin, and J. Kameron. 2009. Marital, family, and interpersonal therapies for depression in adults. In *Handbook of Depression*, 2nd ed., edited by I. H. Gotlib and C. L. Hammen. New York: Guilford.

Beets, M. W., B. R. Flay, S. Vuchinich, F. J. Snyder, A. Acock, K.-K. Li, K. Burns, I. J. Washburn, and J. Durlak. (2009). Using a social and character development program to prevent substance use, violent behaviors, and sexual activity among elementary-school students in Hawaii. *American Journal of Public Health*, 99: 1438–1445.

Biglan, A. 1991. Distressed behavior and its context. *Behavior Analyst* 14: 157–169.

———. 1995. *Changing Cultural Practices: A Contextualist Framework for Intervention Research*. Reno, NV: Context Press.

———. 2003. Selection by consequences: One unifying principle for a transdisciplinary science of prevention. *Prevention Science* 4: 213–232.

————. 2004. *United States v. Philip Morris et al. Direct Written Examination of Anthony Biglan, Ph.D. Submitted by the United States Pursuant to Order #471. Civil No. 99-CV-02496 (GK)*. Available at http://www.justice.gov/civil/cases/tobacco2/20050103%20Biglan_Written_Direct_and_%20Demonstratives.pdf. Accessed June 12, 2014.

————. 2009. The role of advocacy organizations in reducing negative externalities. *Journal of Organizational Behavioral Management* 29: 1–16.

————. 2011. Corporate externalities: A challenge to the further success of prevention science. *Prevention Science* 12: 1–11.

Biglan, A., D. V. Ary, K. Smolkowski, T. E. Duncan, and C. Black. 2000. A randomized control trial of a community intervention to prevent adolescent tobacco use. *Tobacco Control* 9: 24–32.

Biglan, A., P. A. Brennan, S. L. Foster, and H. D. Holder. 2004. *Helping Adolescents at Risk: Prevention of Multiple Problem Behaviors*. New York: Guilford.

Biglan, A., and C. Cody. 2013. Integrating the human sciences to evolve effective policies. *Journal of Economic Behavior and Organization* 90(Suppl): S152–S162.

Biglan, A., B. R. Flay, D. D. Embry, and I. Sandler. 2012. Nurturing environments and the next generation of prevention research and practice. *American Psychologist* 67: 257–271.

Biglan, A., and E. Hinds. 2009. Evolving prosocial and sustainable neighborhoods and communities. *Annual Review of Clinical Psychology* 5: 169–196.

Biglan, A., H. Hops, and L. Sherman. 1988. Coercive family processes and maternal depression. In *Social Learning and Systems Approaches to Marriage and the Family*. New York: Brunner/Mazel.

Binns, H. J., C. Campbell, and M. J. Brown. 2006. Interpreting and managing blood lead levels of less than 10 microg/dL in children and reducing childhood exposure to lead: Recommendations of the Centers for Disease Control and Prevention Advisory Committee on Childhood Lead Poisoning Prevention. *Pediatrics* 120: e1285–e1298.

Blakemore, S. J., and S. Choudhury. 2006. Development of the adolescent brain: Implications for executive function and social cognition. *Journal of Child Psychology and Psychiatry* 47: 296–312.

Boles, S., A. Biglan, and K. Smolkowski. 2006. Relationships among negative and positive behaviors in adolescence. *Journal of Adolescence* 29: 33–52.

Borzekowski, D. L. G., and T. N. Robinson. 2001. The 30-second effect: An experiment revealing the impact of television commercials on food preferences of preschoolers. *Journal of the American Dietetic Association* 101: 42–46.

Bradshaw, C. P., C. W. Koth, L. A. Thornton, and P. J. Leaf. 2009. Altering school climate through school-wide Positive Behavioral Interventions and Supports: Findings from a group-randomized effectiveness trial. *Prevention Science* 10: 100–115.

Bricker, J. B., S. L. Mann, P. M. Marek, J. Liu, and A. V. Peterson. 2010. Telephone-delivered acceptance and commitment therapy for adult smoking cessation: A feasibility study. *Nicotine and Tobacco Research* 12: 454–458.

Brown, A. 2012. With poverty comes depression, more than other illnesses. Available at http://www.gallup.com/poll/158417/poverty-comes-depression-illness.aspx. Accessed June 30, 2014.

Brown, C. H., R. G. Adams, and S. G. Kellam. 1981. A longitudinal study of teenage motherhood and symptoms of distress: The Woodlawn Community Epidemiological Project. *Research in Community and Mental Health* 2: 183–213.

Bullard, L., M. Wachlarowicz, J. DeLeeuw, J. Snyder, S. Low, M. Forgatch, and D. DeGarmo. 2010. Effects of the Oregon model of Parent Management Training (PMTO) on marital adjustment in new stepfamilies: A randomized trial. *Journal of Family Psychology* 24: 485–496.

Campbell, C. A., R. A. Hahn, R. Elder, R. Brewer, S. Chattopadhyay, J. Fielding, T. S. Naimi, T. Toomey, B. Lawrence, and J. C. Middleton. 2009. The effectiveness of limiting alcohol outlet density as a means of reducing excessive alcohol consumption and alcohol-related harms. *American Journal of Preventive Medicine* 37: 556–569.

Capaldi, D. M., T. J. Dishion, M. Stoolmiller, and K. Yoerger. 2001. Aggression toward female partners by at-risk young men: The contribution of male adolescent friendships. *Developmental Psychology* 37: 61–73.

Capaldi, D. M., K. C. Pears, and D. C. R. Kerr. 2012. The Oregon Youth Study Three-Generational Study: Theory, design, and findings. *Bulletin of the International Society of the Study of Behavioural Development* 2: 29–33.

Caprara, G. V., C. Barbaranelli, C. Pastorelli, A. Bandura, and P. G. Zimbardo. 2000. Prosocial foundations of children's academic achievement. *Psychological Science* 11: 302–306.

Carr, J. 2002. With RFK in the delta. *American Heritage* 53: 93. Available at http://www.americanheritage.com/content/rfk-delta. Accessed May 28, 2014.

Carter, S. C. 2000. *No Excuses: Lessons from 21 High-Performing, High-Poverty Schools.* Washington, DC: Heritage Foundation.

CDC (Centers for Disease Control and Prevention). 2008. Smoking-attributable mortality, years of potential life lost, and productivity losses—United States, 2000–2004. *Morbidity and Mortality Weekly Report* 57: 1226–1228.

———. 2011. Quitting smoking among adults: United States, 2001–2010. *Morbidity and Mortality Weekly Report* 60: 1513–1519.

———. 2012. Teen drivers: Fact sheet. Available at http://www.cdc.gov/motor vehiclesafety/teen_drivers/teendrivers_factsheet.html. Accessed May 14, 2014.

————. 2013. Fact sheets: Alcohol use and health. Available at http://www.cdc.gov/alcohol/fact-sheets/alcohol-use.htm. Accessed May 14, 2014.

————. 2014. Overweight and obesity: Adult obesity facts. Available at http://www.cdc.gov/obesity/data/adult.html. Accessed May 27, 2014.

————. n.d. Preventing Teen Pregnancy, 2010–2015. Available at http://www.cdc.gov/TeenPregnancy/PDF/TeenPregnancy_AAG.pdf. Accessed May 14, 2014.

Chaloupka, F. J., M. Grossman, and H. Saffer. 2002. The effects of price on alcohol consumption and alcohol-related problems. *Alcohol Research and Health* 26: 22–34.

Chamberlain, P. 2003. *Treating Chronic Juvenile Offenders: Advances Made Through the Oregon Multidimensional Treatment Foster Care Model.* Washington, DC: American Psychological Association.

Choi, J., B. Jeong, M. L. Rohan, A. M. Polcari, and M. H. Teicher. 2009. Preliminary evidence for white matter tract abnormalities in young adults exposed to parental verbal abuse. *Biological Psychiatry* 65: 227–234.

Clark, K. E., and G. W. Ladd. 2000. Connectedness and autonomy support in parent-child relationships: Links to children's socioemotional orientation and peer relationships. *Developmental Psychology* 36: 485–498.

Clark, T. T., M. J. Sparks, T. M. McDonald, and J. D. Dickerson. 2011. Post-tobacco master settlement agreement: Policy and practice implications for social workers. *Health and Social Work* 36: 217–224.

Conger, R. D., and K. J. Conger. 2008. Understanding the processes through which economic hardship influences families and children. In *Handbook of Families and Poverty*, edited by D. R. Crane and T. B. Heaton. Thousand Oaks, CA: Sage.

Congressional Budget Office. 2011. *Trends in the Distribution of Household Income Between 1979 and 2007.* Washington, DC: Congressional Budget Office.

Connell, A. M., and T. J. Dishion. 2006. The contribution of peers to monthly variation in adolescent depressed mood: A short-term longitudinal study with time-varying predictors. *Development and Psychopathology* 18: 139–154.

Connell, A. M., T. J. Dishion, M. Yasui, and K. Kavanagh. 2007. An adaptive approach to family intervention: Linking engagement in family-centered intervention to reductions in adolescent problem behavior. *Journal of Consulting and Clinical Psychology* 75: 568–579.

Copeland, L. 2013. School cheating scandal shakes up Atlanta. *USA Today*, April 14.

Costello, E. J., S. N. Compton, G. Keeler, and A. Angold. 2003. Relationships between poverty and psychopathology: A natural experiment. *Journal of the American Medical Association* 290: 2023–2029.

Dahl, G., and L. Lochner. 2012. The impact of family income on child achievement: Evidence from the earned income tax credit. *American Economic Review* 102: 1927–1956.

DeBaryshe, B. D., G. R. Patterson, and D. M. Capaldi. 1993. A performance model for academic achievement in early adolescent boys. *Developmental Psychology* 29: 795–804.

Deci, E. L., R. Koestner, and R. M. Ryan. 1999. A meta-analytic review of experiments examining the effects of extrinsic rewards on intrinsic motivation. *Psychological Bulletin* 125: 627–668.

DeNavas-Walt, C., B. D. Proctor, and J. C. Smith. 2010. *Income, Poverty, and Health Insurance Coverage in the United States: 2009.* Washington, DC: US Government Printing Office.

Dennison, B. A., T. A. Erb, and P. L. Jenkins. 2002. Television viewing and television in bedroom associated with overweight risk among low-income preschool children. *Pediatrics* 109: 1028–1035.

De Vries, M. W. 1987. Cry babies, culture, and catastrophe: Infant temperament among the Masai. In *Child Survival.* Dordrecht, Holland: D. Reidel Publishing Company.

Dill, K. 2014. Report: CEOs earn 331 times as much as average workers, 774 times as much as minimum wage workers. Available at http://www.forbes.com/sites/kathryndill/2014/04/15/report-ceos-earn-331-times-as-much-as-average-workers-774-times-as-much-as-minimum-wage-earners. Accessed June 23, 2014.

Dishion, T. J., and D. W. Andrews. 1995. Preventing escalation in problem behaviors with high-risk young adolescents: Immediate and 1-year outcomes. *Journal of Consulting and Clinical Psychology* 63: 538–548.

Dishion, T. J., T. Ha, and M. H. Véronneau. 2012. An ecological analysis of the effects of deviant peer clustering on sexual promiscuity, problem behavior, and childbearing from early adolescence to adulthood: An enhancement of the life history framework. *Developmental Psychology* 48: 703–717.

Dishion, T. J., and K. Kavanagh. 2003. *Intervening in Adolescent Problem Behavior: A Family-Centered Approach.* New York: Guilford.

Dishion, T. J., K. Kavanagh, A. Schneiger, S. Nelson, and N. K. Kaufman. 2002. Preventing early adolescent substance use: A family-centered strategy for the public middle school. *Prevention Science* 3: 191–201.

Dishion, T. J., S. E. Nelson, and B. M. Bullock. 2004. Premature adolescent autonomy: Parent disengagement and deviant peer process in the amplification of problem behavior. *Journal of Adolescence* 27: 515–530.

Dishion, T. J., S. E. Nelson, and K. Kavanagh. 2003. The Family Check-Up with high-risk young adolescents: Preventing early-onset substance use by parent monitoring. *Behavior Therapy* 34: 553–571.

Dishion, T. J., K. M. Spracklen, D. W. Andrews, and G. R. Patterson. 1996. Deviancy training in male adolescent friendships. *Behavior Therapy* 27: 373–390.

Dixon, H. G., M. L. Scully, M. A. Wakefield, V. M. White, and D. A. Crawford. 2007. The effects of television advertisements for junk food versus nutritious food on children's food attitudes and preferences. *Social Science and Medicine* 65: 1311–1323.

Dodge, K. A., T. J. Dishion, and J. E. Lansford. 2006. *Deviant Peer Influences in Programs for Youth: Problems and Solutions.* New York: Guilford.

Domitrovich, C. E., R. C. Cortes, and M. T. Greenberg. 2007. Improving young children's social and emotional competence: A randomized trial of the preschool "PATHS" curriculum. *Journal of Primary Prevention* 28: 67–91.

Douglas Mental Health University Institute. 2014. Prenatal maternal stress. Available at http://www.douglas.qc.ca/info/prenatal-stress. Accessed May 16, 2014.

Eaker, E. D., L. M. Sullivan, M. Kelly-Hayes, R. B. S. D'Agostino, and E. J. Benjamin. 2007. Marital status, marital strain, and risk of coronary heart disease or total mortality: The Framingham Offspring Study. *Psychosomatic Medicine* 69: 509–513.

Eaton, D. K., L. Kann, S. Kinchen, S. Shanklin, K. H. Flint, J. Hawkins, et al. 2012. Youth Risk Behavior Surveillance—United States, 2011. *Morbidity and Mortality Weekly Report* 61: 1–162.

Eifert, G. H., and J. P. Forsyth. 2005. *Acceptance and Commitment Therapy for Anxiety Disorders: A Practitioner's Treatment Guide to Using Mindfulness, Acceptance, and Values-Based Behavior Change Strategies.* Oakland, CA: New Harbinger.

Embry, D. D., and A. Biglan. 2008. Evidence-based kernels: Fundamental units of behavioral influence. *Clinical Child and Family Psychology Review* 11: 75–113.

Engelmann, S., P. Haddox, and E. Bruner. 1983. *Teach Your Child to Read in 100 Easy Lessons.* New York: Simon and Schuster.

Escuriex, B. F., and E. E. Labbé. 2011. Health care providers' mindfulness and treatment outcomes: A critical review of the research literature. *Mindfulness* 2: 242–253.

Fisher, P. A., and P. Chamberlain. 2000. Multidimensional treatment foster care: A program for intensive parenting, family support, and skill building. *Journal of Emotional and Behavioral Disorders* 8: 155–164.

Flay, B. R., C. G. Allred, and N. Ordway. 2001. Effects of the Positive Action program on achievement and discipline: Two matched-control comparisons. *Prevention Science* 2: 71–89.

Forgatch, M. S., G. R. Patterson, D. S. DeGarmo, and Z. G. Beldavs. 2009. Testing the Oregon delinquency model with nine-year follow-up of the Oregon Divorce Study. *Development and Psychopathology* 21: 637–660.

Forrester, K., A. Biglan, H. H. Severson, and K. Smolkowski. 2007. Predictors of smoking onset over two years. *Nicotine and Tobacco Research* 9: 1259–1267.

Fothergill, K. E., M. E. Ensminger, K. M. Green, R. M. Crum, J. Robertson, and H. S. Juon. 2008. The impact of early school behavior and educational achievement on adult drug use disorders: A prospective study. *Drug and Alcohol Dependence* 92: 191–199.

Fryar, C. D., T. C. Chen, and X. Li. 2012. *Prevalence of Uncontrolled Risk Factors for Cardiovascular Disease: United States, 1999–2010.* Hyattsville, MD: National Center for Health Statistics.

Fuchs, L. S., D. Fuchs, S. R. Powell, P. M. Seethaler, P. T. Cirino, and J. M. Fletcher. 2008. Intensive intervention for students with mathematics disabilities: Seven principles of effective practice. *Learning Disability Quarterly* 31: 79–92.

Galobardes, B., J. W. Lynch, and G. D. Smith. 2004. Childhood socioeconomic circumstances and cause-specific mortality in adulthood: Systematic review and interpretation. *Epidemiologic Reviews* 26: 7–21.

Galobardes, B., J. W. Lynch, and G. D. Smith. 2008. Is the association between childhood socioeconomic circumstances and cause-specific mortality established? Update of a systematic review. *Journal of Epidemiology and Community Health* 62: 387–390.

Gandhi, A. 1998. Overcoming hatred and revenge through love. *Fellowship Magazine*, July–August.

Gaudiano, B. A., and J. D. Herbert. 2006. Acute treatment of inpatients with psychotic symptoms using acceptance and commitment therapy: Pilot results. *Behaviour Research and Therapy* 44: 415–437.

Gilpin, E. A., W. S. Choi, C. C. Berry, and J. P. Pierce. 1999. How many adolescents start smoking each day in the United States? *Journal of Adolescent Health* 25: 248–255.

Glantz, S. A. 2003. Smoking in movies: A major problem and a real solution. *Lancet* 362: 258–259.

Glaser, S. R., P. A. Glaser, and A. Matthews. 2006. *Be Quiet, Be Heard: The Paradox of Persuasion.* Eugene, OR: Communications Solutions.

Gonzales, P., T. Williams, L. Jocelyn, S. Roey, D. Kastberg, and S. Brenwald. 2008. *Highlights from TIMSS 2007: Mathematics and Science Achievement of US Fourth- and Eighth-Grade Students in an International Context.* Washington, DC: National Center for Education Statistics, Institute of Education Sciences.

Goodman, L. A., M. Pugach, A. Skolnik, and L. Smith. 2013. Poverty and mental health practice: Within and beyond the 50-minute hour. *Journal of Clinical Psychology* 69: 182–190.

Gordon, J., A. Biglan, and K. Smolkowski. 2008. The impact on tobacco use of branded youth anti-tobacco activities and family communications about tobacco. *Prevention Science* 9: 73–87.

Gottman, J. M., with J. Declaire. 1997. *Raising an Emotionally Intelligent Child.* New York: Simon and Schuster.

Gray, P. 2013. *Free to Learn: Why Unleashing the Instinct to Play Will Make Our Children Happier, More Self-Reliant, and Better Students for Life.* New York: Basic Books.

Greenfeld, L. A. 1998. *Alcohol and crime: An analysis of national data on the prevalence of alcohol involvement in crime.* Washington, DC: US Department of Justice.

Grouzet, F. M. E., T. Kasser, A. Ahuvia, J. M. Fernandez-Dols, Y. Kim, S. Lau, R. M. Ryan, S. Saunders, P. Schmuck, and K. M. Sheldon. 2005. The structure of goal contents across 15 cultures. *Journal of Personality and Social Psychology* 89: 800–816.

Grube, J. W. 1995. Television alcohol portrayals, alcohol advertising, and alcohol expectancies among children and adolescents. In *The Effects of the Mass Media on the Use and Abuse of Alcohol,* edited by S. E. Martin and P. D. Mail. Rockville, MD: National Institute on Alcohol Abuse and Alcoholism.

Grube, J. W., P. A. Madden, and B. Friese 1996. Television alcohol advertising increases adolescent drinking. Poster presented at the annual meeting of the Research Society on Alcoholism, Washington, DC, June 22–27, 1996.

Grube, J. W., and P. Nygaard. 2005. Alcohol policy and youth drinking: Overview of effective interventions for young people. In *Preventing Harmful Substance Use: The Evidence Base for Policy and Practice,* edited by T. Stockwell, P. J. Gruenewald, J. W. Toumbourou, and W. Loxley. New York: Wiley.

Gunn, B., A. Biglan, K. Smolkowski, and D. Ary. 2000. The efficacy of supplemental instruction in decoding skills for Hispanic and non-Hispanic students in early elementary school. *Journal of Special Education* 34: 90–103.

Hacker, J. S., and P. Pierson. 2010a. Winner-take-all politics: Public policy, political organization, and the precipitous rise of top incomes in the United States. *Politics and Society* 38: 152–204.

Hacker, J. S., and P. Pierson. 2010b. *Winner-Take-All Politics: How Washington Made the Rich Richer—and Turned Its Back on the Middle Class.* New York: Simon and Schuster.

Hamlin, J. K., K. Wynn, P. Bloom, and N. Mahajan. 2011. How infants and toddlers react to antisocial others. *Proceedings of the National Academy of Sciences* 108: 19931–19936.

Hanson Bridgett LLP. 2012. Flexible purpose corporation vs. benefit corporation. Available at http://www.hansonbridgett.com/Publications/articles/2012-09-flexible-purpose.aspx. Accessed June 11, 2014.

Harris, R. 2007. *The Happiness Trap: Stop Struggling, Start Living*. Wollombi, New South Wales, Australia: Exisle Publishing.

———. 2009a. *ACT Made Simple: An Easy-to-Read Primer on Acceptance and Commitment Therapy*. Oakland, CA: New Harbinger.

———. 2009b. *ACT with Love: Stop Struggling, Reconcile Differences, and Strengthen Your Relationship with Acceptance and Commitment Therapy*. Oakland, CA: New Harbinger.

Hart, B., and T. R. Risley. 1995. *Meaningful Differences in the Everyday Experience of Young American Children*. Baltimore, MD: Brookes Publishing.

Hawkins, J., S. Oesterle, E. C. Brown, R. D. Abbott, and R. F. Catalano. 2014. Youth problem behaviors 8 years after implementing the Communities That Care Prevention System: A community-randomized trial. JAMA *Pediatrics* 168: 122–129.

Hayes, S. C. 1987. A contextual approach to therapeutic change. In *Psychotherapists in Clinical Practice: Cognitive and Behavioral Perspectives*, edited by N. S. Jacobson. New York: Guilford.

———. 1993. *Analytic Goals and the Varieties of Scientific Contextualism*. Reno, NV: Context.

Hayes, S. C., with S. Smith. 2005. *Get Out of Your Mind and Into Your Life: The New Acceptance and Commitment Therapy*. Oakland, CA: New Harbinger.

Hayes, S. C., L. J. Hayes, H. W. Reese, and T. R. Sarbin, eds. 1993. *Varieties of Scientific Contextualism*. Reno, NV: Context.

Hayes, S. C., K. D. Strosahl, and K. G. Wilson. 1999. *Acceptance and Commitment Therapy: An Experiential Approach to Behavior Change*. New York: Guilford.

Henggeler, S. W., S. K. Schoenwald, C. M. Borduin, M. D. Rowland, and P. B. Cunningham. 2009. *Multisystemic Therapy for Antisocial Behavior in Children and Adolescents*. New York: Guilford.

Henshaw, S. K. 1998. Unintended pregnancy in the United States. *Family Planning Perspectives* 30: 24–29, 46.

Hibbeln, J. R., L. R. Nieminen, T. L. Blasbalg, J. A. Riggs, and W. E. Lands. 2006. Healthy intakes of n-3 and n-6 fatty acids: Estimations considering worldwide diversity. *American Journal of Clinical Nutrition* 83: 1483S–1493S.

Himmelstein, D. U., D. Thorne, E. Warren, and S. Woolhandler. 2009. Medical bankruptcy in the United States, 2007: Results of a national study. *American Journal of Medicine* 122: 741–746.

Hinds, E., C. Cody, A. Kraft, A. Biglan, L. B. Jones, and F. M. Hankins. 2011. Using acceptance and commitment therapy to improve the wellbeing of teachers. In *Evidence-Based Education*, edited by J. S. Twyman and R. Wing. Oakland, CA: Association for Behavior Analysis International and Wing Institute.

Horner, R. H., G. Sugai, K. Smolkowski, L. Eber, J. Nakasato, A. W. Todd, and J. Esperanza. 2009. A randomized, wait-list controlled effectiveness trial assessing school-wide positive behavior support in elementary schools. *Journal of Positive Behavior Interventions* 11: 133–144.

Huesmann, L. R., K. Lagerspetz, and L. D. Eron. 1984. Intervening variables in the TV violence–coaggression relation: Evidence from two countries. *Developmental Psychology* 20: 746–775.

Huxley, A. 1932. *Brave New World*. London: Chatto and Windus.

Ialongo, N. S., L. Werthamer, S. G. Kellam, C. H. Brown, S. Wang, and Y. Lin. 1999. Proximal impact of two first-grade preventive interventions on the early risk behaviors for later substance abuse, depression, and antisocial behavior. *American Journal of Community Psychology* 27: 599–641.

IOM and NRC (Institute of Medicine and National Research Council). 2009. *Preventing Mental, Emotional, and Behavioral Disorders Among Young People: Progress and Possibilities*. Washington, DC: National Academies Press.

IOM (Institute of Medicine) Committee on Food Marketing and the Diets of Children and Youth. 2006. *Food Marketing to Children and Youth: Threat or Opportunity?* Edited by J. M. McGinnis, J. A. Gootman, and V. I. Kraak. Washington, DC: National Academies Press.

Irvine, A. B., A. Biglan, K. Smolkowski, C. W. Metzler, and D. V. Ary. 1999. The effectiveness of a parenting skills program for parents of middle school students in small communities. *Journal of Consulting and Clinical Psychology* 67: 811–825.

Isaacson, W. 2007. "Einstein & Faith." *TIME*. April 5. http://content.time.com/time/magazine/article/0,9171,1607298,00.html

Jablonka, E., and M. J. Lamb. 2014. *Evolution in Four Dimensions, Revised Edition: Genetic, Epigenetic, Behavioral, and Symbolic Variation in the History of Life*. Boston: MIT Press.

Jablonka, E., and G. Raz. 2009. Transgenerational epigenetic inheritance: Prevalence, mechanisms, and implications for the study of heredity and evolution. *Quarterly Review of Biology* 84: 131–176.

Jacobson, E. 1938. *Progressive Relaxation*. Chicago: University of Chicago Press.

Jacobson, N. S., K. S. Dobson, P. A. Truax, M. E. Addis, K. Koerner, J. K. Gollan, E. Gortner, and S. E. Prince. 1996. A component analysis of cognitive-behavioral treatment for depression. *Journal of Consulting and Clinical Psychology* 64: 295–304.

Johnson, S. 2006. *The Ghost Map: The Story of London's Most Terrifying Epidemic— and How It Changed Science, Cities, and the Modern World.* New York: Riverhead Books.

Johnston, L. D., P. M. O'Malley, J. G. Bachman, and J. E. Schulenberg. 2013. *Monitoring the Future National Results on Drug Use: 2012 Overview, Key Findings on Adolescent Drug Use.* Ann Arbor: Institute for Social Research, University of Michigan.

Jones, L. B., K. Whittingham, and L. Coyne. Forthcoming. Cultural evolution in families. In *The Wiley-Blackwell Handbook of Contextual Behavioral Science,* edited by R. D. Zettle, S. C. Hayes, A. Biglan, and D. Barnes-Holmes. Chichester, West Sussex, UK: Wiley and Sons.

Kam, C. M., M. T. Greenberg, and C. A. Kusché. 2004. Sustained effects of the PATHS curriculum on the social and psychological adjustment of children in special education. *Journal of Emotional and Behavioral Disorders* 12: 66–78.

Kasser, T. 2004. The good life or the goods life? Positive psychology and personal well-being in the culture of consumption. In *Positive Psychology in Practice,* edited by P. A. Linley, and S. Joseph. Hoboken, NJ: Wiley.

Kasser, T. 2011. Cultural values and the well-being of future generations: A cross-national study. *Journal of Cross-Cultural Psychology* 42: 206–215.

Kasser, T., S. Cohn, A. D. Kanner, and R. M. Ryan. 2007. Some costs of American corporate capitalism: A psychological exploration of value and goal conflicts. *Psychological Inquiry* 18: 1–22.

Kasser, T., and R. M. Ryan. 1993. A dark side of the American dream: Correlates of financial success as a central life aspiration. *Journal of Personality and Social Psychology* 65: 410–422.

Kasser, T., and R. M. Ryan. 1996. Further examining the American dream: Differential correlates of intrinsic and extrinsic goals. *Personality and Social Psychology Bulletin* 22: 280–287.

Kellam, S. G., C. H. Brown, J. M. Poduska, N. S. Ialongo, W. Wang, P. Toyinbo, et al. 2008. Effects of a universal classroom behavior management program in first and second grades on young adult behavioral, psychiatric, and social outcomes. *Drug and Alcohol Dependence* 95: S5–S28.

Kellam, S. G., C. H. Brown, B. R. Rubin, and M. E. Ensminger. 1983. Paths leading to teenage psychiatric symptoms and substance use: Developmental epidemiological studies in Woodlawn. In *Childhood Psychopathology and Development,* edited by S. B. Guze, F. J. Earls, and J. E. Barrett. New York: Raven.

Kellam, S. G., L. S. Mayer, G. W. Rebok, and W. E. Hawkins. 1998. Effects of improving achievement on aggressive behavior and of improving aggressive behavior on achievement through two preventive interventions: An investigation of causal paths. In *Adversity, Stress, and Psychopathology,* edited by B. P. Dohrenwend. New York: Oxford University Press.

Koh, H. K. 2002. Accomplishments of the Massachusetts Tobacco Control Program. *Tobacco Control* 11: ii1–ii3.

Kohn, A. 1993. *Punished by Rewards: The Trouble with Gold Stars, Incentive Plans, A's, Praise, and Other Bribes.* Boston: Houghton, Mifflin.

Komro, K. A., B. R. Flay, A. Biglan, and the Promise Neighborhoods Research Consortium 2011. Creating nurturing environments: A science-based framework for promoting child health and development within high-poverty neighborhoods. *Clinical Child and Family Psychology Review* 14: 111–134.

Komro, K. A., A. Tobler, A. Delisle, R. O'Mara, and A. Wagenaar. 2013. Beyond the clinic: Improving child health through evidence-based community development. *BMC Pediatrics* 13: 172–180.

Kuhn, T. S. 1970. The structure of scientific revolutions. *International Encyclopedia of Unified Science* 2: 1–210.

Lakein, A. 1973. *How to Get Control of Your Time and Your Life.* New York: Signet.

Landry, S. H., K. E. Smith, P. R. Swank, and C. Guttentag. 2008. A responsive parenting intervention: The optimal timing across early childhood for impacting maternal behaviors and child outcomes. *Developmental Psychology* 44: 1335–1353.

Landry, S. H., K. E. Smith, P. R. Swank, T. Zucker, A. D. Crawford, and E. F. Solari. 2012. The effects of a responsive parenting intervention on parent-child interactions during shared book reading. *Developmental Psychology* 48: 969–986.

Lapham, L. 2004. Tentacles of rage. *Harper's*, September, 31–41.

Leflot, G., P. A. C. van Lier, P. Onghena, and H. Colpin. 2013. The role of children's on-task behavior in the prevention of aggressive behavior development and peer rejection: A randomized controlled study of the Good Behavior Game in Belgian elementary classrooms. *Journal of School Psychology* 5: 187–199.

Leigh, A. 2009. Top incomes. In *The Oxford Handbook of Economic Inequality*, edited by W. Salverda, B. Nolan, and T. Smeeding. London: Oxford University Press.

Lewis, K. M., N. Bavarian, F. J. Snyder, A. Acock, J. Day, D. L. DuBois, P. Ji, M. B. Schure, N. Silverthorn, S. Vuchinich, and B. R. Flay. (2012). Direct and mediated effects of a social-emotional and character development program on adolescent substance use. *International Journal of Emotional Education*, 4: 56–78.

Lewis, K. M., D. L. DuBois, N. Bavarian, A. Acock, N. Silverthorn, J. Day, P. Ji, S. Vuchinich, and B. R. Flay. (2013). Effects of Positive Action on the emotional health of urban youth: A cluster-randomized trial. *Journal of Adolescent Health*, 53: 706–711.

Lewis, K. M., M. B. Schure, N. Bavarian, D. L. Dubois, J. Day, P. Ji, N. Silverthorn, A. Acock, S. Vuchinich, and B. R. Flay. (2013). Problem behavior and urban, low-income youth: A randomized controlled trial of Positive Action in Chicago. *American Journal of Preventive Medicine*, 44: 622–630.

Lewinsohn, P. M. 1975. The behavioral study and treatment of depression. In *Progress in Behavioral Modification*, vol. 1, edited by M. Hersen, R. M. Eisler, and P. M. Miller. New York: Academic Press.

Li, C., L. S. Balluz, C. A. Okoro, C. W. Strine, J. M. Lin, M. Town, et al. 2011. Surveillance of certain health behaviors and conditions among states and selected local areas: Behavioral Risk Factor Surveillance System, United States, 2009. *Morbidity and Mortality Weekly Report Surveillance Summaries* 60, no. 9.

Liebal, K., T. Behne, M. Carpenter, and M. Tomasello. 2009. Infants use shared experience to interpret pointing gestures. *Developmental Science* 12: 264–271.

Lundgren, T., J. Dahl, N. Yardi, and L. Melin. 2008. Acceptance and commitment therapy and yoga for drug-refractory epilepsy: A randomized controlled trial. *Epilepsy and Behavior* 13: 102–108.

Manning, J. 2008. The Midwest farm crisis of the 1980s. Available at http://eightiesclub.tripod.com/id395.htm. Accessed October 28, 2012.

Mayer, G. R. 1995. Preventing antisocial behavior in the schools. *Journal of Applied Behavior Analysis* 28: 467–478.

McLean, B., and J. Nocera. 2010. *All the Devils Are Here: The Hidden History of the Financial Crisis.* New York: Penguin.

McLoyd, V. C. 1998. Socioeconomic disadvantage and child development. *American Psychologist* 53: 185–204.

Menand, L. 2001. *The Metaphysical Club.* New York: Farrar, Straus and Giroux.

Mesmer-Magnus, J., D. J. Glew, and C. Viswesvaran. 2012. A meta-analysis of positive humor in the workplace. *Journal of Managerial Psychology* 27: 155–190.

Metzler, C. W., A. Biglan, J. C. Rusby, and J. R. Sprague. 2001. Evaluation of a comprehensive behavior management program to improve school-wide positive behavior support. *Education and Treatment of Children* 24: 448–479.

Miller, G. E., E. Chen, A. K. Fok, H. Walker, A. Lim, E. F. Nicholls, S. Cole, and M. S. Kobor. 2009. Low early-life social class leaves a biological residue manifested by decreased glucocorticoid and increased proinflammatory signaling. *Proceedings of the National Academy of Sciences* 106: 14716–14721.

Miller, G. E., M. E. Lachman, E. Chen, T. L. Gruenewald, A. S. Karlamangla, and T. E. Seeman. 2011. Pathways to resilience: Maternal nurturance as a buffer against the effects of childhood poverty on metabolic syndrome at midlife. *Psychological Science* 22: 1591–1599.

Miller, T. 2004. The social costs of adolescent problem behavior. In *Helping Adolescents at Risk: Prevention of Multiple Problem Behaviors*, edited by A. Biglan, P. Brennan, S. Foster, and H. Holder. New York: Guilford.

Mrazek, P., A. Biglan, and J. D. Hawkins. 2005. *Community-Monitoring Systems: Tracking and Improving the Well-Being of America's Children and Adolescents.* Falls Church, VA: Society for Prevention Research.

National Cancer Institute. 2008. *The Role of the Media in Promoting and Reducing Tobacco Use.* Bethesda, MD: US Department of Health and Human Services, National Institutes of Health, National Cancer Institute.

National Center for Education Statistics. 2014. The condition of education: Mathematics performance. Available at http://www.nces.ed.gov/programs/coe/indicator_cnc.asp. Accessed June 14, 2014.

National Highway Traffic Safety Administration. 2008. *Traffic Safety Facts 2006.* Washington, DC: US Department of Transportation, National Highway Traffic Safety Administration. Available at http://www-nrd.nhtsa.dot.gov/Pubs/810818.pdf. Accessed May 14, 2014.

National Institute on Alcohol Abuse and Alcoholism. 2013. Underage drinking. Available at http://www.niaaa.nih.gov/alcohol-health/special-populations-co-occurring-disorders/underage-drinking. Accessed May 14, 2014.

National Transportation Safety Board. 2013. *Reaching Zero: Actions to Eliminate Alcohol-Impaired Driving.* Washington, DC: NTSB.

Nestle, M. 2002. *Food Politics: How the Food Industry Influences Nutrition and Health.* Berkeley: University of California Press.

Nyhlén, A., M. Fridell, M. Bäckström, M. Hesse, and P. Krantz. 2011. Substance abuse and psychiatric co-morbidity as predictors of premature mortality in Swedish drug abusers a prospective longitudinal study 1970–2006. *BMC Psychiatry* 11: 122.

Olds, D. L. 2007. Preventing crime with prenatal and infancy support of parents: The Nurse-Family Partnership. *Victims and Offenders* 2: 205–225.

Olds, D. L., P. L. Hill, R. O'Brien, D. Racine, and P. Moritz, P. 2003. Taking preventive intervention to scale: The Nurse-Family Partnership. *Cognitive and Behavioral Practice* 10: 278–290.

Olds, D. L., L. Sadler, and H. Kitzman. 2007. Programs for parents of infants and toddlers: Recent evidence from randomized trials. *Journal of Child Psychology and Psychiatry* 48: 355–391.

Patricelli, L. 2012. *Yummy, Yucky.* Somerville, MA: Candlewick Press.

Patterson, G. R. 1982. *Coercive Family Process. Volume 3.* Eugene, OR: Castalia.

Patterson, G. R., M. S. Forgatch, and D. S. DeGarmo. 2010. Cascading effects following intervention. *Development and Psychopathology* 22: 949–970.

Patterson, G. R., and E. Gullion. 1968. *Living with Children: New Methods for Parents and Teachers.* Champaign, IL: Research Press.

Patterson, G. R., and H. Hops. 1972. Coercion, a game for two: Intervention techniques for marital conflict. In *The Experimental Analysis of Social Behavior*, edited by R. E. Ulrich and P. T. Mountjoy. New York: Appleton-Century-Crofts.

Patterson, G., J. Reid, and T. Dishion. 1992. *Antisocial Boys. Volume 4: A Social Interactional Approach*. Eugene, OR: Castalia.

Paul, G. L. 1966. *Insight vs. Desensitization in Psychotherapy: An Experiment in Anxiety Reduction*. Stanford, CA: Stanford University Press.

Pechmann, C., A. Biglan, J. Grube, and C. Cody. 2011. Transformative consumer research for addressing tobacco and alcohol consumption. In *Transformative Consumer Research for Personal and Collective Well-Being*, edited by D. G. Mick, S. Pettigrew, C. Pechmann, and J. L. Ozanne. New York: Routledge.

Pechmann, C., and S. J. Knight. 2002. An experimental investigation of the joint effects of advertising and peers on adolescents' beliefs and intentions about cigarette consumption. *Journal of Consumer Research* 29: 5–19.

Perie, M., R. Moran, and A. D. Lutkus. 2005. *NAEP 2004 Trends in Academic Progress: Three Decades of Student Performance in Reading and Mathematics*. National Center for Education Statistics, U. S. Department of Education, Institute of Education Sciences.

Pierce, J. P., J. M. Distefan, C. Jackson, M. M. White, and E. A. Gilpin. 2002. Does tobacco marketing undermine the influence of recommended parenting in discouraging adolescents from smoking? *American Journal of Preventive Medicine* 23: 73–81.

Pierce, J. P., E. A. Gilpin, and W. S. Choi. 1999. Sharing the blame: Smoking experimentation and future smoking-attributable mortality due to Joe Camel and Marlboro advertising and promotions. *Tobacco Control* 8: 37–44.

Popova, S., N. Giesbrecht, D. Bekmuradov, and J. Patra. 2009. Hours and days of sale and density of alcohol outlets: Impacts on alcohol consumption and damage: A systematic review. *Alcohol and Alcoholism* 44: 500–516.

Powell, L. F., Jr. 1971. Confidential memorandum: Attack on American free enterprise system. Available at http://scalar.usc.edu/works/growing-apart-a-political-history-of-american-inequality/the-powell-memorandum. Accessed May 28, 2014.

Powell, L. M., G. Szczypka, F. J. Chaloupka, and C. L. Braunschweig. 2007. Nutritional content of television food advertisements seen by children and adolescents in the United States. *Pediatrics* 120: 576–583.

Prinz, R. J., M. R. Sanders, C. J. Shapiro, D. J. Whitaker, and J. R. Lutzker. 2009. Population-based prevention of child maltreatment: The US Triple P System Population Trial. *Prevention Science* 10: 1–12.

Rangel, J. M., P. H. Sparling, C. Crowe, P. M. Griffin, and D. L. Swerdlow. 2005. Epidemiology of *Escherichia coli* O157:H7 outbreaks, United States, 1982–2002. *Emerging Infectious Diseases* 11: 603–609.

Reeves, A., D. Stuckler, M. McKee, D. Gunnell, S. S. Chang, and S. Basu. 2012. Increase in state suicide rates in the USA during economic recession. *Lancet* 380: 1813–1814.

Richardson, J. L., B. Radziszewska, C. W. Dent, and B. R. Flay. 1993. Relationship between after-school care of adolescents and substance use, risk taking, depressed mood, and academic achievement. *Pediatrics* 92: 32–38.

Roberts, D. M., M. Ostapchuk, and J. G. O'Brien. 2004. Infantile colic. *American Family Physician* 70: 735–740.

Robinson, P., and K. Strosahl. 2008. *The Mindfulness and Acceptance Workbook for Depression: Using Acceptance and Commitment Therapy to Move Through Depression and Create a Life Worth Living.* Oakland, CA: New Harbinger.

Roeser, R. W., and J. S. Eccles. 1998. Adolescents' perceptions of middle school: Relation to longitudinal changes in academic and psychological adjustment. *Journal of Research on Adolescence* 8: 123–158.

Rogers, C. R. 1951. *Client-Centered Therapy: Its Current Practice, Implications, and Theory.* Boston: Houghton Mifflin.

Ross, N. A., M. C. Wolfson, J. R. Dunn, J. M. Berthelot, G. A. Kaplan, and J. W. Lynch. 2000. Relation between income inequality and mortality in Canada and in the United States: Cross-sectional assessment using census data and vital statistics. *British Medical Journal* 320: 898–902.

Rozanski, A., J. A. Blumenthal, and J. Kaplan. 1999. Impact of psychological factors on the pathogenesis of cardiovascular disease and implications for therapy. *Circulation* 99: 2192–2217.

Rusby, J. C., K. K. Forrester, A. Biglan, and C. W. Metzler. 2005. Relationships between peer harassment and adolescent problem behaviors. *Journal of Early Adolescence* 25: 453–477.

Sandler, I. N., J. Y. Tein, and S. G. West. 1994. Coping, stress, and the psychological symptoms of children of divorce: A cross-sectional and longitudinal study. *Child Development* 65: 1744–1763.

Sapolsky, R. M. 1994. *Why Zebras Don't Get Ulcers.* New York: Freeman.

Sargent, J. D., M. A. Dalton, M. L. Beach, L. A. Mott, J. J. Tickle, M. B. Ahrens, et al. 2002. Viewing tobacco use in movies: Does it shape attitudes that mediate adolescent smoking? *American Journal of Preventive Medicine* 22: 137–145.

Schmuck, P., T. Kasser, and R. M. Ryan. 2000. Intrinsic and extrinsic goals: Their structure and relationship to well-being in German and US college students. *Social Indicators Research* 50: 225–241.

Seligman, M. E. 1970. On the generality of the laws of learning. *Psychological Review* 77: 406–418.

Shadish, W. R., and S. A. Baldwin. 2005. Effects of behavioral marital therapy: A meta-analysis of randomized controlled trials. *Journal of Consulting and Clinical Psychology* 73: 6–14.

Sheldon, K. M., and T. Kasser. 2008. Psychological threat and extrinsic goal striving. *Motivation and Emotion* 32: 37–45.

Skinner, B. F. 1953. *Science and Human Behavior.* New York: Macmillan Company.

———. 1972. *Beyond Freedom and Dignity.* New York: Bantam Books.

Slovic, P. E. 2000. *The Perception of Risk.* London: Earthscan Publications.

Smith, G. D., and C. Hart. 2002. Life-course socioeconomic and behavioral influences on cardiovascular disease mortality: The collaborative study. *American Journal of Public Health* 92: 1295–1298.

Snyder, F., B. R. Flay, S. Vuchinich, A. Acock, I. Washburn, M. W. Beets, and K.-K. Li. (2010). Impact of the Positive Action program on school-level indicators of academic achievement, absenteeism, and disciplinary outcomes: A matched-pair, cluster randomized, controlled trial. *Journal of Research on Educational Effectiveness*, 3: 26–55.

Snyder, F.J., A. Acock, S. Vuchinich, M. W. Beets, I. Washburn, and B. R. Flay. (2013). Preventing negative behaviors among elementary-school students through enhancing students' social-emotional and character development. *American Journal of Health Promotion*, 28: 50–58.

Snyder, F. J., S. Vuchinich, A. Acock, I. J. Washburn, and B. R. Flay. (2012). Improving elementary-school quality through the use of a social-emotional and character development program: A matched-pair, cluster-randomized, controlled trial in Hawaii. *Journal of School Health*, 82: 11–20.

Soby, J. M. 2006. *Prenatal Exposure to Drugs/Alcohol: Characteristics and Educational Implications of Fetal Alcohol Syndrome and Cocaine/Polydrug Effects.* Springfield, IL: Charles C. Thomas.

Spoth, R., C. Redmond, C. Shin, M. Greenberg, M. Feinberg, and L. Schainker. 2013. Longitudinal effects of universal PROSPER community-university partnership delivery system effects on substance misuse through 6 1/2 years past baseline from a cluster randomized controlled intervention trial. *Preventive Medicine* 56: 190–196.

Stebbins, L. B., R. G. St. Pierre, E. C. Proper, R. B. Anderson, and T. R. Cerva. 1977. *Education as Experimentation: A Planned Variation Model. Volume IV-A: An Evaluation of Follow Through.* Cambridge, MA: Abt Associates.

Strom, S. 2011. Local laws fighting fat under siege. *New York Times*, June 30. Available at http://www.nytimes.com/2011/07/01/business/01obese.html?pagewanted=all&_r=0. Assessed July 1, 2014.

Sugai, G., R. Horner, and B. Algozzine, eds. 2011. *Reducing the Effectiveness of Bullying Behavior in Schools.* Available at http://www.pbis.org/common/cms/files/pbisresources/PBIS_Bullying_Behavior_Apr19_2011.pdf. Accessed May 14, 2014.

Tein, J. Y., I. N. Sandler, D. P. MacKinnon, and S. A. Wolchik. 2004. How did it work? Who did it work for? Mediation in the context of a moderated prevention effect for children of divorce. *Journal of Consulting and Clinical Psychology* 72: 617–624.

Tirch, D. 2012. *The Compassionate-Mind Guide to Overcoming Anxiety: Using Compassion-Focused Therapy to Calm Worry, Panic, and Fear.* Oakland, CA: New Harbinger.

Törneke, N. 2010. *Learning RFT: An Introduction to Relational Frame Theory and Its Clinical Application.* Oakland, CA: New Harbinger.

Truax, C. B., and R. T. Carkuff. 1967. *Toward Effective Counseling and Psychotherapy.* Chicago: Aldine.

Twenge, J. M. 2009. Status and gender: The paradox of progress in an age of narcissism. *Sex Roles* 61: 338–340.

Twenge, J. M., and W. K. Campbell. 2008. Increases in positive self-views among high school students: Birth-cohort changes in anticipated performance, self-satisfaction, self-liking, and self-competence. *Psychological Science* 19: 1082–1086.

Twenge, J. M., and W. K. Campbell. 2009. *The Narcissism Epidemic: Living in the Age of Enlightenment.* New York: Free Press.

Twenge, J. M., and J. D. Foster. 2010. Birth cohort increases in narcissistic personality traits among American college students, 1982–2009. *Social Psychological and Personality Science* 1: 99–106.

Twenge, J. M., S. Konrath, J. D. Foster, W. K. Campbell, and B. J. Bushman. 2008. Further evidence of an increase in narcissism among college students. *Journal of Personality* 76: 919–928.

US Department of Health and Human Services. 1980. *The Health Consequences of Smoking for Women: A Report of the Surgeon General.* Washington, DC: US Department of Health and Human Services, Public Health Service, Office of the Assistant Secretary for Health, Office on Smoking and Health.

———. 1981. *The Health Consequences of Smoking: The Changing Cigarette. A Report of the Surgeon General.* Washington, DC: US Department of Health and Human Services, Public Health Service, Office of the Assistant Secretary for Health, Office on Smoking and Health.

———. 1982. *The Health Consequences of Smoking: Cancer. A Report of the Surgeon General.* Washington, DC: US Department of Health and Human Services, Public Health Service, Office of the Assistant Secretary for Health, Office on Smoking and Health.

———. 1983. *The Health Consequences of Smoking: Cardiovascular Disease. A Report of the Surgeon General.* Washington, DC: US Department of Health and Human Services, Public Health Service, Office of the Assistant Secretary for Health, Office on Smoking and Health.

———. 1984. *The Health Consequences of Smoking: Chronic Obstructive Lung Disease. A Report of the Surgeon General.* Washington, DC: US Department of Health and Human Services, Public Health Service, Office of the Assistant Secretary for Health, Office on Smoking and Health.

———. 1986. *The Health Consequences of Involuntary Smoking. A Report of the Surgeon General.* Washington, DC: US Department of Health and Human Services, Public Health Service, Office of the Assistant Secretary for Health, Office on Smoking and Health.

———. 1988. *The Health Consequences of Smoking: Nicotine Addiction. A Report of the Surgeon General.* Washington, DC: US Department of Health and Human Services, Public Health Service, Office of the Assistant Secretary for Health, Office on Smoking and Health.

———. 1989. *Reducing the Health Consequences of Smoking: 25 Years of Progress. A Report of the Surgeon General.* Washington, DC: US Department of Health and Human Services, Public Health Service, Office of the Assistant Secretary for Health, Office on Smoking and Health.

———. 2014. *The Health Consequences of Smoking—50 Years of Progress: A Report of the Surgeon General.* Atlanta, GA: US Department of Health and Human Services, Centers for Disease Control and Prevention, National Center for Chronic Disease Prevention and Health Promotion, Office on Smoking and Health.

Van Meurs, K. 1999. Cigarette smoking, pregnancy, and the developing fetus. Available at http://med.stanford.edu/medicalreview/smrp14-16.pdf. Accessed May 14, 2014.

Van Ryzin, M. J., and T. J. Dishion. 2013. From antisocial behavior to violence: A model for the amplifying role of coercive joining in adolescent friendships. *Journal of Child Psychology and Psychiatry* 54: 661–669.

Wachlarowicz, M., J. Snyder, S. Low, M. Forgatch, and D. DeGarmo. 2012. The moderating effects of parent antisocial characteristics on the effects of Parent Management Training-Oregon (PMTO). *Prevention Science* 13: 229–240.

Wagenaar, A. C., and S. C. Burris, eds. 2013. *Public Health Law Research: Theory and Methods.* New York: Wiley and Sons.

Wagenaar, A. C., and T. L. Toomey. 2002. Effects of minimum drinking age laws: Review and analyses of the literature from 1960 to 2000. *Journal of Studies on Alcohol Supplement* 14: 206–225.

Walker, O. L., and H. A. Henderson. 2012. Temperament and social problem solving competence in preschool: Influences on academic skills in early elementary school. *Social Development* 21: 761–779.

Washburn, I. J., A. Acock, S. Vuchinich, F. J. Snyder, K.-K. Li, P. Ji, J. Day, D. L. DuBois, and B. R. Flay. (2011). Effects of a social-emotional and character development program on the trajectory of behaviors associated with character development: Findings from three randomized trials. *Prevention Science*, 12: 314–323.

Washington State Institute for Public Policy [WSIPP]. (2014). Per-pupil expenditures: 10% increase for one student cohort from kindergarten through grade 12. Available at http://www.wsipp.wa.gov/BenefitCost/ProgramPdf/182/Per-pupil-expenditures-10-increase-for-one-student-cohort-from-kindergarten-through-grade-12. Accessed August 19, 2014.

WebMD. 2013. Eating right when pregnant. Available online at http://www.webmd.com/baby/guide/eating-right-when-pregnant. Accessed May 14, 2014.

Webster-Stratton, C. 1992. *The Incredible Years: A Trouble-Shooting Guide for Parents of Children Aged 3–8*. Toronto, Ontario, Canada: Umbrella Press.

Webster-Stratton, C., and K. C. Herman. 2008. The impact of parent behavior-management training on child depressive symptoms. *Journal of Counseling Psychology* 55: 473–484.

Webster-Stratton, C., M. J. Reid, and M. Stoolmiller. 2008. Preventing conduct problems and improving school readiness: Evaluation of the Incredible Years Teacher and Child Training Programs in high-risk schools. *Journal of Child Psychology and Psychiatry* 49: 471–488.

Wechsler, H., and T. F. Nelson. 2008. What we have learned from the Harvard School of Public Health College Alcohol Study: Focusing attention on college student alcohol consumption and the environmental conditions that promote it. *Journal of Studies on Alcohol and Drugs* 69: 481–490.

Wegman, H. L., and C. Stetler. 2009. A meta-analytic review of the effects of childhood abuse on medical outcomes in adulthood. *Psychosomatic Medicine* 71: 805–812.

Weiss, R. L., and B. A. Perry. 2002. Behavioral couples therapy. In *Comprehensive Handbook of Psychotherapy. Volume 2: Cognitive-Behavioral Approaches*, edited by F. W. Kaslow and T. Patterson. New York: Wiley and Sons.

Whiting, C. 2004. Income inequality, the income cost of housing, and the myth of market efficiency. *American Journal of Economics and Sociology* 63: 851–879.

Wilkinson, R. 1992. Income distribution and life expectancy. *British Medical Journal* 304: 165–168.

Wilkinson, R., and K. Pickett. 2009. *The Spirit Level: Why Greater Equality Makes Societies Stronger*. New York: Bloomsbury.

Wilson, D. S. 1998. Adaptive individual differences within single populations. *Philosophical Transactions of the Royal Society of London. Series B: Biological Sciences* 353, 199–205.

———. 2003. *Darwin's Cathedral: Evolution, Religion, and the Nature of Science.* Chicago: University of Chicago Press.

———. 2007. *Evolution for Everyone: How Darwin's Theory Can Change the Way We Think About Our Lives.* New York: Delacorte Press.

Wilson, D. S., and M. Csikszentmihalyi. 2008. Health and the ecology of altruism. In *Altruism and Health: Perspectives from Empirical Research*, edited by S. G. Post. New York: Oxford University Press.

Wilson, D. S., S. C. Hayes, A. Biglan, and D. D. Embry. 2014. Evolving the future: Toward a science of intentional change. *Behavioral and Brain Sciences*, 37: 395–416.

Wilson, D. S., D. T. O'Brien, and A. Sesma. 2009. Human prosociality from an evolutionary perspective: Variation and correlations at a city-wide scale. *Evolution and Human Behavior* 30: 190–200.

Wilson, E. O. 1998. *Consilience: The Unity of Knowledge.* New York: Alfred A. Knopf.

Wolpe, J. 1958. *Psychotherapy by Reciprocal Inhibition.* Stanford, CA: Stanford University Press.

Working Group on Extreme Inequality. 2007. *Presenting the findings of the Working Group on Extreme American Inequality.* Available at http://www.zerohedge .com/article/presenting-findings-working-group-extreme-american-inequality. Accessed on July 1, 2014.

Wray-Lake, L., C. A. Flanagan, and D. W. Osgood. 2010. Examining trends in adolescent environmental attitudes, beliefs, and behaviors across three decades. *Environmental Behavior* 42: 61–85.

Zeilberger, J., S. E. Sampen, and H. N. Sloane Jr. 1968. Modification of a child's problem behaviors in the home with the mother as therapist. *Journal of Applied Behavior Analysis* 1: 47–53.

Anthony Biglan, PhD, is a senior scientist at Oregon Research Institute, and a leading figure in the development of prevention science. His research over the past thirty years has helped to identify effective family, school, and community interventions to prevent the most common and costly problems of childhood and adolescence. He is a leader in efforts to use prevention science to build more nurturing families, schools, and communities throughout the world. Biglan lives in Eugene, OR.

Foreword writer **Steven C. Hayes, PhD**, is Nevada Foundation Professor in the department of psychology at the University of Nevada. An author of thirty-four books and more than 470 scientific articles, he has shown in his research how language and thought leads to human suffering. He cofounded acceptance and commitment therapy (ACT)—a powerful therapy method that is useful in a wide variety of areas. Hayes has been president of several scientific societies and has received several national awards, including the Lifetime Achievement Award from the Association for Behavioral and Cognitive Therapies.

Afterword writer **David Sloan Wilson, PhD**, is president of the Evolution Institute and SUNY distinguished professor of biology and anthropology at Binghamton University. He applies evolutionary theory to all aspects of humanity, in addition to the biological world. His books include *Darwin's Cathedral, Evolution for Everyone: How Darwin's Theory Can Change the Way We Think About Our Lives, The Neighborhood Project,* and *Does Altruism Exist?*